丛书主编 周江

海洋·极地·自然资源法研究丛书 国别海洋法系列

印度、巴基斯坦海洋法律体系研究

刘畅 著

知识产权出版社

全国百佳图书出版单位

—北京—

图书在版编目（CIP）数据

印度、巴基斯坦海洋法律体系研究/刘畅著. —北京：知识产权出版社，2022.3
（海洋·极地·自然资源法研究丛书/周江主编. 国别海洋法系列）
ISBN 978 - 7 - 5130 - 7915 - 0

Ⅰ.①印… Ⅱ.①刘… Ⅲ.①海洋法—研究 Ⅳ.①D993.5

中国版本图书馆 CIP 数据核字（2021）第 243401 号

责任编辑：薛迎春　　　　　　　　　责任校对：潘凤越
封面设计：黄慧君　　　　　　　　　责任印制：刘译文

印度、巴基斯坦海洋法律体系研究
刘　畅 ◎ 著

出版发行：**知识产权出版社** 有限责任公司	网　　址：http：//www.ipph.cn
社　　址：北京市海淀区气象路 50 号院	邮　　编：100081
责编电话：010-82000860 转 8724	责编邮箱：471451342@ qq.com
发行电话：010-82000860 转 8101/8102	发行传真：010-82000893/82005070/82000270
印　　刷：三河市国英印务有限公司	经　　销：新华书店、各大网上书店及相关专业书店
开　　本：710mm×1000mm　1/16	印　　张：19.75
版　　次：2022 年 3 月第 1 版	印　　次：2022 年 3 月第 1 次印刷
字　　数：350 千字	定　　价：88.00 元
ISBN 978 - 7 - 5130 - 7915 - 0	

重庆市高校哲学社会科学协同创新团队
"海洋与自然资源法研究团队"阶段性成果

总　序

中国是陆海兼备的海洋大国，海洋开发历史悠久，曾创造了举世瞩目的海洋文明。"鱼盐之利，舟楫之便"是先人认识和利用海洋之精炼概括，仍不悖于当今海洋之时势。然数百年前，泰西诸国携坚船利炮由海而至，先祖眼中的天然屏障竟成列强鱼肉九州之通道。海洋强国兴衰，殷鉴不远。

吾辈身处百年未有之变局，加快建设海洋强国已成为中华民族伟大复兴的重要组成。扎实的海洋工业、尖端的海洋科技及强大的海军战力，无疑为海洋强国之必需。此外，完备的海洋治理体系和卓越的海洋治理能力等软实力亦不可或缺。海洋治理体系之完备，海洋治理能力之卓越，皆与海洋法治息息相关。经由法律的治理以造福生民，为古今中外人类实践之最佳路径。

海洋法治之达致，需赖全体国人之努力，应无沿海内陆之别。西南政法大学虽处内陆，一向以"心系天下"为精神导引。作为中国法学教育研究的重镇，西南政法大学独具光荣的历史传承、深厚的学术底蕴和完备的人才积累。她以党的基本理论、基本路线、基本方略和国家的重大战略需求为学术研究之出发点和归宿。

西南政法大学海洋与自然资源法研究所之成立，正是虑及吾辈应为建设海洋强国贡献绵薄。国际法学院、经济法学院（生态法学院）、国家安全学院相关研究团队，合众为一，同心勠力，与中国海洋法学会合作共建而成。我所将持续系统地研究涉海法律问题，现以"海洋·极地·自然资源法研究丛书"之名，推出首批公开出版成果。

本丛书拟设四大系列：国别海洋法系列、海洋治理系列、极地治理系列及自然资源法系列。系列之间既各有侧重又相互呼应，其共同的目标在于助力中国海洋治理体系与治理能力的现代化。

本丛书推崇创作之包容性，对当下及今后各作者的学术观点，都将予以最大程度的尊重；本丛书亦秉持研究之开放性，诚挚欢迎同人惠赐契合丛书主题及各系列议题的佳作；本丛书更倡导学术的批判性，愿广纳学友对同一问题的补正、商榷甚或质疑。若经由上述努力与坚持，可将本丛书打造为学界交流与争鸣的平台，则是我们莫大的荣幸。

本丛书能由构想变为现实，离不开诸多前辈、领导及同人的关心、指导与支持，我相信，丛书的付梓是对他们玉成此事最好的感谢！

是为序！

2020 年 3 月 31 日

目　录

第 I 部分

印度海洋法律体系研究

一、印度海洋基本情况

印度共和国（Republic of India，以下简称"印度"）是世界四大文明古国之一，于公元前 2500 年至公元前 1500 年创造了印度河文明。公元前 1500 年前后，原居住在中亚的雅利安人进入南亚次大陆，建立了一些奴隶制小国，确立了种姓制度，婆罗门教兴起。公元前 4 世纪，孔雀王朝统一印度大部。阿育王统治时期，印度佛教兴盛并开始向外传播。随着公元前 2 世纪孔雀王朝灭亡，至公元 6 世纪小国林立，印度教逐渐兴起。1526 年，蒙古贵族后裔建立莫卧儿帝国，成为当时世界强国之一。1619 年，英国东印度公司在印度西北部建立首个据点。1757 年起，印度逐渐沦为英国殖民地，至 1849 年被英国全部占领。1947 年 6 月，英国公布"蒙巴顿方案"，将印度分为印度和巴基斯坦两个自治领地。同年 7 月，英国议会通过印度独立法案，该法案规定：第一，建立"两个独立的自治领，即印度和巴基斯坦"；第二，英国政府将于 8 月 15 日将一切权力移交给两自治领制宪议会，对于过去英属印度领土上的政府不再负责；第三，英王对于印度的宗主权将不复存在；第四，双方的一切条约和协定都将失效[1] 1947 年 8 月 15 日，印巴分治，印度宣布独立，首都设在新德里（New Delhi）。1950 年 1 月 26 日，印度共和国正式成立，为英联邦成员国[2]

（一）海洋地理概况

印度全境地处北半球，是南亚领土面积最大的国家，也是世界第七大国家。在地理环境上，一方面，其北面因喜马拉雅山脉而与亚洲大陆大多数国家分隔；另一方面，其东西南三面均由海洋包围。由此，印度的陆上邻国有 6 个，分别是阿富汗、巴基斯坦、中国、不丹、缅甸和孟加拉国，陆地边界约为 15200 公里[3] 同时，作为一个三面环海的国家，印度东临孟加拉湾，西濒阿拉伯海，南面为印度洋，大陆海岸线和群岛海岸线全长 7516.6 公里，[4]

---

〔1〕 孙士海、葛维钧主编：《印度》，社会科学文献出版社 2010 年版，第 109 页。

〔2〕 商务部国际贸易经济合作研究院：《对外投资合作国别（地区）指南——印度（2020 年版）》，载中华人民共和国商务部网站，http：//www.mofcom.gov.cn/dl/gbdqzn/upload/yin-du.pdf，最后访问日期：2021 年 3 月 1 日。

〔3〕 "Profile", Government of India, https：//www.india.gov.in/india-glance/profile, July 1, 2019.

〔4〕 其中，大陆海岸线长 5560 公里。参见中华人民共和国外交部：《印度国家概况》，载中华人民共和国外交部网站，https：//www.fmprc.gov.cn/web/gjhdq_676201/gj_676203/yz_676205/1206_677220/1206x0_677222/，最后访问日期：2020 年 7 月 1 日。

与斯里兰卡隔海相望。印度的古吉拉特邦（Gujarat）、马哈拉施特拉邦（Maharashtra）、果阿邦（Goa）、卡纳塔克邦（Karnataka）和喀拉拉邦（Kerala）位于印度西海岸，泰米尔纳德邦（Tamil Nadu）、安得拉邦（Andhra）、奥里萨邦（Orissa）和西孟加拉邦（West Bengal）位于印度半岛的东海岸。虽然印度在较长时间内都依托内陆河流发展，但印度陆地资源的种类和储量有限，海洋对印度的价值不言而喻。

（二）政治及经济概况

政治方面，印度是一个议会制联邦共和国，总统为国家元首，任期 5 年，但实权由总理掌握。名义上，总统是国家最高元首，享有广泛的行政权，但事实上，政府各部部长皆由总理提名再由总统任命，掌握国家权力的是以总理为首的部长会议。[1] 印度各邦邦长作为总统的代表，是该邦的行政首长，而联邦属地则由总统指派政务官进行管理。每一个邦或联邦属地无论大小，都有各自的民选政府、人口、服饰、节日、语言和历史文化。[2]

虽然印度在国家结构上实行的是联邦制，但是联邦政府高度集权，实质上具有单一制国家的特点。此外，联邦议会的权限很大，其立法范围几乎覆盖了国家所有的重大事项，而各邦的立法权限则限于法律规定的 66 个项目，包括公共秩序、警察、监狱、农林渔业、水利灌溉、邦内的贸易与商业等。[3]

经济方面，印度是金砖五国之一。2018 年，印度人口超过 13.52 亿人，仅次于中国，居世界第二位。[4] 同年，印度国内生产总值达 2.726 万亿美元，是世界第三大经济体，人均国民收入约合 1733 美元。[5] 种姓制的长期盛行，使印度成为一个贫富差距巨大、发展极不平衡的国家，至今全国仍有超过 1.7 亿贫困人口。印度是一个农业大国，耕地面积约 1.6 亿公顷，占世界耕地总面积的 1/10，是世界上最大的粮食生产国之一，农村人口占其总人口的 72%。[6] 渔业在农业中占有重要地位，鱼总产量居世界第六位，淡水

---

〔1〕 孙士海、葛维钧主编：《印度》，社会科学文献出版社 2010 年版，第 109—110 页。

〔2〕 "States and Union Territories", Government of India, https：//knowindia. gov. in/states-uts/, July 1, 2019.

〔3〕 孙士海、葛维钧主编：《印度》，社会科学文献出版社 2010 年版，第 193—194 页。

〔4〕 "Country Profile—India", World Bank, https：//databank. worldbank. org/views/reports/report-widget. aspx? Report _ Name = CountryProfile&Id = b450fd57&tbar = y&dd = y&inf = n&zm = n&country = IND, July 1, 2020.

〔5〕 "Data", World Bank, https：//data. worldbank. org/country/india, July 1, 2019.

〔6〕 中华人民共和国外交部：《印度国家概况》，载中华人民共和国外交部网站，https：//www. fmprc. gov. cn/web/gjhdq_ 676201/gj_ 676203/yz_ 676205/1206_ 677220/1206x0_ 677222/, 最后访问日期：2020 年 7 月 1 日。

鱼产量居世界第二位，是印度重要的出口创汇来源。

自 20 世纪 90 年代开始，印度大力推行经济改革，经济发展模式从半封闭半管制转变为开放自由的市场经济，逐步与世界经济接轨。在工业领域，除涉及国防、安全、铁路、原子能等特殊行业外，一律取消许可证制度，并向私营经济开放。在贸易领域，实行优惠政策，降低投资门槛，大力吸引外商投资。在金融领域，实行财政、税收改革，改善营商环境。得益于经济改革，印度的国民经济结构得到完善，农业所占比重持续下降，服务业所占比重持续上升并成为国民经济最大的组成部分和增长最快的领域，包括商业、酒店业、通信业、IT 业、金融业、保险业、地产业以及社区和社会服务业等在内的服务业得到了快速发展，教育、科技水平不断提高，脱贫工作稳步推进，经济建设取得了重大成就，综合国力大幅提升。

总体来看，印度的外交政策旨在维护自身的国家利益，其首要目标是促进和维持一个和平稳定的外部环境，以实现国内经济的包容性发展，为消灭国内贫困扫清障碍。因此，印度积极参与本区域和全球性的合作，高度重视和平的地缘关系的维护，积极为睦邻友好关系而努力。印度作为人口大国和传统的农业大国，农业在其经济生活中占据着举足轻重的地位。而由于特殊的地理位置和地理条件，印度深受西南季风和气候变化的影响，鉴于这样的特殊国情，印度的外交活动主要围绕气候变化、能源和粮食安全以及经济合作等问题而展开。[1]

印度是《联合国海洋法公约》（以下简称《公约》）的缔约国，同时是国际海事组织（International Maritime Organization）、国际水文组织（International Hydrographic Organization）、印度洋金枪鱼委员会（Indian Ocean Tuna Commission）、上海合作组织（Shanghai Cooperation Organisation）等众多国际组织的成员。

印度与中国于 1950 年 4 月 1 日建交。20 世纪 50 年代，两国领导人共同倡导和平共处五项原则，双方交往密切。1962 年 10 月，两国间由于边境领土问题曾发生大规模武装冲突，外交关系恶化。1976 年双方恢复互派大使后，两国关系逐步改善。近年来，两国边界谈判持续向前推进，边境地区总体保持和平与安宁。[2]

---

〔1〕 "India & the World", Government of India, https://knowindia.gov.in/india-and-the-world/, July 1, 2019.

〔2〕 中华人民共和国外交部：《印度国家概况》，载中华人民共和国外交部网站，https://www.fmprc.gov.cn/web/gjhdq_676201/gj_676203/yz_676205/1206_677220/1206x0_677222/，最后访问日期：2020 年 7 月 1 日。

（三）海洋资源利用现况

根据《公约》的规定，印度拥有 202 万平方公里的专属经济区，其面积相当于印度陆地领土面积的三分之二，这使得印度拥有十分丰富的海洋生物和非生物资源。其中，海洋生物资源主要包括各种鱼类（如飞鱼、金鳍鱼、金枪鱼等）、软体动物和海兽（如海豹、企鹅、海胆、海参、海百合等）。近几十年来，随着世界主要渔业基地对大西洋、太平洋渔业资源的过度开发，印度洋渔业资源的开发潜力越来越受到重视。同时，印度较早即开始了对海洋药物的研究和开发，印度洋地区丰富的藻类资源、浮游生物以及其他植物、动物等为印度海洋药物的研发提供了基础。[1]

在非生物资源方面，印度沿海陆地、专属经济区及大陆架区域蕴含着丰富的金属矿藏，包括锰、钴、铜、锌、铅和镉等在内的矿产资源散布在印度附近洋区的 3000 米—6000 米深的海底。1987 年，印度首次向国际海底管理局筹备委员会（PrepCom for and ITLOS）提出开发多金属结核（polymetallic nodules）的申请并获得批准。[2] 2002 年，印度政府与国际海底管理局（International Seabed Authority）签署了一份为期 15 年的多金属结核的勘探和开采合同，并于 2017 年合同到期后续签 5 年。[3] 2016 年 9 月 26 日，印度政府与国际海底管理局签署了一份为期 15 年的多金属硫化物（polymetallic sulphides）勘探和开采合同。根据该合同，印度申请开发的区域位于印度洋中部超过 10000 平方公里的海域，由上百个区块组成。[4] 目前，印度共在超过 150000 平方公里的海域进行多金属结核的开采和加工。[5] 在港口建设方面，三面环海的地理位置，使印度大约 95% 的对外商品贸易是通过海运完成的，许多港口正在变成航海贸易集散地和海事服务中心，如加瓦拉尔·尼赫鲁港（Jawaharlal Nehru Port）、蒙德拉港（Mundra Port）、锡卡港（Sikka Port）、哈兹拉港（Hazira Port）等，这对确保印度经济持续增长至关重要。然而，港口基础设

---

〔1〕 "Centre for Marine Living Resources and Ecology", Ministry of Earth Sciences, https： //www. godae. org/~ godae-data/GOVST-VII/presentations/4. 6-CMLRE_ GODAE. pdf, July 1, 2020.

〔2〕 "Statement by India", International Seabed Authority, https： //ran-s3. s3. amazonaws. com/isa. org. jm/s3fs-public/files/documents/india_ statements_ council. pdf, August 20, 2019.

〔3〕 "Government of India", International Seabed Authority, https： //www. isa. org. jm/government-india, August 20, 2019.

〔4〕 "The Governmnet of India Signs Exploration Contract with The International Seabed Autority", International Seabed Authority, https： //www. isa. org. jm/news/government-india-signs-exploration-contract-international-seabed-authority, August 20, 2019.

〔5〕 "India Ocean Policy Statement", Ministry of Earth Sciences, https： //moes. gov. in/writereaddata/files/OCEAN_ POLICY_ STATEMENT. pdf, August 20, 2019.

施和港口运营的落后极大地制约着印度港口的升级和现代化。2018—2019年，印度主要港口的周转时间约为 2.5 天，运营效率仍落后于全球平均基准时间 1—2 天。印度陆路货物运输中约有 87% 通过公路和铁路完成，内陆水运占比偏低。由于将港口连接至生产和消费中心的高速公路和铁路的运力限制，货物在转运到港口过程中的效率大大降低，物流成本也随之增加。因此，与港口最后一英里的连通性仍是其货物进出内陆的主要障碍之一。

2015 年 3 月 25 日，印度内阁批准了"萨格尔马拉计划"（Sagarmala Plan），并于 2016 年 4 月 14 日在 2016 年印度海事峰会（The Maritime India Summit 2016）上根据该计划推出了"国家远景计划"（National Perspective Plan，NPP），以全面开发印度丰富的海洋资源，大力推进港口现代化，促进港口运输业的发展。"萨格尔马拉计划"的目标是以最少的基础设施投资来降低进出口和国内贸易的物流成本，具体包括四个方面的内容：第一，通过优化不同运输方式的组合降低国内货物运输成本；第二，通过在沿海地区建立未来的工业产能来降低大宗商品的物流成本；第三，通过发展邻近离散制造业集群的港口来提高出口竞争力；第四，减少进出口集装箱运输的时间和成本。"萨格尔马拉计划"的主要内容包括五个方面：第一，港口现代化和新港口开发，即消除现有港口的不足，扩大其产能，并开发新港口；第二，增强港口连通性，即通过包括国内水道（内陆水运和沿海运输）在内的多式联运物流解决方案，增强港口与内地的连通性，降低货物运输的成本和时间；第三，与港口有关的工业化，即发展与港口相邻的产业集群和沿海经济区，以降低物流成本并减少进出口和国内货物的运输时间；第四，沿海社区发展，即通过技术培训、发展渔业和开发沿海旅游资源等促进沿海社区的可持续发展；第五，沿海航运和内陆水运运输，即以可持续和环境友好的发展模式通过沿海和内陆水运运送货物。[1]

---

〔1〕 "About-sagarmala", Ministry of Shipping, http：//sagarmala. gov. in/about-sagarmala/background, July 1, 2019.

二、海洋事务主管部门及其职能

（一）基本政治结构

印度为联邦制民主共和国，模仿英国式议会制度，以英国威斯敏斯特体制（西敏制）为模型，其政治体制主要由立法机关、行政机关和司法机关组成。

1. 立法机关

印度的立法权由联邦议会行使。联邦议会为两院制，包括联邦院（Council of States）和人民院（House of the People）。联邦院为上院，共 250 席，由总统指定 12 名具有专门学识或实际经验的议员，其余 238 名议员为各邦及中央直辖区代表。人民院为下院，共 545 席，其中 543 席由选民直接选举产生。人民院是印度主要立法机关，基本职能为：制定法律和修改宪法；控制和调整联邦政府的收入和支出；对联邦政府提出不信任案，并有权弹劾总统。议会制定的法律会受到最高法院的司法审查，但是议会对某些行政人员的任免具有决定性的权力，包括总理在内的内阁成员都从议会中选举产生。

2. 行政机关

印度的行政机关由总统、副总统、总理及其领导的内阁会议组成。根据其宪法，印度行政权主要授予总统。总统名义上是国家元首和武装部队统帅，但政府实权由总理领导的内阁掌握。政府以总统名义行使广泛的行政权力。[1]

印度设总统、副总统各一人。总统是名誉元首，也是国家统一的象征。总统的权力主要分为以下几个方面：（1）联邦最高行政权；（2）武装部队最高统帅权；（3）任命总理，并根据总理的提名任免内阁成员，任免最高法院和高等法院的法官，任免检察长、审计长、各邦邦长和直辖区行政专员等；（4）在法律规定的特殊情况发生时有权在全国或者部分地区宣告紧急状态。以上权力，除任命总理外，实际上都是总理以总统的名义行使。[2]

总理是政府的首脑，由总统任命人民院多数党领袖担任。同时，依据宪

---

〔1〕 See Article 53, Chapter I, Part V, The Constitution of India, India Code, https：//www. india. gov. in/my-government/constitution-india，February 11，2020.

〔2〕 See Article 55, Chapter I, Part V, The Constitution of India, India Code, https：//www. india. gov. in/my-government/constitution-india，February 11，2020.

法，设立以总理为首的内阁"在总统行使职权时协助总统，并向其提供建议"[1]。总理的职责主要有：(1) 向总统报告内阁对于管理联邦事务和立法建议的一切决定；(2) 向总统提供关于管理联邦事务和立法建议的资料；(3) 应总统要求，将经某一内阁成员决定而未经部长会议讨论的任何事项提交内阁会议讨论。总理拥有组织和领导政府的权力，总理有权提请总统随时免去某一内阁部长的职务[2]。

3. 司法机关

印度的司法系统由印度最高法院、各邦高等法院和县法院组成。最高法院由总统任命的首席大法官和 30 名陪审法官组成，是最高司法权力机关，有权解释宪法、审理联邦政府与各邦之间的争议问题等。总检察长由总统任命，其主要职责是就执法事项向政府提供咨询和建议，行使宪法和法律规定的检察权，对宪法和法律的执行情况进行监督等[3]。

(二) 海洋管理的专门机构

当前，印度海洋相关管理职能分散在政府的各个部门，除地球科学部 (Ministry of Earth Sciences) 外，没有统一的高层海洋事务协调机构。

1. 初始建立阶段

1981 年 7 月，印度成立了海洋开发局 (Department of Ocean Development)，以加强海洋综合管理，有效保护海洋环境及其资源，从而实现海洋资源的可持续利用。作为内阁秘书处的一部分，海洋开发局由总理直接领导，其职能主要包括：海岸带和海洋环境管理、海洋生物和非生物资源勘探开发、海洋观测与信息服务、海洋科学研究、极地研究和海洋人才培养等。1982 年 3 月，海洋开发局从内阁独立，成为单独的部门。

2. 重组发展阶段

2006 年 2 月，海洋开发局更名为海洋开发部 (Ministry of Ocean Development)。同年，鉴于海洋、大气与地球之间的紧密联系，为了整合印度的科学研究工作，印度政府决定进一步重组海洋开发部。2006 年 7 月，印度政府将印度气象部 (India Meteorological Department)、国家中期数值天气预报中

---

[1] See Article 74, Chapter I, Part V, The Constitution of India, India Code, https://www. india. gov. in/my-government/constitution-india, February 11, 2020.

[2] See Article 75, Chapter I, Part V, The Constitution of India, India Code, https://www. india. gov. in/my-government/constitution-india, February 11, 2020.

[3] See Article 76, Chapter I, Part V, The Constitution of India, India Code, https://www. india. gov. in/my-government/constitution-india, February 11, 2020.

心（National Centre for Medium Range Weather Forecasting）和印度热带气象研究所（Indian Institute of Tropical Meteorology）合并组成地球科学部。

印度地球科学部一方面继承了原海洋开发部的主要职能，另一方面更着重于海洋领域的科学与技术研究以及海洋公益服务的开展。其现有职能主要涉及：海洋科学与服务、大气科学与服务、低温圈/极地科学、海洋资源、海洋技术、近海海洋生态学、气候变化科学、防灾减灾、船舶管理、地球科学领域的研究与研发、相关宣传与教育等。

2007 年 10 月，地球科学部下设地球系统科学组织（Earth System Science Organization），作为地球科学部的执行机构，负责为地球科学部制定政策与计划，包括海洋科学与技术、天气与气候、地球科学和极地科学领域的指导性政策与服务计划，以提高各类预报能力，为印度社会、经济、环境与安全事业服务。其具体任务为：（1）组织地球系统各领域的基础与应用研究，并以印度次大陆及其邻近海域和极地区域为重点区域；（2）为国家提供最高质量的预报服务，包括季风、其他天气气候数据，以及海上自然灾害的早期预警，如地震、海啸等；（3）发展海洋资源调查、勘探与开发技术，为可持续开发利用海洋资源服务。

地球系统科学组织的下属机构有：印度气象局（IMD）、印度热带气象研究所（IITM）、国家中期数值天气预报中心（NCMRWF）、海洋生物资源与生态中心（CMLRE），国家地震学中心（NCS）、国家海岸研究中心（NCCR）、国家极地和海洋研究中心（NCPOR）、国家海洋信息服务中心（INCOIS）、国家海洋技术研究所（NIOT）、国家系统科学中心（NCESS）。[1]

印度地球科学部携其下属机构，开展了一系列与海洋有关的工作。1998 年 1 月，原海洋开发局经内阁批准设立了沿海和海洋区域综合管理项目局（Integrated Coastal and Marine Area Management Project Directorate）。项目局后被划属国家海岸研究中心，专门从事长期的海岸研究（coastal research），旨在促进对沿岸水质、生态系统、海岸线侵蚀、海岸有害物质及污染物等海岸问题的研究与解决。[2] 2012—2017 年，印度政府投入 150 亿卢布开展了名为"海洋生态系统监测与建模"（Monitoring and Modeling of Marine Ecosystems）的项目计划。该计划由国家海岸研究中心和海洋生物资源与生态中心联合开展，从事包括"海洋生物资源技术开发"（Marine Living Resources Technology

---

〔1〕 "Institutes", Ministry of Earth and Science, https：//www. moes. gov. in, November 28, 2019.

〔2〕 "Coastal Research", MoES, https：//www. moes. gov. in/programmes/coastal-research, Feburary 10, 2020.

Development）和"源海药品"（Drugs from the Sea）等在内的多项子计划。其中，"海洋生物资源技术开发"计划涵盖多种经济开发技术，如黑唇珍珠的生产、观赏植物的种植等，也聚焦符合海洋药业要求的深海生物活性分子提取技术。海洋药业方面，印度已在从沿岸水域的生物中提取生物活性分子领域积累了大量技术经验。又由于地球科学部下属的渔业与海洋学研究船"萨加尔塞姆帕达"号（Sagar Sampada）参与了深海生物的采集工作，印度已将生物分子提取技术对象扩展到能更多用于研制新药物的深海微生物及生物上。海洋生物资源与生态中心负责对此类生物进行收集和常规采样，筛选可用于研发新药的提取物。在此过程中，凭借积累下来的专业知识和技术，海洋生物资源与生态中心开展对具有药用潜力生物的大规模培养，建立样本存储库。而"源海药品"计划提供了包括来自南部海洋的具有良好生物活性的深海生物体，实现了商业规模药用生物的养殖，掌握了微生物及酶的提取技术。[1] 此外，国家极地和海洋研究中心负责极地和南印度洋的海洋研究，受地球科学部委托，与国家海洋技术研究所、国家海洋研究所一起开展对专属经济区的调查，绘制专属经济区内的海底地形地貌。[2]

（三）海洋管理的其他行政机构

1. 农业和农民福利部

农业是印度一半以上人口的主要生计来源，其 54.6% 的人口从事农业及相关活动，农业在印度经济中起着至关重要的作用，占该国总附加值的 17.4%。农业和农民福利部（Ministry of Agriculture & Farmers Welfare）是印度农业规章的制定者和农业发展的管理者，由三部分组成：一是农业合作和农民福利部门（Department of Agriculture Co-operation and Farmers Welfare），负责促进农业生产，保障农民福利；二是畜牧、乳制品及渔业部门（Department of Animal Husbandry, Dairying & Fisheries），负责肉类乳品来源的养殖捕捞；三是农业调查和教育部门（Department of Agriculture Research and Education），负责研究农业市场运营和开发技术。[3] 除上述部门外，农业和农民福利部还下设专门的印度渔业调查研究所（Fishery Survey of India, FSI），以满足渔业

---

[1] "Monitoring and Modeling of Marine Ecosystems", MoES, https：//www. moes. gov. in/programmes/ monitoring-and-modeling-marine-ecosystems-mmme, February 10, 2020.

[2] NCPOR, "Survey of the EEZ", http：//www. ncaor. gov. in/pages/researchview/7, February 11, 2020.

[3] Depatrment of Agriculture Cooperation & Farmers Welfare, "Glance", http：//agricoop. nic. in/ department-glance, November 28, 2019.

发展尤其是深海捕捞的动态需求。该渔业调查研究所是印度渔业的国家研究所，由农业和农民福利部于 1983 年设立。该机构致力于研究和调查在印度专属经济区内的传统及深海渔业状况，并负责编写年度渔业资源调查及相关评估与研究计划，以满足传统渔民、中小型船舶经营者和深海工业船队的可持续渔业需求。

渔业调查研究所源于印度政府 1946 年建立的深海渔业研究站（Deep Finishing Station）试点项目。该项目的初衷是发展深海渔业以增加印度的食物供应。1974 年，该项目被命名为"渔业考察计划"（Exploratory Fisheries Project），并逐步获得了勘查机构的地位。其位于沿海各邦的办公基地被称为"近海渔业工作站"（Offshore Fishing Stations），致力于渔业勘探、渔场图绘制、捕捞作业培训和深海捕捞商业可能性的探索。

随着印度专属经济区的划定以及海洋渔业发展重要性的提升，印度对资源信息的需求也日益增加。为了满足相关新兴需要，"渔业考察计划"的勘查机构在 1983 年进行了重大的结构和职能改革，重组为国家级的研究机构并更名为"印度渔业调查研究所"。1988 年，该所再次重组并被承认为国家级的科学技术研究所，从而扩大了其职能的内容和活动的范围。至此，渔业调查研究所成为印度的专门性渔业研究所，主要负责调查和评估印度专属经济区及附近区域的渔业资源，以促进海洋渔业资源的可持续开发和管理。[1]

当前，渔业调查研究所的主要任务是：（1）对印度专属经济区和临近公海的鱼类资源进行调查和评估，并绘制渔场图；（2）监测海洋渔业资源，以便进行渔业监管；（3）以海洋生态系统环境和生态的最大可持续产量概念为参考，对深海捕鱼量的适宜性进行评估；（4）对海洋渔业进行预报，包括在渔业管理中应用遥感等技术；（5）维护深海渔业资源的数据，并向不同的用户群体传播信息；（6）通过培训渔业工人和满足关联机构的师资需求来开发人力资源。[2] 2005 年，海洋工程部（Marine Engineering Division）并入渔业调查研究所，为研究所提供了更多资源和技术上的支持。[3]

2. 环境、森林和气候变化部

环境、森林和气候变化部（Ministry of Environment and Forest and Climate

〔1〕 "About Us", Fishery Survey of India, http：//fsi. gov. in/LATEST-WB-SITE/fsi-ab-us-frm. htm, November 28, 2019.

〔2〕 "Mandate", Fishery Survey of India, http：//fsi. gov. in/LATEST-WB-SITE/fsi-mand-frm. htm, November 28, 2019.

〔3〕 "About Us", Fishery Survey of India, http：//fsi. gov. in/LATEST-WB-SITE/fsi-ab-us-frm. htm, November 28, 2019.

Change）负责印度环境、林业及气候方面的政策与计划之制订和实施，包括保护动植物、森林与野生生物；预防和控制污染；植树造林和恢复退化地区的环境等。为了保护沿海环境，环境、森林和气候变化部拟定了《沿海监管区通告》。该通知于 2011 年、2018 年进行了两次修订。根据该通知，印度政府宣布在沿海各邦划分沿海监管区（Coastal Regulation Zone，CRZ）。环境、森林和气候变化部授权沿海各邦政府和联邦政府的行政机关实行沿海监管区管理计划（Coastal Zone Management Plans），通过该计划保护印度沿海地区的环境并促进经济发展。[1]

2011 年 2 月 8 日，环境、森林和气候变化部根据《1986 年环境（保护）法》［The Environment（Protection）Act］和《沿海监管区通告》，组建了沿海监管区管理局（Coastal Zone Management Authority）。根据《2017 年重组国家沿海监管区管理局》的通告，管理局的权力及职能主要包括：第一，根据《环境（保护）法》以及根据该法制定的规则，或根据与上述目的相关的任何其他法律，协调各邦沿海地区管理当局（SCZMA）和联邦领土沿海地区管理当局（UTZMA）的行动。第二，审查来自各邦沿海监管区管理机构及联邦领土沿海监管区管理机构的、为阐明沿海监管区相关地域及沿海监管区计划而提出的改进或修订性提案，并向中央政府提出特定建议。第三，审核涉及违反《环境（保护）法》及其下相关规则（rules）或任何与《环境（保护）法》宗旨相关的其他法律的案件，无论是依职权还是基于个人、团体或组织的申告；并在必要时依《环境（保护）法》第 5 节作出指示。第四，在不服从上述指示时，依据《环境（保护）法》第 19 节提出诉告。第五，依《环境（保护）法》第 10 节采取相关措施核实与案件有关的各项事实。第六，就保护和改善沿海环境相关事宜，向各邦政府、中央直辖区政府、各邦沿海监管区管理机构、中央直辖区沿海监管区管理机构等各级政府机构及其他必要的机构或组织提供技术援助和指导。第七，审查和批准特定区域管理计划、综合沿海监管区管理计划，并审查和批准各邦沿海监管区管理机构及联邦沿海监管区管理机构就此所提交的修改提案。第八，与沿海监管区管理有关的事宜，就政策和规划、研究和开发、建立英才中心和资金提供等，向中央政府提出建议。第九，处理中央政府所指示的与沿海监管区有关的所有环境问题。第十，将有关会议议程和会议记录的信息通过环境、森林和气候变化部官网等渠道公开发布。第十一，在有需要时，邀请其他专家参与沿海地

---

［1］ "National Coastal Zone Management Authority（NCZMA）", Ministry of Environment，http：// moef. gov. in/en/e-citizen/national-coastal-zone-management-authority-nczma/，November 28，2019.

区管理会议。[1]

3. 港口、航运和水道部

港口、航运和水道部（Ministry of Ports，Shipping and Waterways）在印度历史上经过多次分立重组，是制定和执行有关航运的规章制度和法律的最高机构。1942 年 7 月，印度运输部门拆分成立邮政部（Department of Posts）和战争运输部（Department of War Transport）。其中，战争运输部的职能范围覆盖了主要港口、铁路枢纽、公路及水上交通、汽油配给及天然气生产，其设立初衷在于协调战时的交通需求，并引导推动沿岸航运及主要港口的管理与开发。1957—2004 年，战争运输部历经运输部（Department of Transport），交通、航运与旅游部（Department of Transport，Shipping & Tourism），航运与交通部（Ministry of Shipping and Transport），地面运输部（Department/Ministry of Surface Transport），航运部（Department/Ministry of Shipping）的更名改组，先后隶属运输与通信部（Ministry of Transport & Communications）、运输与航空部（Ministry of Transport and Aviation）、航运与交通部（Ministry of Shipping and Transport）、航运部（Ministry of Shipping）等，最终再次成为独立国家机关。[2] 2020 年 11 月，航运部正式更名为港口、航运和水道部。

当前，印度的航运部下设各航运及港口部门，负责包括造船业和修船业、主要港口、国家水路和内河运输的相关管理与服务，经授权制定上述问题相关的政策和方案并担负其落实和执行。在海运方面，航运部致力于制定一套全面的政策以解决海运领域所面临的各类问题，包括：大幅提升港口的泊位和货物装卸设备的容量，以配合日益增长的海外贸易需求；制定私营部门参与港口建设的综合政策指导方针，以鼓励私营部门参与港口建设等；从而使航运业能够在本国市场承担更高的海上贸易份额。[3]

4. 科学与技术部

科学与技术部（Department of Science & Technology）成立于 1971 年 5 月，其宗旨是开拓科学技术的新领域，并作为节点部门组织、协调和促进全国科技活动的开展深入。在其职责范围内 18 个方向的具体项目和方案中，

---

〔1〕 See Article 4，S. O. 3266 （e）06. 10. 2017-Reconstitution Of National Coastal Zone Management Authority，MOEF，http：//moef. gov. in/wp-content/uploads/2017/11/6-10-2017-NCZMA-NOTI-FICATION. pdf，March 2，2021.

〔2〕 "Organisation History"，Ministry of Shipping，http：//shipmin. gov. in/index1. php？lang = 1&level = 1&sublinkid = 42&lid = 52，November 28，2019.

〔3〕 "Introduction"，Ministry of Ports，Shipping and Waterways，https：//shipmin. gov. in/about-us/introduction，March 3，2022.

科学与工业研究及其技术的推广应用占有重要一席。[1] 隶属于科学与技术部的科学与工业研究委员会（Council of Scientific & Industrial Research，CSIR），是在多个科技领域具有尖端研发知识库的先进研发组织。该委员会拥有覆盖全印度的 38 个国家实验室、39 个外联中心、3 个创新中心和 5 个实验单位，由约 8000 名科技人员组成的团队支持着约 4600 名科学家在各具研发专长和专业经验的领域不断创造。[2] 而成立于 1966 年的国家海洋研究所（National Institute of Oceanography）正为该委员会下设的 40 余个特色实验室之一，是从事海洋科研尤其是北印度洋研究的独立机构。

20 世纪 50 年代，全球海洋学家在对大西洋和太平洋的探索方面取得了很大进展，但对印度洋的了解却相对滞后。1959—1965 年，印度海洋学研究科学委员会（Scientific Committee on Oceanographic Research）和政府间海洋学委员会（Intergovernmental Oceanographic Commission）主导组织了一个名为"国际印度洋远征"（International Indian Ocean Expedition）的项目，其最重要的成果之一即为印度洋生物学中心（Indian Ocean Biological Centre）的成立。1966 年 1 月 1 日，该中心成为国家海洋研究所，并获得国家实验所的地位。

国家海洋研究所的规模不断扩大，目前该研究所共拥有 200 名科学家和 100 名技术支持人员。其主要研究领域既包括海洋生物、海洋化学、地质（地球）物理和海洋物理这四个海洋学传统分支，也包括海洋工程、海洋仪器和海洋考古学等多个新兴研究方向。该研究所在果阿邦的总部以及在各区域中心拥有众多先进的实验室，并拥有印度海洋科学相关藏书最丰富的图书馆。除了基础研究，该研究所还依托行业赞助开展应用性研究，包括海洋数据收集、环境影响评估以及用于预测环境影响的建模等。同时，研究所积极为政府部门及私营部门提供海洋环境保护和沿海地区法规方面的咨询服务。[3]

5. 新能源和可再生能源部

新能源和可再生能源部（The Ministry of New and Renewable Energy，MoNRE）是一个科学性部门，于 1981 年 3 月设立，受两次石油危机的影响，负责实施开发新能源和可再生能源的计划和相关政策。1982 年，新能源和可再生能源部的前身被能源部（Ministry of Energy）的下属机构非传统能源局

[1]　"Introduction"，Department of Science & Technology，https：//dst. gov. in/about-us/introduction，November 28，2019.

[2]　See "About CSIR"，CSIR，https：//www. csir. res. in/about-us/about-csir，November 28，2019；CSIR，"Labs"，https：//www. csir. res. in/csir-labs，November 28，2019.

[3]　"About"，National Institute of Oceanography，http：// www. nio. org，November 28，2019.

(The Department of Non-conventional Energy Sources）合并。1992 年，非传统能源局成为非传统能源部（The Ministry of Non-conventional Energy Sources），后于 2006 年 10 月正式更名为新能源和可再生能源部。[1] 新能源和可再生能源部的任务是确保国家能源安全，提供稳定的能源供应，增强可再生能源包括风能、潮汐能在内的可再生电力的供应能力，促进能源公平和提高能源负担能力。[2]

新能源和可再生能源部下属有五个机构：国立太阳能研究所（National Institute of Solar Energy）、国立风能研究所（National Institute of Wind Energy）、印度太阳能公司（Solar Energy Corporation of India）、国家可再生能源研究所（National Institute of Renewable Energy）、印度可再生能源发展署（The Indian Renewable Energy Development Agency）。[3]

6. 石油和天然气部

早在 2013 年，印度的能源消费量即紧随中国和美国之后，位列全球第三位。尽管拥有丰富的化石燃料资源，但是印度的能源消费仍越来越依赖进口。

石油和天然气部（Ministry of Petroleum and Natural Gas，MoPNG）掌控着国内石油行业全部产业链，包括勘探、开发、炼化、输送和销售，统辖众多国有公司（Public Sector Undertaking，PSU）。其下属机构碳氢化合物总局（Directorate General of Hydrocarbons，DGH）负责石油天然气行业上游勘探开发和监管，包括但不限于就勘探策略和生产政策向石油和天然气部提供咨询；海底可燃冰（Gas Hydrate）、页岩气、页岩油和油页岩等非常规油气资源的勘探与开发；履行其他与此相关而政府不能及时指派的职能。[4] 为开发海底可燃冰，石油和天然气部及碳氢化合物总局已与来自美国、日本、德国的六个国家机构签署《谅解备忘录》，共享科学数据，开展实地研究活动。[5] 国有公司具体实施油气资源的勘探和开发，截至 2016 年 1 月，探明深海、浅海石油天然气矿区总计已有 104 个。64 个石油天然气矿区已投入生

---

〔1〕 "History-background", MoNRE, https：//mnre. gov. in/history-background, February 11, 2020.

〔2〕 "Mission", MoNRE, https：//mnre. gov. in/mission, February 11, 2020.

〔3〕 "Institutes / Agencies", MoNRE, https：//mnre. gov. in/national-institute-solar-energy, February 11, 2020.

〔4〕 "About Us", DGH, http：//dghindia. gov. in/index. php/page? pageId = 24&name = About% 20Us, February 11, 2020.

〔5〕 "Exploration & Production", MoPNG, http：//petroleum. nic. in/exploration-production/about-exploration-production, February 12, 2020.

产。[1] 国有公司中，印度石油天然气公司（ONGC）是印度国内最大的石油生产商，其油气开采大部分来源于孟买西海岸的孟买高地（Mubai High）油田。[2]

（四）海上武装执法机构

印度的海上武装执法职能主要由其海岸警卫队及海军承担。该两者都隶属于印度国防部，但在职责范围、执法方式等方面各有侧重。

1. 印度海岸警卫队

早在 20 世纪 60 年代，印度海军就向政府提议设立实施海商海事法律及执行在印度水域"安全与护卫"职责的辅助性力量，因为在这些领域部署高精尖的战舰及其他设施并非最优选项。随着 70 年代国内外情势的变化，这一提议得到了印度政府的采纳。一则，在这一时期，猖獗的海上走私已经威胁到印度国家经济，而既有的海事机构如海关和渔业部门却无力应对如此大规模的走私行动，甚至无法在领水拦截违法船舶，设立单独海事武装力量成为反走私的必要。二则，随着《联合国海洋法公约》谈判中对沿岸国专属经济区权利的确认，印度也于 1976 年颁布海域划定相关立法，由此所划入其专属管辖的 201 万平方公里海域需要巡查与守护；三则，孟买油田的发现及后续昂贵的沿岸设施开发建设，也需要必要的保护与灾难响应措施。1974 年 9 月，印度成立了一个专门委员会以研究现有机制在应对海上走私及其他非法海事活动时的不足。该委员会于 1975 年提出报告，强烈建议设立"海岸警卫"性质的组织以对印度海域进行普遍监管与巡察。1977 年 2 月 1 日，内阁决定成立一个临时性的海岸警卫机构。1978 年，印度颁布《海岸警卫队法》（Coast Guard Act，1978），印度海岸警卫队由此作为国家一个独立的武装力量于 1978 年 8 月 19 日正式成立。[3]

当前，印度海岸警卫队是印度四个武装部队之一，其使命是守卫印度共和国的海上利益。其主要任务包括：（1）保护包括石油、鱼类及矿产在内的印度海洋及沿岸财富；（2）保护海上生命和财产的安全，包括在海难中协助海员开展救援行动；（3）落实海洋、非法捕捞、走私及毒品贩卖有关的海商事法及相关制度；（4）维护海洋环境及生态并保护珍稀物种；（5）维护人工

---

〔1〕　"Discoveries"，DGH，http：//dghindia. gov. in/index. php/page? pageId = 64&name = Hydrocarbon% 20Scenario，February 12，2020.

〔2〕　"Mubai High Feild"，Offshore Technology，https：//www. offshore-technology. com/projects/mumbai-high-field/，February 12. 2020.

〔3〕　"History"，Indian Coast Guard，https：//www. indiancoastguard. gov. in/content/290_ 3_ History. aspx，November 28，2019.

岛、近岸码头以及其他海上设施的安全；（6）收集相关科研数据；（7）为海军作战提供后援力量。[1]

2. 印度海军

印度海军的建制可以追溯至东印度公司时期的海军陆战队。1612 年，东印度公司组建海军陆战队以保护在该地区的英国商船。随着 18 世纪末至 19 世纪初东印度公司对印度次大陆东部（孟加拉）建立统治，该海军陆战队于 1830 年改称"大英帝国印度海军"（Her Majesty's Indian Navy）。在历经"孟买海军陆战队""大英帝国印度海军陆战队"等名称及编制转变后，其于 1892 年被改组为拥有 50 艘舰艇的"皇家印度海军陆战队"（Royal Indian Marine），并主要作为英军的后勤力量参与第一次世界大战。第二次世界大战前夕，"皇家印度海军陆战队"改制为"皇家印度海军"（Royal Indian Navy），并在战后得到了长足的发展。随着 1950 年 1 月印度共和国成立，"皇家印度海军"正式更名为"印度海军"（Indian Navy）。[2]

近年来，印度军事力量获得一定的发展，尽管由于军工基础薄弱、财力有限，整体而言与预期目标有很大的差距，但印度海军建设仍取得引人瞩目的成果。当前，印度海军建设有水面舰艇部队、海军航空兵部队与水下潜艇部队三支作战单元。其中，水面舰艇部队拥有航空母舰"维克拉马蒂亚"号，"加尔各答"级导弹驱逐舰、"德里"级与"拉吉普特"级驱逐舰、"什瓦里克"级与"塔尔瓦"级护卫舰约 26 艘，以及多艘轻巡洋舰、两栖登陆船坞、登陆艇等；水下潜艇部队则拥有"歼敌者"号核潜艇 1 艘、新锐常规动力"鲉鱼"级潜艇、"基洛"级潜艇 9 艘、"西舒玛"级潜艇 4 艘。[3]

从高强度的正式战争到人道主义援助和救灾行动，印度对其海军作出了极为广泛的角色定位，也因而将其职能事项划分为四大部分：第一，军事职能（Military Role）。通过在海上或从海上威胁使用武力或使用武力，以防范敌对海上力量破坏自己的国家安全和利益，既包括在对敌方领土和贸易的进攻行动中使用海洋武装力量，也包括在保护本国军队、领土和贸易的防御行动中使用海洋武装力量。第二，外交职能（Diplomatic Role）。即使用海军力

---

[1] "Mission", Indian Coast Guard, https：//www. indiancoastguard. gov. in/content/248_3_Mission. aspx, November 28, 2019.

[2] "Mission", Indian Coast Guard, https：//www. indiancoastguard. gov. in/content/248_3_Mission. aspx, November 28, 2019.

[3] See "Surface Ships", Indian Navy, https：//www. indiannavy. nic. in/surface-ships-0, November 29, 2019; "Submarines Active", Indian Navy, https：//www. indiannavy. nic. in/content/submarines-active, November 29, 2019.

量来支持外交政策目标，一方面建立"友谊的桥梁"以加强国际合作，另一方面表明威慑潜在对手的能力和意图。海军外交将有利于塑造海洋环境，维护国家利益，促进外交政策的执行与国家安全目标的实现。第三，警察职能（Constabulary Role）。海军的警察职能是应对日益增加的海上犯罪。海军所担负的警察职责主要在于执行相关国际条约制度及国内立法以维持良好的海上秩序，武力仅作为自卫或执行过程中的最后手段。执行海上警察职能并非海军的首要任务。随着 1978 年印度海上警卫队的成立，印度管辖海域内的警察执法任务已由其全面接管，印度海军仅负责印度管辖海域以外的海洋执法。不过，受 2008 年孟买恐怖袭击的影响，印度海军被授权在与国家及各邦海岸警卫队、中央及各邦政府，以及各地港口管理当局的紧密协作下，负责印度海岸的总体安全。第四，和平职能（Benign Role）。和平职能主要涉及人道主义援助、救灾、搜索和救援（SAR）、军械处理、潜水援助、打捞作业、水道测量等相关工作。武力或武力威胁在这一职能实施过程中基本没有使用的必要和空间，但海军特遣部队固有的机动性、可达性和耐久力在危机早期阶段的救济物资提供、急救和援助等方面极有价值。国家海岸警卫队是印度国家搜救行动的指定机构，但海军仍可根据需要被投入救援，并可能在专门性民事机构的后续接管阶段被部署为补充力量。[1]

根据印度海军的海洋战略蓝图，其将按照功能分别组编保卫海岸线和港口的浅海海军以及由远洋立体舰队组成的深海海军，以遏阻印度洋上大国海军的行动为基本任务，以反潜作战为基本形式，在广阔的印度洋水域中实施水下、海上、空中的立体打击，从而保卫印度漫长的海岸线、岛屿领土以及专属经济区，并且将具备控制苏伊士运河、霍尔木兹海峡、马六甲海峡等印度洋战略要地的能力，最终实现把印度洋变为"印度湖"的"宏愿"。印度海洋军事愿景的勃勃野心可见一斑。[2]

---

〔1〕 "Role of Navy", Indian Navy, https：//www. indiannavy. nic. in/content/role-navy, November 29, 2019.

〔2〕 "Blueprint to Bluewater", Indian Navy, https：//www. indiannavy. nic. in/node/1421, November 29, 2019.

三、国内海洋立法

由于古代印度次大陆主要为印度教徒的居所，其法律制度源于印度教的宗教和社会习俗，以印度教社会的独特种姓制度和共同家庭制度为基础。而随着公元 11 世纪前后穆斯林人对印度的入侵，印度的大部分地区逐渐接受穆斯林的统治，并建立起穆斯林法律体系和穆斯林司法机构。自公元 17 世纪开始，以商人身份进入印度的英国人逐渐征服整个次大陆。在长达一个多世纪的征服与统治之中，英国统治者建立法院和任命法官，从而使现代印度的法律体系、司法机构及相关术语和概念都承袭、模仿英国。值得注意的是，就人身法的适用而言，在印度，往往需要根据具体主体的宗教信仰而分别适用印度教法或穆斯林法，这也是在英国统治时期即被采用的惯常做法。不过，即使仍然保留区分适用的实践，两种传统法律在印度独立后的成文化进度呈现明显反差：一方面，大部分印度教法都已被编纂成法律；另一方面，穆斯林法尚无成文法，法院只能根据权威评论和司法判例适用穆斯林法。

除《印度宪法》以外，当今印度的法律渊源分为主要渊源和次要渊源两个层级。其中，主要渊源包括：联邦议会和各邦议会通过的成文法，联邦议会通过的叫中央法案（Central Act），各邦议会通过的叫邦法案（State Act）；总统和邦长在联邦议会或各邦议会闭会期间发布的条例（Ordinance），但这些条例自联邦议会或各邦议会重新召开六个星期后失效；由议会通过的成文法所授权行政机关制定的规则（Rule）和法规（Regulation）。此外，还包括主要由行政机关使用的通报（Circular）、命令（Order）、通知（Notification）等规范性文件，但不应将其视为主要渊源。

而印度的次要法律渊源是最高法院、高等法院和一些专门法庭的判决。依据《印度宪法》第 141 条、第 142 条第 1 款，最高法院宣布的法令对印度境内的所有法院具有约束力；最高法院行使其司法管辖权时，为了充分公平处理任何未决诉讼或案件，可以发布必要的法令或命令，这种法令或命令应在印度全国范围内予以执行。由是，印度不仅承袭了判例法传统，还在典型的"法官造法"上似有所超越。[1]

---

〔1〕 Ramakrishnan Viraraghavan，"UPDATE：Guide to Indian Laws"，https：//www.nyulawglobal.org/globalex/India1.html#_ edn157，February 11，2020.

（一）划定管辖海域的法

1. 关于国家领土和管辖海域的基本规定

《印度宪法》于 1949 年 11 月 26 日由制宪议会通过，并于 1950 年 1 月 26 日生效。1951 年至 2015 年，印度共颁布了 100 个宪法修正案[1]。根据《1949 年印度宪法》第 1 条第 3 款规定："印度领土包括：一、各邦领土；二、第一附表所列之中央直辖区领土；三、将来取得之其他领土。"[2] 除该条之外，《印度宪法》中再无其他涉及海洋领土的规定，也未直接对管辖海域作出划定，仅在《印度宪法》第 297 条提出：领海、大陆架（1963 年第 15 次宪法修正案加入）[3] 有价值的资源和专属经济区（1976 年第 40 次宪法修正案加入）内的资源，均属于联邦。1976 年的第 40 次修正案中还规定：印度领海海域及大陆架上的土地、矿物及其他有价值的资源均属于联邦政府，应由联邦支配其用途；印度专属经济区的所有其他资源也属联邦所有，应由联邦支配其用途；印度领海大陆架、专属经济区与其他海洋区域的范围由议会法律随时确定。[4]

可以看到，作为拥有较广袤陆地领土的国家，印度更侧重于对陆地领土的保护和规定，对海洋的重视则不足，体现在宪法中便是对海洋的专门性规定较少，仅局限于概括性的规定；另一方面，印度制定《印度宪法》的时间节点正好是印度独立初期，此时的印度急于摆脱殖民统治，其立宪重心尚未放在海洋主权及相关海洋利益上。但是随着世界各国对海洋的关注，以及随着联合国三次海洋法会议的召开及海洋法公约的谈判，印度对于海洋权益的重视程度日渐加深，立法上也随之有所改变，其几个宪法修正案的颁布正是说明。

2. 关于领海宽度以及领海基线的规定

1976 年，印度议会通过《领海、大陆架、专属经济区及其他海洋区域

[1]　"The Constitution of India", India Code, https：//www. india. gov. in/my-government/constitution-india, February 11，2020.

[2]　See Article 1（3），The Constitution of India，India Code，https：//www. india. gov. in/sites/upload_ files/npi/files/coi_ part_ full. pdf，February 11，2020.

[3]　See Artile 9："Amendment of article 297. —In article 297 of the Constitution，after the words 'territorial waters'，the words 'or the continental shelf' shall be inserted"，The Constitution（Fifteenth Amendment）Act，1963，India Code，https：//www. india. gov. in/my-government/constitution-india/amendments/constitution-india-fifteenth-amendment-act-1963，February 11，2020.

[4]　See Artile 2，The Constitution（Fortieth Amendment）Act，1976，India Code，https：//www. india. gov. in/my-government/constitution-india/amendments/constitution-india-fortieth-amendment-act-1976，February 11，2020.

法》（Territorial Waters，Continental Shelf，Exclusive Economic Zone and Other Maritime Zones Act，1976，以下简称《1976 年海域法》）。该法共包括 16 条规定，除了第 5 条关于毗连区及第 7 条关于专属经济区的相关规定单独由中央政府专门发布政府公报（Official Gazette）宣布生效以外（已于 1977 年发布公报生效），其余条款于发布之时（1976 年 8 月 25 日）立即生效。

根据该法第 3 条，印度的主权及于印度的领海、领海的海床及底土以及领海上空。其领海的外部界限为一条其每一点与领海基线最近点的距离等于 12 海里的线。该法同时指出，如果中央政府依据国际法或本国实践认为有必要的，可以于任何时间于政府公报中作出通知后，更改领海外部界限，并在经过议会两院批准后发布。与此同时，该法第 4 条对外国军舰无害通过领海的权利作出了限制，规定外国军舰进入印度领海必须事先通知印度中央政府。[1]

2009 年，印度先于 5 月 11 日颁布了《外交部通告》（Ministry of External Affairs Notification，以下简称《2009 年通告》），对领海基线的基点坐标作出了明确规定，并于 11 月 20 日颁布了《外交部勘误表》（Ministry of External Affairs Corrigendum，以下简称《2009 年勘误表》）对前述通知的部分内容进行更正，并向联合国提交了这两份文件。在文件中印度指出，印度的领海基线的划定，交替采用正常基线和直线基线。[2] 其划定基线的各基点坐标如第 I 部分表 1、表 2、表 3、表 4 所示：

第 I 部分 表 1 印度划定的西海岸基线体系基点坐标

基点	地理名称	地理坐标	
		纬度（北）	经度（东）
1	Sir Mouth N.	23°40′20.80″	68°04′31.20″
2	Sir Mouth S.	23°36′30.30″	68°07′00.90″
3	Pir Sanai Creek	23°36′15.20″	68°07′28.50″
4	Kori Creek	23°24′14″	68°20′49″
5	Veraya Thar	23°18′24″	68°27′48″

---

[1] "The Territorial Waters，Continental Shelf，Exclusive Economic Zone and Other Maritime Zones Act，1976"，India Code，https：//www. indiacode. nic. in/handle/123456789/1484？sam _ handle = 123456789/1362，March 10，2020.

[2] UN Office of Legal Affairs，"Ministry of External Affairs Notification"，https：//www. un. org/Depts/los/LEGISLATIONANDTREATIES/PDFFILES/DEPOSIT/ind _ mzn7x _ 2009. pdf，February 11，2020.

续表

基点	地理名称	地理坐标	
		纬度（北）	经度（东）
6	Kharo Creek	23°15′40″	68°30′50″
7	Bari Bn.	23°11′03″	68°36′33″
8	Kachchigad （Thence following low water line to baseline point 9）	22°18′36″	68°55′58″
9	Diu Head W.	20°41′24″	70°49′18″
10	Tarapur Pt.	19°50′32″	72°38′13″
11	Mahim Cr.	19°37′40″	72°41′16″
12	Ussapur Rk.	19°32′26″	72°42′00″
13	Poshpir Is.	19°20′15″	72°44′58″
14	Outer Is.	19°15′52″	72°45′36″
15	Mehti Khada	19°08′00″	72°46′27″
16	Outer Rf. Back Bay	18°55′21″	72°47′21″
17	Prongs Rf.	18°52′33″	72°47′42″
18	Kanhoji Angre	18°42′12″	72°48′48″
19	Whale Rf.	18°16′16″	72°54′53″
20	Kumbaru Pt.	18°13′01″	72°55′55″
21	Srivardhan Lt.	18°03′14″	72°59′28″
22	Srivardhan Pt.	18°01′12″	73°00′09″
23	Bankot	17°58′08″	73°01′10″
24	Dighi	17°56′31″	73°01′50″
25	Ranvi Pt.	17°33′20″	73°08′16″
26	Boria Pt	17°24′18″	73°10′00″
27	Jaigarh Lt.	17°17′53″	73°11′27″
28	Miria Head	17°01′36″	73°15′12″
29	Mushroom Rk.	16°32′17″	73°18′36″
30	Girye Bay	16°30′40″	73°18′59″
31	Burnt Is.	15°53′18″	73°27′21″
32	Saint George Is.（Sail Rock）	15°20′38″	73°45′40″
33	Cape Rama	15°05′00″	73°54′46″
34	Mangalgudda Is.	14°48′54″	74°03′18″

续表

基点	地理名称	地理坐标	
		纬度（北）	经度（东）
35	Basavarajadurg Is.	14°18′43″	74°23′54″
36	Netrani Is.	14°00′37″	74°19′22″
37	Coconut Is. （North）	13°24′06″	74°38′57″
38	Mulki Rks.	13°11′54″	74°40′18″
39	Mangalore S.	12°50′58″	74°49′32″
40	Bekal	12°24′30″	75°00′32″
41	Kotte Kunnu	12°00′20″	75°12′04″
42	Sacrifice Rk.	11°29′30″	75°31′40″
43	Ponnani N.	10°47′24″	75°54′36″
44	Chetwai	10°31′30″	76°01′42″
45	Sand Patch （off Kochi）	09°58′27″	76°13′18″
46	Alleppey （Thence following low water line including offlying islands to baseline point 47）	09°30′22″	76°18′48″
47	Vivekananda Memorial	08°04′24″	77°33′24″
48	Idindakarai	08°10′33″	77°44′48″
49	Manappad Pt.	08°22′24″	78°04′12″
50	Tiruchchendur Pt.	08°29′44″	78°07′54″
51	Tuticorin Jetty Lt. House	08°44′48″	78°13′48″
52	Nalla Tanni Is.	09°06′03″	78°34′48″
53	Musal Tivu	09°11′24″	79°05′18″
54	Adam's Bridge （Thence join by straight line on East Coast to baseline point 55）	09°05′36″	79°31′48″

第Ⅰ部分 表2 印度划定的东海岸基线体系基点坐标

基点	地理名称	地理坐标	
		纬度（北）	经度（东）
55	Adam's Bridge N.	09°06′24″	79°31′36″
56	Devils Point （Thence following low water line to baseline point 57）	09°19′00″	79°20′12″
57	Pt. Calimere W.	10°17′30″	79°52′42″

续表

基点	地理名称	地理坐标	
		纬度（北）	经度（东）
58	Pt. Calimere NE.	10°18′30″	79°53′20″
59	Pt. Calimere N. (Thence following low water line to baseline point 60)	10°19′30″	79°52′50″
60	Caverippattinam N.	11°11′50″	79°51′30″
61	Coleroon S.	11°21′00″	79°50′45″
62	Cuddalore	11°42′22″	79°47′00″
63	Malakkanam	12°13′15″	79°59′37″
64	Palar R.	12°26′48″	80°08′45″
65	Mamallapuram	12°36′24″	80°12′30″
66	Covelong Pt.	12°46′54″	80°15′24″
67	Ennur N.	13°16′36″	80°20′48″
68	Kattupalli	13°18′25″	80°20′56″
69	Tangal	13°20′36″	80°20′36″
70	Pulicat	13°26′36″	80°19′36″
71	Point Pudi	13°46′54″	80°15′20″
72	Penner R.	14°34′40″	80°11′50″
73	Motumala	15°29′45″	80°12′45″
74	False Divi E.	15°43′25″	80°56′30″
75	Golumuttapaya R.	15°46′00″	81°00′40″
76	Divi Pt.	15°58′00″	81°09′24″
77	Narsapur Pt.	16°17′40″	81°42′00″
78	Bandamurlanka	16°23′40″	81°57′30″
79	Karakutippa	16°34′15″	82°19′20″
80	Jonnala Konda	17°35′24″	83°12′54″
81	Kalingapatnam	18°19′00″	84°08′03″
82	Bavana Padu S.	18°33′22″	84°21′32″
83	Ganguvada (Thence following low water line to baseline point 84)	18°47′40″	84°33′30″
84	Devi Pt.	19°57′00″	86°22′30″
85	Dowdeswell Is.	20°20′30″	86°47′33″
86	Wheeler Is.	20°44′30″	87°06′06″
87	West Spit	21°22′42″	88°43′30″

续表

基点	地理名称	地理坐标	
		纬度（北）	经度（东）
88	New Moore Is. S.	21°33′54″	89°08′45″
89	New Moore Is. E.	21°34′37″	89°12′23″

第Ⅰ部分 表3 安达曼和尼科巴群岛基线体系（西）基点坐标

基点	地理名称	地理坐标	
		纬度（北）	经度（东）
90	Cape Land Fall E.	13°40′29″	93°01′12″
91	Cape Land Fall W.	13°40′30″	93°00′52″
92	Landfall Is. NE.	13°39′57″	92°59′03″
93	Land Fall Island W.	13°39′44″	92°58′39″
94	West Is. N.	13°35′50″	92°53′28″
95	West Is. S.	13°34′46″	92°52′58″
96	Point Is. N.	13°25′27″	92°48′32″
97	North Reef Is.	13°05′12″	92°41′10″
98	Interview Is.	12°51′40″	92°39′00″
99	Flat Is.	12°32′00″	92°40′12″
100	North Sentinel Is.	11°35′06″	92°11′50″
101	South Sentinel Is.	10°58′36″	92°12′36″
102	Little Andaman Is. （Sandy Pt.）	10°32′15″	92°23′10″
103	Car Nicobar Is.	09°09′28″	92°43′02″
104	Teressa Island	08°16′24″	93°04′48″
105	Great Nicobar Is. （Teesta Pt）	07°00′18″	93°39′32″
106	Great Nicobar Is. SW. （Thence following low water line to baseline point 107）	06°45′33″	93°48′16″
107	Indira Pt.	06°45′16″	93°50′15″
108—120	待后另行通告		

第Ⅰ部分 表4 拉克沙群岛基线体系基点坐标

基点	地理名称	地理坐标	
		纬度（北）	经度（东）
121	Cherbaniani Reef	12°23′15″	71°51′48″
122	Byramgore Reef NW.	11°57′48″	71°43′20″

续表

基点	地理名称	地理坐标	
		纬度（北）	经度（东）
123	Byramgore Reef SW.	11°52′30″	71°45′00″
124	Peremul Par	11°10′30″	71°59′50″
125	Suheli Par	10°01′00″	72°14′00″
126	Viringili Is. （Minicoy）NW. （Thence following low water line to baseline point 127）	08°16′34″	73°00′36″
127	Kodi Pt.	08°19′27″	73°04′52″
128	Kalpeni Is.	10°03′30″	73°38′56″
129	Cheriyan Is.	10°08′15″	73°39′55″
130	Androth Is.	10°48′47″	73°42′10″
131	Kiltan Is.	11°29′14″	73°00′38″
132	Cherbaniani	12°23′50″	71°53′10″
133	Cherbaniani North Pt. （Thence join by straight line to baseline point 121）	12°24′00″	71°52′30″

2011 年 12 月，巴基斯坦对印度公布的上述基点提出异议。其在与联合国秘书长的通信中指出，印度所确定的多处基点侵犯了巴基斯坦及国际社会海洋权益。如，印度在上述基点 1—3 间的连线，侵犯了巴基斯坦在爵士湾地区（Sir Creek area）的领土主权并侵占其主权管辖范围内的领海，其基线划定方式违背了《公约》第 7 条第 6 款的规定，即"一国不得采用直线基线制度，致使另一国的领海同公海或专属经济区隔断"。[1]

3. 关于毗连区的基本规定

《1976 年海域法》第 5 条规定，印度毗连区为领海以外邻接领海的一带海域，毗连区的外部界限为一条其每一点与领海基线最近点的距离等于 24海里的线。根据该条规定，除海关、移民、财政、卫生外，中央政府还可以就印度的国家安全问题在毗连区内行使相应的权力和采取必要的措施。印度的这一规定，无疑是对《公约》中沿岸国毗连区相关权力的扩大。同时，中央政府认为有必要时，根据国际法或国内实践，可以通过颁布政府公报的形式对毗连区的外部界限或管辖事项进行调整，并可以在上述公报中制定相应

---

[1]　UN Office of Legal Affairs，"Communication from The Government of Pakistan dated 6 December 2011"，https：//www. un. org/Depts/los/LEGISLATIONANDTREATIES/PDFFILES/DEPOSIT/communicationsredeposit/mzn76_ 2011_ pak. pdf. March 20，2021.

条款以促进相关文件的执行，以上颁布的公报、条款等文件应如同在印度领土适用一样在毗连区产生效力。

4. 关于专属经济区和大陆架的基本规定

依据《1976 年海域法》第 7 条，印度的专属经济区为印度领海以外且邻接领海的区域，从测算领海宽度的基线量起延至 200 海里。第 6 条规定，印度的大陆架为印度领海以外本国陆地领土的全部自然延伸，扩展到大陆边外缘的海底区域的海床和底土，如果从领海基线量起至大陆架外缘的距离不足 200 海里，则扩展至 200 海里。同时，印度对其大陆架享有完全的、排他的主权权力。

在《1976 年海域法》之后，针对大陆架的相关问题，印度陆续颁布了10 个相关通知，这些通知主要内容包括：对大陆架区域上人工岛屿和人工设施的坐标及其周边 500 米区域进行划定，对指定区域可航行船舶种类进行扩展和调整，对相关法律进行扩展适用，对相关坐标进行增加和勘误。[1] 针对专属经济区的相关问题，印度共发布了 11 个通知，其中大部分与前述大陆架的通知内容一致，仅 2006 年发布的《规定的扩展适用》（Extension of Application of Provisions）是单独适用于专属经济区的，其规定将 1958 年的《商船运输法》的第 3 条第 2 款和第 407 条扩展适用到专属经济区。[2]

5. 关于历史性水域的基本主张

《1976 年海域法》第 8 条对历史性水域的规定为：印度中央政府可以政府公报的形式对邻接其陆地领土的印度历史性水域的界限作出具体规定，印度的主权应延伸并一直延伸至其历史性水域，包括其下的海床和底土，其上的空气空间，以及水域本身。1974 年，印度和斯里兰卡就历史性水域问题签订了《印度共和国政府与斯里兰卡共和国政府关于历史性水域边界的协定》（Agreement between The Government of the Republic of India and The Government of the Republic of Sri Lanka on the boundary in historic waters，以下简称《1974 年协定》）。[3]

1977 年，印度根据《1974 年协定》以及《1976 年海域法》，发布了

〔1〕 "Notifications", India Code, https：//indiacode. nic. in/show-data？actid＝AC_ CEN_ 10_ 10_ 00002 _ 197680 _ 1517807318455&sectionId＝19117&sectionno＝6&orderno＝6，March 10, 2020.

〔2〕 "Extension of Application of Provisions", India Code, https：//upload. indiacode. nic. in/showfile？actid＝AC_ CEN_ 10_ 10_ 00002_ 197680_ 1517807318455&type＝notification&filename＝SO2168% 20Extension% 20of% 20application% 20of% 20provisions% 20 （22. 12. 2006 ）. pdf, March 10, 2020.

〔3〕 关于《1974 年协定》的具体内容，请参见本书第 I 部分中"五、海洋争端解决"。

《1977 年 1 月 15 日印度对历史性水域海洋区域界限的说明》（Description of
The Area of Sea of Limits of Historic Waters of India Jan 15，1977，以下简称
《1977 年说明》）。根据《1977 年说明》，印度在保克海峡（Palk Strait）和
保克海湾（Palk Bay）的历史性水域的界限为一条从北纬 10°17.5′、东经
79°52.7′到北纬 10°05.0′、东经 80°03.0′的弧线；在马纳尔海湾（Gulf of Man-
nar）的历史性水域界限为一条从北纬 08°30.0′、东经 78°07.9′到北纬 08°22.2′、
东经 78°55.4′的弧线。[1]

2009 年，印度在《2009 年通告》和《2009 年勘误表》中再次强调，印
度与斯里兰卡在保克海峡、保克海湾和马纳尔海湾三个地区的历史性水域的
界限应以《1977 年说明》为准。[2]

（二）海上安全相关立法

1957 年，印度议会通过了《海军法》（Navy Act，1957），合并和修改了
与印度海军有关的法律及政府法规。该法共 22 章，主要对《海军法》的适
用对象、术语解释、关于护送商船的纪律性规则、海军军官和其他船员服役
的法律责任及特权豁免，以及入伍、载船、离船、叛变、与敌军交流等相关
纪律规则及违反相关规则的惩处进行了详细规定，是印度维护海上安全军事
力量的基础性立法。[3]

1978 年，印度颁布了《海岸警卫队法》（Coast Guard Act，1978）。该法
案旨在通过组建和管理确保海洋安全的专门武装部队以维护印度在相关区域
和事项上的海洋权益和国家利益。该法共 13 章，123 条，主要涉及海岸警卫
队的组建、纪律、人事任免、法律责任以及相应的程序性权利，根据该法第
14 条的规定，海岸警卫队的主要职责在于：确保印度管辖的人工岛屿、人工
设施、码头及其他建筑和装置的安全；保护印度渔民包括协助他们在海上脱
困；保护海洋环境，防止及控制海洋污染；协助海关等相关机构打击走私；

---

〔1〕　"Description of The Area of Sea of Limits of Historic Waters of India Jan 15，1977"，India Code，
　　　https：//upload. indiacode. nic. in/showfile? actid = AC_ CEN_ 10_ 10_ 00002_ 197680_
　　　1517807318455&type = notification&filename = Description% 20of% 20the% 20area% 20of% 20sea%
　　　20of% 20limits% 20of% 20historic% 20waters% 20of% 20India% 20Jan% 2015，% 201977. pdf，
　　　March 12，2020.
〔2〕　UN Office of Legal Affairs，"Ministry of External Affairs Notification"，https：//www. un. org/
　　　Depts/los/LEGISLATIONANDTREATIES/PDFFILES/DEPOSIT/ind_ mzn7x_ 2009. pdf，March
　　　12，2020.
〔3〕　"The Navy Act，1957"，India Code，https：//www. indiacode. nic. in/bitstream/123456789/1400/
　　　1/AAA1957_ _ _ _ 62. pdf#search = Navy% 20Act，February11，2020.

协助相关海区法律文件的落实；包括保护海上生命和财产安全，收集海上科研数据在内的其他被授权的事项。[1] 1993 年，印度政府批准了《国家石油泄漏灾害应急计划》（National Oil-spill Disaster Contingency Plan），其中明确指出，印度海岸警卫队被指定为负责印度海域石油泄漏的国家主管部门，该计划使海岸警卫队保护海洋环境的职责进一步明确。[2]

2000 年，印度分别加入了《制止危及海上航行安全非法行为公约》（Convention for the Suppression of Unlawful Acts against the Safety of Maritime Navigation）和《制止危及大陆架固定平台安全非法行为议定书》（Protocol for the Suppression of Unlawful Acts against the Safety of Fixed Platforms Located on the Continental Shelf），为了落实印度所承担的相关义务，印度于 2002 年通过了《制止危害海上航行安全和大陆架固定平台安全的非法行为法》（Suppression of Unlawful Acts Against Safety of Maritime Navigation and Fixed Platforms on Continental Shelf Act，2002）。该法共分三章，分别为前言、违法行为及杂项，其中第二章对危害船舶、固定平台、船上货物、海上航行设施的犯罪行为，相关法院、司法程序、引渡条件等作出规定。[3]

（三）海洋渔业相关立法

1. 《1949 年印度宪法》

印度对渔业投入了相当的关注，在印度宪法中已有对渔业管理和发展的基础性规定。《印度宪法》主要通过列表的方式明确各级政府在渔业方面的管理及立法权限。《印度宪法》附表 6 第 3 条规定了地区自治议会与区自治议会的立法权，确认了某些自治地区渔业的立法权，第 6 条还规定了自治地区的自治议会可以在本地区内设立、建设或管理养鱼场。附表 11 则涉及赋予村务委员会（Panchayats）在渔业方面管理的权力。附表 7 尤其对中央政府和各邦政府有关渔业的立法权限作出划分。根据附表 7 表 A 第 57 条，联邦在领水以外的渔业和渔业捕捞事项有专属的排他的立法权，表 B 第 21 条则规定，

---

〔1〕 "The Coast Guard Act, 1978", India Code, https：//www. indiacode. nic. in/bitstream/123456789/ 1734/1/197830. pdf#search = Coast% 20Guard% 20Act, February11, 2020.

〔2〕 "National Oil-spill Disaster Contingency Plan", Indian Coast Guard, https：//indiancoastguard. gov. in/WriteReadData/bookpdf/201512281221565793127NOSDCPCGBR771. pdf, March 11, 2020.

〔3〕 "The Suppression of Unlawful Acts Against Safety of Maritime Navigation and Fixed Platforms on Continental Shelf Act, 2002", India Code, https：//www. indiacode. nic. in/bitstream/123456789/ 2009/1/A2002-69. pdf#search = Suppression% 20of% 20Unlawful% 20Acts% 20Against% 20Safety% 20of% 20Maritime, February11, 2020.

各邦对各邦下的渔业有专属的立法权限[1] 据此，印度各级政府关于渔业的管辖权问题得到充分明晰，这也为印度渔业的管理提供了基础性框架。

2. 《1897 年印度渔业法》

1897 年颁布的《印度渔业法》（Indian Fisheries Act，1897）是印度渔业方面最早的专门性立法，其适用的水域是从海岸线向海洋方向量起的 3 海里的海域。但随着渔业的发展，以及国家利益需求的变化，该法已于 2015 年被废止。该法共 7 条，所涉内容包括术语解释、适用范围、违反该法的逮捕规定等。其中第 2 条规定，该法应视为对其他渔业法的补充，这些法案包括《1886 年阿萨姆邦土地和税收条例》（Assam Land and Revenue Regulation，1886）、《1889 年私人渔业保护法案》（Private Fisheries Protection Act，1889）、《1879 年尼尔吉里斯竞赛及鱼类保护法案》（Nilgiris Game and Fish Preservation Act，1879）、《1914 年旁遮普渔业法案》（Punjab Fisheries Act，1914）；第 4 条规定禁止使用炸药等爆炸物进行捕鱼；第 5 条规定禁止使用毒药等有害物质进行捕鱼；第 6 条则授权地方政府可以就固定引擎的安装与使用、渔网的尺寸和种类以及使用方式、在特定水域连续性捕鱼的禁止等相关问题制定规则。尽管该法案已并非印度的现行立法，但该法在 19 世纪末就已经对固定引擎、私人水域等用语进行解释，对使用爆炸物和毒药等非法捕捞方式作出禁止性规定，同时明确地方政府的职责，从而为印度渔业资源保护构建了初步框架，成为印度早期渔业立法中较具代表性的成果。[2]

3. 《1972 年海产品出口发展局法》

1972 年，印度议会颁布了《海产品出口发展局法》（Marine Products Export Development Authority Act，1972），其旨在为印度的海产品工业发展建立一个专门的机构。根据这一法案，印度中央政府于 1982 年正式成立海产品出口发展局（Marine Products Export Development Authority，MPEDA）。该法第 4 条规定，海产品出口发展局至少有 10 名成员，其中 5 名应分别代表农业部门、财政部门、对外贸易部门、工业部门、运输及交通部门。同时，该法也对海产品出口发展局的主要职能进行规定，包括：第一，采取适当措施促进由中央政府控制的相关海产品工业的发展，尤其是出口方面的发展；第二，发展和规范近海和深海捕鱼，并采取措施保护和管理近海和深海渔业；第三，为用于海产品或海产品运输的渔船、加工厂或仓库提供注册；第四，为

---

[1]　"Constitution Schedule", India Government, https://www.india.gov.in/sites/upload_files/npi/files/coi-eng-schedules_1-12.pdf, February 11, 2020.

[2]　"Indian Fisheries Act, 1897", India Code, http://extwprlegs1.fao.org/docs/pdf/ind42223.pdf, February 11, 2020.

出口的海产品确立质量标准，规范海产品出口并开发印度海产品的海外市场；第五，收集海产品相关的数据和信息，为海产品行业的各方面提供信息和培训，等等。[1]

4. 海上捕鱼监管相关立法

20世纪60年代以来，印度小型机械船的使用不断增加，到了70年代，有近53000艘此类船舶在沿海进行捕鱼活动，与此同时，渔民还对鲭鱼和沙丁鱼等远洋浅滩鱼类实行围捕。正是在这样的背景下，1976年3月22—23日在新德里举行的中央渔业委员会第十次会议认识到维护传统渔民利益的必要性和可能性，中央政府根据会议建议，于1976年5月成立了一个委员会，以研究划定不同类型船只的捕鱼范围问题。委员会于1978年12月提交了一份报告，并附《海上捕鱼监管草案》（Marine Fisheries Regulations Bill）范本。1979年，该范本被分发给沿海各邦，以让各邦制定适当的法律。

依据《海上捕鱼监管草案》以及《印度渔业法》，印度沿海各邦陆续制定了《海上捕鱼监管法》（Marine Fishing Regulation Acts），对在领海范围内的捕鱼管理和养护措施进行规定。这些规定主要包括：调节网眼尺寸，以免捕获幼鱼；可捕捞的最小和最大鱼类规格；调节渔具，以避免过度捕捞特定物种；保留传统渔民的保护区；休渔期的确定。这些法案还规定了在领水划定捕鱼区，以供非机械化和机械化渔船捕鱼，同时视各邦具体情况的不同，每个邦划定的区域距离岸边的远近也不同，但通常来说，将预留5—10公里供手工（非机械）船操作。[2]

2019年，印度发布《海洋渔业（监管和管理）草案》［Marine Fisheries (Regulation and Management) Bill, 2019］。该草案共有5章，23条，其目的主要在于：对印度专属经济区和公海渔业进行监督和管理，并保护海洋渔业资源以使其可持续使用；在印度海域维护法律和秩序（为了捕鱼和与捕鱼有关的活动）；关注渔民和渔业工作者，特别是传统和小型渔民的社会保障、生计和海上安全问题。草案对禁止未经许可的捕鱼、费用的征收和豁免、渔业管理计划、许可证的取消或暂停等作出了详细规定，该立法文本的通过将

---

〔1〕 "The Marine Products Export Development Authority Act, 1972", India Code, https://www.indiacode. nic. in/bitstream/123456789/1665/3/A1972-13. pdf # search = Marine% 20Products% 20Export% 20Development% 20Authority% 20Act，February 11，2020.

〔2〕 Rajesh K. M.，"Fisheries Legislation in India"，http://eprints. cmfri. org. in/9871/1/Rajesh_ 8. pdf? nsukey = Tr1jmSWoUzsdpB15jvX5OmPrMin8lGlCr4VPWFg1% 2BOcxh4qgzcHqOwdyw7% 2F3l W% 2FCUwOHXb2D7YUi7H4c2b6E0kQQk5dUDSczTzj7idUiaBmkCPVlLdHWRUlgElVTsYaX2LWV b4sphpGjxFuClbwFro% 2B% 2B4ynwHK0LmlfuDyYWgtFB% 2Bb6EvwjX8QFnpIAMGBngRROboeoV DT0zycw7iVviIA% 3D% 3D，February 11，2020.

会为印度的捕鱼监管提供更加完善的保障。[1]

5. 本国渔船监管的相关立法

1958 年，印度政府颁布了《商船运输法》（Merchant Shipping Act, 1958），该法共 18 章，461 项条款。其中第十五部分是关于渔船的规定，主要涉及渔船注册、渔船检验的相关事项，包括渔船注册的义务、可进行渔船注册的港口、注册申请、注册证明书、检验证书、安全设备的检验等内容。[2] 之后，根据该部分第 435U 条的授权，印度中央政府于 1988 年 9 月颁布了《商船法（印度渔船检验）规则》［Merchant Shipping (Indian Fishing Boats Inspection) Rules, 1988］。该规则共 12 条，主要对印度渔船的检验事项进行详细规定。其中第 6 条是对渔船检查内容的规定，包括船体的机械设备能够满足预期的使用要求且效率高；船舱、船体的其他开口及上层建筑部分都能够有效关闭，并且在各个方面都满足预期的使用要求；通风器、空气管、侧舷窗、排水孔、排水口和其他海上连接设施都足够有效等。同年 11 月，印度政府又颁布了《商船法（印度渔船注册）规则》［Merchant Shipping (Registration of Fishing Boat) Rules, 1988］，进一步对《商船法》中提及的渔船注册事项进行细化。该规则共 23 条，主要内容包括注册证明书的申请、渔船的命名及名字变更、官方编号、渔船吨位的确定方式等。[3]

不难看出，印度对于其渔业的重视也体现在其对渔船的管理上，通过上述几项立法，印度从多个方面对其渔船的监管问题进行了详细规定，较好地为渔船的运营提供了法律保障，从而促进印度渔业的发展。

6. 有关外国船只在印度海域捕捞的监管立法

为了遏制在印度管辖海域内外国船只的非法捕捞活动，印度政府分别于 1981 年和 1982 年通过了《印度海洋区域（外国船只捕鱼监管）法》［Maritime Zones of India (Regulation of Fishing by Foreign Vessels) Act, 1981，以下简称《外国船只捕鱼监管法》] 和《印度海洋区域（外国船只捕鱼监管）规则》［Maritime Zones of India (Regulation of Fishing by Foreign Vessels) Rules, 1982，以下简称《外国船只捕鱼监管规则》]。其中，《外国船只捕鱼监管法》共 5 章，26 条，《外国船只捕鱼监管规则》是在其基础上的进一步细化。

---

［1］　ICSF, " Marine Fisheries (Regulation and Management) Bill, 2019 ", https：//indianlegal. icsf. net/images/resources/externalNews/docs/legal _ india/documents/65005543. pdf, February 11, 2020.

［2］　该法具体内容参见本节"海上运输相关立法"部分。

［3］　See MUMBAL, "Fishing Boats", https：// www. dgshipping. gov. in/Content/PageUrl. aspx? page_ name = ShipManualChap9, February 20, 2021.

根据上述立法和规则，印度对在其领水和专属经济区内参与捕捞的外国船只作出以下规定：第一，明确外国船舶在上述海域参与捕捞的条件、资格、程序、目的等内容；第二，授权相关执法机关对违反上述规定的外国船舶进行搜查、扣押；第三，列明对从事非法捕捞的外国船舶的惩处和刑罚。[1]

7.《2005 年沿海水产养殖管理局法》

2005 年，印度通过了《沿海水产养殖管理局法》（Coastal Aquaculture Authority Act，2005），以建立专门机构规范沿海区域的水产养殖相关活动，这一法案包括 5 章，共 20 条。根据这一法案，管理局应以一名高等法院法官为主席，至少包含一名沿海水产养殖领域的专家，一名由政府任命的沿岸生态学专家，一名环境保护或污染控制领域的专家，两名分别来自农业部门和商业部门的代表，以及四名来自沿海各邦的代表。该局的职能包括：第一，制定水产养殖场建设和营运的相关规章；第二，监测沿岸水产养殖场对沿岸海洋环境的影响；第三，为沿岸水产养殖场进行登记；第四，经听证后取消或拆除任何会造成污染的沿岸水产养殖场，等等。印度的中央政府通过建立这一机构对沿海水产养殖进行有效的监管和指导，以确保沿岸海洋环境的养护和沿海水产养殖的可持续性发展。

同时，为了落实各项法案的规定，印度陆续出台了多项相关政策，以进一步细化在渔业发展方面的规定。[2]

（四）海洋能源相关立法

1. 涉及海上能源开发的一般性法律规定

第一，《石油法》。1934 年，印度政府针对石油及相关产品的进口、运输、仓储、生产及混合提炼问题出台了《石油法》（Petroleum Act，1934）。该法共 4 章，32 条，其中第 30 条、第 32 条及所附列表已经被废止。根据该法现行有效条款，其主要就石油进口、运输等环节的监管和控制，石油产品的检验和取样，以及在上述环节中的违法行为的惩处及相关程序分别作出规定。尽管该法没有直接涉及海洋区域，但是在海洋石油产业涉及相关环节时

---

〔1〕 "The Maritime Zones of India（Regulation of Fishing by Foreign Vessels）Act，1981"，India Code，https：//www. indiacode. nic. in/bitstream/123456789/1817/1/198142. pdf#search = Maritime% 20Zones% 20of% 20India，February 11，2020.

〔2〕 "The Coastal Aquaculture Authority Act，2005"，India Code，https：//www. indiacode. nic. in/bitstream/123456789/2068/1/200524. pdf # search = Coastal% 20Aquaculture% 20Authority% 20Act，February 11，2020.

仍可能受到上述立法的调整和监管。[1]

第二，《油田（管理和开发）法》。1948 年，印度通过《油田（管理和开发）法》［Oil Fields（Regulation and Development）Act, 1948］，旨在为公众利益而对油田的管理及矿物油（mineral oil）的开发等相关问题制定规则。该法案共 14 条，分别对油田开采的授权条件、管理油田开采活动的机构及职权、油田开采特许权的费用缴纳、修改既存特许权协议的权力及条件等作出规定。[2]

第三，《石油和天然气委员会（权益转让和废止）法》。1959 年，印度曾通过《石油和天然气委员会法》（Oil and Natural Gas Commission Act, 1959）设立石油天然气委员会，以专门管理石油及相关产品的生产和销售事项，该 1959 年立法及上述委员会为印度当时及其后较长时间国内油气勘探和生产提供了基本的管理框架。1993 年，印度通过了《石油和天然气委员会（权益转让和废止）法》［Oil and Natural Gas Commission（Transfer of Undertaking and Repeal）Act, 1993，以下简称《1993 年石油天然气法》］，将石油天然气委员会的资本、财产、职权及相关或附带事项全部转移至石油天然气公司（Oil and Natural Gas Corporation），上述 1959 年立法也随之废止。《1993 年石油天然气法》详细规定了石油天然气委员会应向石油天然气公司转移的有形的、无形的资产范围。授权石油天然气公司颁发执照、特许许可，给予其免税等特权和豁免，授权其检查石油天然气相关的供应情况，允许其就该法所赋予的相关职权制定实施细则，同时，对其职员和雇员的权利和义务作出相应规定。[3]

---

〔1〕　"The Petroleum Act, 1934", India Code, https：//www. indiacode. nic. in/bitstream/123456789/2401/1/A1934-30. pdf#search = Petroleum% 20Act, February 11, 2020.

〔2〕　"The Oilfields（Regulation and Development）Act, 1948", India Code, https：//www. indiacode. nic. in/bitstream/123456789/1397/3/A1948-53. pdf#search = Oilfields, February 11, 2020.

〔3〕　See "The Oil And Natural Gas Commission Act, 1959", Indian Kanoon, https：//indiankanoon. org/doc/783396/? _ _ cf_ chl_ jschl_ tk_ _ =4019eb7a2c46393e4311a764e4c350372541f39d-1617540153-0-ASR33zjG-BHsPdxq0SkW254uulFjy7LDnTU9Mcgfr-ZYI8-UozvFhXlFX3cskjC5U9FRu61QV9vs9dT_ oCIt7LYOlyQEScKEJLhOJ9PQ4ooQSHkvjsXiPW3u_ MO6kpxwLLoeoNdGFkK8RQCBIf4-JfdGIgy1L36C5CoCttoRIrawf048rde1uK0ynJwVSURK4Army1AikYo2ujVkk_ se_ oYiyV3YjDVtIRvcXtNgssPo-wCk6U3Gb2pOhHeEspnLkyrH3UjZosQ8XO_ qQveyOaqlnD3cQOA6TIs7T_ mzk9gZ_ Knp7C0DRUiDsllyL2rxntEpZnvDkhi-i6LaYD3j19eAhiFCFCFG7kWfVgUMjHgc6yAzb_ t2sLxHONoziXkJBZJPT9STRyQKJK6Wdk6tIE67Wmvnk6S2I1bXo_ kWZNGRSp_ l-MzNbzm_ z5Fi8eaR1NWZx5fQPzwa7OSHDzwdXVY, March 12, 2020；"The Oilfields（Regulation and Development）Act, 1948", IndiaCode, https：//www. indiacode. nic. in/bitstream/123456789/1397/3/A1948-53. pdf # search = Oilfields, March 12, 2020.

2. 涉及海上能源开发的专门性法律规定

《离岸区域矿产（开发和管理）法》〔Offshore Areas Mineral（Development and Regulation）Act，2002，以下简称《2002 年离岸矿产法》〕虽然在 2002 年即已出台，但直至 2010 年 1 月 15 日才生效。该法共 6 章 38 条，分别就印度领水、大陆架、专属经济区及其他海域矿产资源的开发和管理的一般性规则，进入相关设施以及检查、搜查、扣押的相关权力和机构，违反前述条款的责任及惩处等作出规定。[1]

2006 年，根据《2002 年离岸矿产法》第 35 条的相关授权，印度政府颁布了《离岸区域矿产特许规则》（Offshore Areas Mineral Concession Rules，2006）。该规则进一步对离岸区域矿产开发相关事项作出细化，如颁发勘探许可及续期，颁发开采执照及续期，颁发生产执照，海洋环境的保护，相关的安全性条款，勘探、开采、生产中的具体操作环节的要求，以及对相关管理不服的申诉权利和程序。该立足于《2002 年离岸矿产法》的授权而制定的 2006 年规则，与前述 2002 年立法同样于 2010 年生效，并于 2019 年进行了修订。[2] 与此同时，印度通过颁布相关政策以探索印度的石油和天然气资源，满足其不断增长的石油和天然气需求。

（五）海上运输相关立法

1. 《1908 年印度港口法》

1908 年 12 月生效的《印度港口法》（Indian Ports Act，1908）是对在其之前生效的印度港口及港务费用相关制定性文件的合并与集成。依据该法第 1 条第 2 款，该法适用于该法附表一所列各港口，以及《1855 年第二十号法案》《1875 年印度港口法》《1889 年印度港口法》中所载的与上述港口相通的可航行河流及运河，并排除了相关条款对军舰及政府公务船舶的适用。

---

〔1〕 "The Offshore Areas Mineral（Development and Regulation）Act，2002"，India Code，https：// www. indiacode. nic. in/bitstream/123456789/2040/1/200317. pdf # search = Offshore% 20Areas% 20Mineral，March 12，2020.

〔2〕 See "Offshore Areas Mineral Concession Rules，2006"，India Code，https：//upload. indiacode. nic. in/showfile? actid = AC _ CEN _ 15 _ 16 _ 000010 _ 200317 _ 1517807327201&type = rule&filename = Offshore% 20Areas% 20Mineral% 20Concession% 20Rules,% 202006. pdf，March 12，2020；"Offshore Areas Mineral Concession（Amendment）Rules，2019"，IndiaCode，ht- tps：//upload. indiacode. nic. in/showfile? actid = AC _ CEN _ 15 _ 16 _ 000010 _ 200317 _ 1517807327201&type = rule&filename = oamdr _ amendment _ rules, _ 2019. pdf，March 12，2020.

在其现行有效的 8 章共 68 条规定中，有关港口管理的权力划分、相关港口管辖机构的职权职责、船舶在港口的航行安全、港口设施的维护、港口及其设施使用的相关税费、船舶入港的吊装与引航、违反上述规定的惩处措施及额度等都得到专章的相应覆盖，并特别对船舶进港的号旗使用、外国船员的叛逃、授权港口为临时船员驻地、港口管制及防卫权力行使以及紧急状态下的机构职责等作出额外规定。[1]

2.《1925 年印度海上货物运输法》

1922 年 10 月，在比利时布鲁塞尔举行的国际海事大会上，与会代表一致同意建议本国政府采纳提单相关的某些统一规则，并在随后的 1923 年会议上就该统一规则草案作出进一步的修订。作为英国海外领地，印度对于这一主要由英国推动的统一规则草案作出了积极回应，在《1924 年统一提单的若干法律规定的国际公约》[International Convention for the Unification of Certain Rules of Law relating to Bills of Lading，以下简称《海牙规则》] 正式签署之前，即在本国开始了《印度海上货物运输法》（Indian Carriage of Goods by Sea Act，1925，以下简称《1925 年海运法》）配套性立法，该法于 1925 年 9 月正式生效。

该法包括规范海上货物运输的正文与提单相关规则的附件。与其所立足之国际立法相适应，正文部分相对简单，仅以 7 项条文就法案适用范围、法案正文与附件规则的效力范围、适航绝对义务的排除、提单规则在运输合同中的明示纳入、特定规则适用范围的修改、保留及溯及力作出总括性规定；而附件的提单相关规则却相对周详，除对"承运人""运输合同""货物运输""船舶"等术语作出明确界定外，对于承运人的运输风险类型、承运人责任类型、承运人免责及责任限制的事由与条件、承运人责任的放弃或加重、特别条款适用等都作出了较为细致的安排。[2]

作为国际海商事立法的国内法转化与体现，《1925 年海运法》显示出限制承运人责任、保护承运人利益的明显倾向。同时，随着相关公约尤其是提单相关《海牙规则》的修正发展，这一法案也陆续于 1968 年、1979 年有所

---

〔1〕 "The Indian Ports Act, 1908", India Code, https：//www. indiacode. nic. in/bitstream/1234567 89/2344/1/A1908-15. pdf#search = Indian% 20Ports% 20Act，March 12，2020.

〔2〕 "The Indian Carriage of Goods by Sea Act, 1925", India Code, https：//www. indiacode. nic. in/ bitstream/123456789/2384/1/AAA1925_ _ _ _ 26. pdf#search = Indian% 20Carriage% 20of% 20Goods% 20by% 20Sea% 20Act，March 12，2020.

修订。[1]

3. 《1958 年商船运输法》

印度于 1958 年 10 月通过《商船运输法》，意在以国家利益为目标促进并确保印度商业船队的高效经营与发展，建立国家航运委员会（National Shipping Board）为印度船舶提供登记、认证、安全等相关服务，同时将此前相关立法进行整合。这一立法在经过 1986 年、2002 年、2009 年、2011 年、2015 年、2016 年、2018 年的历次修订及增补之后，至今仍是印度调整监管商船及商船运输相关行为最为重要详尽的单行法典。[2]

根据其第 2 条，该法典适用于所有在印度注册登记的船舶、所有按该法应该在印度注册登记的船舶、任何由符合该法相关条款的个人所拥有的船舶以及其他在印度领水范围内的船舶。对于这一范畴内的船舶及其航运，该法以第四章至第十八章分别就一般管理机构及职权，印度船舶的登记，在船人员类别、资格、注册、义务、雇佣、财产，旅客运输，船舶建造及航行安全，帆船、渔船、核动力船等特别类型船舶，船舶及港口设施的安保，船舶碰撞等海上事故，海上责任限制，海上污染损害民事责任，国际油污损害赔偿基金，航行规则，调查与质询，海难与海难救助，沿岸运输规范，惩处措施及程序等问题作出较为全面的规则设计。同时，按照该法第二章，在该法之下建立的国家航运委员会应包含来自议会、中央政府、船东、船员及其他利益相关方的代表，从而能够就印度航运及其发展事项以及中央政府所提出的与该法案有关的事项向中央政府提供有效建议。[3]

4. 《1963 年海上保险法》

作为海上客货运输的重要风险分担环节，海上保险规则体系的建立于整个海上运输事业发展而言不可或缺。1963 年的《海上保险法》（Marine Insurance Act，1963）正是印度对海上保险相关规则的编纂和成文化努力。

---

〔1〕 1968 年 2 月及 1979 年 12 月分别于布鲁塞尔通过了《修改统一提单若干法律规定的国际公约议定书》（Protocol to Amend the International Convention for the Unification of Certain Rules of Law Relating to Bills of Lading）、《修正（经 1968 年议定书修正的）1924 年统一提单某些法律规定的国际公约的 1979 年议定书》[Protocol amending the International Convention for the Unification of Certain Rules of Law relating to Bills of Lading of 25 August 1924（The Hague Rules），as amended by the Protocol of 23 February 1968]。

〔2〕 See "All Acts and Its Sub-ordinate Legislation about Merchant Shipping Act"，India Code，https：//indiacode. nic. in/handle/123456789/1362/simple-search? page-token = 14fbfab08d2a&page-token-value = 97afd0bdf938e06d385640dd51fd0a60&nccharset = 0F471165&query = Merchant + Shipping + Act&btngo = &searchradio = all，March 12，2020.

〔3〕 "The Merchant Shipping Act，1958"，India Code，https：//www. indiacode. nic. in/bitstream/123456789/1562/5/A1958-44. pdf#search = Merchant% 20Shipping% 20Act，March 12，2020.

在其现行有效的 91 条中，该法分别就海上保险相关术语、海上保险基本适用范围、可保利益的类型及含义、可保价值、合同相关信息披露、海上保单、双重保险、担保条款、保单转让、海上航程相关风险、保险费用、船舶灭失及委付、赔偿限额、保险人权利等进行了调整，旨在对船、货、航程相关的海洋保险业务作出规范。同时，1963 年《海上保险法》也与 1938 年《保险法》（The Insurance Act，1938）等同体系在先立法保持协调，如要求相关船只也必须遵守 1938 年《保险法》第 64VB 条关于在风险开始之前支付保险费的规定，等等。[1]

5. 其他海上运输相关立法

1993 年，印度通过《货物多式联运法》（The Multimodal Transportation of Goods Act，1993），旨在对基于多式联运合同从印度境内一地至印度境外任何地点的货物运输及相关事项提供相应规范。根据这一法案，其所规范的"承运人"包括通过公路、铁路、内河水路、海运或空运履行或承诺履行货物运输或部分货物运输的相关人。这使得其下有关多式联运登记、多式联运文书、多式联运从业者的责任及承担、多式联运争端解决等各项规定对海上货物运输同样具备适用的可能。[2]

2016 年，印度通过《国家水道法》（The National Waterways Act，2016），对现有国家水道以及被宣布为国家水道的部分内陆水道统一制定规则，并以航行与运输为目标促进相关国家水道的规范与发展。随着该法案的出台，《1982 年国家水道（恒河巴吉拉蒂-胡格利河的阿拉哈巴德-哈尔迪亚河段）法》[National Waterway（Allahabad-Haldia Stretch of the Ganga Bhagirathi-Hooghly River）Act，1982]，《1988 年国家水道（布拉马普特拉河的萨迪亚-杜布里段）法》[National Waterway（Sadiya-Dhubri Stretch of Brahmaputra River）Act，1988]，《1992 年国家水道（西海岸运河的科兰-科塔普拉姆段及夏帕卡拉与尤迪约格曼达运河）法》[National Waterway（Kollam-Kottapuram Stretch of West Coast Canal and Champakara and Udyogmandal Canals）Act，1992]，《2008 年国家水道（达喀尔-达姆拉河的延伸、东海岸运河的延伸、马泰河的一段与马哈那迪三角洲河流）法》[National Waterway（Talcher-Dhamra Stretch of Rivers，Geonkhali-Charbatia Stretch of East Coast Canal，Char-

---

[1] "The Marine Insurance Act，1963"，India Code，https：//www.indiacode.nic.in/bitstream/123456789/1520/1/196311.pdf#search = Merchant% 20Shipping% 20Act，March 12，2020.

[2] "The Multimodal Transportation of Goods Act，1993"，India Code，https：//www.indiacode.nic.in/bitstream/123456789/1946/1/a1993-28.pdf # search =% 20Multimodal% 20Transportation，March 12，2020.

batia-Dhamra Stretch of Matai River and Mahanadi Delta Rivers） Act，2008］，
《2008 年国家水道（卡基纳达-本迪治里运河段与卡路威利水库，戈达瓦里河
的巴德拉查兰-拉贾赫穆恩德尔伊段与克利须那河的瓦兹拉巴德-维杰亚瓦达
段）法》 ［National Waterway （Kakinada-Puducherry Stretch of Canals and the
Kaluvelly Tank，Bhadrachalam-Rajahmundry Stretch of River Godavari and Waz-
irabad-Vijayawada Stretch of River Krishna） Act，2008］都被废止。1985 年的
《印度内陆水道管理局法》（Inland Waterways Authority of India Act，1985）的相
关内容也依该法进行了修改。

从其正文及附表来看，《2016 年国家水道法》的调整对象主要为印度内
河及运河，但作为与海洋相通的可航水域，《国家水道法》的相关规定仍会
对印度海上航行的发展与潜力、规范化与现代化有所影响。[1]

（六）海洋环境保护相关立法

1. 海洋水体保护相关立法

印度于 1974 年 3 月通过《水污染防治法》，旨在防止和控制水污染，维
护或恢复水体的清洁卫生状况，并为此目的成立防止和控制水污染委员会，
同时就该委员会相关权力和职能的授予和分配作出规定。

根据该法第 2 条，其所指"水流"包括河流、河道（无论处于丰水期还
是枯水期）、内陆水（无论自然形成还是人工形成）、地下水以及由各邦政府
明确适用于本法的海水及潮汐水。为保护或治理上述水域环境，《1974 年水
污染防治法》授权印度中央政府及各邦政府分别建立中央及各邦的水污染防
治委员会，并就两级委员会的组成方式、成员构成、成员职责、委员会会
议、委员会主席代表、成员空缺时程序及委员会雇员等作出安排。其中，中央
水污染防治委员会的主要职责在于提高各邦水流及水井的清洁度，具体包括：
（1）就水污染防治相关事宜向中央政府提出建议；（2）协调各邦委员会的行动
并解决由此产生的纠纷；（3）为各邦委员会提供技术性支持与指导，并支持
或实施水污染防治相关的调查和研究；（4）通过规划和组织，为水污染防治
相关项目的参与人员提供培训；（5）策划有关水污染防治的大众传媒节目；
（6）收集、整理及公开水污染相关的技术与统计数据、有效防控污染的措施
与说明、有关污水处理的规章与指南；（7）在与各邦协商的情形下，制定、
修改或废止水流及水井的水质标准；等等。而各邦水污染防治委员会，除在

---

〔1〕 "The National Waterways Act，2016"，India Code，https：//www. indiacode. nic. in/bitstream/
123456789/2159/1/A2016-17. pdf#search＝National% 20Waterways，March 12，2020.

各邦范围内配合中央一级委员会执行上述相关职能外,将对本邦内生活污水、工业废水等相关的产业和企业、相关防治措施的施行等担负起更为具体的监管职责。除此之外,有关水污染防治的资金账目及核算、惩处措施及程序、报告及政府协助等也在该法的后续章节得以展开。

需要注意的是,《1974 年水污染防治法》并不当然适用于印度全境。根据《印度宪法》附表七中"列表 B"的规定,"水"相关事项属于各邦的独立立法权限。只有在符合《印度宪法》第 252 条的例外规定时,经相关邦同意,联邦议会才能就此类事项统一立法并适用于作出同意表示的各邦。因此,根据 1974 年《水污染防治法》的特别说明,除联邦领地外,该法仅适用于阿萨姆邦、比哈尔邦等十个邦。这一适用范围在经过 1975 年及 2011 年的修订后并未改变。[1]

2. 海洋生物保护相关立法

1972 年,印度通过《野生动植物保护法》(Wildlife Protection Act, 1972),通过列表方式保护特定动植物种群,同时建立具有生态意义的保护区域网络。该法共含八章 60 项规定,根据这一立法,中央及各邦政府有权宣布任何区域为野生动物保护区、国家公园或相关禁区;除经授权或许可相关人员,在动物危及人类生命或财产、残疾或患病且无法康复时采取的行动外,禁止猎杀动物。除此之外,该法对保护特殊植物、野生动物及动物制品贸易、相关管理机构的权力及分配、相关违法行为的惩处及程序等都作出了相应规定。[2]

依据《1972 年野生动植物保护法》附表一至附表六,鱼类、腔肠动物类、软体动物类等多种海洋生物都被纳入该法保护范围。而在该法颁布以来多次发布的修订补充文件中,获得保护的海洋生物种群还在不断增加。如原

---

〔1〕 "The Water (Prevention and Control of Pollution) Act, 1974", India Code, https://www. indiacode. nic. in/handle/123456789/1612? view_ type = search&sam_ handle = 123456789/1362, March 12, 2020.

〔2〕 该法分别于 2002 年及 2006 年进行了修订,分别就法律名称表述、相关术语解释、专门性监管机构等进行了修改、删减或添加,如 2006 年修订就老虎种群的保护及相关违法犯罪行为的监管设立了专门性机构,由此原第四章后增添了"第四 B"及"第四 C"章。"The Wildlife (Protection) Act, 1972", India Code, https://www. indiacode. nic. in/bitstream/123456789/12931/1/wildlife_ % 28protection% 29_ act% 2c_ 1972_ no. _ 53_ of_ 1972_ date_ 09. 09. 1972. pdf#search = Wildlife% 20Protection, March 12, 2020; "The Wildlife Protection Amendment Act, 2002", India Code, https://www. indiacode. nic. in/bitstream/123456789/6199/1/wild_ act_ 2002. pdf#search = Wildlife% 20Protection, March 12, 2020; "The Wildlife Protection Amendment Act, 2006", India Code, https://www. indiacode. nic. in/bitstream/123456789/6200/1/wildlife_ protection_ amendment_ 2006. pdf#search = Wildlife% 20Protection, March 12, 2020.

印度环境和森林部依据该法授权分别于 2001 年 7 月及 12 月发布两份政府公告，在鱼类列表中增加了鲨鱼、海马、鞍带石斑鱼及细化种类共 9 项，在腔肠动物列表中增加了黑珊瑚等 5 项，在软体动物列表中增加了法螺、水字螺等 61 项，在棘皮动物列表中增加了海参 1 项，从而为海洋生物群提供了更完善的保护。[1]

1992 年，印度签署《联合国生物多样性公约》（United Nations Convention on Biological Diversity）。随着该公约于 1993 年生效，印度开始推进履行公约相关义务，并于 2002 年颁布了立足于该公约的《生物多样性法》（The Biological Diversity Act，2002）。这一立法的主要目标在于，保护生物多样性，为遗传性资源的保护、可持续利用、公平惠益与分享提供规范，这显示出印度对生物性资源相关主权权利的高度重视。根据该法相关规定，其所适用的"生物资源"包括除人体资源物质以外的所有动植物、微生物及其部分、其遗传物质及具有实际或可能用途或价值的副产品。尽管该法并无海洋生物资源的专门性条款，但无疑为海洋生物多样性保护及遗传资源的利用规范提供了相应指引和规范。[2]

3. 海洋区域环境相关立法

1972 年，联合国人类环境会议在斯德哥尔摩召开。作为与会国，印度认为应采取适当步骤及进一步的必要措施以推进会议相关决定的实施，保护和提升人类生活环境，防止环境因素对人类及其他生物物种与财产的危害，并于 1986 年 5 月颁布《环境（保护）法》。该法明确了中央政府在环境保护方面的基本职能，并对相关当事方在环境保护和防止消除污染中的应有行为及责任作出要求。作为印度环境保护的综合性立法，该法同样为海洋区域的环境保护提供了基础性原则与框架性规定。[3]

2011 年，原印度环境和森林部依据上述 1986 年立法第 3 条的授权发布

〔1〕 See "Ministry of Environment and Forests Notification（2001）", India Code, https：//upload. indiacode. nic. in/showfile? actid = AC_ CEN_ 16_ 18_ 00007_ 197253_ 1517807324579&type = notification&filename = MINISTRY% 20OF% 20ENVIRONMENT% 20AND% 20FORESTS% 20SO665E. pdf, March 12, 2020; "Ministry of Environment and Forests Notification（2001）", India Code, https：//upload. indiacode. nic. in/showfile? actid = AC_ CEN_ 16_ 18_ 00007_ 197253_ 1517807324579&type = notification&filename = the_ wildlife_（protection）_ act, _ 1972_（53_ of_ 1972）_ 05_ 12_ 2001_ 1972）_ 04_ 09_ 2010. pdf, March 12, 2020.

〔2〕 "The Biological Diversity Act, 2002", India Code, https：//www. indiacode. nic. in/bitstream/ 123456789/2046/1/200318. pdf#search = Biological% 20Diversity% 20Act, March 12, 2020.

〔3〕 "The Environment（Protection）Act, 1986", India Code, https：//www. indiacode. nic. in/bitstream/123456789/1876/1/a1986-29. pdf#search = Environment% 20（Protection）, March 12, 2020.

《沿海监管区通告》（Coastal Regulation Zone Notification，2011，以下简称《2011 年通告》），将部分印度海岸延伸地带宣布为"沿海监管区"并纳入该通告监管之下。《2011 年通告》的适用，引发了联邦领地及沿海各邦在海洋及海岸生态系统管理与保护、沿海区域开发、生态旅游、沿海人群生计与可持续发展等诸多方面的问题反馈。印度环境、森林和气候变化部由此成立了专门委员会就《2011 年通告》执行过程中的相关问题及各利益方诉求进行调查，并于 2018 年获得该委员会所提交的报告草案。立足于该报告草案的结论与建议，印度于 2019 年 1 月发布《2018 年沿海监管区（CRZ）通告》[Coastal Regulation Zone（CRZ）Notification，2018，以下简称《2018 年通告》]，废止《2011 年通告》，对除安达曼群岛（Andaman）、尼科巴群岛（Nicobar）、拉克沙群岛（Lakshadweep）以外的沿岸及海洋区域环境保护和可持续发展作出新一轮规定。

根据《2018 年通告》，沿海监管区包括从高潮线向陆地方向 500 米范围内的沿海陆地、受潮汐影响的从高潮线向陆地方向 50 米或入海河流宽度相当的陆地区域、从低潮线至领水外部界限的水体和海床、从海岸一侧低潮线至另一侧低潮线受潮汐影响的水体。对上述沿海区域及海洋水域，《2018 年通告》基于其各区域的环境敏感及脆弱程度将其划分为四个等级。其中，第一等级（CRZ-I）为环境价值最为关键之区域，其 A 组区域尤其具有高度的生态敏感性且其地貌对维持海岸整体性具有重要作用，包括红树林、珊瑚及珊瑚礁、沙丘、具有生物活性的浅滩、盐沼、海龟繁育地、马蹄蟹栖息地、鸟类筑巢地以及国家公园、海洋公园、自然保护区、森林保护区等 11 类；第二等级（CRZ-II）主要为较发达地区的沿海延伸地带；第三等级（CRZ-III）为人类活动相对较少、相对安宁，如较为偏远的陆地区域；第四等级（CRZ-IV）为前述监管区范围内的海水区域。《2018 年通告》对在上述区域中禁止从事的活动进行了统一规定，并按相应等级对在上述区域可以进行的活动分别作出安排，要求将其纳入相关管理机构的特别考量。[1]

在相关争端解决及程序方面，印度于 2010 年 6 月通过《国家绿色法庭法》（National Green Tribunal Act，2010），以建立一个由司法专家或环境专家组成的专门性法庭，从而高效便利地处理环境保护及森林等自然资源养护的相关案件，包括环境相关法律权利的行使以及对个人或财产受到的损害进行

---

[1] "Coastal Regulation Zone（CRZ）Notification，2018"，India Code，https：//upload. indiacode. nic. in/showfile？actid＝AC＿CEN＿16＿18＿00011＿198629＿1517807327582&type＝notification&filename＝gsr37（e）＿dated＿18. 01. 2019-crz＿notification＿2018. pdf，March 15，2020.

赔偿和救济等相关诉讼。这一"绿色法庭"的设立，使得印度成为继澳大利亚和新西兰之后第三个拥有专门性法庭处理环境相关案件的国家。[1] 而印度早期与环境诉讼相关的《1995 年国家环境法庭法》（National Environmental Tribunal Act, 1995）及《1997 年国家环境上诉机构法》（The National Environment Appellate Authority Act, 1997）亦随着该 2011 年立法的颁布而废止。[2]

（七）海洋科研相关立法

2008 年 11 月，《印度海事大学法》（The Indian Maritime University Act, 2008）颁布。依据这一法案建立的印度海事大学为国家级教学及协作型大学（teaching and affiliating university），总部设于金奈（Chennai），并在金奈、孟买（Mumbai）、加尔各答（Kolkata）、维萨卡帕特南（Vishakhapatnam）等地建有校区。按照该法相关规定，印度海事大学的宗旨在于：（1）促进在海洋法、海事历史、海商事法律、海事安全、海洋搜救、危险货物运输、海洋环境等前沿领域的学习、培训、研究及其他拓展性工作；（2）在相关教育教学项目中为特定科学技术及关联学科的综合性课程提供先进知识的积累与储备；（3）采取措施促进教学方法、跨学科研究的创新，并对印度人民的教育、经济利益及社会福利的提高给予特别关注；（4）促进铭刻于宪法中的自由、平等及社会公平，从而在社会经济转型中弘扬对国家发展至关重要的基本观念与核心价值；（5）紧密联系本地的、地区的及国家的发展事项，从而扩大传播有益于个人及社会发展的知识与技能。除此之外，这所大学的权力范围、组织结构、监管主体、领导职责、资金来源、规章制定、雇员要求、年度报告、争端解决等都在该法 50 项条款中有所明确，并陆续出台了 8 项通告作出进一步细化和调整。作为对印度所有阶层、种姓及宗教群体开放的大学，国家对其在海洋科学技术及环境领域取得卓越的教学及科研成就寄予厚望。[3]

---

[1] "The National Green Tribunal Act", Law Teacher, https：//www. lawteacher. net/free-law-essays/constitutional-law/the-national-green-tribunal-act-law-essays. php, March 15, 2020.

[2] "The National Green Tribunal Act, 2010", India Code, https：//indiacode. nic. in/bitstream/123456789/2025/1/A2010-19. pdf, March 15, 2020.

[3] "The Indian Maritime University Act, 2008", India Code, https：//www. indiacode. nic. in/bitstream/123456789/2093/1/200822. pdf # search = Indian% 20Maritime% 20University, March 15, 2020.

四、缔结和加入的国际海洋法条约

（一）联合国框架下的海洋法公约

印度于 1982 年 12 月 10 日签署《联合国海洋法公约》，并于 1995 年 6 月 29 日批准《公约》及《关于执行 1982 年 12 月 10 日〈联合国海洋法公约〉第十一部分的协定》（Agreement relating to The Implementation of Part XI of The United Nations Conventions on the Law of the Sea, 10 December 1982）。2003 年 8 月 19 日，印度批准《执行 1982 年 12 月 10 日〈联合国海洋法公约〉有关养护和管理跨界鱼类种群和高度洄游鱼类种群的规定的协定》（Agreement for the Implementation of the Provisions of the United Nations Convention on the Law of the Sea of 10 December 1982 relating to the Conservation and Management of Straddling Fish Stocks and Highly Migratory Fish Stocks）。印度于 2005 年 11 月 14 日加入《国际海底管理局特权和豁免议定书》（Protocol on the Privileges and Immunities of the International Seabed Authority），并于同日加入《国际海洋法法庭特权和豁免协定》（Agreement on the Privileges and Immunities of the International Tribunal for the Law of the Sea）。对于《公约》，印度作出两项声明：（1）保留在适当时机发表涉及第 287 条、第 298 条争端解决的声明；（2）公约未授予他国在专属经济区及大陆架进行军事活动的权利。[1]

印度并未签署 1958 年日内瓦海洋法公约体系下的四公约，即《领海及毗连区公约》（Convention on the Territorial Sea and the Contiguous Zone）、《公海公约》（Convention on the High Seas）、《捕鱼及养护公海生物资源公约》（Convention on Fishing and Conservation of the Living Resources of the High Seas）和《大陆架公约》（Convention on the Continental Shelf）。

（二）国际海事组织框架下的相关条约

印度于 1961 年 1 月 18 日签署《1948 年国际海事组织公约》（Convention on the International Maritime Organization, 1948），该公约于同日对印度生效。

---

[1] "United Nations Convention on the Law of the Sea-Declarations and Reservations", UN Treaty Collection, https：//treaties. un. org/pages/ViewDetailsIII. aspx? src = TREATY&mtdsg_ no = XXI-6&chapter = 21&Temp = mtdsg3&clang = _ en#EndDec, July 13, 2019.

在国际海事组织（International Maritime Organization）框架下，印度加入了总计30多项国际海事条约，这些条约主要涉及以下方面：船舶管理、防治海洋污染、海上航行安全、海员管理、赔偿和责任等。[1]

其中，与船舶及船员管理有关的条约包括：印度于1968年加入的《1966年国际船舶载重线公约》（International Convention on Load Lines, 1966），于1976年加入的《1965年便利国际海上运输公约》（Convention on Facilitation of International Maritime Traffic, 1965），于1977年加入的《1969年国际船舶吨位丈量公约》（International Convention on Tonnage Measurement of Ships, 1969），于1984年加入的《1978年海员培训、发证和值班标准国际公约》（International Convention on Standards of Training, Certification and Watchkeeping for Seafarers, 1978）等。

与防治海洋污染有关的条约包括：印度于1987年加入的《1969年国际油污损害民事责任公约》（International Convention on Civil Liability for Oil Pollution Damage, 1969），于1997年加入的《1990年国际油污防备、反应与合作公约》（International Convention on Oil Pollution Preparedness, Response and Co-operation, 1990），于1986年加入的《1973年国际防止船舶造成污染公约的1978年议定书》附则一及附则二（International Convention for the Prevention of Pollution from Ships, 1973 as modified by the Protocol of 1978 relating thereto, Annex I, II），于2011年加入的《修订经1978年议定书修订的〈1973年国际防止船舶造成污染公约〉1997年议定书》（Protocol of 1997 to Amend the International Convention for the Prevention of Pollution from Ships, 1973, as modified by the Protocol of 1978 relating thereto），于2000年加入的《1969年国际干预公海油污事故公约》（International Convention relating to Intervention on the High Seas in Cases of Oil Pollution Casualties, 1969），于2015年加入的《控制船舶有害防污底系统国际公约》（International Convention on the Control of Harmful Anti-Fouling Systems On Ships, 2001）等。

与海上航行安全有关的条约包括：印度分别于1976年、1986年、2000年加入的《1974年国际海上人命安全公约》（International Convention for the Safety of Life at Sea, 1974）及其1978年议定书与1988年议定书，于1973年加入的《1972年国际海上避碰规则公约》（Convention on the International Regulations for Preventing Collisions at Sea, 1972），于1978年加入的《国际海

---

[1] "List of Convention", International Maritime Organization, http：//www.imo.org/en/About/Conventions/ListOfConventions/Pages/Default.aspx, July 29, 2019.

事卫星组织公约》（Convention on the International Mobile Satellite Organization, 1976）及《国际海事卫星组织业务协定》（Operating Agreement on the International Mobile Satellite Organization, 1976），于 1995 年加入的《1989 年国际救助公约》（International Convention on Salvage, 1989），于 2001 年加入的《1979 年国际海上搜寻救助公约》（International Convention on Maritime Search and Rescue, 1979），于 1978 年加入的《1972 年国际集装箱安全公约》（International Convention for Safe Containers, 1972），于 2011 年加入的《2007 年内罗毕国际船舶残骸清除公约》（Nairobi International Convention of Removal of Wrecks, 2007），于 1999 年加入的《1988 年制止危及海上航行安全非法行为公约》（Convention for the Suppression of Unlawful Acts against the Safety of Maritime Navigation, 1988），于 1999 年加入的《1988 年制止危及大陆架固定平台安全非法行为议定书》（Protocol for the Suppression of Unlawful Acts against the Safety of Fixed Platforms Located on the Continental Shelf, 1988），于 1976 年加入的《1971 年特种业务客船协定》（Special Trade Passenger Ships Agreement, 1971）及其 1973 年议定书等。

与损害赔偿责任有关的条约包括：印度分别于 1987 年、1999 年加入的《1969 年国际油污损害民事责任公约》（International Convention on Civil Liability for Oil Pollution Damage, 1969）及其 1992 年议定书，于 2000 年加入的《修正〈1971 年设立国际油污损害赔偿基金国际公约〉的 1992 年议定书》（Protocol of 1992 to amend the International Convention on the Establishment of an International Fund for Compensation for Oil Pollution Damage, 1971），分别于 2002 年、2011 年加入的《1976 年海事索赔责任限制公约》（Convention on Limitation of Liability for Maritime Claims, 1976）及其 1996 年议定书等。[1]

（三）渔业资源相关条约

1.《鲸鱼管制国际公约》

印度于 1981 年加入于 1948 年生效的《鲸鱼管制国际公约》（International Convention for the Regulation of Whaling）。[2] 依照该公约，各缔约国组成国

---

[1]　See "Status of IMO Treaties", International Maritime Organization, https：//www.imo.org/localresources/en/About/Conventions/StatusOfConventions/Status% 20-% 202021. pdf, January 23, 2021.

[2]　"International Convention for the Regulation of Whaling", Ecolex, https：//www.ecolex.org/details/treaty/international-convention-for-the-regulation-of-whaling-tre-000074/? q = + the + International + Convention + for + the + Regulation + of + Whaling&xdate_ min = &xdate_ max = , August 5, 2019.

际鲸鱼委员会（International Whaling Commission），以实现保护所有种类的鲸鱼，避免过度捕捞，为后代保存鲸鱼种群所关联的大量自然资源，并建立鲸鱼渔业国际监管体系的目标。[1]

2.《保护南极海洋生物资源公约》

《保护南极海洋生物资源公约》（Convention for the Conservation of Antarctic Marine Living Resources，CCAMLR）生效于 1982 年 4 月 7 日，旨在保护南极海洋生态系统，运用基于生态系统的管理方法，避免海洋生物资源（尤其是南极地区的磷虾资源）的过度捕捞。[2] 印度于 1985 年 6 月 17 日加入《保护南极海洋生物资源公约》。该公约于同年 7 月 17 日对印度生效。[3]

3.《建立印度洋金枪鱼委员会协定》

《建立印度洋金枪鱼委员会协定》（The Agreement for the Establishment of the Indian Ocean Tuna Commission，以下简称《建立协定》）生效于 1996 年 3 月 27 日，旨在设立一个政府间组织——印度洋金枪鱼委员会（The Indian Ocean Tuna Commission，IOTC），以统筹印度洋地区的海洋生物资源，并通过促进缔约国与非缔约国之间合作的方式，实现保护海洋资源与各个国家可持续发展的目标。印度于 1995 年 3 月 13 日批准《建立协定》。1996 年 3 月 17 日，《建立协定》对印度生效。[4]

4.《建立亚洲及太平洋水产养殖中心网络的协定》

《建立亚洲及太平洋水产养殖中心网络的协定》（Agreement for the Establishment of the Network of Aquaculture Centres in Asia and the Pacific，NACA）是一个旨在促进各缔约国国内水产养殖业发展的多边条约。印度于 1992 年 6

---

[1] "History and Purpose", International Whale Comission, https://iwc.int/history-and-purpose, August 9, 2019.

[2] "About CCAMLR", CCAMLR, https://www.ccamlr.org/en/organisation, August 9, 2019.

[3] "Status List", CCAMLR, http://www.austlii.edu.au/au/other/dfat/treaty _ list/depository/CCAMLR.html, August 9, 2019.

[4] See "The Commssion", Indian Ocean Tuna Commission, https://www.iotc.org/node/1, August 12, 2019; "Structure", Indian Ocean Tuna Commission, https://www.iotc.org/about-iotc/structure-commission, August 15, 2019; "The Agreement for the Establishment of the Indian Ocean Tuna Commission", Ecolex, https://www.ecolex.org/details/treaty/agreement-for-the-establishment-of-the-indian-ocean-tuna-commission-tre-001227/? q = + Indian + Ocean + Tuna + Commission, August 15, 2019.

月 4 日批准该公约。同日，该公约对印度生效。[1]

得益于优越的地理位置，海洋渔业已成为印度水产业的重要组成部分。印度周围的热带海域栖息着种类繁多的海洋生物。但是，受限于渔业资金缺乏和技术设备落后，印度的海洋渔业生产与资源地区分布不协调，生产空间十分有限。鉴于此，印度国内多家研究机构均积极参与该中心的研究工作，以期推动印度在单纯捕捞外的渔业潜力开发。[2]

5. 《建立亚太地区渔业产品市场信息及科技咨询服务政府间组织的协定》

《建立亚太地区渔业产品市场信息及科技咨询服务政府间组织的协定》（Agreement for the Establishment of the Intergovernmental Organization for Marketing Information and Technical Advisory Services for Fishery Products in the Asia and Pacific Region，INFOFISH）于 1985 年签署、1987 年生效，当前共有 13 个缔约国。印度于 1986 年加入该协定，成为最早接受该条约约束的五个国家之一。

该协定旨在确认渔业作为国家发展核心部门在部分亚太国家的重要地位。对于在较大程度上依赖渔业收益的亚太国家，建立有关渔业产品的国际市场信息及科技咨询服务，将引导更为平衡的市场供求情势，促进更有规律的价格模式，并鼓励对渔业资源的最佳利用。根据该协定，相关缔约方将建立专门性的政府间国际组织，通过区域合作实现辅助相关国家、社会群体渔业发展的目标。[3]

6. 渔业相关的双边条约

除上述多边性公约外，印度亦主要立足于资金援助、技术合作与相关国际组织及国家签署多项渔业相关双边协定。前者如《1992 年印度与国际开发协会开发信贷协定（虾及鱼养殖项目）》［Development Credit Agreement（Shrimp and Fish Culture Project）between India and International Development Association］；后者如 1973 年的《印度与挪威有关在印度发展渔业的协定》（Agreement between India and Norway regarding Development of Fisheries in India），1973 年的《印度与波兰海洋渔业合作协定》（Agreement between India and Poland on Coop-

---

〔1〕 "Agreement for the Establishment of the Network of Aquaculture Centres in Asia and the Pacific", Ecolex, https：//www. ecolex. org/details/treaty/agreement-for-the-establishment-of-the-network-of-aqua-culture-centres-in-asia-and-the-pacific-tre-001112/? q = Agreement + on + the + Network + of + Aquacul-ture + Centres + in + Asia + and + the + Pacific% 2C&xdate_ min = &xdate_ max = , August 16, 2019.

〔2〕 The Network of Aquaculture Centres in Asia and the Pacific, "Participating R&D Centres", ht-tps：//enaca. org/? id = 42&title = participating-research-centres, August 16, 2019.

〔3〕 "INFOFISH", UN Treaty Collection, https：//treaties. un. org/Pages/showDetails. aspx? objid = 08000002800ce5ad&clang = _ en, August 16, 2019.

eration in Marine Fisheries)，1975 年的《印度与马尔代夫有关鱼类加工企业合作的谅解备忘录》（MOU between India and Maldives on Cooperation in Fish Processing Enterprise），2003 年的《印度与法国有关农业、渔业、农村发展、林业及食品工业的合作协定》（Agreement between India and France on Cooperation in Agriculture，Fisheries，Rurual Development，Forestry and Food Industries），2005 年的《印度与意大利有关渔业与水产产品的谅解备忘录》（MOU on Fishery and Aquaculture Products between India and Italy），2007 年的《印度与越南有关在渔业及水产领域双边合作的谅解备忘录》（MOU on Bilateral Cooperation in the Field of Fisheries and Aquaculture between India and Vietnam），2011 年的《印度与孟加拉国关于渔业领域合作的谅解备忘录》（MOU between India and Bangladesh on Cooperation in the Field of Fisheries），2014 年的《印度与摩洛哥有关海洋渔业合作的谅解备忘录》（MOU between India and Morocco on Cooperation in Marine Fisheries），2015 年的《印度与孟加拉国在孟加拉湾与印度洋地区关于蓝色经济与海事合作领域的谅解备忘录》（MOU between India and Bangladesh in the Field of Blue Economy and Maritime Cooperation in the Bay of Bengal and the Indian Ocean Region），2016 年的《印度与印度尼西亚关于打击非法、不管制、不报告（IUU）捕鱼及促进可持续性渔业治理的联合公报》［Joint Communique on Voluntary International Cooperation to Combat Illegal，Unregulated and Unreported（IUU）Fishing and to Promote Sustainable Fisheries Governance between India and Indonesia］，2016 年的《印度与韩国港口相关产业的谅解备忘录》（MOU between the Republic of India and the Republic of Korea on Cooperation in Port Related Industry），2016 年的《印度与巴西关于遗传资源、农业、畜牧业、自然资源及渔业领域合作的谅解备忘录》（MOU between India and Brazil on Cooperation in the Field of Genetic Resources，Agriculture，Animal Husbandry，Natural Resources and Fisheries），2018 年的《印度与英国有关在畜牧业、乳制品业及渔业部门领域合作的谅解备忘录》（MOU between India and the United Kingdom of Great Britain and Northern Ireland for Cooperation in the Field of Animal Husbandry，Dairying and Fisheries Sectors），2019 年的《印度与冰岛有关在可持续渔业发展领域合作的谅解备忘录》（MOU between India and Iceland on Cooperation in the Field of Sustainable Fisheries Development）。[1]

---

〔1〕 See "Treaty / Agreement"，Ministry of External Affairs，https：//www. mea. gov. in/TreatyList. htm? 1，August 16，2019；UN Treaty Collection，"United Nations Treaty Series Online"，https：//treaties. un. org/Pages/UNTSOnline. aspx? id = 3&clang = _ en，August 16，2019.

（四）与周边国家缔结的划定管辖海域的条约

为解决海上边界划界问题，印度已与周边国家达成系列协议。印度与斯里兰卡两国已于 20 世纪 70 年代，通过协议划定了保克海峡、马纳尔湾、孟加拉湾（Bay of Bengal）周边的海上边界。同样是在 20 世纪 70 年代，印度也与马尔代夫就阿拉伯海区域、与泰国就安达曼海区域达成协议以解决彼此间的海上划界问题。[1]

---

〔1〕　各相关划界协议的详细内容，请参阅本部分"五、海洋争端解决"。

五、海洋争端解决

（一）通过协议解决的海洋争端

1. 印度与斯里兰卡之间的划界协定

印度南部的泰米尔纳德邦（Tamil Nadu）与斯里兰卡东北部隔保克湾相望。保克湾长约 137 公里，宽度在 67—137 公里之间，其北端通过保克海峡与孟加拉湾相连，南端则穿过亚当桥（Adam's Bridge）与马纳尔湾相通。尽管拥有 15000 平方公里的水域面积，从泰米尔纳德邦到斯里兰卡海岸的海水深度却鲜少超过 15 米。一方面，基于保克湾尤其是其在亚当桥附近的浅水状态，外国船舶难以进入和通过，该海湾几乎专为印度与斯里兰卡两国船舶所用。另一方面，作为多样海洋生物汇聚的天堂，其较浅的水域和丰富的渔业资源也令这一海湾自古以来即为上述两国人民的传统捕捞区与重要海上交互通道。印度与斯里兰卡由此围绕这一海域谈判签订了系列海上边界协定。

（1）《1974 年斯里兰卡与印度两国间关于历史性水域边界及相关事项的协定》

坐落于保克湾中的卡此沙提武岛（Kachchativu），长期由印度及斯里兰卡两国的泰米尔渔民共同使用，并曾因领土归属引发印度与斯里兰卡间的争端。该岛位于印度的拉梅斯沃勒姆岛（Rameswaram）与斯里兰卡的纳顿岛（Neduntivu）之间，仅 1.15 平方公里，陆地资源贫瘠，无永久居民，但其周边海床却拥有对虾、珊瑚、珍珠、牡蛎等丰富的海洋资源。[1] 该岛的归属问题自 1921 年在印度和斯里兰卡划定渔业界限的会议上被提出之后，就一直出现在两国海洋边界划定相关事项的系列讨论与谈判之中，却迟迟未能达成一致。[2] 至 1974 年，两国签署《斯里兰卡与印度两国间关于历史性水域边界

---

〔1〕 "Katchatheevu: The Big Issue over A Small Island", Livemint, https://www.livemint.com/Politics/acjYPxP6XuKnlTLqJ2P3QI/Katchatheevu-The-big-issue-over-a-small-island.html, March 15, 2020; "Road to Kachchativu Feast-2017", Department of Government Information, https://www.dgi.gov.lk/news/latest-news/763-road-to-kachchativu-feast-2017, March 15, 2020.

〔2〕 斯里兰卡政府提出，印度政府的测量官早在 1876 年就把该岛视为当时锡兰（现在的斯里兰卡）的一部分。而从葡萄牙及后来的英国殖民统治时期至今，卡此沙提武岛一直处于斯里兰卡的管辖之下。"Maritime Boundary Dispute between India and Sri Lanka", ACADEMIA, https://www.academia.edu/4940394/Maritime_Boundary_Dispute_between_India_and_Sri_Lanka, August 14, 2019.

及相关事项的协定》（Agreement between Sri Lanka and India on the Boundary in Historic Waters between the two Countries and Related Matters，26 and 28 June 1974，以下简称《1974 年协定》），首次就该岛主权归属及其周边历史性水域界限等问题达成合意。[1]

根据《1974 年协定》，印度与斯里兰卡两国在从历史、法律、其他证据等角度进行审查之后，确认印度和斯里兰卡从亚当桥到保克海峡的海上分界线为连接 6 个坐标点（第 I 部分 表5）形成的系列弧线。

第 I 部分 表5　印度与斯里兰卡在保克海峡的海上界限坐标点

坐标点	纬度（北）	经度（东）
1	10°05′	80°03′
2	09°57′	79°35′
3	09°40′15	79°22′60
4	09°21′80	79°30′70
5	09°13′	79°32′
6	09°06′	79°32′

表5 中坐标点及其在该区域海上及海床的实际位置由两国分别委任的测绘人员认定和标注。两国对所划定界限的各自一侧的水域、岛屿、大陆架及其底土均拥有主权、专属管辖权和控制权。同时，如果存在跨越本协定所规定界限的单一地质结构的石油、天然气或其他矿藏时，对此类资源的任何部分或全部的开发利用及其利益分配都应由两国进行协商。[2]

随着《1974 年协定》对保克湾海上边界的划定，卡此沙提武岛也被划归斯里兰卡。根据该协定第 5 条、第 6 条，印度渔民和朝圣者仍然享有前往卡此沙提武岛的自由，无须由斯里兰卡颁发签证等旅行证件，两国船舶也将继续在对方水域享有传统上应有之权利。[3] 不能否认，上述条款着意体现了两国基于"历史性水域"与"历史性权利"的友好姿态，但所谓"传统享有"

---

[1]　该条约在印度外交部官网所载名称为：《印度政府和斯里兰卡共和国政府关于历史性水域边界的协定》（Agreement between The Government of India and The Government of The Republic of Sri Lanka on The Boundary in Historic Waters）。"Boundary Agreement in Historic Waters"，Ministry of External Affairs，https：//mea. gov. in/bilateral-documents. htm？ dtl/6290/Boundary ＿ Agreement＿ in＿ Historic＿ Waters，March 15，2020.

[2]　UN Office of Legal Affairs，"Agreement between Sri Lanka and India on the Boundary in Historic Waters between the Two Countries and Related Matters，1974"，https：//www. un. org/Depts/los/LEGISLATIONANDTREATIES/PDFFILES/TREATIES/LKA-IND1974BW. PDF，August 14，2019.

[3]　Ibid.

(traditionally enjoyed) 的权利并不明晰, 渔民前往卡此沙提武岛的权利是否包括在其周边捕鱼亦未澄清, 这使得两国后续在该海域的资源开发、环境保护、行为监管中时有摩擦、难归安宁。[1]

(2)《1976 年斯里兰卡与印度两国间在马纳尔湾和孟加拉湾的海上边界及相关事项的协定》

《1974 年协定》生效后, 印度和斯里兰卡进一步就马纳尔湾和孟加拉湾的海洋边界进行谈判, 以期《1974 年协定》所确定的双方海洋边界有所延伸。1976 年, 两国在印度新德里签署了《斯里兰卡与印度两国间在马纳尔湾和孟加拉湾的海上边界及相关事项的协定》(Agreement between Sri Lanka and India on the Maritime Boundary between the Two Countries in the Gulf of Mannar and the Bay of Bengal and Related Matters, 23 March 1976, 以下简称《1976 年协定》)。

立足《1974 年协定》中所划界限, 两国在《1976 年协定》中进一步明确: 第一, 印度和斯里兰卡在马纳尔湾的海洋边界为连接 13 个坐标点 (第Ⅰ部分 表6) 的系列弧线段; 第二, 印度和斯里兰卡在孟加拉湾的海洋边界为连接 7 个坐标点 (第Ⅰ部分 表7) 的系列弧线段; 第三, 相关坐标点及其在该区域海上及海床的实际位置由两国分别委任的测绘人员认定和标注。[2]

第Ⅰ部分 表6 印度与斯里兰卡在马纳尔湾的海上界限坐标点

坐标点	纬度 (北)	经度 (东)
1	09°06′. 0	79°32′. 0
2	09°00′. 0	79°31′. 3
3	08°53′. 8	79°29′. 3
4	08°40′. 0	79°18′. 2
5	08°37′. 2	79°13′. 0
6	08°31′. 2	79°04′. 7

---

[1] 事实上, 自 1974 年卡此沙提武岛划归斯里兰卡起, 该协定便遭到了印度泰米尔纳德邦的强烈反对, 并在数十年间采取了多种政治及法律手段意图使《1974 年协定》无效并 "收复" 卡此沙提武岛。而即使存在《1974 年协定》的初步分界, 两国渔业捕捞的传统权利仍然无法得到持续保障, 如斯里兰卡内战 (1983—2009) 所带来的不利影响等。V. Suryanarayan, "The India-Sri Lanka Fisheries Dispute: Creating a Win-Win in the Palk Bay", https://carnegieendowment. org/files/Suryanaryanan_ Fisheries_ Dispute_ . pdf, August 15, 2019.

[2] 有关印度与斯里兰卡在孟加拉湾海上界限的示意图, 参见 US Bureau of Oceans and International Environmental and Scientific Affairs, "Maritime Boundaries: India-Sri Lanka", Limits in the Seas, No. 77, https://www. state. gov/wp-content/uploads/2019/11/LIS-77. pdf, March 20, 2021.

续表

坐标点	纬度（北）	经度（东）
7	08°22′.2	78°55′.4
8	08°12′.2	78°53′.7
9	07°35′.3	78°45′.7
10	07°21′.0	78°38′.8
11	06°30′.8	78°12′.2
12	05°53′.9	77°50′.7
13	05°00′.0	77°10′.6

第Ⅰ部分 表7　印度与斯里兰卡在孟加拉湾的海上界限坐标点

坐标点	纬度（北）	经度（东）
1 b	10°05′.0	80°03′.0
1 ba	10°05′.8	80°05′.0
1 bb	10°08′.4	80°09′.5
2 b	10°33′.0	80°46′.0
3 b	10°41.7	81°02′.5
4 b	11°02′.7	81°56′.0
5 b	11°16′.0	82°24′.4
6 b	1.1°26′.6	83°22′.0

按照该协定，两国对边界各自一侧的历史性水域、领海以及岛屿拥有主权，对边界各自一侧的大陆架、专属经济区及其资源（包括生物资源和非生物资源）享有主权权利和专属管辖权；但同时两国都应尊重对方根据相关国际国内法律在本国领海及专属经济区的航行权。对于边界附近区域的资源开发，一如《1974 年协定》已作出的规定，若存在跨越本协定所规定边界的单一地质结构的各类矿藏，两国应就利益分配及如何有效地开发利用该资源进行协商。[1]

（3）《1976 年斯里兰卡与印度两国间在马纳尔湾从 13 号位置至斯里兰卡、印度及马尔代夫三国交界点（点 T）的海上边界延伸的补充协定》

根据《1976 年协定》第 1 条，对于超出 13 号位置的边界延伸，需要在

---

[1]　UN Office of Legal Affairs, "Agreement between Sri Lanka and India on the Maritime Boundary between the two Countries in the Gulf of Mannar and the Bay of Bengal and Related Matters, 23 March 1976", https：//www. un. org/Depts/los/LEGISLATIONANDTREATIES/PDFFILES/TREATIES/LKA-IND1976MB. PDF, August 15, 2019.

嗣后谈判中进一步确定。随着 1976 年 7 月印度、斯里兰卡和马尔代夫三国有关马纳尔湾三国交界点的协定签署,[1] 印度和斯里兰卡于同年 11 月签订《斯里兰卡与印度两国间在马纳尔湾从 13 号位置至斯里兰卡、印度及马尔代夫三国交界点（点 T）的海上边界延伸的补充协定》[Supplementary Agreement between Sri Lanka and India on the Extension of the Maritime Boundary between the two Countries in the Gulf of Mannar from Position 13 m to the Trijunction Point between Sri Lanka, India and Maldives（Point T）, 22 November 1976, 以下简称《补充协定》], 进一步将两国在马纳尔湾的海上边界从 13 号坐标点位置延伸至三国交界点 T。

作为 1974 年及 1976 年两份划界协定的补充文本,该协定仅有两条,明确:第一,印度和斯里兰卡在马纳尔湾超出《1976 年协定》附件所载的第 13 号位置的海上边界,应为连接第 13 号位置（05°00′.0 N, 77°10′.6 E）与印度、斯里兰卡、马尔代夫三国协定中所载的三国交界点 T（04°47′.04 N, 77°01′.40 E）的弧线段;第二,《补充协定》是《1976 年协定》的补充及不可分割的一部分,《1976 年协定》第 3—7 条的规定,经比照应适用于《补充协定》。[2]

2. 印度与马尔代夫之间的划界协定

阿拉伯海北接巴基斯坦和伊朗,西临亚丁湾、阿拉伯半岛,南至印度半岛南端,是北印度洋的重要海域。尽管该海域的渔业及石油等矿产资源均不丰沛,但其沿岸共有九个国家、多个重要港口,且向北由阿曼湾经霍尔木兹海峡可接波斯湾,向西由亚丁湾过曼德海峡可通红海,是世界性的海上交通贸易要道。

印度与马尔代夫分别位于阿拉伯海的东部与东南部。两国之间长期维持睦邻友好关系,并未因在该海域的相关权利主张发生过争端。1976 年,印度、马尔代夫和斯里兰卡通过协定明确了三国在马纳尔湾的交界点,并进一步推动印度与马尔代夫双方在阿拉伯海域海上边界的划定。1976 年 12 月 8 日,两国签订《印度与马尔代夫间在阿拉伯海的海上边界及相关事项的协定》（Agreement between India and Maldives on Maritime Boundary in The Arabian Sea and Related Matters）。

---

[1] 该协定内容详见下文 "6. 印度涉及的多国间划界协定" 部分。

[2] See UN Office of Legal Affairs, "Supplementary Agreement between Sri Lanka and India on the Extension of the Maritime Boundary between the Two Countries in the Gulf of Mannar from Position 13 m to the Trijunction Point between Sri Lanka, India and Maldives（Point T）", https://www.un.org/Depts/los/LEGISLATIONANDTREATIES/PDFFILES/TREATIES/LKA-IND1974BW.PDF, November 20, 2020.

根据该协定，两国政府共同派员协商确定印度和马尔代夫在阿拉伯海划定海洋边界的地理坐标点（第 I 部分 表 8）及其在海上和海床的实际位置，并以连接上述地理坐标点所形成的弧线作为两国在该区域的海上边界线。[1]

第 I 部分 表 8　印度与马尔代夫在阿拉伯海的海上界限坐标点

坐标点	纬度（北）	经度（东）
T	04°47′04″	77°01′40″
1	04°52′15″	76°56′48″
2	05°05′35″	76°43′15″
3	05°13′56″	76°36′48″
4	06°28′14″	75°41′34″
5	06°33′21″	75°38′31″
6	06°51′06″	75°25′46″
7	07°15′27″	75°16′19″
8	07°24′00″	75°12′06″
9	07°25′19″	75°11′18″
10	07°51′30″	74°56′09″
11	07°48′30″	74°29′45″
12	07°41′50″	73°38′34″
13	07°39′02″	73°19′38″
14	07°40′52″	73°03′23″
15	07°42′19″	72°49′30″
16	07°42′54″	72°42′26″
17	07°49′05″	72°03′45″
18	08°05′38″	70°15′08″
19	07°57′27″	69°35′45″

除有关海上边界位置及走向的核心条款之外，该协定第 4 条、第 5 条同样对两国对边界各自一侧的历史性水域、领海、岛屿以及大陆架、专属经济区及其资源的主权、主权权利和专属管辖权作出规定；在尊重对方船舶相关航行权利的同时，要求共同协商对跨越边界资源的勘探开发。其内容乃至措

---

[1]　有关印度与马尔代夫在阿拉伯海的海上界限的示意图，参见 US Bureau of Oceans and International Environmental and Scientific Affairs, "Maritime Boundary: India-Maldives and Maldives' Claimed 'Economic Zone'", Limits in the Seas, No. 78, https://www.state.gov/wp-content/uploads/2019/11/LIS-77.pdf, March 20, 2021。

辞都与前述印度及斯里兰卡间的《1976 年协定》的第 5 条、第 6 条如出一辙[1] 值得注意的是，从联合国条约数据库的收录情况来看，印度与马尔代夫间这一双边协定并未进入联合国的条约登记清单。这意味着，尽管两国都确认这一协定的真实存在，但该协定的生效状况存疑，且该协定将不能在包括国际法院在内的联合国相关机构中得以援引。[2]

3. 印度与缅甸之间的划界协定

印度与缅甸在安达曼海（Andaman Sea）、科科海峡（Coco Channel）和孟加拉湾的划界问题主要围绕科科群岛（Coco Islands）及其所属的安达曼群岛（Andaman Islands）展开。

安达曼群岛距印度次大陆约 800 公里，距缅甸约 197 公里，其连同尼科巴群岛（Nicobar Islands）将孟加拉湾与安达曼海分隔开来。安达曼群岛于 19 世纪末成为英属印度的一部分，并在印度独立后由印度所继承。相较于安达曼群岛的主体部分，科科群岛的位置距印度更为偏远。为便利管理，殖民时期的英国当局决定将科科群岛交给缅甸政府，并于 1882 年使其正式成为英属缅甸的一部分。科科群岛也由此随着缅甸的独立由缅甸继承。

1986 年 12 月 23 日，印度与缅甸签订《缅甸联邦社会主义共和国与印度共和国间关于在安达曼海、科科海峡与孟加拉湾划定海上边界的协定》（Agreement between the Socialist Republic of the Union of Burma and the Republic of India on the Delimitation of the Maritime Boundary in the Andaman Sea, in the Coco Channel and in the Bay of Bengal, 23 December 1986），就两国在上述海域的划界问题达成协议。该协定以缅甸语、印度语及英语同时作准，于 1987 年 9 月 14 日正式生效。

按照该协议：其一，印度与缅甸在安达曼海和科科海峡之间海上边界为连接坐标点 1 至坐标点 14 的直线段（第 I 部分 表 9）；而从坐标点 1 延伸至缅甸、印度、泰国在安达曼海的三国交界点之间的海上界限，将由三国嗣后协商确定该交界点后划定。其二，印度和缅甸在孟加拉湾的海上边界为连接坐标点 14 至坐标点 16 的直线段（第 I 部分 表 10）；而在坐标点 16 以外在孟

---

[1] US Bureau of Oceans and International Environmental and Scientific Affairs, "Maritime Boundary: India-Maldives and Maldives' Claimed 'Economic Zone'", Limits in the Seas, No. 78, https://www. state. gov/wp-content/uploads/2019/11/LIS-78. pdf, March 20, 2021.

[2] 印度外交部官网并未收录这一协定；而马尔代夫在向联合国大陆架界限委员会（CLCS）提交的文件中确认了该协定的存在，却并未提供该协定的本国官方文本，而是援引了美国国务院研究报告 "Limits in the Seas" 中所载的相关内容。CLCS, "Submission by the Republic of Maldives", https://www. un. org/Depts/los/clcs_ new/submissions_ files/mdv53_ 10/MAL-ES-DOC. pdf, November 20, 2020.

加拉湾上海上边界的延伸将由嗣后协商完成。

第 I 部分 表9　印度与缅甸在安达曼海、科科海峡的海上边界坐标点

坐标点	纬度（北）	经度（东）
1	09°38′00″	95°35′25″
2	09°53′14″	95°28′00″
3	10°18′42″	95°16′02″
4	10°28′00″	95°15′58″
5	10°44′53″	95°22′00″
6	11°43′17″	95°26′00″
7	12°19′43″	95°30′00″
8	12°54′07″	95°41′00″
9	13°48′00″	95°02′00″
10	13°48′00″	93°50′00″
11	13°34′18″	93°40′59″
12	13°49′11″	93°08′05″
13	13°57′29″	92°54′50″
14	14°00′59″	92°50′02″

第 I 部分 表10　印度与缅甸在孟加拉湾的海上边界坐标点

坐标点	纬度（北）	经度（东）
14	14°00′59″	92°50′02″
15	14°17′42″	92°24′17″
16	15°42′50″	90°14′01″

　　与印度早前签订的其他海上划界协定类似，印度与缅甸间的这一协定也规定相关坐标点在海上以及海床和大陆架上的实际位置应由经双方共同授权的测绘人员商定；同时明确两国对协定中海上边界本国一侧的现有岛屿、任何可能出现的岛屿、海洋区域拥有主权、主权权利或管辖权。但作为《公约》开放签署后所缔结的海洋划界协定，两国特别要求对各自管辖海域的权利行使应以《公约》为据；并添加争端解决条款，明确应通过磋商或谈判解决该协定相关争议。[1]

---

〔1〕　UN Office of Legal Affairs，"Agreement between the Socialist Republic of the Union of Burma and the Republic of India on the Delimitation of the Maritime Boundary in the Andaman Sea，in the Coco Channel and in the Bay of Bengal，23 December 1986"，https：//www. un. org/Depts/los/LEGIS-LATIONANDTREATIES/PDFFILES/TREATIES/MMR-IND1986MB. PDF，November 20，2020.

4. 印度与泰国之间的划界协定

印度与泰国在印度洋东北部的边缘海安达曼海上存在较长的海上边界。安达曼海向北与缅甸的伊洛瓦底江（Irrawaddy River）三角洲相通，向东与缅甸半岛、泰国和马来西亚相接，向南抵印度尼西亚的苏门答腊岛（Island of Sumatra）和马六甲海峡，向西至印度的安达曼群岛和尼科巴群岛。由于该海域海洋生物资源并不丰富，矿产资源也相对匮乏，印度和泰国长期以来在该区域并无海洋权益争端，也未有确定该区域海上边界的迫切愿望。1978 年6 月，为维系并加强两国间的传统友谊，两国签署《泰王国政府与印度共和国政府间关于划定两国在安达曼海海床边界的协定》（Agreement between the Government of the Kingdom of Thailand and the Government of the Republic of India on the Delimitation of Seabed Boundary between the Two Countries in the Andaman Sea，22 June 1978），划定两国在安达曼海海床的边界，以永久性地确定两国政府在相关地区行使主权权利的界限。

按照这一协定，依据泰国海道测绘局主任（Director of Hydrographic Department）与印度首席水文测量师（Chief Hydrographer）共同商定的测绘方式：第一，两国在安达曼海的海床边界线为从坐标点 1 依次连接至坐标点 7 的系列直线段；第二，该边界线两端的延伸，应分别从坐标点 1 延伸至泰国、印度及印度尼西亚的三国交界点，以及从坐标点 7 延伸至泰国、印度及缅甸的三国交界点（第 I 部分 表11）。[1]

第 I 部分 表 11　印度与泰国在安达曼海海床的边界坐标点

坐标点	纬度（北）	经度（东）
1	07°48′00″	95°32′48″
2	07°57′30″	95°41′48″

---

〔1〕 这两处的三国交界点已分别由 1978 年及 1993 年的相关协定所明确。See UN Office of Legal Affairs，"Agreement between the Government of the Kingdom of Thailand，the Government of the Republic of India and the Government of the Republic of Indonesia concerning the Determination of the Trijunction Point and the Delimitation of the Related Boundaries of the three Countries in the Andaman Sea，22 June 1978"，https：//www. un. org/Depts/los/LEGISLATIONANDTREATIES/PDFFILES/TREATIES/THA-IND-IDN1978TP. PDF，November 20，2020；UN Office of Legal Affairs，"Agreement between the Government of the Union of Myanmar，the Government of the Republic of India and the Government of the Kingdom of Thailand on the determination of the Trijunction Point between the Three Countries in the Andaman Sea，27 October 1993"，https：//www. un. org/Depts/los/LEGISLATIONANDTREATIES/PDFFILES/TREATIES/MMR-IND-THA1993DT. PDF，November 20，2020.

续表

坐标点	纬度（北）	经度（东）
3	08°09′54″	95°39′16″
4	08°13′47″	95°39′11″
5	08°45′11″	95°37′42″
6	08°48′04″	95°37′40″
7	09°17′18″	95°36′31″

立足于该海床分界线，两国均确认了对方在各自一侧海床及底土的主权权利，并约定将通过磋商或谈判和平解决与本协定的解释或执行相关的任何争议。同时，一如前述各协定，对可能存在的跨越该协定所载边界的单一地质结构的任何矿藏，两国政府应就该矿藏的最有效开发方式及收益分配进行协商。[1]

5. 印度与印度尼西亚之间的划界协定

（1）《印度共和国政府与印度尼西亚共和国政府关于两国间大陆架划界的协定》

《印度共和国政府与印度尼西亚共和国政府关于两国间大陆架划界的协定》（Agreement between the Government of the Republic of India and the Government of the Republic of Indonesia relating to the Delimitation of the Continental Shelf Boundary between the Two Countries）签署于 1974 年 8 月 8 日。根据该协定，依照印度首席水文测量师与印度尼西亚国家测绘协调机构主任（Director of Coordinating Body for National Survey and Mapping）共同商定之方法，两国在大尼科巴和苏门答腊之间的大陆架界限，为连接坐标点 1 至坐标点 4 的系列直线段。相关坐标点的具体位置见第 I 部分 表12。

第 I 部分 表12　印度与印度尼西亚的大陆架界限坐标点

坐标点	纬度（北）	经度（东）
1	6°38′5″	94°38′0″
2	6°30′0″	94°32′4″
3	6°16′2″	94°24′2″
4	6°0′0″	94°10′3″

---

〔1〕 UN Office of Legal Affairs, "Agreement between the Government of the Kingdom of Thailand and the Government of the Republic of India on the Delimitation of Seabed Boundary between the two Countries in the Andaman Sea, 22 June 1978", https://www.un.org/Depts/los/LEGISLATIONANDTREATIES/PDFFILES/TREATIES/THA-IND1978SB. PDF, August 10, 2019.

作为与自然资源主权息息相关的大陆架区域划界，除明确界限走向、要求和平解决相关争议外，该协定再次强调，在单一地质结构跨越边界时，两国政府应彼此交换资讯，就寻求最有效开采及平等分享开采达成协议；同时双方承诺在国内层面采取一切必要手段推动协定条款的落实。[1]

（2）《印度共和国政府与印度尼西亚共和国政府关于延伸两国 1974 年在安达曼海与印度洋的大陆架边界的协定》

《印度共和国政府与印度尼西亚共和国政府关于延伸两国 1974 年在安达曼海与印度洋的大陆架边界的协定》（Agreement between the Government of the Republic of India and the Government of the Republic of Indonesia on the Extension of the 1974 Continental Shelf Boundary between the Two Countries in the Andaman Sea and the Indian Ocean）签订于 1977 年 1 月 14 日，旨在以 1974 年两国大陆架划界协议为基础，进一步明确双方在安达曼海与印度洋的大陆架边界。

根据该协定，依照双方主管机关共同商定之方法：其一，两国在安达曼海海床的界限为依次连接坐标点 1 到坐标点 O 的系列直线段（第 I 部分 表 13）；其二，两国在印度洋的海床的界限为依次连接坐标点 4 到坐标点 U 的系列直线段（第 I 部分 表 14）。

第 I 部分 表 13　印度与印度尼西亚在安达曼海海床的边界坐标点

坐标点	纬度（北）	经度（东）
1	06°38′05″	94°38′00″
K	07°02′24″	94°55′37″
N	07°40′06″	95°25′45″
O	07°46′06″	95°31′12″

第 I 部分 表 14　印度与印度尼西亚在印度洋海床的边界坐标点

坐标点	纬度（北）	经度（东）
4	06°00′00″	94°10′30″
R	05°25′20″	93°41′12″
S	04°27′34″	92°51′17″
T	04°18′31″	92°43′31″
U	04°01′40″	92°23′55″

---

[1] US Bureau of Oceans and International Environmental and Scientific Affairs, "Continental Shelf Boundary: India-Indonesia", Limits in the Seas, No. 62, https://2009—2017. state. gov/documents/organization/61495. pdf, December 28, 2020.

　　除上述核心条款外，该 1977 年协定在互相承认海床及底土主权权利、跨边界的单一地质结构矿藏、和平解决协定相关争议等方面基本承继了两国 1974 年协定的相关思路与立场。[1]

　　6. 印度涉及的多国间划界协定

　　（1）斯里兰卡、印度和马尔代夫在马纳尔湾的三国交界点的协定

　　一如前述，印度于 1976 年与斯里兰卡签署了双边划界协定以明确两国在马纳尔湾的海上边界，并于同年与马尔代夫就确定两国在阿拉伯海的海上边界完成了磋商。在三国间两两达成双边合意的基础之上，印度、马尔代夫和斯里兰卡均表达了在马纳尔湾海域确定三国交界点的愿望和需要，并最终于 1976 年 7 月 31 日缔结《斯里兰卡、印度和马尔代夫间关于确定在马纳尔湾的三国交界点的协定》（Agreement between Sri Lanka, India and Maldives concerning the Determination of the Trijunction Point between the Three Countries in the Gulf of Mannar, 23, 24 and 31 July 1976）。

　　按照这一协定，印度、斯里兰卡和马尔代夫在马纳尔湾以外的海上的三国界限交点被确定为点 T，该点至印度、斯里兰卡和马尔代夫海岸的最近点的距离相等，其经三方共同协商确定的具体坐标见第Ⅰ部分 表 15。

第Ⅰ部分 表 15　印度、斯里兰卡、马尔代夫在马纳尔湾的三国交界点 T 的坐标[2]

坐标点	纬度（北）	经度（东）
T	04°47′04″	77°01′40″

　　该三国交界点在海上和海底的实际位置分别由三国政府为此目的授权的测量人员共同商定的方法确定。出于三国间长期以来的友好关系及该海域划界的稳固共识，该协定无须批准，自三国签字之日起即可生效，若三国协定签订日期不同，将以最后签字之日为生效日期。[3]

---

〔1〕 UN Office of Legal Affairs, "Agreement between the Government of the Republic of India and the Government of the Republic of Indonesia on the Extension of the 1974 Continental Shelf Boundary between the two Countries in the Andaman Sea and the Indian Ocean 14 January 1977", http://www. un. org/Depts/los/LEGISLATIONANDTREATIES/PDFFILES/TREATIES/IND-IDN1977CS. PDF, December 30, 2019.

〔2〕 有关印度、斯里兰卡和马尔代夫在马纳尔湾的三国交界点 T 的位置示意图，参见 UN Treaty Collection, "Map Details", https://treaties. un. org/doc/Treaties/1977/07/19770719% 2006-53% 20AM/I-15805-vol-1049-map-BW. pdf, December 30, 2019。

〔3〕 UN Office of Legal Affairs, "Agreement between Sri Lanka, India and Maldives concerning the Determination of the Trijunction Point between the three Countries in the Gulf of Mannar, 1976", https://www. un. org/Depts/los/LEGISLATIONANDTREATIES/PDFFILES/TREATIES/LKA-IND-MDV1976TP. PDF, August 10, 2020.

（2）印度、印度尼西亚与泰国划定三国交界点及安达曼海相关边界的协定

1978 年 6 月 22 日，印度尼西亚、印度和泰国签订了《印度共和国政府、印度尼西亚共和国政府与泰王国政府有关确立三国交界点及划定三国在安达曼海相关边界的协定》（Agreement between the Government of Republic of India, the Government of the Republic of Indonesia and the Government of the Kingdom of Thailand Concerning the Delimitation of the Tri-junction Point and the Delimitation of the Related Boundaries of the Three Countries in the Andaman Sea）。该协定于 1979 年 3 月 2 日生效。依据该协定，三国边界的交界点位于 07°47′00″N、95°31′48″E 的坐标处。[1] 因此，印度尼西亚与印度间的大陆架边界（boundary of the continental shelf）为从该交界点向西南延伸至坐标点 O（07°46′06″N，95°31′12″E）的一条直线。[2] 泰国至印度之间的海床边界（seabed boundary）为从该交界点向东北延伸至坐标点 1（07°48′00″N，95°32′48″E）的一条直线。[3] 泰国至印度尼西亚的海床边界为从该三国交界点向东南延伸至点 L（07°46′01″N，95°33′01″E）的一条直线。[4]

（3）印度、缅甸和泰国关于在安达曼海的三国交界点的协定

安达曼海以西为印度所属的安达曼群岛，以北坐落有缅甸所属的科科群岛，东南则与泰国的南端陆地相接。尽管在英国殖民时期，英国政府对安达曼群岛以及科科群岛的主权有所分配，但对两处岛屿附近的海域并未有明晰的界限划分。历史遗留原因以及安达曼海为三国陆地围绕的地理特征，使得印度、缅甸、泰国三方有在该海区进一步明确其管辖界域的必要与动力。

一如前述各三国间协定，印度、缅甸及泰国间同样已通过两两间的双边

---

〔1〕 有关印度、印度尼西亚与泰国在安达曼海的三国交界点的示意图，参见 US Bureau of Oceans and International Environmental and Scientific Affairs, "Continental Shelf Boundaries: India-Indonesia-Thailand", Limits in the Seas, No. 93, https://2009—2017. state. gov/documents/organization/58818. pdf, December 30, 2020。

〔2〕 该坐标点 O 由两国在 1977 年签订的《印度共和国政府与印度尼西亚共和国政府关于延伸两国 1974 年在安达曼海与印度洋大陆架边界的协定》中确立。参见 "5. 印度与印度尼西亚之间的划界协定" 相关内容。

〔3〕 该坐标点 1 由两国在 1978 年签订的《泰王国政府与印度共和国政府间关于划定两国在安达曼海海床边界的协定》中确立。参见 "4. 印度与泰国之间的划界协定" 相关内容。

〔4〕 该坐标点 L 由两国在 1975 年签订的《泰王国政府与印度尼西亚共和国政府关于在安达曼海划定两国间海床边界的协定》中确立。UN Office of Legal Affairs, "Agreement between the Government of the Kingdom of Thailand and the Government of the Republic of Indonesia relating to the Delimitation of the Seabed Boundary between the two Countries in the Andaman Sea 11 December 1975", https://www.un. org/Depts/los/LEGISLATIONANDTREATIES/PDFFILES/TREATIES/THA-IDN1975SB. PDF, March 20, 2020。

协定为三国间的最终合意铺平了道路。根据印度与泰国于 1978 年达成的关于安达曼海两国海床边界的协定，缅甸和泰国于 1980 年达成的关于安达曼海的划界协定，以及缅甸与印度于 1986 年达成的关于安达曼海、科科海峡和孟加拉湾的划界协定，该三项双边协定中的部分海上边界线的最终划定都取决或依赖于三国在安达曼海的三国交界点的明确。1993 年 10 月 27 日，三国签订《缅甸联邦政府、印度共和国政府与泰王国政府间关于确立在安达曼海的三国交界点的协定》（Agreement between the Government of the Union of Myanmar, the Government of the Republic of India and the Government of the Kingdom of Thailand on the Determination of the Trijunction Point between the Three Countries in the Andaman Sea, 27 October 1993），就该关键交界点的位置及划定程序等作出明确规定。

按照该协定，印度、缅甸和泰国之间的三国交界点为点 T，该点至三国海岸的最近点的距离相等。点 T 的地理坐标（第 I 部分 表 16）取自英国 1975 年出版、1987 年修订的第 830 号航海图。

第 I 部分 表 16　印度、缅甸、泰国在安达曼海的三国交界点 T 的坐标

坐标点	纬度（北）	经度（东）
T	09°38′00″	95°35′25″

而 T 点在海上的实际位置将参照上述海图及坐标，依据三国政府授权人员共同商定的方法最终测量确定。[1]

（二）通过国际仲裁解决的海洋争端

如前所述，印度展现出通过谈判协商解决与周边国家海洋争端的积极姿态。不过，对与其历史及地缘关联最为紧密的两个邻国——巴基斯坦与孟加拉国，印度却迟迟未能取得突破性的进展。对于与巴基斯坦的海洋争议，无论是通过政治手段或是法律手段都仍面临僵局；而对于与孟加拉国的海洋摩擦，两国已通过国际仲裁寻求最终解决的希望。

1. 争端的背景

印度与孟加拉的海上划界争端源于英国殖民统治者 1947 年炮制的印巴分

---

[1] UN Office of Legal Affairs, "Agreement between the Government of the Union of Myanmar, the Government of the Republic of India and the Government of the Kingdom of Thailand on the Determination of the Trijunction Point between the Three Countries in the Andaman Sea, 27 October 1993", https://www. un. org/Depts/los/LEGISLATIONANDTREATIES/PDFFILES/TREATIES/MMR-IND-THA1993DT. PDF, December 28, 2020.

治方案（"蒙巴顿方案"）。基于这一方案，原孟加拉地区被一分为二，其中东孟加拉作为巴基斯坦的一部分隔着印度与西巴基斯坦遥遥相望。地理上的隔绝以及民族、文化的巨大差异，最终使东巴基斯坦于1971年独立为孟加拉国。自此，印度与巴基斯坦在东部边境的相关争议也随之由孟加拉国继承。[1]

早在孟加拉国独立之前，印巴两国即围绕东、西孟加拉地区的划界长期存在争议。1947年1月，时任印度总督组建"孟加拉边界委员会"（Bengal Boundary Commission），该委员会于同年8月提交报告以明确两地区间的边界走向。这一被称为"拉德克利夫裁定"（Radcliffe Award）的划界报告并未获得预想中的一致认可。两国于1949年将由该报告所产生的相关争议提交国际仲裁，并于1950年获得仲裁庭关于报告相关解释的裁决。不过，由于"拉德克利夫裁决"并未涉及两国在孟加拉地区的海上边界划分，上述1950年的仲裁裁决对于两国在这一区域的海洋争议解决并无助益。

1970年，在一次飓风过后，印孟天然界限哈拉帕汗嘎河（Harappahanga River）注入孟加拉湾的入海口又"新增"了一个大约2500平方米的新岛屿，即新摩尔岛（New Moore Island）。[2] 印度和孟加拉国随即都宣称对该岛拥有主权，并就该岛具有丰富油气资源的专属经济区归属产生争议。可以认为，这正是印度与孟加拉国将争议焦点转向海洋的重要动机：一方面，地理上作为印孟天然界限的哈拉帕汗嘎河在注入孟加拉湾的入海口处，制造了包括新摩尔岛在内的许多冲积三角洲及小岛，双方均有意获取这些三角洲和小岛的主权；另一方面，孟加拉湾拥有的巨量油气储备令周边国家垂涎，而海上岛屿及沙洲的归属无疑也将决定相关国家的自然资源主权权利范围。为此，1974—2009年，两国进行了约10轮谈判，但未能达成任何协议。[3] 2009年10月8日，两国同意组成《公约》附件七下的仲裁庭，依据《公约》第15条、第74条及第83条相关规定就两国在孟加拉湾的领海、专属经济区、200

---

〔1〕 余双、季谐：《美媒鼓吹以印孟模式解决南海争端 美化国际仲裁》，载环球时报，http://world. huanqiu. com/exclusive/2014-08/5092720. html？agt = 15425，最后访问日期：2019年7月23日。

〔2〕 孟加拉国称为南达尔帕蒂岛（South Talpatti）。

〔3〕 关于两国谈判情况，印度方面称共进行8轮谈判、2轮专家级会谈，孟加拉国方面称进行了不少于11轮的谈判。See Counter-Memorial of The Republic of India (Volume I), People's Republic of Bangladesh v. Republic of India, 31 July 2012, Arbitration under Annex VII of The United Nations Convention on The Law of The Sea, p. 51；Memorial of Bangladesh (Volume I), People's Republic of Bangladesh v. Republic of India, 31 May 2011, Arbitration under Annex VII of The U-nited Nations Convention on The Law of The Sea, p. 47.

海里以内及以外的大陆架界限作出划定。

2. 双方的主张

对于领海、专属经济区及 200 海里以内大陆架的划界，印度坚持依等距离线划分两国管辖海域，认为等距离线已成为被普遍接受的海洋划界"原则"，且印度也依据这一"原则"与 6 个邻国成功完成划界，从 1974 年到 2009 年的 35 年印度从未改变过这一主张。而孟加拉国则反复申明，一方面，由于本国海岸地形存在的特殊"内凹现象"（effect of the concavity），适用等距离方法无法在两国间获得公平的结果，且随着周期性潮汐、土壤侵蚀及其他因素，这一"内凹"地形会不断扩大，孟加拉国的领海基线会朝着"侵蚀孟加拉国领土"的方向推进，从而使"等距离线"朝向孟加拉国"偏移"；[1] 另一方面，等距离线仅为划界的方法之一而非划界的"原则"，不应以这一方法违背国际法所要求的公平原则。孟加拉国据此主张在划界时适用 180 度角平分线 （180°angle bisector） 以替代等距离线方法。[2]

而对于 200 海里以外的外大陆架的划界，印度与孟加拉国分别于 2009 年 5 月及 2011 年 2 月向联合国大陆架界限委员会 （Commission on the Limits of the Continental Shelf, CLCS） 提交了其 200 海里以外大陆架划界案。孟加拉国以印度的外大陆架划界涉及印度、孟加拉国及缅甸的争议地区为由，反对印度提交的划界案；印度则未对孟加拉国的外大陆架划界案表示异议。两国划界案都被联合国大陆架界限委员会决定推迟审议。[3]

3. 争议焦点及仲裁结果

（1） 关于管辖权

对仲裁庭而言，能否对 200 海里外大陆架的划界进行管辖是本次仲裁需考量的前置问题之一。仲裁庭承认，适用于 200 海里以外大陆架划界的国际法理论及规则十分有限。但结合相关司法实践及法理分析，仲裁庭仍然认为：第一，争端双方都对 200 海里外大陆架提出过权利主张，双方都认为孟加拉湾存在 200 海里以外的大陆架，且双方一致同意，仲裁庭对 200 海里以外大陆架有管辖权；第二，尽管《公约》第 76 条及附件七并未解决大陆架

〔1〕 "Insights", American School of International Law, https：//www. asil. org/insights/volume/18/is-sue/20/annex-vii-arbitral-tribunal-delimits-maritime-boundary-between, November 10, 2019.

〔2〕 Memorial of Bangladesh （Volume I）, People's Republic of Bangladesh v. Republic of India, 31 May 2011, Arbitration under Annex VII of The United Nations Convention on The Law of The Sea, pp. 47-49, 72.

〔3〕 Memorial of Bangladesh （Volume I）, People's Republic of Bangladesh v. Republic of India, 31 May 2011, Arbitration under Annex VII of The United Nations Convention on The Law of The Sea, pp. 50-51.

外部界限问题，但也并无规定禁止仲裁庭在 200 海里外大陆架的外部界限确定前划分其侧面边界；第三，无论是规定了大陆架概念的《公约》第 76 条还是涉及大陆架划界的《公约》第 83 条，都没有对 200 海里以内或以外的大陆架适用作出区分；第四，尽管联合国大陆架界限委员会对大陆架外部界限的确定负有特别职责，但划定大陆架的外部边界线与划定两国之间在外大陆架的分界线是不同的；第五，在联合国大陆架界限委员会决定推迟审议两国的外大陆架划界案的情形下，依两国此前谈判的消极局面，若仲裁庭拒绝管辖，两国在 200 海里外大陆架上的权益将难以确立和行使。因此，仲裁庭认为，其对在 200 海里以内和 200 海里以外双方主张区域的大陆架划界均具有管辖权。[1]

（2）关于海上边界的划界起点

两国同意，应将两国间陆地边界的终点作为其海上边界的起点，此陆地边界的终点应根据孟加拉边界委员会 1947 年的"拉德克利夫裁定"来确定。按照这一裁定，两国的陆地边界终点为库尔纳地区（District of Khulna）及"24 帕嘎纳斯地区"（District of 24 Parganas）间的分界线与孟加拉湾的交会处。而上述两区域的分界线于 1925 年由当时的孟加拉总督在《第 964 号通告》中划定。两国由此对"拉德克利夫裁定"及《第 964 号通告》中相关表述的解释发生争议，并就对方提交的地图、换文等证据等提出异议。[2]

对此，仲裁庭认为：第一，1925 年《第 964 号通告》中所述的库尔纳地区与"24 帕嘎纳斯地区"间的边界线，应为哈里汉加河（Haribhanga River）的主航道汇入孟加拉湾处，而非四条河流（Ichhamati and Kalindi, Raimangal and Haribhanga）在两两交汇后的分别入海点；第二，这一通告中的"目前"一词确实在表面上具有歧义，但结合 1950 年关于解释"拉德克利夫裁定"相关仲裁裁决，该措辞须理解为哈里汉加河在 1947 年"拉德克利夫裁定"作出时的主航道走向，而无论其以后流域出现何种变化；第三，印度所提交的 1951 年印度政府和巴基斯坦政府（孟加拉独立前）之间的往来信函，仅能视为政府公务员之间的信件，不能作为两国间 1947 年"拉德克利夫裁定"的后续协议；第四，通过对一系列同期地图（包括"拉德克利夫裁定"中使用的地图）的比较与选择，最终确定两国陆地边界终点位置的坐标为北

---

〔1〕 Award, People's Republic of Bangladesh v. Republic of India, 7 July 2014, Arbitration under Annex VII of The United Nations Convention on The Law of The Sea, pp. 38-39.

〔2〕 Award, People's Republic of Bangladesh v. Republic of India, 7 July 2014, Arbitration under Annex VII of The United Nations Convention on The Law of The Sea, pp. 40-60

纬 21°38′40.2″,东经 89°09′20.0″。[1]

（3）关于领海划界

为划定两国的领海分界线,仲裁庭需要:第一,确定海上等距离线可依赖的两国海岸基点,它们将贯穿后续所有海洋区域（包括领海、专属经济区及大陆架）的边界划定过程;第二,确定本案情形中领海划界的适宜方式。印度与孟加拉国分别向仲裁庭提交了各自认定的本国及对方海岸线的基点坐标,但均遭到对方的质疑。同时,尽管随着国际海洋法法庭（International Tribunal for the Law of the Sea,ITLOS）于 2012 年对孟加拉国与缅甸在孟加拉湾海洋划界争议作出判决,孟加拉国对角平分线的适用立场有所松动,同意先确立一条临时等距离线以供调整,但两国围绕低潮高地地位、海岸环境侵蚀、领海划界方法等仍存在诸多争议。

对于领海划界所依赖的海岸基点的位置,两国都同意领海分界线应以陆地边界的终点为起点,并一致排除两国直线基线在领海划界中的适用,对于其海岸基点具体位置的分歧,仲裁庭认为:①相邻海岸间的海洋区域划界不应将低潮高地纳入考量,《公约》第 13 条所规定的是领海宽度的测量,却并不涉及低潮高地在相邻或相向国家海洋边界划定中的适用。②根据卫星地图的显示,新摩尔岛（孟加拉国称南达尔帕蒂岛）位置确实存在某种海洋地形地物,其或长期被海水淹没或为低潮高地;但无论其地理状况如何,这一地形都无法被视为坐落于海岸线上的"海岸点突起"（protuberant coastal point）,新摩尔岛由此不能作为确立基点的适当位置。③最终确立的适于划定领海中间/等距离线的基点,分别为孟加拉国一侧海岸的基点 B-1（21°39′04″N,89°12′40″E）以及位于印度一侧海岸的摩尔岛低潮线基点（21°38′06″N,89°05′36″E）。[2]

对于如何调整临时等距离线以划定领海分界线,仲裁庭认为:①所谓气候变化对海岸侵蚀的影响并不是划界的关键,能否就本案情况反映当前海岸的基本走向才是需要考虑的对象;未来海岸线的可能变化不会危害已经确立的海洋边界,已经消失的地形也可通过技术手段予以确认,孟加拉国的这一主张不能构成偏离等距离线的"特别情况"（special circumstances）。②孟加拉国所援引的海岸线内凹现象与领海的狭长水域的划界无甚关联,所涉及的莱曼加河的入海口（Raimangal estuary）在地形上同时影响着印度和

---

〔1〕 Award, People's Republic of Bangladesh v. Republic of India, 7 July 2014, Arbitration under Annex VII of The United Nations Convention on The Law of The Sea, pp. 25-56.

〔2〕 Award, People's Republic of Bangladesh v. Republic of India, 7 July 2014, Arbitration under Annex VII of The United Nations Convention on The Law of The Sea, pp. 83-86

孟加拉国，这一内凹也并未产生显著的"截断效应"，亦不能作为调整等距离线的"特别情况"。③"拉德克利夫裁定"中所确立的陆地边界终点并不在仲裁庭所选定的基点的等距离线上，有必要将该陆地边界终点与仲裁庭划定领海的中间线相连接，这构成调整临时等距离线的"特别情况"。由上，仲裁庭确认，两国间的领海分界线应为一条长 12 海里的大地线，由陆地边界终点大致向南延伸，并于北纬 21°26′43.6″、东经 89°10′59.2″处与中间线交会。[1]

(4) 关于专属经济区和大陆架划界

对于专属经济区和大陆架的划界，两国的分歧主要在于：第一，等距离/相关情况方法在划界时的中心地位；第二，是否存在应适用角平分线为替代方法的情形；第三，若适用等距离/相关情况方法，临时等距离线是否需要进行调整。

对于两种划界方法的采用，仲裁庭认为，一方面应考虑划界方法的适用前提，另一方面应顾及特定划界方法在本案中的适用实际。鉴于此，仲裁庭认定：①等距离/相关情况方法更为客观，临时等距离线就是基于客观的几何标准作出，而基于直线海岸线的角平分线方法则包含较多的主观因素；②等距离/相关情况方法的分步划界方式可保证划界过程中更高的透明度，而角平分线方法即使说理充分也无法具备类似的高度透明性；③孟加拉国主张的内凹地形并未影响其海岸基点的确认，亦不存在所谓该海岸地貌无法反映孟加拉湾北部地形的情况。由上，仲裁庭表达了在本案中适用等距离/相关情况方法的明确倾向。[2]

对于是否存在"相关情况"（relevant circumstances）以调整临时等距离线甚至适用替代划界方法，仲裁庭分析后认为：①有关莱曼加河与哈里汉加河口海岸的不稳定性，不足以成为调整专属经济区与大陆架划界的临时等距离线的"相关情况"；正如仲裁庭在领海界限部分所强调的，只有划界当时的地理状况具有关联性，而基于气候变化等的未来预测无须被纳入考量。②基于孟加拉国海岸的"内凹"地形，临时等距离线确实构成对孟加拉国向海延伸的"截断效应"，并成为调整临时等距离线的"相关情况"。一方面，临时等距离线使孟加拉国的海洋边界无法延伸至国际法允许的最大宽度；另一方面，临时等距离线从点 Prov-3 开始向东的明显弯折对孟加拉国构成不

〔1〕 Award, People's Republic of Bangladesh v. Republic of India, 7 July 2014, Arbitration under Annex VII of The United Nations Convention on The Law of The Sea, pp. 73-74, 82-83, 86-87.

〔2〕 Award, People's Republic of Bangladesh v. Republic of India, 7 July 2014, Arbitration under Annex VII of The United Nations Convention on The Law of The Sea, pp. 104-106.

利。仲裁庭由此须调整临时等距离线以避免不合理的"截断效应"对孟加拉国的损害。③有关孟加拉国因其人民极度依赖在孟加拉湾渔业捕捞而需要调整临时等距离线的主张，由于孟加拉国未能提交充分证据以证明这一依赖性以及临时等距离线对此造成的不公后果，仲裁庭对该"相关情况"不予支持。[1]

对于 200 海里以外大陆架的划定，仲裁庭多次提出，当事国之间需要划分的为一块单一的大陆架（single continental shelf），无论对于 200 海里以内还是 200 海里以外的大陆架，划界所立足的基点与专属经济区完全等同，等距离线/相关情况方法一并适用，而作用于 200 海里以内大陆架划界的"相关情况"同样对 200 海里以外大陆架划界产生影响。[2]

综上，仲裁庭参照该地区的地理综合情况，评估了海洋区域分配的比例性，在遵循等距离为基本划界方法的同时，适当对等距离线进行调整后，划定了两国专属经济区和 200 海里以内及以外的大陆架分界线。[3]

随着 2014 年 7 月 7 日海牙常设仲裁法庭对印度和孟加拉国海洋划界一案作出最终裁决，两国在孟加拉湾海域的划界争议解决取得阶段性成果。依照裁决结果，在对临时等距离线作出调整之后，争议相关地区约 106613 平方公里被划归孟加拉国，约 300220 平方公里则置于印度管辖之下，两国所获得区域比例约为 1∶2.81。孟加拉国获得了超过其此前所要求的海域范围；印度则让出约 1.95 万平方公里此前主张的管辖海区，获得哈拉帕汗嘎河口附近海域的控制权以及时隐时现的新摩尔岛。[4] 值得注意的是，仲裁庭划定的海洋分界线导致孟加拉国 200 海里以外大陆架海域与印度 200 海里以内的专属经济区海域出现重叠，形成了所谓的"灰色区域"（gray area）。这意味着，在仲裁庭所划界限以东的这一"灰色区域"，孟加拉国拥有勘探大陆架、开采海床和底土的矿物及其他非生物资源以及属于定居物种的生物体的主权权利，而印度还拥有大陆架上覆水域的专属经济区的主权权利。仲裁庭认为，这是出于公平依据"相关情况"调整等距离线后出现的不可避免的情形，在该

〔1〕　Award, People's Republic of Bangladesh v. Republic of India, 7 July 2014, Arbitration under Annex VII of The United Nations Convention on The Law of The Sea, pp. 119-126.

〔2〕　Award, People's Republic of Bangladesh v. Republic of India, 7 July 2014, Arbitration under Annex VII of The United Nations Convention on The Law of The Sea, pp. 130, 138-142.

〔3〕　有关仲裁庭为印度与孟加拉国在孟加拉湾所划定的海上分界线的示意图，参见 Award, People's Republic of Bangladesh v. Republic of India, 7 July 2014, Arbitration under Annex VII of The United Nations Convention on The Law of The Sea, p. 163。

〔4〕　"Insights", American School of International Law, https：//www. asil. org/insights/volume/18/issue/20/annex-vii-arbitral-tribunal-delimits-maritime-boundary-between, November 10, 2019.

地带的权利分配及行使即交由当事国双方自行决定以作出协调性安排。[1]

(三) 未决的海洋争端

印度与斯里兰卡、马尔代夫、泰国、孟加拉国之间先后通过双边或多边协定完成了有关的海洋划界。目前,只余与巴基斯坦之间的海洋划界争端尚未解决。

爵士湾(Sir Creek)是印度与巴基斯坦交界处的一片争议水域,将印度的古吉拉特邦(Gujarat State)和巴基斯坦的信德省(Sindh Province)分开。爵士湾全长96公里,其本身是块无人居住的沼泽地,面向阿拉伯海,一年中有近半年的时间都被海水淹没,水域面积仅有38平方公里,但是却涉及近800平方公里海域的归属。由于该地区蕴藏着丰富的油气资源和渔业资源,具有重要的战略和经济意义,爵士湾至今未完成划界,并直接影响印巴两国海洋边界的确定。[2]

1. 争议背景

在遭受英国殖民之前,印度统治着喀奇及其周边地区。1760年,穆斯林统治者征服了喀奇邦(Kutch State),并一直持续至1813年。1843年,信德被英国征服。1853年后,信德省成为印度统治的孟买政府(Hindu Dominated Bombay Presidency)的一部分。1935年,信德成为一个独立的省份,并在随后的英国殖民期间一直将喀奇置于其管辖之下。1947年,巴基斯坦独立,信德省作为一个穆斯林聚居区,成为巴基斯坦的一个省。

而印巴间有关爵士湾的划界争议亦可追溯到英国殖民时期。1907年,喀奇的伐木人在信德砍伐树木的行为被信德行政长官报告至孟买政府。孟买政府遂要求喀奇的统治者给出合理解释。当时的喀奇统治者认为,喀奇的边界位于爵士湾的右岸,因此伐木的区域并不属于信德管辖。1914年,孟买政府为解决这一争端,作出了一份"1192号决议"(Resolution 1192)。一方面,该决议第9段将爵士湾认定为信德的一部分,并由此在该决议所附地图[3]上将边界划在爵士湾的东岸,称为"绿线"(当前巴基斯坦所主张边界);但另一方面,该决议的第10段却指出,由于爵士湾在一年中的大部分时间可以

[1] Award, People's Republic of Bangladesh v. Republic of India, 7 July 2014, Arbitration under Annex VII of The United Nations Convention on The Law of The Sea, pp. 147-149.

[2] Sir-creek, "Home", https://historypak.com/sir-creek/, August 20, 2019.

[3] 该决议所附地图参见"Sir-creek-disput", India Today, https://www.indiatoday.in/india/north/story/sir-creek-dispute-gujarat-chief-minister-narendra-mod-rann-of-kutchmaritime-boundary-124418-2012-12-16, August 20, 2019。

通航，因此根据国际法和"航道中间线原则"（Thalweg Principle），边界只能固定在航行通道的中间，称为"红线"（当前印度所主张边界），并由此将信德和喀奇分隔开来。[1]

2. 双方主张

这一"红线"与"绿线"的含混不明，导致印巴两国独立后有关喀奇地区领土划界争议的长期存在。印度方面认为，喀奇全境属于印度。而巴基斯坦方面则认为，应以喀奇中部或北纬 24 度线作为分界线，将喀奇分属于两国管辖。1965 年，印度声称巴基斯坦军队在北纬 24 度线附近非法巡逻，巴基斯坦军队则向印度哨所开火，随后双方均在喀奇部署了数千名士兵。针对印巴两国加剧的敌对状态，英国出面调停并促成两国于 1965 年 6 月 30 日达成停火协议，同意通过仲裁解决该争端。仲裁庭于 1968 年 2 月 19 日作出裁决，将喀奇争议区域 90% 的领土判归印度，剩余 10% 判归巴基斯坦。由此，喀奇地区的领土争端通过仲裁方式成功解决。但由于该仲裁裁决中并未提及爵士湾，有关爵士湾的划界问题至今仍不明晰。

当前，印度方面认为，爵士湾边界的划定直接影响印巴两国海洋边界的划定，应采用"航道中间线原则"划定爵士湾的边界，继而划定海上边界。而巴基斯坦方面则坚持以爵士湾右岸的绿线作为边界线，并依此进行海上划界。

3. 发展现状

在 1968 年后的数年里，由于印巴两国政治关系紧张，有关爵士湾划界的谈判一直停滞不前，直到印巴两国都签署并批准《公约》后，这一问题才又开始有所推进。在进行正式划界谈判前，鉴于爵士湾在过去几十年中的地理变化，两国均认为有必要在开展进一步对话前对爵士湾的陆地和水道展开新的地质调查。2005—2007 年，两国成立联合调查队，对爵士湾开展了两轮联合调查。调查结果表明，与 1914 年地图相比，爵士湾在水深、地形、流向等方面均已发生变化。[2] 2008 年，在伊斯兰堡举行的印巴第四轮双边对话中，双方认可根据此前的联合调查所绘制的一份区域地图。2011 年 5 月 21 日，印巴举行双边会谈后发表联合声明，该声明中提到"有必要划定爵士湾地区的陆地边界以及巴基斯坦与印度之间的国际海上边界"。2012 年 6 月 19 日，

---

[1] "Everything You Need To Know About The Dispute Over Sir Creek Between India And Pakistan", India Times, https：//www.indiatimes.com/news/everything-you-need-to-know-about-the-dispute-over-sir-creek-between-india-and-pakistan-260071.html, August 20, 2019.

[2] "India and Pakistan-Up Sir Creek", The economist, https：//www.economist.com/asia/2007/01/18/up-sir-creek, August 20, 2019.

双方在印巴双边会谈中重申通过和平友好方式解决该地区问题的意愿。[1]

在印巴两国的领土争端中，有关爵士湾的争端因政治敏感度较低，一度被认为是最易解决的双边争端之一，并将对两国和平完成其他领土划界带来良好的示范效果。然而，这片曾经相对不重要的狭长水域，如今却由于丰富的渔业资源和可能潜藏着丰富的油气资源而逐渐得到重视。2012年，现任印度总理莫迪在就任古吉拉特邦邦长时，就积极关注该问题，并致信联邦政府请求其必须坚守对爵士湾的主权主张。[2] 诚如前述，印巴之间已经就爵士湾的划界问题进行了多轮谈判，但由于双方均难以作出明确让步，该海上边界争端的解决之策至今仍处于迷雾之中。由于海上边界争端迟迟未能解决，该海域的渔业争端时有发生，海上货运安全也难以保障。

---

〔1〕 "Sir-Creek-Disput", India Today, https：//www. indiatoday. in/india/north/story/sir-creek-dispute-gujarat-chief-minister-narendra-mod-rann-of-kutchmaritime-boundary-124418-2012-12-16，August 20，2019.

〔2〕 Nasir Aijaz, "Absence of maritime boundary between India and Pakistan Brings Miseries to Fishermen of Two Nations", http：//www. theasian. asia/archives/88317, August 20, 2019.

六、国际海洋合作

（一）海洋防务合作

1. 与周边国家的合作

对印度而言，为在印度洋地区掌握海上主导权力，其与周边国家的海洋防务合作具有战略意义。如何利用与周边国家的友好关系来推进自己的战略目标实现，一直都是印度所思考的问题。除双边关系之外，印度还逐步在印度洋地区组织中发挥更重要的领导作用，如在环印度洋区域合作联盟（The Indian Ocean Rim Association，IORA）的经济与外交论坛以及印度洋海军论坛（Indian Ocean Naval Symposium，IONS）中的行动推进。印度正不断强化其与印度洋地区国家间的安全联系，通过防务合作以巩固并加大其在印度洋的影响力。[1]

在印度周边国家中，基于与斯里兰卡间特殊的地缘关系以及马尔代夫在印度洋的战略价值，印度非常重视与该两国间的海洋安全关系。就斯里兰卡而言，因其战略需求与地理环境，斯里兰卡希望将自己定位为印度洋的一个枢纽，并通过与印度洋沿岸国家的接触，实现其海事和安全利益目标。而就马尔代夫而言，由于恐怖主义对马尔代夫一直以来的威胁，海上安全成为其关注的防务重点。自1991年以来，印度同马尔代夫每两年举行一次代号为"多斯蒂"（Dosti）的联合海上军事演习。[2] 2012年，该双边联合军演升级为"三国海岸警卫队联合演习"，由印度、马尔代夫、斯里兰卡三国共6艘军舰，包括2艘印度海岸警卫队军舰、3艘马尔代夫军舰、1艘斯里兰卡军舰，在马尔代夫首都马累（Male）海域参加了代号为"多斯蒂十一"（Dosti XI）的为期5天的演习。[3] 2014年10月28—31日，三国同在马累海域举行了代号为"多斯蒂十二"（Dosti XII）的海岸防卫演习，此次演习的重点是海上搜救、人道主义援助及救灾、海洋污染应对和反海盗行动，这对于解决

---

〔1〕 叶贝茜：《外媒称中国挺进印度洋并未削弱印度影响力》，载腾讯新闻，https：//news. qq. com/a/20130225/001425. htm，最后访问日期：2020年1月9日。

〔2〕 "Trilateral Joint Exercise Dosti-14 to Commence Nov. 26", Sun, https：//en. sun. mv/50879, January 10, 2020.

〔3〕 "Current-Affairs", Gk Today, https：//www. gktoday. in/current-affairs/exercise-dosti-xi/, January 10, 2020.

印度洋上的海盗行为和相关的海上安全问题至关重要。[1] 自 2012 年起，该三国联合演习已经举办至第十四届（XIV，2019 年），致力于地区海洋作业协调与合作能力的训练与加强。

在与斯里兰卡的双边合作方面，自 2005 年起，印度就与斯里兰卡进行"斯里兰卡—印度海军演习"（Sri Lanka India Naval Exercise，SLINEX）。联合军事演习的目的在于增进两国海军对彼此操作程序、沟通程序和实践规范等相关环节的了解，定期进行演习以巩固已积累的相关经验，从而有效增强两国海军在复杂海上行动中共同作业的信心。[2] 因斯里兰卡安全局势的动荡，该演习一度被中断，直至 2011 年才在斯里兰卡的亭可马里（Trincomalee）进行第二次演习。"SLINEX 2011"是斯里兰卡当时最大规模的海军演习，共分四个阶段进行，包括在亭可马里进行的港口培训计划和在亭可马里附近海域进行的海上培训计划。[3] 此后，两国分别于 2013 年、2015 年、2017 年、2018 年继续开展该代号下的联合海上军演。2019 年 9 月，印度与斯里兰卡在孟加拉湾进行了第七届斯里兰卡—印度军事演习，两国共派出四艘军舰，并进行飞机追踪、海上航行等一系列演习。在入海阶段之前，双方海军还在维萨卡帕特南港（Visakhapatnam）进行了为期 3 天的专业互动、培训活动、文化活动和体育交流。[4] 此外，为加强军事联系，印度于 2018 年在菩提加耶（Bodh Gaya）接待了 160 名斯里兰卡军人及其家属代表。[5] 2019 年 4 月，印度和斯里兰卡同意在包括地区安全在内的安全和国防领域加强合作，印度同意为斯里兰卡培训国防人员。[6]

除双边联合军演外，由于南亚区域合作联盟（South Asian Association For Regional Cooperation）运行受挫，在区域一级，印度与斯里兰卡积极利用"环孟加拉湾多领域经济技术合作倡议"（The Bay of Bengal Initiative for Multi-

---

〔1〕 Sona, "Dil Dosti Dance 12th November 2014 Written Episode Update", https：//www. tellyup-dates. com/dil-dosti-dance-12th-november-2014-written-episode-update/，January 10，2020.

〔2〕 "Indian Navy Ships Enter at Trincomalee for SLINEX-15", India navy, https：//www. indiannavy. nic. in/content/slinex-15-sri-lanka-india-exercise, January 10，2020.

〔3〕 Raja Raja Cholan, "Indo-Sri Lankan Naval Drills", https：//www. iaspreparationonline. com/slinex-indo-sri-lankan-naval-drills/，January 10，2020.

〔4〕 "Sri Lankan Naval Ships Sindhurala and Suranimala Arrive Viskhapatnam to Participate in Sri Lanka-India Exercise（SLINEX）", India navy, https：//www. indiannavy. nic. in/content/sri-lankan-na-val-ships-sindhurala-and-suranimala-arrive-viskhapatnam-participate-sri-lanka--，January 10，2020.

〔5〕《印度加强与斯里兰卡的国防合作》，载印度世界广播网，http：//airworldservice. org/chi-nese/archives/22318，最后访问日期：2020 年 1 月 10 日。

〔6〕 "India to Train Sri Lankan Military", ONLANKA, https：//www. onlanka. com/news/india-to-train-sri-lankan-military. html，January 11，2020.

Sectoral Technical and Economic Cooperation，BIMSTEC）平台加强安全联系，并从 2018 年起参与该平台国家联合军事演习。同时，斯里兰卡于 2010 年启动"加勒对话"（Galle Dialogue）年度论坛，意在为各国及其他国际利益相关者提供一个共同平台，以讨论和审议海事相关问题，对话中尤其强调加强海上安全的合作以及它们之间的知识和信息共享。[1]

在与马尔代夫的双边合作方面，印度和马尔代夫的国防部长于 2019 年 1 月 24 日在新德里举行会谈时表示，两国将继续加强国防关系。印度国防部在有关该会谈的正式声明中指出，"双方商定，两国将继续保持密切的传统友谊，并推动海事安全、反恐和医疗合作"。[2] 其中，"Ekuverin"演习是两国自 2009 年以来每年都要进行的军事演习。"Ekuverin"一词在马尔代夫语中意为"朋友"，该演习旨在通过反恐、反叛乱和两栖作战演练，提升双方的协同作战能力。2009—2019 年，两国共举行了 11 届"Ekuverin"演习，每届演习时间为 14 天，演习地点在印度和马尔代夫两国间轮换。如，2017 年 12 月 15 日，在印度卡纳塔克邦（Karnataka）举行了第 8 届年度联合演习，该次演习重点是增强两支部队在半城市环境中进行反恐行动的协同操作性；[3] 2018 年的演习于 12 月 15 日在马尔代夫的马菲拉佛施（Maafilaafushi）举行，演习内容与 2017 年类似；[4] 2019 年 10 月 7 日开始的 2019 年度演习展开多种联合训练，包括在联合国的授权下对半城市环境中的反叛乱和反恐行动中的特遣队进行联合培训，发展这两个特遣队之间的协同操作性和凝聚力。[5]

此外，印度虽与巴基斯坦接壤，但两国基于历史关系及战略规划等多方面原因，在海洋上基本没有防务合作。美国桑迪亚国家实验室（Sandia National Laboratories）在其 2003 年出具的一份名为《海洋信任措施的建立：印度和巴基斯坦的机会》（Confidence Building Measures at Sea：Opportunities for

---

〔1〕 "Galle Dialogue：International Maritime Conference"，Galedialogue，http：//galledialogue. lk/index. php？id＝3，January 11，2020.

〔2〕 Mandeep Singh，"India，Maldives build strong defense partnership"，https：//ipdefenseforum. com/india-maldives-build-strong-defense-partnership/，January 11，2020.

〔3〕 Abdul Junaid，"India-Maldives Bilateral Military Exercise EKUVERIN 2017"，https：//www. ssbcrack. com/2017/12/india-maldives-bilateral-military-exercise-ekuverin-2017. html，January 11，2020.

〔4〕 "Ex Ekuverin Commences"，Forceindia，http：//forceindia. net/ex-ekuverin-commences/，January 11，2020.

〔5〕 "Indo-Maldives Joint Military Exercise Ekuverin-2019 Concludes"，Hindu Times，https：//www. hindustantimes. com/cities/indo-maldives-joint-military-exercise-ekuverin-2019-concludes/story-bHIePlB8bGO4493jD15ySN. html，January 11，2020.

India and Pakistan) 的报告中指出，尽管目前印度和巴基斯坦的海上部队比陆上部队有更多的合作机会，但仍然缺乏缓解紧张局势或促进行动协调的可靠机制。因此，可行的海洋信任措施建立以及合作务实机制的发起和维持都需要认真研究。[1]

2. 与东盟国家的合作

印度的"东向"（Look East）政策是印度政府为加强和巩固与东南亚国家的经济和战略关系而于 1991 年提出的。为塑造并强化其地区大国的形象，印度在海洋防务合作方面与东南亚国家展开了密切的交流。莫迪就任印度总理后，不仅延续了印度与东南亚国家之间已有的海上安全合作机制，更基于国际和地区安全形势及新政府的认知变化，将"东向"政策升级为"东进"（Act East）政策，并在经济、军事和文化等多层次多领域推进这一政策，强调印度是地区负责任的利益攸关方。

在军事合作方面，一方面，发展海上安全力量，实施远洋战略，在地区海洋安全问题上扮演更加突出的角色，是莫迪"东进"政策的重要组成部分；另一方面，对于"东进"政策的重要伙伴国，印度继续强调东盟国家在"东进"政策中的核心位置并不断拓展和加深彼此间的合作。由此，双方的海上安全合作从形式到规模都得以不断丰富壮大。于 2012 年 12 月 20 日在印度首都新德里举行的"东盟—印度纪念峰会"（Asean-India Commemorative Summit）上，印度发表声明宣布与东盟升级为"战略伙伴"关系。该峰会通过了指导印度与东盟未来 20 年关系发展的《东盟—印度纪念峰会愿景声明》（ASEAN-India Vision Statement 2020），[2] 提出双方将在政治、安全、经济、社会及文化发展等方面加强合作，包括定期举行高官级安全对话以共享信息，在确认海洋安全、航行自由、资源获取、海上交通要道安全等方面深化合作等。[3]

依据《2015 年印度海洋安全战略》所划分的海洋利益区：缅甸、泰国、马来西亚和印度尼西亚被划归一类，属于印度直接邻接的孟加拉湾、安达曼海沿海国；泰国、马来西亚、新加坡和印度尼西亚四个国家则被划归另一

---

〔1〕 "Confidence Building Measures at Sea: Opportunities for India and Pakistan", Sandia National Laboratories, https://www.sandia.gov/cooperative-monitoring-center/_assets/documents/sand2004-0102.pdf, January 11, 2020.

〔2〕 "ASEAN-India Commemorative Summit 2012", MoEA, https://mea.gov.in/in-focus-article.htm? 20295/ASEANIndia + Commemorative + Summit + 2012, January 11, 2020.

〔3〕 陈雪莲：《印度东盟升级为战略伙伴关系将加强海上安全合作》，载新浪网，http://mil.news.sina.com.cn/2012-12-21/0714710355.html，最后访问日期：2020 年 1 月 11 日。

类，它们扼守着对印度来说最为重要的印度洋边缘要道——马六甲海峡。上述五个国家（缅甸、泰国、马来西亚、印度尼西亚、新加坡）由此都处于印度的首要海洋利益区之内。此外，中国南海、西太平洋及其邻近海域被界定为印度的次要海洋利益区，而越南、柬埔寨、马来西亚、文莱、印度尼西亚和菲律宾恰好位于这片海域之内。因此，除了老挝这一内陆国家之外，所余东南亚国家都被纳入印度的海洋安全战略的利益区划之中，整个东南亚地区在印度海洋安全战略中的重要地位显而易见。在莫迪政府愈加重视海上安全的大背景及《2015 年印度海洋安全战略》的指导下，印度与东南亚国家海上安全合作的具体实践也呈现出活跃的动态图景。[1]

（1）与缅甸的合作

从 2013 年 3 月始，印度便与缅甸海军开展联合巡航，并随后将这一联合巡航常态化。2016 年 2 月，两国于第四届联合巡航闭幕式时正式签署了《标准操作程序》（The Standard Operating Procedure，SOP），缅甸由此成为继泰国和印度尼西亚之后第三个与印度签订此类正式协议的国家。《标准操作程序》的签署是一项重大成就，因为两国在具有战略意义的安达曼海和孟加拉湾都拥有较长的海洋边界，该文件的签署将促进两国之间协调巡逻的顺利进行。[2]与此同时，印度为缅甸提供了大量海上军事装备。2017 年 3 月，双方在印缅国防会议上签署了一项 3790 万美元鱼雷购销合同。2019 年 7 月，印度和缅甸再度签署了一项防务合作协议。印度国防部在该协议中表示，本阶段合作旨在加强总体性的国防合作与交流，包括加大印度为缅甸国防人员提供培训的力度、探讨强化海上安全合作的方式等。[3]

（2）与泰国的合作

自 2003 年以来，泰国皇家海军与印度海军每年均开展两次联合巡逻（India-Thailand Coordinated Patrol），旨在确保《公约》中有关海洋自然资源养护及海洋环境保护等条款的有效实施，从而预防和抑制非法及不受监管的捕鱼活动、预防及打击毒品走私与海盗行为、交换信息以预防偷渡与非法移民、联合进行海上搜救等。可见，彰显海上军事实力、维持印度洋区域秩

---

〔1〕 刘磊、于婷婷：《莫迪执政以来印度与东南亚国家的海上安全合作》，载搜狐网，http：//www. sohu. com/a/292842388_ 618422.，最后访问日期：2020 年 1 月 11 日。

〔2〕 "India-Myanmar Naval Ships Takes Part in Coordinated Patrolling Exercise", ANI, https：//www. india. com/news/india/india-myanmar-naval-ships-takes-part-in-coordinated-patrolling-exercise-958862/, January 11, 2020.

〔3〕 "India, Myanmar Sign Defence Cooperation Agreement", The Economic Times, https：//economic-times. indiatimes. com/news/defence/india-myanmar-sign-defence-cooperation-agreement/articleshow/70439116. cms, January 11, 2020.

序、护卫海上航行安全是两国军事演习及相关军事合作的重心。2015 年，双方举行了海上合作与司法合作联合特遣部队第一次会议。2016 年，泰国总理访问印度，双方共同发声呼吁加强包括反海盗合作在内的海上合作，通过海岸警卫队合作保证海上通道安全，从而维护地区和平并确保印度洋航行顺畅。两国由此决定增加在印度洋的联合军事演习和联合巡逻，同时签署了《白色航运协定》（White Shipping Agreement）。[1] 2019 年 9 月 5—15 日，两国第 28 次联合巡逻在泰国曼谷举行，双方再次表达了通过在地区内构建良好海洋秩序以实现印度洋和平防卫的强烈愿望。[2] 除了每年例行的双边联合巡航、高层互访、港口访问，双方的军工合作领域也有所拓展，2015 年五家印度国防生产公司参与在曼谷举行的防务与安全展览即可见一斑。[3]

（3）与印度尼西亚的合作

同与泰国的合作实践相似，印度与印度尼西亚间的海上防务合作也较早地通过两国间的"联合巡逻"方式展开。自 2002 年以来，两国海军每年两次在两国"国际海上边界线"（The International Maritime Boundary Line）的两侧进行联合巡逻，以确保相关各方能够在印度洋这一重要区段安全可靠地从事商业运输、国际贸易及其他合法海洋活动。2019 年 3 月 19 日—4 月 4 日，印度与印度尼西亚开展了第 33 次联合巡逻，正式巡逻分三个阶段于 3 月 22—31 日进行，双方的舰艇和飞机沿 236 海里的"国际海上边界线"展开巡航。[4]

与此同时，印度与印度尼西亚间的海上防务合作也通过港口互访、军事技术协作、联合军事演习等渠道不断拓展。2014 年，印度海军、海岸警卫队和印度尼西亚海军互访港口，军方高层代表团同步实现互访，双方均认为这种专业性互动增强了其政策的协同性。2015 年，双方又通过举行第四届军事人员对话和第七届海军人员对话，实现了作战、训练和能力建设领域的合作。2017 年，印度国防秘书莫汉·库马尔（Mohan Kumar）访问印度尼西亚时，提出向印度尼西亚提供潜艇技术训练的计划，以期进一步深化双边海上防

---

[1] "bilateral-documents", Ministry of External Affairs, https://www.mea.gov.in/bilateral-documents.htm? dtl/26923/IndiaThailand + Joint + Statement + during + the + visit + of + Prime + Minister + of + Thailand + to + India, January 11, 2020.

[2] "28th India-Thailand Coordinated Patrol-05-15 Sep 19", India navy, https://www.indiannavy.nic.in/content/28th-india-thailand-coordinated-patrol-05-15-sep-19, January 11, 2020.

[3] 刘磊、于婷婷：《莫迪执政以来印度与东南亚国家的海上安全合作》，载搜狐网，http://www.sohu.com/a/292842388_618422，最后访问日期：2020 年 1 月 11 日。

[4] "about us", India navy, https://www.indiannavy.nic.in/node/22310, January 11, 2020.

务合作。2018 年 5 月，莫迪访问印度尼西亚，与印度尼西亚总统佐科（Joko Widodo）会晤后签署国防合作协议，将加强军事对话、联合演习、海上安全及恐怖主义合作等问题囊括其中，同时宣布两国将共同开发具有重要战略意义的印度尼西亚西部港口城市沙璜（Sabang）。[1] 2018 年 11 月，印度与印度尼西亚海军举行了有史以来首次双边联合演习，旨在加强双边关系，扩大海上合作，增强操作协同并交流最佳做法，演习项目包括机动演习、水面作战演习、防空演习、武器射击训练、直升机作战和登船作战等。[2]

（4）与越南的合作

印度和越南长期保持良好邦交，并无历史包袱和现实利益的尖锐纠葛。冷战期间，印度和越南的关系主要体现在政治和道义上的相互支持，两国在安全领域和海洋领域的合作几乎是空白。二战结束之初，为了争取民族独立与解放，时任越南领导人胡志明曾向时任印度总理尼赫鲁求助，但印度仅给予了道义上的支持，未能提供实质性的帮助。越南民主共和国成立后，尼赫鲁总理于 1954 年访问越南，成为第一个访问越南的外国元首。20 世纪 70 年代，尽管印度和越南皆有反华立场，但两国安全合作并无进展。如越南在 1978 年曾向印度求助提升越南武器的自给能力，但被印度婉拒。

冷战结束后，印度和越南于 1994 年签署《防务合作谅解备忘录》，印度开始参与越南近海油气资源的勘探和开发。进入 21 世纪，印越关系进展迅速，两国开启海洋安全领域合作。2000 年，越南总理潘文凯（Phan Van Khai）访问印度，印度国防部长称越南为"最值得信赖的伙伴和盟友"，表示将加强两国间安全合作，开展联合防务训练，为越南提供先进武器，并提议印度海军进驻越南金兰湾军事基地。随后，越南和印度在海洋安全领域的合作逐步铺开。2007 年，越南总理阮晋勇访问印度，印度与越南的关系上升为战略伙伴关系，建立战略对话机制。总体来看，2011 年以前，印度与越南的海洋安全合作虽不断推进，但合作方式较为单一、进展不快。至 2011 年，越南国家主席张晋创访问印度，时任印度总理曼莫汉·辛格表示："印度和越南都是海洋国家，面临着共同的安全威胁，我们相信确保重要海上通道的安全至关重要，我们同意将加强在海洋领域的合作。"2015 年，印度与越南发表《2015—2020 年印越国防合作共同愿景声明》（The Joint Vision Statement on Viet Nam-India Defence Cooperation for the Period of 2015-2020），强调和明确了

---

〔1〕　刘磊、于婷婷：《莫迪执政以来印度与东南亚国家的海上安全合作》，载搜狐网，http：//www.sohu.com/a/292842388_618422，最后访问日期：2020 年 1 月 11 日。

〔2〕　Jvs, "Samudra Shakti: Indian Navy-Indonesian Navy Bilateral Exercise", https：//www.jatinverma.org/samudra-shakti-indian-navy-indonesian-navy-bilateral-exercise, January 11, 2020.

双方扩大海上安全合作的决心与举措，印度随后为越南海军提供了大量设备援助和技术培训。2017 年，印度与越南确立"全面战略合作伙伴关系"之后，双方的海上安全合作层次再度得到提升。越南明确将印度视作平衡中国的一种力量，欢迎印度在东南亚尤其是南海发挥更大作用。

联合军演已成为印越海洋合作的传统项目。早在 2000 年，印度和越南就开启了海上联合军演项目。随着两国关系的升级，印越海上联合军演更趋频繁和常态化，两国于 2013 年 6 月、2015 年 8 月和 2018 年 5 月在南海举行的联合军演尤其令人关注。两国海上力量频繁举行联合军演，是印度和越南海洋合作不断深化的表现。尽管越南自冷战结束之初就一直在谋求对外关系的多元化，尤其重视与域外大国发展关系，但在 2016 年 2 月与日本开展海军联合演习前，印度是唯一一个与越南开展例行海军联合演习的国家。2018 年 5 月，印度与越南进行首次双边海军联合演习，双方都派出了本国最先进的舰艇。2018 年 11 月，印度总统科温德（Ram Nath Kovind）访问越南，在发表的声明中，双方同意举行首次海事安全对话，并进一步鼓励双方海军和海岸警卫队舰艇停靠对方港口。

而在港口访问方面，因越南海军实力总体相对落后，两国的海军往来中主要是由印度军舰单向对越南港口进行访问。近年来，随着两国海洋合作升温，印度军舰频繁访问越南港口，所访问港口从最南部的胡志明市港口逐步延伸到中部和北部的芽庄港、岘港、海防港，亦包括濒临南海、极为敏感的金兰湾。2011 年 7 月，印度海军"埃拉瓦特"号（Airavat）坦克登陆舰应邀访问芽庄港，这是外国海军舰船首次获准进入芽庄港口。此后，印度军舰分别于 2013 年 6 月、2015 年 10 月、2018 年 5 月三次访问越南海防港；于 2014 年 8 月、2017 年 9 月两次访问海防港；于 2016 年 5 月访问金兰湾。相比他国，印度海军近年来到访金兰湾的频率明显较高。2018 年 1 月，越南驻印度大使再次表示欢迎印度在越南专属经济区进行油气田投资并随时欢迎印度海军访问越南港口。[1]

与此同时，印度持续帮助越南海军提升军事水平，并不断加大支持力度。自 2000 年开始，帮助越南提升海上力量就一直是印越海洋合作的重要内容。从两国近年的相关实践来看，印度对越南海军提升军力的支持主要围绕帮助越南培训海军人才，为越南提供海上军事装备等内容展开。在海军人才培训方面，越南从俄罗斯采购基洛级潜艇后，印度即根据与越南签署的

---

〔1〕 刘磊、于婷婷：《莫迪执政以来印度与东南亚国家的海上安全合作》，载搜狐网，http：//www. sohu. com/a/292842388_ 618422，最后访问日期：2020 年 1 月 11 日。

《2011—2013 行动计划》同意帮助越南进行舰艇人员培训。2013 年 11 月，印度海军宣布将对 500 名越南潜艇人员进行水下作战培训。而在军备支持方面，印度目前已仅次于俄罗斯成为越南第二大军事合作伙伴，提升越南海军军备水平已经成为印度与越南两国近年来武器和装备技术合作领域的重要目标。2014 年 9 月，时任印度总统慕克吉访越时承诺向越南提供 1 亿美元的军购贷款，以协助越南从印度采购 4 艘巡逻艇，并准备向越南提供印度海军最先进的"布拉莫斯"超音速巡航导弹。同年 10 月，时任越南总理阮晋勇访问印度，双方会谈的重要议题之一便围绕印度即将向越南出售的 4 艘海军巡逻艇展开。2016 年 9 月，印度总理莫迪在访越期间承诺为越南提供 5 亿美元的国防信贷额度，简化了有关国防设备的购买手续，并就印度帮助越南建造海上巡逻艇事宜签署相关协议。2018 年 3 月，时任越南国家主席陈大光访印，印方重申继续强化与越南的防务合作，支持越南军队提升军力；两国同意加快落实印度为帮助越南建造高速巡逻舰而提供 1 亿美元贷款的协议，并表示有望尽早签署印方 2016 年承诺的提供 5 亿美元国防信贷额度的框架性协议。[1]

（5）与其他东盟国家的合作

相较之下，印度与马来西亚、柬埔寨、菲律宾等国的海上合作起步相对较晚并发展缓慢，但以港口访问、军事演习和高层互访等为主要形式的双边海上安全合作亦在持续开展。

"米兰"（Milan）军演是印度于 1995 年开始举办的一项军事演习，该演习的目的是建立一个有效的交流平台，以讨论印度洋地区国家共同关切的问题，并加强友好海军之间更深层次的合作。1995 年的第一届军演仅有 5 个国家参加，除印度外还包括印度尼西亚、新加坡、斯里兰卡、泰国，[2] 而至 2014 年的"米兰"军演已有共 17 个国家的 15 艘军舰参加，并且首次吸纳了菲律宾和柬埔寨两国的参与。[3] 第十届演习于 2018 年 3 月 11—13 日举行，该次演习共有 20 艘船参加，这使其成为在安达曼海进行的最大规模的多边

〔1〕 邵建平：《"东进"遇上"西看"：印越海洋合作新态势及前景》，载《国际问题研究》2019 年第 4 期，第 82—95 页。
〔2〕 "India to Host Mega Naval Exercise amid China's Manoeuvring in High Seas", The Economic Time, https：//economictimes. indiatimes. com/news/defence/india-to-host-mega-naval-exercise-amid-chinas-manoeuvring-in-high-seas/articleshow/63069995. cms, January 11, 2020.
〔3〕 "Milan 2014：An Unequivocal Success", India navy, https：//www. indiannavy. nic. in/content/milan-2014-unequivocal-success, January 11, 2020.

演习。[1]

2015 年 5 月和 11 月，印度海岸警卫队总干事毕希特上将和海军舰艇"萨亚德里"号访问菲律宾马尼拉；同年 6 月和 11 月印度海军"兰维尔"号导弹驱逐舰和"卡莫尔塔"号反潜舰两次对柬埔寨西哈努克港进行访问，并与柬埔寨海军和当地社区医疗组进行联合训练演习。2016 年，印度海军访问马来西亚巴生港（Kelang），并与马来西亚海军进行沙盘演练。印度与新加坡的海上军事演习从反潜作战演习扩展到更复杂的模拟行动及主要水面舰艇的部署训练。此外，双方于 2017 年 11 月签署了一项海军合作协议，希望通过联合演习、相互使用海军设施和提供后勤支持来加强海上安全合作。[2]

3. 与域外大国的合作

（1）与美国的合作

冷战结束后，印美双方即在海上安全领域开展合作，两国于 2005 年签署《印美国防关系新框架》（New Framework for the India-U. S. Defense Relationship），迎来了双边国防关系飞速发展的十年，并使美国和印度走上了日益广泛、复杂的战略合作道路。[3] 自印度总理莫迪上任后，印度和美国的高级官员互访更为频繁，积极推动两国在印度洋地区的海上安全合作进入新阶段。

2015 年 1 月，时任美国总统奥巴马访问印度并出席印度共和国日阅兵式，双方随后共同发表《美印关于亚太和印度洋地区事务的联合战略构想声明》（U. S. -India Joint Strategic Vision for the Asia-Pacific and Indian Ocean Region），就印度洋区域的海上安全合作划定方向。2015 年 6 月，美国时任国防部长卡特在访印期间确立了指导双方未来十年防务关系的"印美防务关系新框架"，这一防务框架所依赖的双边关系在 2015 年 9 月印度总理莫迪二度访美时得到进一步强化。2016 年 2 月，美国海军作战部部长约翰·理查德森访

---

〔1〕 第十一届"米兰"军演原定于 2020 年 3 月在印度维萨卡帕特南举行，来自南亚、东南亚、非洲和欧洲的 30 余个国家受邀参与，但因新冠肺炎疫情被推迟。据印度方面于 2021 年 10 月所发布的消息，新一届"米兰"军演将于 2022 年 2 月举行，涵盖印度洋及周边 40 余个国家的此次军演将是其军演史上最大规模的一次海军演习。"MILAN 2018"，India navy, https：//www. indiannavy. nic. in/content/milan-2018, Januanry 11, 2020; Shaurya Karanbir Gurung, "RIndian Navy postpones multilateral exercise Milan 2020 due to coronavirus", https：//economictimes. indiatimes. com/news/defence/indian-navys-multilateral-exercise-milan-2020-postponed-due-to-coronavirus/articleshow/74461918. cms, July 19, 2020. NEXT IAS, "Exercise MILAN", https：//www. nextias. com/current-affairs/07-10-2021/exercise-milan, December 15, 2021.

〔2〕 "Singapore, India Navies Ink Bilateral Deal", Navaltoday, https：//navaltoday. com/2017/11/30/singapore-india-navies-ink-bilateral-deal/, January 11, 2020.

〔3〕 "Fact Sheet：U. S. -India Defense Relationship", US DoD, https：//dod. defense. gov/Portals/1/Documents/pubs/US-IND-Fact-Sheet. pdf, January 11, 2020.

问印度并参加了印度海军主办的国际海上舰队大阅兵。2016 年 6 月，莫迪上任后第四次访问美国，双方随后公布《亚太及印度洋联合战略愿景》（Joint Strategic Vision for the Asia-Pacific and Indian Ocean Region），声明将在亚太和印度洋地区开展更深入的合作。

特朗普政府时期，印美在维护印太地区海上安全方面延续了奥巴马在任时两国高层的深入交流势头。2017 年 2 月，特朗普刚刚就任不久，美国国防部长马蒂斯便与印度防长通话，表示"要继续推动双边的防务合作"。2017 年 6 月，莫迪第五次对美国进行国事访问，特朗普表示美国和印度之间的关系从未如此密切和强大。2017 年 11 月 13 日下午，莫迪与特朗普在菲律宾举办的东盟峰会期间举行双边会晤，就两国在地区和全球事务上加强合作事宜进行商谈。

在联合军演方面，"马拉巴尔"（Malabar）系列军事演习是美印两国之间级别最高、规模最大的海上联合军事演习。该联合演习项目始于 1992 年，因其初始演习地点在印度马拉巴尔海滩而得名，原为美国和印度间的双边演习。自 2015 年起，日本加入"马拉巴尔"系列海上军演，该演习由此成为一个长期性的三方海上联合军事演习。[1] 事实上，"马拉巴尔 2014"海上联合军演即于 2015 年 7 月在位于日本四国南部到冲绳东部的西太平洋海域进行，此次演习已有日本海上自卫队的参与，并被认为是美国重返亚太的重要一步，但出于对中国态度的顾虑，当时印度政府对日本参加印度洋军演并不支持。[2] 直至 2015 年 10 月在印度洋东北部孟加拉湾举行的"马拉巴尔 2015"联合军事演习中，日本海军才首次以年度三边联合军演的一个长期成员而非外国受邀者身份正式参与，与美国及印度共同完成了投入三国最先进设备的空中海上侦查演习行动。在随后的 2016—2019 年，美印日三国的"马拉巴尔"联合军演分别在日本九州长崎县的美国佐世保海军基地、印度洋东北部的孟加拉湾海域、关岛海域附近的菲律宾海等开展。其中，"马拉巴尔 2016"联合军演使当时中国东海的安全形势一度恶化，令钓鱼岛争端进一步加剧；"马拉巴尔 2017"联合军演中，美国"尼米兹"号航母战斗群、日本"出云"号轻型航母和印度"维克拉马蒂亚"号航母齐聚孟加拉湾，在"马拉巴尔"25 年军演史上三国航母首次联合亮相；"马拉巴尔 2018"联合军演首次在西太平洋美国领土关岛附近海域举行，同时包括港口水域阶段

〔1〕《美日印将举行海上联合军演 日本出动准航母参加》，载环球网，https：//baijiahao. baidu. com/s？ id = 1645701862832716051&wfr = spider&for = pc. ，最后访问日期：2020 年 1 月 11 日。

〔2〕 王欢：《美日印马拉巴尔军演今起举行 日本"重返"印度洋》，载环球网，https：//world. huanqiu. com/article/9CaKrnJQykv，最后访问日期：2020 年 1 月 11 日。

演习和海上行动阶段演习，并以海上行动阶段的反潜作战为核心；而"马拉巴尔 2019"再返日本九州佐世保及其关东南部海域，是日本主办该演习的"首秀"。[1]

在双边协定方面，美印两国国防部长于 2015 年 6 月联合签署了《美印 2015 防务合作框架协议》（2015 Framework for the U. S. -India Defense Relationship），以增进双方在防务领域合作的安全性。这一新的防务合作框架下的内容主要包括：①再一次明晰美印两国联合防务小组的指导性作用，并重新确定其 5 个下属小组的责任和义务；②建立防务贸易和技术倡议小组以减少双方合作的阻碍；③促进两国军事技术和投资的流动，以提高联合开发和生产新型军备的能力。2015 年 1 月，美国国防部挂牌成立了"印度快速反应小组"，专门负责推动落实印度和美国在军备贸易和技术倡议下的各项合作项目。2016 年 8 月 29 日，美印在华盛顿正式签署《后勤交换备忘录协定》（Logistics Exchange Memorandum of Agreement，LEMOA），规定两军在联合行动期间的军事物资、设备维护和供应费用问题。依据这一协定，美国和印度的军队可以使用另一方的陆海空军事基地来进行包括补给、维护和休整在内的后勤相关作业。据此，印度军队理论上可以进入世界各地的美军基地寻求后勤援助，而美国在印度、太平洋地区海域的活动也可从印度的军事基地及附属设施中获得便利并得到一定保障。该协定由此被认为对包括南亚地区、中东地区和东亚地区在内的国际安全局势产生了较大影响。除直接的军事合作外，2016 年 5 月美国和印度签订的《白色航运协定》（White Shipping Agreement）在加强两国之间商船信息的数据共享的基础上，也为双方提升在印度洋海域的感应能力、联合开展反潜作战军事演习等提供一定支持。可以认为，莫迪执政以来通过签署或者更新印美间的一系列协议，为印美海上安全合作提供了良好的机制保障，使两国的双边合作建设保持在较高水平。[2]

（2）与俄罗斯的合作

印度洋地区一直在俄罗斯的战略规划中占据重要地位。苏联曾着力于稳固其在印度洋地区的存在感；而苏联解体后，俄罗斯曾因受限于国内局势而对该地区的关注度有所下降，但最近十年其在印度洋区域表现再度活跃。尽

---

〔1〕 "Malabar 2019 Strengthens U. S. -Japan-India Naval Cooperation"，US Embassy and Consulate in Japan，https：//jp. usembassy. gov/malabar-2019-strengthens-japan-india-u-s-naval-cooperation/，January 11，2020.

〔2〕 刘磊、寇鹏程：《析莫迪执政以来印度与美国海上安全合作》，载《国际关系研究》2018 年第 5 期，第 79—95 页。

管与该地区的贸易和安全关系仍然较为有限，其在印度洋事务中也多被视为仅扮演边缘角色或根本不扮演角色，但作为全球性强国，俄罗斯仍坚持其在印度洋地区具有至关重要的经济和战略利益。作为其"向东转"（Pivot to the East）战略的一部分，俄罗斯将与印度洋域内国家在战略、贸易和科学等领域建立更牢固的多元化联系作为其外交政策重点之一。[1] 印度亦由此成为俄罗斯在印度洋地区寻求合作的重要力量。

俄罗斯与印度的海洋防务合作关系首先体现在武器装备的交易方面。2017 年，斯德哥尔摩国际和平研究所（Stockholm International Peace Research Institute）公布的一项研究表明，2012—2016 年，印度进口武器中的 68% 来自俄罗斯，14% 来自美国，7.2% 来自以色列。[2] 2018 年 11 月，时任印度海军司令苏尼尔·兰巴（Sunil Lanba）上将访问俄罗斯，印度和俄罗斯着手讨论在印度造船厂以非常经济的价格联合建造和开发一艘核潜艇。根据相关提议，两国计划联合开发一艘造价不高于 2 亿美元的原型艇，俄罗斯公司将把技术诀窍和相关文件转让给印度造船厂。2016 年，印度和俄罗斯达成一项协议，协议内容为印度将从俄罗斯购买 4 艘排水量 3620 吨的"格里格罗维奇海军上将"级护卫舰，其中两艘护卫舰由俄罗斯制造，另有两艘护卫舰将在印度南部果阿的一家国有造船厂建造。[3] 两国在 2018 年正式签署购买合同，这成为发展俄印军事和技术合作的又一重要事件。[4] 另外，印度已经从俄罗斯租借了两艘核动力潜艇，包括目前正在服役的"查克拉"号。[5] 在 2019 年 9 月举行的"第 20 届印度—俄罗斯年度峰会"中，双方表示，在国防领域，双方已逐渐从单纯的买卖关系向合作伙伴关系转型，其中包括军事装备的联合生产以及贸易和投资的其他合作。俄罗斯联邦军事技术合作局局长德米特里·舒加耶夫（Dmitry Shugayev）表示，印俄此次签订了一项破纪录的

〔1〕 Ksenia Kuzmina, "Russia and the Indian Ocean Security and Governance", https：//russiancouncil. ru/en/analytics-and-comments/analytics/russia-and-the-indian-ocean-security-and-governance/ d, January 11, 2020.

〔2〕 孙亚辉、谭利娅：《报告显示俄罗斯仍然是印度最大防务伙伴》，载环球网，https：// world. huanqiu. com/article/9CaKrnK0KoR. ，最后访问日期：2020 年 1 月 11 日。

〔3〕 "Russia, India Prepare Contract for Four Project 11356 Frigates", Navy Recogniton, http：//navyrecognition. com/index. php/news/defence-news/2018/april-2018-navy-naval-defense-news/6154-russia-india-prepare-contract-for-four-project-11356-frigates. html, January 11, 2020.

〔4〕 Joanne Stocker, "India Signs Contracts to Purchase 4 Admiral Grigorovich-class Frigates from Russia", https：//thedefensepost. com/2018/11/20/india-russia-4-admiral-grigorovich-project-11356-frigates/, January 11, 2020.

〔5〕 丁宏：《印度海军司令访俄寻求合作建造核潜艇》，载搜狐网，http：//www. sohu. com/a/278291575_ 313834，最后访问日期：2020 年 1 月 11 日。

价值 145 亿美元的武器及其他军事装备买卖合同。[1] 同时,印俄商定准备构建互惠的后勤支持合作框架,使双方可以在印度洋以及北极地区,互用对方的港口和军事基地,从而更有效地利用"国际南北运输走廊"(International North-South Transport Corridor, INSTC)并推进其建设。[2]

而在联合军演方面,"因陀罗"(Indra)作为俄罗斯与印度联合演习的代号始于 2003 年。该演习最初为两年一次,其目的仅在于训练双方的协同作战能力以进行海上执法及打击海盗、恐怖活动和毒品走私等非法活动。但随着俄罗斯实力逐步恢复以及印度扩大本国影响力的愿望强烈,双方从 2012 年起将演习改为一年一次,并增加了演练科目。2017 年,双方又将演习升格为海陆空三军联合演习。2017 年 10 月,"因陀罗-2017"在俄罗斯远东地区的谢尔盖耶夫斯基 249 训练场和符拉迪沃斯托克附近的日本海水域举行。印度方面有来自陆海空军的共计 910 名军人参演,大多数演练装备包括苏-30 战机都由俄罗斯提供。[3] 2018 年 11 月,"因陀罗-2018"在印度北方邦举行,来自俄罗斯和印度的 500 名军事人员参加,双方在演习期间演练了维和行动的联合规划,训练陆军参谋部与分队之间的协同程序并成功消灭"恐怖分子"团伙。[4] 2019 年 12 月,"因陀罗-2019"军演在印度帕纳吉市莫尔穆加奥港及印度洋分陆海两阶段展开。除派出的约 700 名军人、40 架各种用途的飞行器(15 架歼击机、约 20 架军用运输机、5 架军用直升机)外,俄罗斯首次派出波罗的海舰队舰艇参加这一军演。[5] 演习科目包括伞兵登陆、攻占和消灭"恐怖分子"营地训练等,并由印俄混合乘组驾驶印度空军苏-30MKI 飞机对抗战舰。作为军备交流的环节之一,印度空军还邀请俄军飞行员体验试驾了印度国产的"光辉"战斗机(LCA)。[6] 可以认为,除了加

〔1〕 Mu Xuequan, "Russia, India Agree to Boost Joint Military Production, Trade Cooperation", http://www.xinhuanet.com/english/2019-09/05/c_138365558.htm, January 11, 2020.
〔2〕 Indrani Talukdar, "Challenges for India — Russia Strategic Partnership", https://russiancouncil.ru/en/analytics-and-comments/columns/asian-kaleidoscope/challenges-for-india-russia-strategic-partnership/, January 11, 2020.
〔3〕 《俄印首次海陆空三军"因陀罗-2017"联合演习结束》,载中国网,http://www.china.com.cn/military/2017-11/01/content_41827439.htm,最后访问日期:2021 年 1 月 12 日。
〔4〕 赵范旨、黄子娟:《俄印"因陀罗-2018"演习收官之战在印举行》,载环球网,http://military.people.com.cn/n1/2018/1129/c1011-30432086.html.,最后访问日期:2020 年 1 月 12 日。
〔5〕 周洪新:《俄印加深军事合作,"因陀罗-2019"演习即将开始,陆海空兵种全覆盖》,载搜狐网,http://www.sohu.com/a/341705728_587233.,最后访问日期:2020 年 1 月 12 日。
〔6〕 参见宋鹏超:《俄印"因陀罗-2019"军演 专家:军事合作促政治互信》,载神州网,http://www.szmag.net/show/437695.html,最后访问日期:2020 年 1 月 12 日;徐璐明:《俄飞行员兴奋体验印度光辉战机 落地后竖起大拇指》,载环球网,https://3w.huanqiu.com/a/c36dc8/3wHzCMJARlt,最后访问日期:2020 年 1 月 12 日。

强军事互信、提高联合作战水平外，推进两国在军工领域的密切合作亦是印俄军演的重要目标。

（3）与澳大利亚的合作

印度和澳大利亚于 2008 年签署了《安全与合作联合公报》（Joint Declaration on Security and Cooperation），希望通过"安全合作框架"将两国的战略观点融合在一起。该公报的主要内容之一即是要在战略层面加强两国海上合作的优势地位。澳大利亚是印度雄心勃勃希望成为区域"网络安全提供者"（Net Security Provider）愿景的支持者之一，其旨在通过与印度建立更深入的海上合作关系作为对华的平衡力量。较长时间以来，澳大利亚都通过目标多样的海上演习，如 2019 年 3 月的"印度洋—太平洋奋进"（Indo-Pacific Endeavour）演习，来加强与印度的安全合作。同时，澳大利亚也希望借此避免在美国和中国的对抗中被卷入任何一方。[1]

（4）与日本的合作

除了前述美印日三方联合进行的"马拉巴尔"演习，印日也就海上防务进行过多项双边合作。2018 年 10 月，印度和日本海军在印度洋展开高强度空中反潜演习，印度海军一架 P‐8I 远程海上侦查反潜机和日本海上自卫队两架 P-3"猎户座"反潜机参加演习。[2] 在同年举行的印日两国年度双边峰会上，双方就"海域态势感知"（MDA）的实施安排问题签署协议，认为在印度洋—太平洋海域扩展海域态势感知能力并加强交流将有助于地区和平与稳定，同时通过协议加深印度海军与日本海上自卫队之间的合作。两国还建立了外交部长和国防部长"2＋2"对话安排，以加强包括双边国防部长对话、国防政策对话、国家安全顾问对话、军种参谋长级对话等在内的现有机制。[3] 在 2019 年 12 月举行的新一轮两国"2＋2"对话中，印度和日本再次表现出对初步签署《物资劳务相互提供协议》（Acquisition and Cross-Servicing Agreement，ACSA）的关注与期待。该协议将允许印度军方和日本自卫队互相使用基地并提供后勤支持，被视为两国间国防合作进一步深化的表征。2020 年 9 月，印度与日本最终成功签署《物资劳务相互提供协议》。印度成

---

〔1〕 Kanchi Mathur，"Challenges and Prospects for India-Australia Maritime Cooperation"，http：//www. internationalaffairs. org. au/australianoutlook/challenges-and-prospects-for-india-australia-maritime-cooperation/，January 11，2020.

〔2〕 姜舒译：《日本自卫队两架 P-3 飞抵印度 与印军展开反潜演习》，载人民日报海外网，http：//baijiahao. baidu. com/s？id＝1582671043901320726&wfr＝spider&for＝pc&isFailFlag＝1.，最后访问日期：2020 年 1 月 12 日。

〔3〕 程大树：《印度与日本签署海事协议加强印太海域舰艇活动监控》，载国防信息网，http：//www. dsti. net/Information/News/112359，最后访问日期：2020 年 1 月 12 日。

为继美国、英国、法国、加拿大及澳大利亚之后与日本签署该协定的第六个国家。[1]

（二）海洋油气资源合作

依据美国能源信息署（EIA）发布的《印度油气行业分析报告》，截至2015年年底，印度已探明石油储量接近57亿桶，大部分储量位于印度西部地区。印度国内石油供不应求，从而导致深水油田和边际油田的开采力度不断加大，同时已开采油田的采收率也在不断提高。另外，印度国家石油公司也在加快购买海外油田的速度，以保证国内的能源供应。根据《石油与天然气杂志》（*The Oil & Gas Journal*）的数据，2015年年底，印度已探明的石油储量接近57亿桶。过去几年间，印度的海上已探明储量不断增长，而陆地石油产量却在降低。截至2015年4月，印度的海上油田可采储量已经略微超过了国内总可采储量的50%。大部分的可采储量位于印度的西部地区，特别是孟买附近的近海海域以及古吉拉特邦的陆上油田。阿萨姆邦—若开邦（Assam-Arakan）盆地是印度国内另外一个重要的产油区，其可采储量占全国的22%。由于深海油田开采难度高且投资不足，印度的监管环境又较为恶劣，印度的海洋石油开发并不是十分充分。[2]

与此同时，2013年印度的能源消费量紧随中国和美国之后，已经居于全球第三位。随着其国内经济增速以及现代化进程的加快，印度的能源需求量持续攀升。2020年，英国石油公司发布的第69版《英国石油公司统计评论》（*BP Statistical Review*）指出，印度石油日消费量增幅位居全球第三，为15.9万桶，仅次于中国的68.1万桶和伊朗的18.3万桶。[3] 美国能源信息署在2019年发布的《国际能源展望》（*International Energy Outlook* 2019）中曾指出，至2050年印度将是全球能源消费增长速度最快的国家，到21世纪40年

---

〔1〕 See Huma Siddiqui, "Act East Policy: India and Japan ACSA Expected to Be Signed Later This Year, sources", https://www.financialexpress.com/defence/act-east-policy-india-and-japan-acsa-expected-to-be-signed-later-this-year-sources/1698440/, January 12, 2020; The Hindu, "India-Japan Call upon Pakistan to Act on Terror", https://www.thehindu.com/news/national/india-japan-call-upon-pakistan-to-act-on-terror/article30125707.ece, January 12, 2020; Prashant Dhawan, "India Japan to Sign ACSA Agreement", https://www.studyiq.com/blog/india-japan-sign-acsa-agreement-free-pdf/, January 12, 2020.

〔2〕 "Country Analysis Brief: India", U.S. Energy Information Administration, https://www.eia.gov/international/analysis/country/IND, February 11, 2020.

〔3〕 "India 2nd Biggest Driver Of Global Energy Consumption In 2019: BP Statistical Review", IBEF, https://www.ibef.org/research/newstrends/india-2nd-biggest-driver-of-global-energy-consumption-in-2019-bp-statistical-review, July 20, 2020.

代中期，印度将比美国消耗更多的能源；到 2050 年，印度的能源消耗将仅次于中国。[1] 因此，尽管拥有较为丰富的化石燃料资源，印度的能源消费越来越依赖进口，并对油气资源开采的国际合作持开放态度。[2] 事实上，印度政府和国外公司已经加大了对前沿技术和边际油田的投资，以弥补老油田产量的下降。近几年，位于拉贾斯坦邦（Rajasthan）的巴默（Barmer）盆地和位于近海的克里希纳-哥达瓦里（Krishna-Godavari）盆地陆续有重大油气发现，这有望给印度的石油开发带来更多的活力。[3]

1. 对本国海洋油气资源的合作开发

直到 20 世纪 70 年代末，印度的油气勘探和生产行业仍然由两家国有石油公司——印度石油天然气公司（Oil and Natural Gas Corporation，ONGC）和印度石油有限公司（Indian Oil Corporation，OIL）所主导，这两家公司均获国家推荐颁发的石油勘探许可证（Petroleum Exploration Licenses，PELs），勘探主要局限于陆地和浅海。1979 年，印度政府采取战略措施，通过提供 32 个勘探区块（17 个海上区块和 15 个陆上区块）来吸引外国投资和技术，以应对印度石油经济的未来承诺和挑战。政府一开始通过招标的方式系统地提供区块，这些招标回合也被称为"新勘探许可政策前的勘探回合"（Pre-NELP Exploration Round）[4]，但 1980—1986 年的三个回合都不是很成功。在1986 年年底进行的勘探区块的第三轮国际招标中，印度曾提出如果发现可开采油田，上述两家公司将仅获合资企业 40% 的股份；但该回合中却几乎没有外国公司参与，也没有值得信赖的勘探或突破性的发现。1989 年，印度石油有限公司在拉贾斯坦邦的塔诺特地区（Tanot，Mata Temple），印度石油天然气公司在孟买近海的希拉地区（Heera）南部都发现了天然气。1990 年，第四轮国际招标首次允许印度本土公司与外国公司共同参与，然而这一伙伴关系的构建尝试仍没有取得海油勘探开发的重要成果。1991 年，印度政府采取自由化的经济政策，取消了包括石油部门在内的核心集团的许可证，并采取了包括部分取消政府份额的投资在内的其他措施。为了推动印度石油部门的发展，印

[1] "EIA Analysis Explores India's Projected Energy Consumption", U. S. Energy Information Administration, https：//www. eia. gov/todayinenergy/detail. php? id=42295, July 20, 2020.

[2] 《(2016) EIA 报告：印度油气行业现状》，载石油圈网，http：//www. oilsns. com/article/63246，最后访问日期：2020 年 2 月 11 日。

[3] "Country Analysis Brief：India", U. S. Energy Information Administration, https：//www. eia. gov/international/analysis/country/IND, February 11, 2020.

[4] NELP，即新勘探许可政策（New Exploration Licensing Policy），由印度政府在 1997—1998 年制定，旨在为油气勘探和生产领域的公共部门和私营公司提供公平的竞争环境。"NELP Rounds", DGH, http：//dghindia. gov. in/index. php/page? pageId=59. , February 11, 2020.

度政府在 1994 年提出更有利可图的报价，然而这也导致生产分成协议中的分歧。至 1996 年，印度政府共进行了 5 轮招标，提供了 126 个面积在 1 平方公里至 50000 平方公里的区块。除了国家石油公司和印度私营公司，壳牌（Shell）、安然（Enron）、美国石油公司（Amoco）和西方石油公司（Occidental）等大型公司也参与了勘探，并与印方签署开发合同。

随着 1991—1996 年印度政府的不懈努力，印度石油和天然气行业的开放进程变得更加顺畅，许多私营企业也加入这个行业。新勘探许可政策在为印度私人资本提供进入油气开发行业途径的同时，也为外国公司进入印度油气行业开辟了新途径。该政策的主要目标是从印度和外国公司吸引巨额风险资本、最先进的技术，并学习新的地质概念和最佳管理实践，以便推动在印度的石油和天然气资源勘探，从而满足国家不断增长的石油和天然气需求。印度的新勘探许可政策于 1997 年获得批准后，于 1999 年 2 月生效。在该政策框架下，勘探区块通过国际竞争性招标程序被授予印度国有或私营公司及外国公司，印度石油天然气公司和印度石油有限公司也平等参与这一竞争。新勘探许可政策不仅加速了印度的油气勘探，也给印度带来了最先进的技术以及大幅提升的运营、管理效率。印度政府根据该政策的相关制度与国有石油公司、私营（包括印度和外国）公司、合资公司共签署了 254 份合同，采用地球物理勘测和探索性钻探对几个未勘探和勘探不充分的地区，特别是近海和深水地区进行了评估[1] 新勘探许可政策下公开透明的国际化招标程序吸引了大批世界知名公司，同时引进私人资本和外国资本的方式为印度的油气开发行业注入了新的活力。可以认为，新勘探许可政策在促进勘探与生产行业发展的同时，也极大地促进了印度油气开发行业的自由化。通过新勘探许可政策勘探回合授权开发的区域如第 Ⅰ 部分 表 17 所示。

第 Ⅰ 部分 表 17　在新勘探许可政策勘探回合中授权的区块[2]

回合	获得区块			
	深海（个）	浅海（个）	陆地（个）	总计（个）
Ⅰ	7	16	1	24
Ⅱ	8	8	7	23
Ⅲ	9	6	8	23

---

〔1〕 "Pre-NELP Exploration Blocks", National Date Repository, https：//www. ndrdgh. gov. in/NDR/? page_ id =579, February 11, 2020.

〔2〕 "NELP Rounds", Directorate General of Hydrocarbons, http：//dghindia. gov. in/index. php/ page? pageId =59, February 11, 2020.

续表

回合	获得区块			
	深海（个）	浅海（个）	陆地（个）	总计（个）
Ⅳ	10	0	10	20
Ⅴ	6	2	12	20
Ⅵ	21	6	25	52
Ⅶ	11	7	23	41
Ⅷ	8	11	13	32
Ⅸ	1	3	15	19
总计	81	59	114	254

根据印度工业和内部贸易促进部（Department for Promotion of Industry and Internal Trade）发布的数据，2000 年 4 月—2019 年 3 月，印度的石油和天然气行业吸引了 70.18 亿美元的外国直接投资。石油和天然气部部长达曼德拉·普拉丹（Dharmendra Pradhan）表示，由于印度希望至 2022 年将对石油进口的依赖减少 10%，因此外国投资者将有机会在印度投资价值 3000 亿美元的项目。[1] 以天然气水合物（Gas Hydrate）为例，其在世界范围内尚处于研发阶段，为了应对天然气水合物探索的挑战，印度石油和天然气部（Ministry of Petroleum and Natural Gas）下的碳氢化合物总局（Directorate General of Hydrocarbon）已与多家机构签署了谅解备忘录，以共享知识和科学数据，这些机构包括：美国地质勘探局（United States Geological Survey），美国能源部（United States Department of Energy），美国海洋能源管理局（US-Bureau of Ocean Energy Management），日本国家石油天然气和金属公司（Japan Oil，Gas and Metals National Corporation），以及德国亥姆霍兹波茨坦中心（Helmholtz-Centre Potsdam-German Research Centre for Geosciences，又称德国地学中心）和亥姆霍兹基尔海洋研究中心（Helmholtz Centre for Ocean Research Kiel）等。[2]

2. 对他国海洋油气资源的合作开发

（1）与周边国家的合作

尽管印度的"大周边"思想可以追溯到其独立前的尼赫鲁时代，但与能

---

〔1〕　"Oil & Gas Industry in India"，India Brand Equity Foundation，https：//www.ibef.org/industry/oil-gas-india.aspx，February 11，2020.

〔2〕　"About Exploration & Production"，Ministry Of Petroleum and Natural Gas，http：//petroleum.nic.in/exploration-production/about-exploration-production，February 11，2020.

源相关联进而构建印度"大周边"能源合作网络，却是 21 世纪以来的发展态势。21 世纪初，随着能源供应压力的不断加大、能源价格不断上涨，印度开始推动"大周边"能源建设。2005 年，印度正式提出"构建南亚地区能源中心"的战略构想，标志着"大周边"能源合作战略正式启动。[1]

印度一直将东南亚视为"东向行动政策"的优先方向之一，与东盟和绝大多数东南亚国家保持着密切的外交关系，并着重与越南和缅甸开展能源外交。长期以来，越南是印度的石油供应国之一，印度则是最早参与开发越南石油资源的国家。2013 年 11 月，越南为印度提供了 7 个南海石油勘探区块，其中 3 个区块允许印度享有独家开采权。2014 年 10 月，越南又向印度提供了 2 个南海油气勘探区块。2016 年，印度总理莫迪访问越南，两国政府首脑一致同意将双边关系提升为全面战略伙伴关系，并表示将进一步提升双边能源合作的水平与规模。随着两国关系的升温，印度对越南油气开发的投资力度也在不断加大，越南对印度出口石油的总量也将不断上升。

印度也把缅甸视为东向能源外交的重点国家之一。缅甸是离印度最近的东南亚国家，具有较为丰富的天然气资源，其天然气探明储量为 1.2 万亿立方米，是印度东向最重要的天然气供应国。2005 年，印度、孟加拉国和缅甸达成修建缅—孟—印天然气管道（MBI）的协议，计划将缅甸的天然气途经孟加拉国输往印度东部城市加尔各答。该管道全长 900 千米，建成后预计每年向印度供应 110 亿立方米天然气。2006 年，印缅达成天然气进口协议，印度取得了缅甸海上天然气的开发权。2010 年，印缅签署了一份价值达 13.5 亿美元的油气开发协议，并将向缅甸海上 A-1 和 A-3 油田追加投资。2016 年，时任缅甸总统吴廷觉和国务资政昂山素季先后访问印度，两国签署了相关能源合作协议。[2] 2020 年，印度与缅甸在能源、基础设施等领域交换了 10 项协议，其中，能源领域备忘录的内容主要是关于石油产品领域的合作。[3]

（2）与中东国家的合作

印度的大部分油气进口来自中东地区，印度也因此通过积极开展首脑外交，带动与伊朗、沙特阿拉伯和科威特等国的能源外交。2001 年，时任印度

---

[1] 杨思灵：《印度与其"大周边"地区的能源合作》，载《亚非纵横》2009 年第 3 期，第 26—32 页。

[2] 张帅、任欣霖：《印度能源外交的现状与特点》，载《国际石油经济》2018 年第 3 期，第 83—90 页。

[3] Sangeeta Nair, "India, Myanmar Exchange 10 Agreements in Various Fields Including Energy, Infrastructure", https://www.jagranjosh.com/current-affairs/india-and-myanmar-exchange-10-agreements-in-various-fields-including-energy-infrastructure-transport-1582806326-1, July 20, 2020.

总理瓦杰帕伊访问伊朗推动了两国的能源合作，两国建立了副部长级联合委员会和伊朗石油出口印度的常态机制，签署了开展能源合作的框架协议并很快得到落实。2002 年，印度和伊朗签署油田勘探开发协议，这是印度首次进入伊朗油气资源勘探开发领域。2003 年，时任伊朗总统哈塔米访印期间与印度达成能源合作共识，表示伊朗将进一步加大对印度的石油出口，积极推进天然气管道建设。同年 5 月，印伊双方签署协议，伊朗承诺未来 25 年每年向印度提供 500 万吨液化天然气，2004 年每天向印度提供 10 万桶石油。2005 年，印伊双方的石油公司对伊朗南帕尔斯气田的一个区块进行了联合勘探。同时，双方签署液化天然气购买协议，2009—2034 年，伊朗将每年向印度供应 500 万吨液化天然气，印度则向伊朗提供能源生产和利用的多项先进技术。此外，印度获得伊朗最大陆上油田亚达瓦兰（Yadavaran）20% 的股份和朱菲伊尔油田（Jufeyr）100% 的股份，这两个油田每天将分别向印度供应原油 6 万桶和 3 万桶。[1]

（3）与俄罗斯的合作

如前所述，印度对于能源的需求巨大，而俄罗斯是全球主要的石油和天然气生产国和出口国，两国的能源战略需求高度互补。两国曾多次表示将加强油气方面的合作，印度也积极参与在俄罗斯及周边地区的油气资源的勘探开发，推进油气管道建设。

2001 年，印度石油天然气公司投入巨资参与俄罗斯远东地区萨哈林群岛的石油开采项目，并获得 20% 的份额油[2]开采比例。在印俄两国政府的积极推动下，两国的能源企业签订相关协议，同意双方在对方领土以及在包括中亚、里海地区在内的第三国合作勘探开采油气资源。目前，俄罗斯和印度之间的能源合作侧重于核能和石油投资方面，在液化天然气、天然气运输和能源金融市场等新领域的合作是俄罗斯和印度在能源领域发展伙伴关系的一种特别有

---

[1]　参见张力：《从伊朗核危机看印度—美国战略关系》，载《南亚研究季刊》2007 年第 4 期，第 1 页；张帅、任欣霖：《印度能源外交的现状与特点》，载《国际石油经济》2018 年第 3 期，第 83—90 页。

[2]　"份额油"为经济术语，是指一国在对外石油建设项目中参股或投资，每年从该项目的石油产量中分取一定的份额。这种方式能减轻对国际油价的冲击，并减小价格波动风险，因此在我国对外石油投资中被广泛采用。参见厉以宁、王武龙主编：《中国企业投资分析报告》，经济科学出版社 2006 年版，第 169—175 页；时光慧、祁艺主编：《能源工业 中国石油天然气集团公司发展概况》，载中华人民共和国年鉴编辑部主编：《中华人民共和国年鉴》，中华人民共和国年鉴社 2017 年版，第 473—475 页。

效的方式，印度各石油公司在俄罗斯油田的数笔投资均超过 100 亿美元。[1]

（4）与中国的合作

印度与中国的合作主要体现在共同开发上，早在 1997 年中印两国的国家石油公司就共同开发第三国的石油资源达成谅解备忘录。在哈萨克斯坦的石油开采中，两国的石油公司在互惠条件下开展了一系列的合作。中印在苏丹的石油开采项目中也都拥有较大比例的股份。2005 年 12 月，中国石油天然气集团公司与印度石油天然气公司首次联手，以各占 50% 的比例共同收购了加拿大石油公司在叙利亚一个油田 38% 的股份。印度方面对于此次同中国的能源合作反响热烈，印度石油和天然气部秘书特里帕提在接受当地媒体采访时表示，中印两国石油公司此次联合在海外进行石油竞标"是一个具有里程碑意义的行动"，对于未来两国能源合作"有着极为重要的指导作用"。[2]

在此基础上，两国能源外交关系也朝着制度化的方向迈进。2006 年，印度石油和天然气部部长拉奥访华期间提出了构建中印能源合作领域机制化合作框架的倡议，双方签署了关于联合勘探开发和投资第三国油气资源的谅解备忘录。[3] 2006 年 8 月，中印两国石油公司联手收购了哥伦比亚公司油田 50% 的股权。2007 年，印度燃气公司与中国燃气控股有限公司联手成立了各持股 50% 的合资公司，这是中国公司首次投资印度的石油天然气行业。2019 年 1 月 12 日，印度石油和天然气部部长与中国国家发展和改革委员会主任马凯在北京签署了"加强石油与天然气合作"的备忘录，这份文件旨在促进两国加强能源领域合作，对确保能源安全和稳定亚洲能源市场价格起到推动作用。同时，两国将建立一个工作组，每年至少会晤一次，推动合作的进展。

（三）海洋渔业合作

1. 印度洋沿岸国家之间的渔业合作

海洋渔业资源是印度洋沿岸各国最重要的海洋资源之一，渔业资源对沿岸国家在确保粮食安全、消灭贫困、创造就业和增加收入等方面均具有重要意义。然而，近年来，过度捕捞和气候变化的双重影响造成印度洋区域内主要渔业资源的锐减。作为印度洋沿岸国家中的重要一员，印度历来十分重视

---

〔1〕 Zoya Burbeza, "The Viewpoint: Collaboration between India and Russia in the Oil and Gas Sector", https://barandbench.com/india-russia-oil-gas-sector/, January 11, 2020.

〔2〕《中印联手到海外买石油（经济观察）》，载新浪网，http://news.sina.com.cn/o/2005-12-26/09157818105s.shtml，最后访问日期：2020 年 7 月 20 日。

〔3〕 张春梅：《中国与印度签署"加强石油与天然气合作"备忘录》，载央广网，http://www.cnr.cn/news/t20060114_504154760.html，最后访问日期：2020 年 1 月 12 日。

与印度洋沿岸其他国家的渔业合作。

（1）与孟加拉国的合作

2011 年 9 月 6 日，印度和孟加拉国签署了《印度和孟加拉国有关渔业领域合作的备忘录》（MOU between India and Bangladesh on Co-operation in the Field of Fisheries）。该备忘录有效期为 5 年，主要涉及两国交换渔业信息、开展渔业联合行动、促进渔业和水产养殖业的合作等内容。[1]

2016 年 4 月 13 日，印度官方发布了一份公告，介绍了印度与孟加拉国间前述 2011 年备忘录的实施情况。公告中明确："印度和孟加拉国签署的（2011 年）备忘录，加强了两国的友好关系，促进了渔业和水产养殖业的合作。备忘录即将到期，经双方同意，很可能进一步延期至较长时间。"[2]

（2）与斯里兰卡的合作

印度与斯里兰卡之间的渔业争端由来已久。这一争端根源于 1974 年和 1976 年印度与斯里兰卡之间的海上划界协定。该系列协定划定了两国的海上边界，但没有为两国渔民建立任何共享合作机制。[3]

2008 年 10 月 26 日，两国达成《有关捕鱼安排的联合声明》（Joint Statement on Fishing Arrangements），这一联合声明的达成，使两国间由于渔业冲突而引发的暴力事件大幅减少。2011 年 3 月 28—29 日，印度—斯里兰卡渔业联合工作组第三次会议在新德里举行，双方回顾了两国自上次会议（2006 年 1 月于科伦坡举行）以来的渔业合作情况，重申渔民及其生计问题的重要性，强调必须以人道的方式对待所有渔民，确保渔民的安全，在任何情况下均不得对渔民使用武力。[4] 2014 年 8 月 29 日，印度—斯里兰卡渔业相关问题联合委员会第一次会议（The First Meeting of India-Sri Lanka Joint Committee on Fisheries Related Issues）在印度新德里举行。双方探讨了渔业双边合作的

---

〔1〕 "MOU between India and Bangladesh on Co-operation in the Field of Fisheries", Ministry of External Affairs, https：//mea. gov. in/bilateral-documents. htm？ dtl/5189/MOU + between + India + and + Bangladesh + on + cooperation + in + the + field + of + fisheries, November 2, 2019.

〔2〕 "MoU between India and Bangladesh on Cooperation in the Field of Fisheries", PMINDIA, https：//www. pmindia. gov. in/en/news ＿ updates/mou-between-india-and-bangladesh-on-cooperation-in-the-field-of-fisheries/, Novermber 2, 2019.

〔3〕 "Exploring Regional Solutions to Fishermen Disputes in South Asia", The London School of Economics and Political Science, https：//blogs. lse. ac. uk/southasia/2017/07/18/exploring-regional-solutions-to-fishermen-disputes-in-south-asia/, November 2, 2019.

〔4〕 "Meeting of India Sri Lanka JWG on Fisheries-Joint Press Statement", Ministry of External Affairs, https：//mea. gov. in/bilateral-documents. htm？ dtl/4524/Meeting + of + India + Sri + Lanka + JWG + on + Fisheries + + Joint + Press + Statement, November 2, 2019.

途径，如建立渔业合资机制，加强双方在渔业能力研究和建设方面的合作等[1]。2015 年，随着斯里兰卡新政府的上台，印度与斯里兰卡两国的政治关系得到改善，印度就保克湾的渔业问题与斯里兰卡重启对话。双方重申了本国立场，表示愿共同"寻求永久解决渔业问题的办法"[2]。2017 年 4 月 26 日，印度与斯里兰卡就促进两国经济合作签订协议，该协议特别提及印度渔民的深海捕鱼活动以及斯里兰卡对印度渔民的人道主义待遇问题，要求在任何情况下斯里兰卡都不得对印度渔民使用任何形式的武力[3]。

（3）与印度尼西亚的合作

2005 年 11 月 23 日，印度与印度尼西亚签署了《印度共和国农业部与印度尼西亚海洋事务与渔业部间有关海洋及渔业合作的谅解备忘录》（Memorandum of Understanding between the Ministry of Agriculture of Republic of India and the Ministry of Marine Affairs and Fisheries of Republic of Indonesia on Marine and Fisheries Cooperation），并成立"印度—印度尼西亚渔业合作技术联合委员会"（Joint Technical Committee，JTC）。该委员会的第一次会议于 2012 年 12 月 6—7 日在雅加达举行，两国明确了在渔业领域进行合作，特别是加强在加工、销售和研发水产品方面的合作[4]。该谅解备忘录于 2015 年 11 月到期[5]。

2016 年 11 月上旬，印度表示同意续签该备忘录，而印度尼西亚方面则建议签署新的谅解备忘录。2018 年，印度再次提议延长或更新已到期的谅解

---

[1] "Joint Press Statement on India-Sri Lanka Joint Committee Meeting on Fisheries Related Issues", Ministry of External Affairs, https：//mea. gov. in/press-releases. htm? dtl/23957/joint + press + statement + on + indiasri + lanka + joint + committee + meeting + on + fisheries + related + issues, November 2, 2019.

[2] "The India-Sri Lanka Fisheries Dispute：Creating a Win-Win in the Palk Bay", Carnegieindia, https：//carnegieindia. org/2016/09/09/india-sri-lanka-fisheries-dispute-creating-win-win-in-palk-bay-pub-64538, November 2, 2019.

[3] "India, Sri Lanka Ink Pact for Economic Cooperation", Theindubusinessline, https：//www. theindubusinessline. com/economy/policy/india-sri-lanka-ink-pact-for-economic-cooperation/article9665788. ece#!, November 2, 2019.

[4] 《印度与印度尼西亚进行渔业合作》，载中国水产科学研究院网，http：//www. cafs. ac. cn/info/1053/4166. htm，最后访问日期：2019 年 11 月 2 日。

[5] "Memorandum of Understanding between the Ministry of Agriculture of Republic of India and the Ministry of Marine Affairs and Fisheries of Republic of Indonesia on Marine And Fisheries Cooperation", Ministry of External Affairs, https：//mea. gov. in/bilateral-documents. htm? dtl/7077/memorandum + of + understanding + between + the + ministry + of + agriculture + of + republic + of + india + and + the + ministry + of + marine + affairs + and + fisheries + of + republic + of + indonesia + on + marine + and + fisheries + cooperation, November 2, 2019.

备忘录，而不是签署新的谅解备忘录，因为印度尼西亚所提出的新谅解备忘录草案的内容与已到期的谅解备忘录内容一致。[1]

2018 年 5 月，印度总理莫迪对印度尼西亚进行了正式访问，并就有关海洋生物资源的科学管理和保护，打击和制止"非法、不报告和不管制"（Illegal，Unreported and Unregulated，IUU）捕鱼，认定新兴的有关渔业的犯罪，发展海洋蓝色经济（Blue Economy）等方面与印度尼西亚总统达成一致意见。[2]

2. 与其他国家的合作

（1）与中国的合作

2013 年 5 月 20 日，印度海产品出口发展局（MPEDA）与原中国国家质检总局签署《关于合作开展渔业产品进出口贸易的谅解备忘录》（MoU on Cooperation for Import and Export Trade of Fishery Products）。谅解备忘录旨在促进印度和中国之间的渔业产品贸易，推动两国此类产品贸易的健康发展。印度期望通过这种合作向中国出口更多的鱼类产品。[3]

2018 年 11 月 28 日，中国海关总署代表团访问印度，双方就两国间渔业、水果、烟草等合作进行商讨，并于会后签署了《有关印度向中国出口鱼粉和鱼油的卫生和检验要求的议定书》（Protocol on Hygiene and Inspection Requirements for the Export of Fish Meal and Fish Oil from India to China）。该议定书的签署意味着双方在印度向中国出口鱼粉和鱼油的卫生和检验要求上达成共识，并为印度向中国出口鱼油和鱼粉等相关产品铺平了道路。[4]

（2）与越南的合作

2007 年，印度与越南签署《印度和越南有关渔业和水产养殖领域双边合作的谅解备忘录》（MOU on Bilateral Cooperation in the Field of Fisheries and Aquaculture between India and Vietnam）。该备忘录主要包括四方面的内容：第一，信息和数据交换；第二，两国间政府官员、渔业推广人员、专家、研究人员之间的交流；第三，在渔业和水产养殖行政管理人员、研究人员和人

---

〔1〕 "International cooperation", Deparment of Fisheries, http：//dof. gov. in/international-cooperation, November 2，2019.

〔2〕 "Shared Vision of India-Indonesia Maritime Cooperation in the Indo-Pacific", Ministry of External Affairs, https：//www. mea. gov. in/bilateral-documents. htm? dtl/29933/Shared_ Vision_ of_ IndiaIndonesia_ Maritime_ Cooperation_ in_ the_ IndoPacific, November 2，2019.

〔3〕 "India, China Sign MoUs to Address Concerns on Trade Deficit", Press Information Bureau, https：//pib. gov. in/newsite/PrintRelease. aspx? relid＝96098，November 2，2019.

〔4〕 "India to Export Fish Meal and Fishoil to China Protocol Signed Today", Press Information Bureau, https：//pib. gov. in/newsite/PrintRelease. aspx? relid＝186003，November 2，2019.

力资源培训领域进行合作；第四，促进和鼓励双方企业在渔业、水产养殖、鱼品加工、渔业进出口及其他与渔业有关的行业中进行投资和技术方面的直接合作。谅解备忘录自双方签字之日起生效，并长期有效。[1]

2014年9月15日，两国再次签署谅解备忘录，协商确定在印度开展巨鲶育种等相关活动。根据该备忘录的规定，印度将组成一个联合技术委员会，以提供指导、审查相关活动的进展并促进谅解备忘录下的合作。2017年9月14日，经双方一致同意，进一步延长了该备忘录下的合作期限。

（3）与挪威的合作

早在20世纪50年代，印度与挪威即已开始渔业合作。1952年秋，挪威与印度当局合作开展了"印度喀拉拉邦（Kerala）项目"（以下简称"喀拉拉邦项目"）。这是挪威在印度的第一个发展援助项目，涉及印度喀拉拉邦两个村庄的渔业发展。1959—1960年，双方合作开发了一种25英尺长的新型机动渔船，这些渔船取代了传统的非机动渔船，可以用来拖网捕虾，大幅提高了渔民的捕鱼量，为鱼类出口创造了条件。除了新型渔船，"喀拉拉邦项目"的内容还包括在陆地上建立鱼产品加工企业、改善供水条件等。1961年，挪威协助印度建立了一个现代渔业中心。通过"喀拉拉邦项目"，挪威帮助印度喀拉拉邦和其他邦提高了鱼类捕获量，增加了渔民的就业机会和收入，促进了当地的经济增长。[2]

2010年3月，印度与挪威签署了有关海洋渔业的进一步合作协议，除任意一方书面通知终止外，该协议长期有效。根据该协议，双方每年定期举行相关会议商讨渔业合作问题。其中，第五次会议于2016年4月8日在新德里举行。第六次会议原定于2017年8月召开，但由于行政原因未能召开。[3]

2019年1月，印度与挪威签署了《印度—挪威海洋对话谅解备忘录》（MoU on India-Norway Ocean Dialogue），并依据该谅解备忘录成立了"蓝色经济"联合特别工作组，以促进海洋渔业、水产养殖等方面的多部门合作。[4]

[1] "MOU Between India and Vietnam on Bilateral Cooperation in the Field of Fisheries and Aquaculture", Thefishsite, https：//thefishsite. com/articles/mou-between-india-and-vietnam-on-bilateral-cooperation-in-the-field-of-fisheries-and-aquaculture, November 2, 2019.

[2] "India", Vorad, https：//norad. no/en/landsider/asia-og-oseania/india/, November 2, 2019.

[3] Deparment of Fisheries, "International Cooperation", http：//dof. gov. in/international-cooperation, November 2, 2019.

[4] "India, Norway Ink MoU to Boost Blue Economy", Indiatoday, https：//www. indiatoday. in/mail-today/story/india-norway-ink-mou-to-boost-blue-economy-1426724-2019-01-09, November 2, 2019.

（四）海洋科研合作

1. 与中国的合作

2003 年 6 月 23 日，印度与中国签署了《中华人民共和国国家海洋局与印度共和国政府海洋开发部海洋科技领域合作谅解备忘录》。随着印度国内机构调整，海洋开发部并入地球科学部。此后直到 2015 年，两国在相关领域无政府层面进一步合作。

2015 年 5 月 15 日，印度与中国签署了《中华人民共和国国家海洋局和印度共和国地球科学部关于加强海洋科学、海洋技术、气候变化、极地科学与冰冻圈领域合作的谅解备忘录》（以下简称《备忘录》）。根据《备忘录》，双方将开展海洋科学、海洋技术、海气相互作用、气候波动与变化、海洋生物化学研究和生态系统、地质和地球物理方面的合作。[1]

2016 年 5 月 17 日，中印海洋科技合作联合委员会（以下简称"联委会"）第一次会议在北京召开。该会议是落实 2015 年《备忘录》的一项重要会议。双方总结肯定了 2015 年《备忘录》推行实施取得的显著成果，讨论并通过了印度环流与季风气候研究等 8 个合作项目。双方决定，将定期举行中印海洋科技合作联委会会议和研讨会，成立联合指导委员会，指定项目负责人，推动合作项目的实施。同时，双方同意加强在政府间海洋学委员会和其他多边机制下的合作，共同参与第二次国际印度洋考察计划等。[2]

2. 与俄罗斯的合作

印度与俄罗斯存在长期稳定的双边科学合作关系，该合作始于 1972 年印度和苏联签署的《印度与苏联间科学技术协议》（Science and Technology Agreement between India and USSR），并随着其后的"科学合作综合长期计划"（The Integrated Long Term Programme，ILTP）而得到进一步加强。为深化合作，两国于 1993 年成立了印俄科学技术合作工作组（IRWGS&T），该工作组下设六个工作小组以具体决定并实施协作研究项目。其中，第六工作小组专注于海洋学方面的科学合作，主要由印度国家海洋研究所和俄罗斯教育科学部牵头进行。[3]

---

〔1〕《中印签署海洋领域合作文件 将在气候变化等方面合作》，载环球网，https：//china. huan-qiu. com/article/9CaKrnJL3B6，最后访问日期：2019 年 11 月 2 日。

〔2〕陈君怡：《进一步推进中印海洋领域合作》，载新华网，http：//www. xinhuanet. com/politics/2016-05/20/c_ 129001102. htm，最后访问日期：2019 年 11 月 2 日。

〔3〕Dr. Shishir Shrotriya，"Indo-Russian S&T Cooperation"，https：//www. indianembassy-moscow. gov. in/indo-russian-s-t-cooperation. php，November 2, 2019.

2017 年 6 月，第一届印俄科技合作联合委员会（India-Russia Joint Committee on Science and Technology Cooperation）在俄罗斯新西伯利亚市召开。两国在会上确定了在海洋技术、深海工程、信息技术和太空技术等领域的合作。印度方面表示，俄罗斯是印度在高科技领域的首选合作伙伴，两国间的新合作将进一步推动双边伙伴关系的发展。[1]

2019 年 7 月底，印度金奈国家海洋技术研究所（The National Institute of Ocean Technology，NIOT）与俄罗斯克雷洛夫州研究中心（Krylov State Research Centre，KSRC）签署了谅解备忘录，以共同开发用于深海矿物开采的机器和技术。该谅解备忘录还提到了在开发深海作业载人潜水器方面的合作。[2]

3. 与日本的合作

2016 年 11 月，莫迪总理访问日本期间，印度地球科学部和日本海洋与地球科学技术厅（Japan Agency for Marine-Earth Science and Technology，JAMSTEC）签署了《海洋与地球科学技术互助合作谅解备忘录》（Memorandum of Understanding on Mutual Cooperation in Marine and Earth Science and Technology）。该谅解备忘录旨在通过联合调查、巡航和技术研发等方式，在平等互利的基础上，建立和促进两国在海洋和地球科学技术领域的合作。双方确定了 3 个合作项目，分别是有关季风预测的气候建模、深海勘探及安达曼海地震和海啸预警研究。

除了官方合作，印度与日本之间还有广泛的民间海洋研究合作。如印度国家海洋研究所（CSIR-National Institute of Oceanography）、印度德里大学（Delhi University）等机构与日本海洋科学技术厅、日本东京大学（Tokyo University）等之间都存在不同形式的海洋科研合作。[3]

4. 与孟加拉国的合作

2015 年 6 月 6 日，印度与孟加拉国签署了《印度与孟加拉国在孟加拉湾和印度洋地区有关蓝色经济和海事合作领域的谅解备忘录》（Memorandum of Understanding between the Government of the Republic of India and the Govern-

---

〔1〕 Jitesh Jha，"1st India-Russia Joint Committee on Science and Technology Cooperation held"，https：//www. jagranjosh. com/current-affairs/1st-indiarussia-joint-committee-on-science-and-technology-cooperation-held-1498103560-1，November 2, 2019.

〔2〕 M. Ramesh，"NIOT Teams Up with Russian Research Unit to Mine for Minerals in the Deep Sea"，https：//www. thehindubusinessline. com/news/variety/niot-teams-up-with-russian-research-unit-to-mine-for-minerals-in-the-deep-sea/article28787172. ece，November 2, 2019.

〔3〕 "Bilateral Cooperation in the field of Science & Technology between India and Japan"，Embassy of India，https：//www. indembassy-tokyo. gov. in/st_ cooperation. html，November 2, 2019.

ment of the People's Republic of Bangladesh in the Field of Blue Economy and Maritime Co-operation in the Bay of Bengal and the Indian Ocean Region）。该谅解备忘录第 2 条第 1 款明确了双方在海洋生物技术研究和发展方面的合作，第 2 条第 3 款则强调了两国在海洋科学和蓝色经济领域的技术合作。[1]

5. 与法国的合作

2016 年 3 月，印度与法国国家科研中心（CNRS）和法国索邦大学（Sorbonne University）合作建立了海洋生物研究所（National Institute of Marine Biology and Biotechnology）。双方据此共同致力于研究气候变化对世界海洋的影响，并有意加强海洋生物研究和海洋生态学研究方面的合作。[2]

（五）区域性国际合作

1. 环印度洋联盟

环印度洋联盟（The Indian Ocean Rim Association，IORA）是成立于 1997 年的政府间国际组织。[3]环印度洋联盟现有 22 个成员国、10 个对话伙伴国及 2 个观察员国，其协调秘书处设于毛里求斯的埃比尼（Ebene）。环印度洋联盟的核心任务是促进成员国间的贸易和投资，旨在通过开展一致同意的区域性合作，增进成员间特别是印度洋沿岸成员间的互信与合作，为更广范围和更具深度的合作构建顺畅良好的运行机制。[4]

作为创始成员国之一，印度积极参与环印度洋联盟的合作事宜。如，"印度洋对话"（Indian Ocean Dialogue）即是由环印度洋联盟所倡导的旗舰倡议（a flagship initiative），其首次活动举办于印度的喀拉拉邦，是成员国的学者、专家、政府官员及分析人士等商讨包括经贸合作、海上安全、灾难救助等重要议题的关键对话平台。[5] 2011—2013 年，身为环印度洋联盟主席国

〔1〕 Ministry of External Affairs, "Memorandum of Understanding between the Government of the Republic of India and the Government of the People's Republic of Bangladesh in the Field of Blue Economy and Maritime Co-operation in the Bay of Bengal and the Indian Ocean Region", https：// www. mea. gov. in/Portal/LegalTreatiesDoc/BG15B2419. pdf, October 13, 2020.

〔2〕 "First Marine Biology Institute for India", Indiabioscience, https：//indiabioscience. org/columns/indian-scenario/first-marine-biology-institute-for-india, November 2, 2019.

〔3〕 环印度洋地区 14 国于 1997 年 3 月成立环印度洋地区合作联盟（The Indian Ocean Rim Association for Regional Cooperation—IOR-ARC）。该组织于 2013 年 11 月由其第 13 届部长理事会会议决定更名为环印度洋联盟（The Indian Ocean Rim Association—IORA）。

〔4〕 "About IORA", The Indian Rim Association, https：//www. iora. int/en/about/about-iora, October 25, 2020.

〔5〕 "The Indian Ocean Dialogue", The Indian Rim Association, https：//www. iora. int/en/flagship-projects/the-indian-ocean-dialogue, October 25, 2020.

的印度，决心加强该机构的能力与活力。印度在其担任主席国期间，提出的六个优先领域和两个重点领域，现已成为环印度洋联盟各成员国促进均衡稳定发展的共识，并已纳入该机构的工作规划中。这六个优先领域分别是：海上安全与安保（Maritime Safety & Security）、贸易和投资便利化（Trade & Investment Facilitation）、渔业管理（Fisheries Management）、灾难风险管理（Disaster Risk Management）、旅游和文化交流（Tourism & Cultural Exchanges）、学术、科学和技术（Academic，Science & Technology）。而两个重点领域同样与海洋有所关联，分别是蓝色经济（Blue Economy）和女性的经济自主（Women's Economic Empowerment）。[1]

2. 环孟加拉湾多领域经济技术合作倡议

环孟加拉湾多领域经济技术合作倡议（Bay of Bengal Initiative for Multi-Sectoral Technical and Economic Cooperation，BIMSTEC，以下简称《经济技术合作倡议》），是由孟加拉湾沿岸及邻近孟加拉湾地区的国家所组成的地区性组织。1997 年 6 月 6 日，《经济技术合作倡议》根据《曼谷宣言》（The Bankok Declareation）宣告成立，以印度、孟加拉国、斯里兰卡、泰国为创始会员国。随后，缅甸（1997 年 12 月）、不丹和尼泊尔（2004 年 2 月）也相继加入。《经济技术合作倡议》在南亚地区和东南亚地区搭建起了地区间交流与合作的平台，代表了成员国间紧密的合作关系，其宗旨在于建立一个在多领域开展互利合作，从而推动成员国经济增长的地区协作联盟。

与众多地区性组织不同，《经济技术合作倡议》是一个以核心领域合作为主导的组织。1997 年，该组织即在成员国间展开包括贸易、技术、能源、交通、旅游、渔业在内的六大领域的合作。2008 年，该组织在成员国间再次铺开新的八大领域的合作，包括农业、公共健康、扶贫、反恐、环境、文化、人员交流和气候变化。[2]

在第一届《经济技术合作倡议》首脑会议上，印度提出在成员国间共享农业、环境和灾难管理的遥感信息。在此基础之上，印度进一步提出在新德里建立《经济技术合作倡议》的天气与气候中心。2014 年 3 月 4 日，该组织各成员国在缅甸内比都（Nay Pyi Taw）签署了《设立天气与气候中心的备忘录》（The Memorandum of Association on the establishment of BIMSTEC Centre for Weather and Climate）。2018 年 7 月 30 日，天气与气候中心理事会和科学咨询

---

〔1〕 "Priorities-Focus-Areas"，The Indian Rim Association，https：//www. iora. int/en/priorities-focus-areas/overview，October 25，2020.

〔2〕 "About BIMSTEC"，BIMSTEC，https：//bimstec. org/? page_ id = 189，November 1，2019.

委员会的第一次会议在印度新德里召开，并于次日举办了题为“《经济技术合作倡议》地区的恶劣天气与气候灾害预警”的讲习班。该中心自设立后一直运行于印度的中期数值天气预报国家中心之下，并持续为其提供研究数据。[1]

3. 《亚洲地区反海盗及武装劫船合作协定》

《亚洲地区反海盗及武装劫船合作协定》（The Regional Cooperation Agreement on Combating Piracy and Armed Robbery against Ships in Asia，ReCAAP）是亚洲第一个关于加强反海盗和武装抢劫船舶合作的区域性政府间协定。该协定在 2004 年 11 月 11 日正式签订，并于 2006 年 9 月 4 日生效实施，而印度是该协定的发起及缔约方之一。[2] 截至 2020 年，该协定共有 20 个缔约国，包括 14 个亚洲国家、1 个美洲国家（美国）、1 个大洋洲国家（澳大利亚）及 4 个欧洲国家（挪威、荷兰、丹麦、英国）。根据这一合作协定，缔约国协力创建了亚洲地区反海盗及武装劫船合作协定信息共享中心（ReCAAP Information Sharing Centre，ISC）。该信息共享中心于 2006 年 11 月 29 日在新加坡正式成立，旨在通过信息共享、能力建设及合作安排加强区域协调，从而更有效地打击海盗及海上武装抢劫行为。[3] 该信息共享中心能够在接到报告后作出快速反应并为遇险船舶提供尽可能的帮助。该中心也同包括国际海事组织和国际刑警组织（INTERPOL）等在内的国际组织合作，共同打击针对船舶的海上相关犯罪。经 2018 年《亚洲地区反海盗及武装劫船合作协定》第 12 届理事会会议确认，该中心已满足相关条件成长为打击海盗及海上武装抢劫船舶的杰出的信息共享中心。[4]

（六）全球性国际组织框架下的合作

1. 国际海事组织

国际海事组织成立于 1959 年 1 月，总部设在伦敦，原名政府间海事协商组织（Inter-Governmental Maritime Consultative Organization），1982 年 5 月改称国际海事组织。国际海事组织是负责全球海上航行安全、防止船舶污染的

---

〔1〕 “Centres”，BIMSTEC，https：//bimstec. org/？page_ id = 1292，November 2，2019.

〔2〕 《Recaap 发布亚洲海盗和武装抢劫船报告》，载国际船舶网，http：//www. eworldship. com/html/2016/ship_ inside_ and_ outside_ 1211/122869. html，最后访问日期：2019 年 10 月 26 日。

〔3〕 “Vision & Mission”，ReCAAP，http：//www. recaap. org/vision_ mission_ of_ ReCAAP-ISC，November 2，2019.

〔4〕 “Executive Director's Message”，ReCAAP，http：//www. recaap. org/message_ by_ recaap-isc_ ed，October 27，2019.

联合国专门机构，其宗旨在于促进各国间的航运技术合作，鼓励各国在促进海上安全、提高船舶航行效率、防止和控制船舶对海洋污染方面采取统一的标准，并处理相关法律问题。印度已于1959年成为其会员国。[1]

为应对船舶压载水的有害有机物造成的海洋污染，国际海事组织同全球环境基金（The Global Environment Facility）[2]、联合国开发计划署（United Nations Development Programme）于2000年开展了全球压载水管理计划（Global Ballast Water Management Programme）。鉴于发展中国家生物多样性易遭破坏的特点，该计划的第一阶段就确定了首先于包括印度在内的六个发展中国家开展活动。这些活动包括：示范港之间的交流与教育宣传、港口的风险评估和调查、压载水管理法规的审查、合规执法和监控能力的建设等。目前该计划已进行到第二阶段。印度已加入该组织项下30多项国际条约，涉及国际海洋污染防治、海员管理、船舶管理、港口管理、海上航行安全、海事赔偿和责任等多项内容。[3]

2. 联合国粮食及农业组织

联合国粮食及农业组织（Food and Agriculture Organization of the United Natios，FAO）是联合国系统内最早的常设专门机构之一。其宗旨是提高各国人民的营养水平和生活标准，改进农产品的生产和分配，改善农村和农民的经济状况，促进世界经济的发展并保证人类免于饥饿。[4] 作为该组织的194个成员国之一，印度与该组织合作推动的优先领域包括：（1）可持续农业发展；（2）粮食及营养安全；（3）跨境合作；（4）可能的情形下性别与气候变化的交叉问题。近年来，对水、土壤及其他自然资源可持续管理以及渔业发展都成为在组织框架下被关注的中心问题。[5]

在联合国粮食及农业组织第三届大会的建议下，亚洲—太平洋渔业委员会（Asia-Pacific Fishery Commission，APFIC）于1948年11月正式设立。该委员会通常每两年举行一届会议，旨在通过发展和管理捕捞及养殖活动，以

---

〔1〕 "Memberstates", International Maritime Organization, http：//www. imo. org/en/About/Membership/Pages/MemberStates. aspx, October 27, 2019.

〔2〕 全球环境基金成立于1992年，旨在帮助解决全球最严重的的环境问题。"About US", Globe Environment Facility, https：//www. thegef. org/about-us, October 29, 2019.

〔3〕 "The GEF-UNDP-IMO GloBallast Programme", International Maritime Organization, http：//www. imo. org/en/About/Events/Rio2012/Documents/Report% 20card% 20leaflet% 20GloBallast% 20Rio. pdf#search = India, October 29, 2019.

〔4〕 "About FAO", FAO, http：//www. fao. org/about/en/, October 30, 2019.

〔5〕 "India", FAO, http：//www. fao. org/countryprofiles/index/en/? iso3 = IND. , October 30, 2019.

及通过符合成员目标的相关加工和销售活动，促进水生生物资源的全面及恰当利用。[1] 目前该委员会有 21 个成员国，印度是成员方之一。[2]

亚太区域渔业产品销售信息及咨询服务政府间组织（Intergovernmental Organisation for Marketing Information and Technical Advisory Services for Fishery Products in the Asia and Pacific Region，INFORFISH）最初为联合国粮食及农业组织于 1981 年启动的试点工程。自 1987 年以来，该组织逐渐成长为专门针对亚太地区及其他地区的渔业行业提供市场信息和技术咨询服务的政府间国际组织，共有包括印度在内的 13 个成员国。亚太地区存在数个世界最大的渔业国，而总部设在马来西亚吉隆坡的亚太区域渔业产品销售信息及咨询服务政府间组织，已经成为该地区渔业生产及出口方最重要的市场营销后援力量。[3]

----

[1]　"About the Asia-Pacific Fishery Commission", FAO, About the Asia-Pacific Fishery Commission, October 30, 2019.

[2]　"Membership", FAO, http：//www. fao. org/apfic/background/about-asia-pacific-fishery-commission/membership/en, October 31, 2019.

[3]　"Member Countries", InfoFish, http：//infofish. org/v3/index. php/about-us, October 30, 2019.

七、对中国海洋法主张的态度

（一）对"南海仲裁案"的态度

2014年5月莫迪政府上台后，印度不断介入南海问题，积极与东盟国家在南海问题上共同发声，加强与美、日等国在南海问题上的战略性互动，努力扩大其在南海地区的战略影响力，以更大限度地服务于其国家利益。

对于中菲"南海仲裁案"，印度虽然并未明确表示立场，却表现出对裁决结果的极大关注，并多次在正式的外交场合提及该案相关内容。2016年7月12日，国际仲裁庭对"南海仲裁案"作出所谓的"最终裁决"，判决菲律宾"胜诉"，否定了中国"九段线"的主张，并宣称中国对南海海域没有"历史性所有权"。对此，印度政府迅速作出反应。在裁决公布的当天，印度外交部即发表了《关于根据〈公约〉附件七作出的"南海仲裁案"裁决的声明》（Statement on Award of Arbitral Tribunal on South China Sea Under Annexure VII of UNCLOS）。在该《声明》中，印度表示："印度注意到依据《公约》附件七所设仲裁庭已就菲律宾和中国问题作出裁决。印度支持《公约》所体现的以国际法原则为基础的航行和飞越自由，支持贸易畅通。印度认为，各国应在不使用武力或以武力相威胁的情况下，通过和平手段解决争端，在可能使影响和平与稳定的争端复杂化或升级的活动中保持克制。南海航道是维护南海和平稳定、繁荣发展的重要通道。作为《公约》缔约国，印方敦促各方切实尊重《公约》及其所确立的国际海洋法律秩序。"[1]

2016年9月2日，印度总理莫迪对越南进行正式访问并同越南发表了联合声明。双方在声明中重申共同维护亚洲和平、稳定和发展繁荣的愿望和决心。对于根据《公约》附件七设立的仲裁庭所作的裁决，双方再次表达"对于建立在《公约》及其他国际法基本原则基础上的和平、稳定、安全、自由航行和飞越以及自由贸易的支持"，并"呼吁各国保持克制，在不使用武力或以武力相威胁的情况下，通过和平方式解决争端，避免冲突升级影响和平与稳定，尊重外交和法律程序，全面遵守《南海各方行为宣言》，并尽快落

---

〔1〕 "Statement on Award of Arbitral Tribunal on South China Sea Under Annexure VII of UNCLOS", Ministry of External Affairs, https：//www. mea. gov. in/press-releases. htm? dtl/27019/statement + on + award + of + arbitral + tribunal + on + south + china + sea + under + annexure + vii + of + unclos, August 20，2020.

实 '南海行为准则'"。双方强调 "南海作为重要的海上通道对地区和平、稳定和繁荣的重要性,并敦促各方尽最大努力遵守并尊重《公约》及其所确立的国际海洋法律秩序"[1]

2016 年 9 月 8 日,印度总理莫迪在第 11 届东亚峰会 (East Asia Summit) 上发表讲话,强调南海是全球商品贸易的重要通道,其和平稳定与开放对区域和全球利益至关重要。除了一贯地呼吁各方遵守《公约》、尊重《公约》及国际法基本原则所规定的航行和飞越自由,莫迪还特别指出,印度和孟加拉国在解决海洋边界问题上的做法,为解决这类问题树立了良好榜样[2]

2016 年 11 月,莫迪对日本进行正式访问,双方发表了联合声明。该声明重申两国对基于《公约》及国际法基本原则的海上航行和飞越自由的尊重,敦促各方保持克制,通过和平手段解决争端,避免使用武力或以武力相威胁,避免采取单方面行动以加剧局势的紧张,呼吁各国尽最大努力尊重《公约》及其所确定的国际海洋法律秩序。关于南海问题,双方强调各争议方应遵守包括《公约》在内的国际法,采取和平方式妥善解决争议[3]

可以看到,一方面,印度在正式外交场合频频提及 "南海仲裁案",另一方面,印度又始终避免过于鲜明地表达自己对于 "南海仲裁案" 的立场。应注意到,虽然印度没有直接肯定裁决结果,但是却支持仲裁庭的成立,还曾援引通过仲裁庭裁决解决的印度与孟加拉国间的海洋边界问题作为例子,可见其态度并非完全中立。

(二) 对《南海各方行为宣言》的态度

2002 年 11 月 4 日,东盟与中国签署了《南海各方行为宣言》 (The Declaration on the Conduct of Parties in the South China Sea, DOC)。《南海各方行为宣言》实质上是一份政治性文件,并不具有国际法上条约的约束力,但该

---

[1] "Joint Statement between India and Vietnam during the visit of Prime Minister to Vietnam", Ministry of External Affairs, https://www.mea.gov.in/bilateral-documents.htm? dtl/27362/Joint + Statement + between + India + and + Vietnam + during + the + visit + of + Prime + Minister + to + Vietnam, August 20, 2020.

[2] "Remarks by Prime Minister at the 11th East Asia Summit held on 8 September 2016 in Vientiane, Lao PDR", Ministry of External Affairs, https://mea.gov.in/Speeches-Statements.htm? dtl/27552/Remarks + by + Prime + Minister + at + the + 11th + East + Asia + Summit + held + on + 8 + September + 2016 + in + Vientiane + Lao + PDR, August 20, 2020.

[3] "India-Japan Joint Statement during the visit of Prime Minister to Japan", Ministry of External Affairs, https://mea.gov.in/bilateral-documents.htm? dtl/27599/IndiaJapan + Joint + Statement + during + the + visit + of + Prime + Minister + to + Japan, August 20, 2020.

宣言仍旧被视为一项重要的冲突预防措施。[1]

印度并非南海争端的直接当事国，亦非东盟成员国，更不是《南海各方行为宣言》的签署国，但其仍自视在南海有巨大的国家利益。从经济现状上看，南海是印度最重要的海上通道之一，印度对外贸易量的 55% 要经由南海的海上通道运输。[2] 而在政治策略上，东盟十国又是印度"东进政策"的核心。[3] 因此，印度历来对南海的和平稳定、航行和飞越自由、贸易自由等十分关切，不仅在正式场合公开表达对《南海各方行为宣言》的支持，也在多个双边、多边国际场合呼吁有关各方遵守和落实《南海各方行为宣言》，寄望在协商一致基础上尽快制定"南海行为准则"。

2014 年 9 月，印度总统慕克吉（Pranab Kumar Mukherjee）访问越南，访问结束后双方发表联合声明称："双方认为南海航行自由不应该受到阻碍，并呼吁有关各方保持克制，避免使用武力或以武力相威胁，根据《联合国海洋法公约》等国际法，通过和平手段解决争端。双方欢迎有关各方遵守和执行《南海各方行为宣言》，并致力于推动制定'南海行为准则'。"同年 10 月，越南总理阮晋勇访印期间双方发布联合声明时重申了上述立场。

2014 年 11 月，第九届东亚峰会在缅甸首都内比都举行，印度总理莫迪在会上表示："为了南海的和平与稳定，每个人都应遵守包括 1982 年《联合国海洋法公约》在内的国际法律规范。我们也希望相关各方能成功落实《南海各方行为宣言》，尽快在协商一致的基础上完成'南海行为准则'的制定。"[4] 这是印度政府首次在国际多边场合公开评论南海问题，显示出印度新一届政府对南海局势的深刻关切。[5]

2016 年 4 月 18 日，印度、中国和俄罗斯三国外长在莫斯科举行了印中俄外长第十四次会晤并在会后发表联合公报，该公报第 21 条指出："中国、俄罗斯、印度承诺维护基于国际法原则的海洋法律秩序，该秩序显著体现在

---

[1] 参见刘复国、吴士存主编：《2013 年度南海地区形势评估报告》，载中国南海研究院网站，http://www.nanhai.org.cn/index.php/Index/Research/work_ c/id/101.html.，最后访问日期：2020 年 8 月 20 日。

[2] "Question No. 808 Trade Through South China Sea", Ministry of External Affairs, https://www.mea.gov.in/rajya-sabha.htm? dtl/28041/question + no808 + trade + through + south + china + sea, August 20, 2020.

[3] "'Look East' Policy Now Turned Into 'Act East' Policy", The Hindu, https://www.thehindu.com/news/national/look-east-policy-now-turned-into-act-east-policy-modi/article6595186.ece, August 20, 2020.

[4] "Modi 'Acts East' at East Asia Summit", The Diplomat, https://thediplomat.com/2014/11/modi-acts-east-at-east-asia-summit/, August 20, 2020.

[5] 龚大明：《印度莫迪政府的南海政策》，载《东南亚南亚研究》2015 年第 4 期，第 8—14 页。

《联合国海洋法公约》中。所有相关争议应由当事国通过谈判和协议解决。外长们呼吁全面遵守《联合国海洋法公约》、《南海各方行为宣言》及落实《南海各方行为宣言》后续行动指针。"[1] 这被认为是印度对《南海各方行为宣言》及中国南海立场的明确支持。[2]

2018 年 7 月，在第三届东盟国防部长会议（ASEAN Defence Ministers' Meeting）上，印度国防部长强调根据现有国际法在国际水域自由航行和飞越、无障碍地贸易和获取资源的重要性。他表示，印度希望"南海行为准则"能够在协商一致的基础上尽快达成。[3]

可以看到，印度虽然不是东盟成员国，但是由于其在南海的利益需求，印度历来对《南海各方行为宣言》持积极正面姿态，并希望尽快制定"南海行为准则"，以营造一个有利于包括印度在内的周边国家和平稳定的南海环境。

（三）在"一带一路"框架下与中国合作的态度

1. 印度对"一带一路"态度的转变

作为南亚次大陆最大国家和"一带一路"沿线最大的发展中国家，目前印度对"一带一路"的参与不甚积极，甚至带有一定程度的敌视和反对。因此，印度既是中国实施"一带一路"倡议的关键，又在某种意义上成为推进"一带一路"建设的重大障碍。总体来看，印度对"一带一路"倡议经历了态度模糊、积极响应和拒绝抵制三个阶段。

（1）态度模糊阶段。2013 年下半年至 2014 年上半年，印度对"一带一路"倡议尚处于认知阶段，民间认可与反对声音并存，官方层面没有明确表态是否参与。在重要的外交场合和对话中，印度都尽量回避这一话题。

（2）积极响应阶段。2014 年上半年至 2016 年上半年，尽管印度国内对"一带一路"倡议还存在多种质疑，但在两国高层互访的推动下，印度官方层面对"一带一路"建设持正面态度，并以实际行动给予中国正面回应。2014 年 2 月，中印边界问题特别代表第 17 轮会谈在新德里举行，中方正式

---

〔1〕《中华人民共和国、俄罗斯联邦和印度共和国外长第十四次会晤联合公报》，载中华人民共和国外交部网站，https：//www. mfa. gov. cn/web/zyxw/t1356650. shtml，最后访问日期：2020 年 8 月 23 日。

〔2〕《中、俄、印三国外长就南海问题联合发声》，载中华人民共和国驻印度大使馆网站，https：//www. fmprc. gov. cn/ce/cein/chn/zgyw/t1358198. htm，最后访问日期：2020 年 8 月 23 日。

〔3〕 "India Calls for Early Conclusion of South China Sea Code of Conduct", The Economic Times, https：//economictimes. indiatimes. com/news/defence/india-calls-for-early-conclusion-of-south-china-sea-code-of-conduct/articleshow/49658921. cms，August 20，2020.

邀请印度参与"21世纪海上丝绸之路"建设。时任印度总理辛格在会见中印边界问题中方特别代表杨洁篪时表示，印方将积极参与孟中印缅经济走廊和"丝绸之路经济带"建设。[1] 2015年5月，中国国家主席习近平在陕西西安会见印度总理莫迪，习近平表示，双方可以就"一带一路"、亚洲基础设施投资银行等合作倡议以及莫迪总理提出的"向东行动"政策加强沟通，找准利益契合点，实现对接，探讨互利共赢的合作模式，促进共同发展。莫迪则表示，印中两国都向南亚有关国家提供帮助和支持；中方提出了"一带一路"倡议，印方同样重视南亚地区互联互通建设，这将促进本地区的发展繁荣，印方愿加强同中方在这一领域的合作。[2]

（3）抵制拒绝阶段。在2016年6月的核供应国集团（NSG）首尔年会上，中国未能支持印度申请加入核供应国集团的诉求，导致中印间潜在矛盾因"具体问题"而公开化和表面化。这成为印度对"一带一路"态度的转折点。2017年5月，印度以"中巴经济走廊"经过印巴争议地区克什米尔从而破坏了其主权与领土完整为由，拒绝参加"一带一路"国际合作高峰论坛，成为唯一一个缺席该论坛的经济大国。[3] 对此，印度外交部发言人表示："不能接受一个无视其主权和领土完整核心利益的项目。"[4] 2019年4月，印度再次拒绝参加第二届"一带一路"国际合作高峰论坛。[5] 对此，中国外交部发言人陆慷在论坛召开前答记者问时表示，"一带一路"是开放包容的经济合作倡议，从不介入有关方面的领土争议问题。中国在与有关国家共建"一带一路"进程中，始终坚持平等开放透明，坚持以企业为主体的市场化运作，按照市场规律和通行的国际规则行事。[6]

---

〔1〕 陈雪莲：《印度总理辛格会见杨洁篪》，载人民网，http：//politics. people. com. cn/n/2014/0212/c70731-24337835. html，最后访问日期：2020年8月20日。

〔2〕 谭晶晶、王慧慧、梁娟：《习近平会见印度总理莫迪》，载中国一带一路网，https：//www. yidaiyilu. gov. cn/xwzx/xgcdt/6828. htm，最后访问日期：2020年8月20日。

〔3〕 Darshana M. Baruah，"India's Answer to the Belt and Road"，https：//carnegieendowment. org/files/WP_ Darshana_ Baruah_ Belt_ Road_ FINAL. pdf，August 20，2020.

〔4〕 "Official Spokesperson's Response to A Query on Participation of India in OBOR/BRI Forum"，Ministry of External Affairs，https：//www. mea. gov. in/media-briefings. htm？dtl/28463/official + spokespersons + response + to + a + query + on + participation + of + india + in + oborbri + forum，August 20，2020.

〔5〕 "What to Make of India's Absence from the Second Belt and Road Forum"，The Diplomat，https：//thediplomat. com/2019/05/what-to-make-of-indias-absence-from-the-second-belt-and-road-forum/，August 20，2020.

〔6〕 《2019年4月15日外交部发言人陆慷主持例行记者会》，载中华人民共和国外交部网站，https：//www. fmprc. gov. cn/web/fyrbt_ 673021/jzhsl_ 673025/t1654510. shtml，最后访问日期：2020年8月20日。

2020 年 4 月以来，印度边防部队单方面在印中边界西段实际控制线中方一侧的加勒万河谷地区持续抵制修建道路、桥梁等设施。在中方就此多次提出交涉和抗议后，印度边防部队于 5 月 6 日凌晨在加勒万河谷地区越线进入中国领土，构工设障，阻拦中方边防部队正常巡逻，蓄意挑起事端，试图单方面改变边境管控现状。6 月 6 日，两国边防部队举行军长级会晤，就缓和边境地区局势达成共识，印方承诺不越过加勒万河口巡逻和修建设施，双方通过现地指挥官会晤商定分批撤军事宜。然而，6 月 15 日晚，印方一线边防部队公然打破双方军长级会晤达成的共识，在加勒万河谷现地局势已经趋缓的情况下，再次跨越实控线蓄意挑衅，并暴力攻击中方前往现地交涉的官兵，进而引发激烈肢体冲突，造成人员伤亡。[1] 加勒万河谷事件使印中双边关系陷入紧张状态。[2] 6 月底，印度宣布封禁 59 款中国手机应用程序，[3] 印度交通部长宣布将禁止中资企业参与印度道路建设项目。此外，来自中国的进口货物在印度的一些港口也遇到清关障碍。[4] 可见，由于印中双边关系恶化，印度对"一带一路"的抵制态度更加明显和坚决。

2. 印度应对"一带一路"的主要战略选择

（1）通过个别项目参与，分享"一带一路"红利

尽管印度国内对"一带一路"有诸多否定的声音，但印度也看到了"一带一路"建设对印度经济发展的有利之处，其在某些方面采取了灵活的务实主义路线，最突出的是参与亚投行的筹建。2014 年 10 月，印度作为亚投行首批意向创始成员国在北京签约，其内阁于 2015 年 6 月正式批准加入。印度出资 84 亿美元，成为亚投行第二大股东，并获得第二大表决权份额。[5] 2017 年，上海合作组织给予印度成员国地位，印度正式成为上合组织八个成员国之一。同年，印度总理莫迪出席金砖国家领导人第九次会晤，围绕"深

---

〔1〕《2020 年 6 月 19 日外交部发言人赵立坚主持例行记者会》，载中华人民共和国外交部网站，https：//www.fmprc.gov.cn/web/fyrbt_ 673021/jzhsl_ 673025/t1790422. shtml，最后访问日期：2020 年 7 月 26 日。

〔2〕刘思伟：《加勒万河谷事件：中印关系的大转折?》，载环球网，https：//opinion. huan-qiu. com/article/3ytIXIWU4gg，最后访问日期：2020 年 7 月 26 日。

〔3〕《2020 年 6 月 19 日外交部发言人赵立坚主持例行记者会》，载中华人民共和国外交部网站，https：//www.fmprc.gov.cn/web/fyrbt_ 673021/jzhsl_ 673025/t1790422. shtml，最后访问日期：2020 年 7 月 26 日。

〔4〕黄惠馨、杨弘杨：《印度宣布将禁止中资企业参与印度道路建设项目 外交部回应》，载中国一带一路网，https：//www. yidaiyilu. gov. cn/xwzx/gnxw/135473. htm，最后访问日期：2020 年 7 月 26 日。

〔5〕"Members and Prospective Members of the Bank"，AIIB，https：//www. aiib. org/en/about-aiib/governance/members-of-bank/index. html，August 24，2020.

化金砖伙伴关系，开辟更加光明未来"的主题，就全球政治经济形势、金砖合作、国际和地区热点问题等与其他金砖国家领导人深入交换意见。[1]

（2）基于本土互联互通计划，展开对"一带一路"的对抗和竞争

2014 年 6 月，莫迪政府推出"季风计划"，尝试"借古谋今"，深化环印度洋地区的互利合作。通过"季风计划"的实施，印度谋求可持续的区域战略利益，保障更加牢固的地区领导权，进而实现印度的全球战略抱负。[2]"季风计划"一经提出，就被印度各界普遍解读为印度版的"21 世纪海上丝绸之路"，是能够同中国"一带一路"相抗衡的重大战略构想。[3]。除"季风计划"外，印度还提出了"香料之路""棉花之路""佛教之路"，其与"季风计划"异曲同工，均是意图通过一些历史文化符号，把印度与周边地区串联起来，形成与"一带一路"不同维度的互联互通计划，与"一带一路"开展战略竞争。

（3）借助于其他大国提出的互联互通计划和区域合作计划，平衡对冲"一带一路"的影响

针对"一带一路"，日本于 2015 年提出了"高质量基础设施伙伴计划"，准备未来五年投入 2000 亿美元用于日本、东南亚和南亚地区的互联互通。印度对该计划不断高调表示支持。2016 年，莫迪访问伊朗，两国签署了《关于恰巴哈尔港的开发与运营的双边协议》，[4] 印度、阿富汗、伊朗三方也签署了《建立恰巴哈尔港运输与过境走廊的三方协定》，根据协议，印度将投资 5 亿美元用于翻新和建设恰巴哈尔港，该港口将为印度的货物和产品开辟一条通往阿富汗和中亚的中转路线，避免经过巴基斯坦的陆路，这一举措将与其临近的中巴经济走廊形成巨大竞争。[5] 2017 年 5 月 22—26 日，在印度举行的第 52 届非洲开发银行年会（The 52nd Annual Meeting of the African Develop-

〔1〕《金砖国家（BRICS）》，载中华人民共和国外交部网站，https：//www. fmprc. gov. cn/web/wjb_ 673085/zzjg_ 673183/gjjjs_ 674249/gjzzyhygk_ 674253/jzgj_ 674283/gk_ 674285/，最后访问日期：2020 年 8 月 22 日。

〔2〕王沥慷：《印度：季风计划》，载中国一带一路网，https：//www. yidaiyilu. gov. cn/zchj/gjjj/1060. htm，最后访问日期：2020 年 8 月 20 日。

〔3〕梅冠群：《印度对"一带一路"倡议的态度及成因》，载《东南亚南亚研究》2018 年第 1 期，第 52—60 页。

〔4〕"India, Iran Moving Forward on Redeveloping Chabahar Port", JOC. com, https：//www. joc. com/port-news/international-ports/india-iran-move-forward-redevelopment-chabahar-port_ 20160509. html, August 24, 2020.

〔5〕"Chabahar port：India, Afghanistan, Iran Agree on Routes for Trade and Transit Corridors", Livemint, https：//www. livemint. com/Politics/8kwV0d4RJafJ1zGkqJ7GgP/Chabahar-port-India-Afghan-istan-Iran-agree-on-routes-for. html, August 24, 2020.

ment Bank Summit）上，印度和日本宣布了共同构想的“亚非增长走廊”（Asia-Africa Growth Corridor，AAGC）。莫迪在声明中表示，印度和日本都致力于在非洲实现更紧密的发展合作。非洲和日本代表出席了这次会议，使这一宣布具有重要意义。值得注意的是，这份声明是在 2017 年 5 月 14—15 日在北京举行的“一带一路”高峰论坛背景下作出的，而印度并未参加本次论坛。分析人士认为，印度此举是有意为之，其目的是抗衡中国的“一带一路”倡议，尤其是“一带一路”倡议中所涉及的非洲和印度洋地区的项目。[1]

可以看到，一方面，印度担心中国的“一带一路”倡议对其构成威胁，拒绝、排斥、反对参与“一带一路”的相关合作，并积极采取一系列对冲措施进行战略对抗；另一方面，在“一带一路”建设取得巨大成果的情况下，印度又不忍错过重要的发展机遇，因而有选择地与中国进行合作。虽然对印度而言，这些合作都并非在“一带一路”的名义之下进行，但对中国来说，这些合作无疑都是“一带一路”框架下的合作。

结　语

总体而言，作为南亚次大陆第一大国，印度的海洋渔业及矿物资源都十分丰富，扼守着世界上最为重要的海洋通道之一，其海洋战略的图谋与海洋经济的潜力都令人侧目。印度国内虽保有传统的印度教法和穆斯林法等宗教法，但是也深受英国殖民时期遗留的普通法体系的影响。印度是 1982 年《公约》的缔约国，其积极缔结主要的国际海洋法条约，也是国际海事组织的成员国，还加入了涉及印度洋及附近地区渔业资源的国际条约。印度与周边国家在海洋划界问题上倾向于先协商和谈判，并达成协定遵守，对彼此分歧较大的争端才以诉诸国际司法机制的方式解决。印度对中菲之间的“南海仲裁案”采取的立场并非中立，因其既支持仲裁庭的成立，也多次在外交场合与越南、日本等国呼吁确保南海地区的“航行自由”，并将其与孟加拉国之间的海洋争端解决树立为国际社会的榜样。针对中国提出的“一带一路”倡议，印度呈现出防范心态下谨慎平衡与有限合作的基本姿态。

---

〔1〕 Jagannath P. Panda，“Asia-Africa Growth Corridor（AAGC）：An India-Japan Arch in the Making?”，http：//isdp. eu/publication/asia-africa-growth-corridor-aagc-india-japan/，August 24，2020.

第 II 部分

巴基斯坦海洋法律体系研究

一、巴基斯坦海洋基本情况

巴基斯坦伊斯兰共和国（The Islamic Republic of Pakistan，以下简称"巴基斯坦"），建国时间虽短，却有着悠久的历史和文化。早在 5000 年前，这里就孕育了灿烂的印度河文明。作为与印度历史同源的国家，1858 年其作为印度之一部分沦为英国殖民地，成为英属印度的一部分。1940 年 3 月，全印穆斯林联盟通过了关于建立巴基斯坦的决议。1947 年 6 月，英国公布"蒙巴顿方案"，实行印巴分治。同年 8 月 14 日，巴基斯坦宣告独立，成为英联邦的一个自治领，分为东、西巴基斯坦。1956 年 3 月 23 日，巴基斯坦伊斯兰共和国成立，仍为英联邦成员国，曾于 1972 年退出，后于 1989 年重新加入英联邦。1971 年，因国内矛盾尖锐和大国势力介入，巴基斯坦发生分裂，东巴基斯坦独立为孟加拉人民共和国。[1]

（一）海洋地理概况

巴基斯坦位于南亚次大陆西北部，东接印度，东北与中国毗邻，西北与阿富汗交界，西邻伊朗，南濒阿拉伯海，国土面积为 79.6 万平方公里（不含巴控克什米尔的 1.3 万平方公里），海岸线全长 980 公里。除南部属热带气候外，其余属亚热带气候。南部湿热，受季风影响，雨季较长；北部地区干燥寒冷，部分地区终年积雪。[2]

巴基斯坦全境五分之三为山区和丘陵地形，地势北高南低、西高东低。北部的高山区主要由喀喇昆仑山脉（the Karakoram）、兴都库什山脉（the Hindukush）和部分喜马拉雅山脉（the Himalayas）构成，分布着大量的冰川、高山湖泊和巨大山谷，并拥有包括世界第二高峰乔戈里峰（Qogir，亦称"K-2 峰"，海拔 8611 米）在内的 35 座海拔超过 7300 米的山峰。西部低山区则覆盖了开伯尔-普什图赫瓦省（Khyber Pukhtoonkhwa Province）的大部分地区，山区被山谷和山口切断，包括著名的开伯尔山口（Khyber Pass），其

---

〔1〕 中华人民共和国商务部：《对外投资合作国别（地区）指南——巴基斯坦（2018 年版）》，载中国一带一路网，https：//www.yidaiyilu.gov.cn/wcm.files/upload/CMSydylgw/201902/2019 02010412036.pdf，最后访问日期：2019 年 11 月 22 日。

〔2〕 中华人民共和国外交部：《巴基斯坦国家概况》，载中华人民共和国外交部网站，https：//www.fmprc.gov.cn/web/gjhdq_676201/gj_676203/yz_676205/1206_676308/1206x0_676310/，最后访问日期：2019 年 11 月 22 日。

全长 56 公里，是连接中亚和南亚次大陆的要塞。东部平原区主要包括旁遮普平原（The Punjab Plain）和信德平原（The Sindh Plain），同时分布着大片的沙漠。南部沿海也有沙漠分布。[1] 发源于中国的印度河全长 2300 千米，自东北向西南流经巴基斯坦全境，最后汇入阿拉伯海，是巴基斯坦第一大河。[2]

总体来看，国土较为狭长的巴基斯坦只有南部偏少比例的国境邻接海洋，其总共不足 1000 公里的海岸线也无法与其邻国印度比肩。但自古以来，巴基斯坦地区就与阿富汗一并被视为南亚、中亚、西亚的"十字路口"，其面向阿拉伯海的出海口更使其成为周边国家的战略要冲。除印度外，巴基斯坦的陆地邻国中，阿富汗及虽未相接却仅数十公里相隔的塔吉克斯坦为内陆国家，巴基斯坦是其通向世界大洋的必由之路；而尽管中国有着面向东海及南海的漫长海岸线，巴基斯坦仍是中国当前通往印度洋最为重要和便利的战略要道；同时，伊朗虽在波斯湾有着较明显的地理优势，但波斯湾相对水域狭长曲折且周边局势复杂，巴基斯坦的阿拉伯海出口则仍扼守其通向印度洋的海上要道。

（二）政治概况

巴基斯坦实行多党制，现有大约 200 个政党，派系众多，全国性大党主要有：正义运动党（Pakistan Tehreek-e-Insaf）、巴基斯坦穆斯林联盟（谢里夫派）（Pakistan Muslim League-Nawaz）、巴基斯坦人民党（Pakistan People's Party）、巴基斯坦穆斯林联盟（领袖派）［Pakistan Muslim League（QA）］等。现任总统为阿里夫·阿尔维（Arif Alvi），于 2018 年 9 月 9 日宣誓就职。现任总理为伊姆兰·汗（Imran Khan），2018 年 8 月 18 日就任。

行政区划上，巴基斯坦全国共有四大省及伊斯兰堡首都特区（Islamabad Capital Territory）。四大省分别是俾路支省（Province of Balochistan）、开伯尔-普什图赫瓦省（Khyber Pakhtunkhwa）、旁遮普省（Province of Punjab）和信德省（Province of Sindh）。首都位于伊斯兰堡（Islamabad）。伊斯兰教为巴基斯坦国教，全国 95% 以上的居民信奉伊斯兰教，少数人信奉基督教、印度教

〔1〕 "Pakistan", Thecommonwealth, https：//thecommonwealth. org/our-member-countries/pakistan, March 20, 2021.

〔2〕 中华人民共和国驻巴基斯坦大使馆经济商务参赞处：《巴基斯坦概况》，载中华人民共和国商务部网站，http：//pk. mofcom. gov. cn/article/ddgk/，最后访问日期：2020 年 11 月 22 日。

和锡克教等。[1]

（三）经济概况

经过多年的发展，巴基斯坦的经济已逐渐从建国之初的农业经济发展为如今的半工业化经济，在经济建设和经济改革方面取得了巨大成就。2018 财年，巴基斯坦的国民生产总值为 3125.7 亿美元，年增长率达 5.4%。[2] 世界银行发布的《2020 年全球营商环境报告》显示，由于积极推进监管措施改革，巴基斯坦的营商环境排名较之前上升 28 名，升至第 108 位，跻身全球十大营商环境改善国之列。[3]

然而，农业仍为巴基斯坦的支柱产业，农业产值占国内生产总值的近 20%。2018 年，全国 2.12 亿人口中，贫困人口比例占全国总人口的 24.3%。[4] 由于深受季风影响，气候异常和自然灾害对巴基斯坦的农业构成直接而巨大的威胁。同时，巴基斯坦的工业基础仍较为薄弱，工业结构发展不均衡，工业体系不够健全。纺织业是巴基斯坦最大及最重要的工业部门，贡献了近 1/4 的工业增加值，并为 40% 的工业劳动力提供了就业岗位，在国家对外出口中占据 60% 的份额。[5]

2018—2019 财年，巴基斯坦的出口额为 200.9 亿美元，较前一财年下降 1.9%。出口的商品主要为棉花、纱线产品、大米、纺织品和皮革等，进口的商品主要为重型机械、运输车辆、原材料和石油等，主要对外贸易伙伴为中国、欧盟、阿联酋、美国和沙特阿拉伯。其中，中国是其最大的对外贸易伙伴。[6]

---

〔1〕 中华人民共和国外交部：《巴基斯坦国家概况》，载中华人民共和国外交部网站，https://www.fmprc.gov.cn/web/gjhdq_676201/gj_676203/yz_676205/1206_676308/1206x0_676310/，最后访问日期：2020 年 11 月 22 日。

〔2〕 "Country Profile-Pakistan", The World Bank, https://databank.worldbank.org/views/reports/reportwidget.aspx? Report_Name = CountryProfile&Id = b450fd57&tbar = y&dd = y&inf = n&zm = n&country = PAK, March 20, 2021.

〔3〕 "Doing Business2020", TheWorld Bank, https://www.doingbusiness.org/, March 20, 2021.

〔4〕 "Country Profile-Pakistan", The World Bank, https://databank.worldbank.org/views/reports/reportwidget.aspx? Report_Name = CountryProfile&Id = b450fd57&tbar = y&dd = y&inf = n&zm = n&country = PAK, March 20, 2021.

〔5〕 中华人民共和国商务部：《对外投资合作国别（地区）指南——巴基斯坦（2018 年版）》，载中国一带一路网，https://www.yidaiyilu.gov.cn/wcm.files/upload/CMSydylgw/201902/201902010412036.pdf，最后访问日期：2019 年 11 月 22 日。

〔6〕 "Index", Pakbj, http://www.pakbj.org/index.php? m = content&c = index&a = show&catid = 29&id = 2, March 20, 2021.

（四）外交关系

1. 外交政策及目标

巴基斯坦奉行独立自主和不结盟的外交政策，注重发展同伊斯兰国家和中国的关系，致力于维护南亚地区的和平与稳定，并支持中东的和平进程，主张销毁大规模杀伤性武器。在加强同发展中国家团结合作的同时，巴基斯坦也积极发展同西方国家的关系，积极参与各类国际组织和国际活动，主张建立公正合理的国际政治经济新秩序。[1]

巴基斯坦《宪法》第 40 条规定，其国家外交政策的准则为："国家应在伊斯兰统一的基础上，维持和加强伊斯兰国家间的友好关系，支持亚洲、非洲和拉丁美洲人民的共同利益，促进国际和平与安全，与各国建立友好关系，并倡导以和平方式解决国际争端。"巴基斯坦外交政策的六大目标可概括为：第一，促进巴基斯坦成为一个充满活力、进步、温和、民主的伊斯兰国家；第二，与世界各国，尤其是主要大国和邻国发展友好关系；第三，维护国家安全及包括克什米尔在内的地缘战略利益；第四，巩固与国际社会的经贸合作；第五，维护巴基斯坦海外侨民的利益；第六，确保最大程度地利用国家资源进行区域和国际合作。[2]

2. 与印度的关系

巴基斯坦和印度于 1947 年、1965 年和 1971 年三次爆发战争。1971 年巴印断交，1976 年复交。2004 年以来，巴印启动全面对话进程，双边关系持续缓和，但双边摩擦仍时有发生。2018 年 5 月，巴、印达成一致，同意遵守2003 年签订的停火协议，恢复查谟和克什米尔地区的和平。同年 7 月，印度总理莫迪同巴基斯坦正义运动党主席伊姆兰·汗通话，对其带领的正义运动党在大选中获胜表示祝贺。同年 8 月，莫迪总理向伊姆兰·汗总理致就职贺信，提议双方开展建设性互动。同年 9 月，印度外交部确认两国外长将在纽约第 73 届联大期间会见。此后，印媒爆出所谓巴方残杀印控克区警察和巴基斯坦发行克区"自由战士"邮票等消息，印度外交部宣布取消两国外长会面，巴印关系改善势头受挫。同年 11 月，巴印启动印度锡克教徒赴巴基斯坦朝圣边境走廊建设，巴基斯坦举行奠基仪式，伊姆兰·汗总理、多名巴基斯坦军政高官与印度官员共同出席仪式。但双方政府在此前后多次就克什米尔

---

〔1〕 中华人民共和国外交部：《巴基斯坦国家概况》，载中华人民共和国外交部网站，https：//www. fmprc. gov. cn/web/gjhdq＿676201/gj＿676203/yz＿676205/1206＿676308/1206x0＿676310/，最后访问日期：2019 年 11 月 22 日。

〔2〕 "Profile"，Ministryof Foreign Affairs，http：//www. mofa. gov. pk/，March 20，2021.

问题相互指责[1]。由于两国间的矛盾涉及复杂的历史、政治、文化原因，可以预见，在未来相当长时间内，要彻底消除影响两国关系发展的障碍仍较为困难。

3. 与中国的关系

巴基斯坦是最早承认新中国的国家之一。自 1951 年 5 月巴中建交以来，两国关系始终密切友好。多年来，两国关系不断深化，已发展成为"全天候战略伙伴关系"，巴基斯坦视中国为其最亲密的朋友和伙伴之一，中国视巴基斯坦为"铁兄弟"[2]。政治上，两国高层经常互访并开展政治对话；经济上，中国是巴基斯坦最大的贸易伙伴和主要投资者，特别是在基础设施建设和能源领域，两国合作密切。巴基斯坦是中国"一带一路"倡议的坚定支持者，"中巴经济走廊"（China-Pakistan Economic Corridor）则是中国"一带一路"倡议南线的重点项目。2019 年 11 月 5 日，中巴经济走廊联合合作委员会第九次会议在巴基斯坦首都伊斯兰堡召开。来自巴中两国政府、金融机构和企业的代表约 200 人参加会议。巴中双方签署了本次联委会会议纪要，签署并交换了在医疗卫生、青年交流和瓜达尔港建设方面的三个合作文件[3]。

（五）海洋资源利用情况

巴基斯坦拥有漫长的海岸线，并依据《公约》主张拥有 290000 平方公里的专属经济区及大陆架，海洋资源十分丰富。其中，海洋生物资源主要包括以下几种：第一，各种珍稀的脊椎动物。如，阿拉伯座头鲸、鳍鲸、蓝鲸、抹香鲸、虎鲸、宽吻海豚和飞旋海豚等。第二，各种鱼类、贝类和无脊椎动物。巴基斯坦沿岸地区的鳍鱼类和贝类超过 1500 种，其中用于商业捕捞的约有 200 种。虾是最主要的出口商品，螃蟹、龙虾、鱿鱼、墨鱼和一些软体动物也大量出口。鳍鱼类中，沙丁鱼、金枪鱼、黄花鱼、鲷鱼、鲳鱼、鲨鱼、鲶鱼、梭鱼、河豚和鳗鱼是重要的捕捞对象。第三，海龟。巴基斯坦拥有世界上七种海龟中的五种，包括绿海龟、榄蠵龟、棱皮龟、玳瑁龟和赤蠵

〔1〕　中华人民共和国外交部：《巴基斯坦国家概况》，载中华人民共和国外交部网站，https：//www. fmprc. gov. cn/web/gjhdq_676201/gj_676203/yz_676205/1206_676308/1206x0_676310/，最后访问日期：2019 年 11 月 22 日。

〔2〕　巴基斯坦驻华大使馆在介绍巴中双边关系时称："Pakistan considers China as one of its closest friend and partner and China considers Pakistan as its 'Iron Brother'"。See Embassy of the Islamic Republic of Pakistan Beijing, "Bilateral Relations Relations between Pakistan and China", http：//www. pakbj. org/index. php? m = content&c = index&a = show&catid = 29&id = 10, July 25, 2020。

〔3〕　《中巴经济走廊联委会举行第九次会议》，载中国一带一路网，https：//www. yidaiyilu. gov. cn/slxwzy/108915. htm，最后访问日期：2019 年 11 月 22 日。

龟。第四，珊瑚、海藻和红树林。巴基斯坦拥有 29 种珊瑚、200 余种海藻以及丰富的红树林资源。其中，全国大约 97% 的红树林都分布在印度河三角洲地区。该地区曾经有 8 种红树林树种，但由于环境恶化，其中 4 种已经灭绝。现存的红树林主要是白骨壤（Avicennia marina）红树林，占比达到 90%。近年来，由于过度捕捞、气候变化以及海洋污染等问题的加重，巴基斯坦海洋动物和植物的生存受到了严重威胁。为此，巴基斯坦也通过制定专门法律、建立生态保护区和海洋保护区、加强地区合作等方式积极保护各类海洋生物资源。[1]

在非生物资源方面，巴基斯坦的勘探开采活动并不顺利。早在 20 世纪 60 年代，各大石油公司就先后在巴基斯坦沿海进行石油勘探活动，但一直未有收获。美国石油巨头埃克森美孚公司（ExxonMobil）曾在巴基斯坦近海投入巨额资金，与意大利埃尼石油公司（ENI）、巴基斯坦国家石油天然气开发有限公司（Pakistan State-owned Oil and Gas Development Company Limited）和巴基斯坦石油有限公司（Pakistan Petroleum Limited）共同进行海洋油气资源开发，并一度认为该海域油气储量或超科威特。[2] 2019 年 3 月，巴基斯坦总理也对外宣称，巴基斯坦即将发现巨大的海洋油气储存，这将使巴基斯坦跃升为世界重要的产油国，巴基斯坦将不再需要进口石油，国内能源短缺的局面将大大改善。他同时表示，4 月会正式公布勘探结果。[3] 然而至该年 5 月，巴基斯坦遗憾地宣布，在经过 17 次尝试之后，在该海域并未发现任何油气资源。[4]

在海洋运输和港口建设方面，巴基斯坦本国海运能力较弱，全国仅有 15 艘远洋货轮，总载重量为 63.6 万吨，因此，其进出口货物多依赖外轮。巴基斯坦国家航运公司（Pakistan National Shipping Corporation）是巴基斯坦唯一的国营航运公司，拥有各类货轮 9 艘。目前，巴基斯坦共有三大海港，分别是卡拉奇港（Karachi Port）、卡西姆港（Port Qasim）和瓜达尔港（Gwadar Port）。其中，卡拉奇港是巴基斯坦主要的集装箱港，卡西姆港是煤炭、液化

---

〔1〕 "Ahandbookon Pakistan's Coastaland Marine Resources", IUCN, https：//www.iucn.org/sites/dev/files/pk_coastal_resources_handbook.pdf, March 20, 2021.

〔2〕 "ExxonMobil Close to Hitting Huge Oil Reserves in Pakistan, Bigger than Kuwait's", Arabnews, https：//www.arabnews.com/node/1351556/world, March 20, 2021.

〔3〕 "Pakistan's Massive Oil and Gas Discovery Report to be Out in April", Gulfnews, https：//gulfnews.com/world/asia/pakistan/pakistans-massive-oil-and-gas-discovery-report-to-be-out-in-april-1.62968777, March 20, 2021.

〔4〕 "No Oil, Gas Reserves Found off Pakistan Shore", Tribune, https：//tribune.com.pk/story/1975799/2-18th-drilling-attempt-fails-find-oil-gas-reserves-off-pakistan-shore/, March 20, 2021.

天然气、水泥进出口港。2018—2019 财年，卡拉奇港的吞吐量为 35361000 吨，卡西姆港的吞吐量为 36580000 吨，共承担了巴基斯坦 99% 的国际货物贸易量。中国援建的瓜达尔港位于波斯湾海域霍尔木兹海峡（The Strait of Hormuz）湾口处，距卡拉奇约 460 公里，距伊朗边境约 120 公里，是一个温水深海港。2013 年，中国海外港口控股有限公司（China Overseas Ports Holding Company Limited，以下简称"中国港控公司"）、瓜达尔港务局（Gwadar Port Authority）和新加坡港务集团（Port of Singapore Authority）三方签署《特许经营权协议》，中国港控公司接管了 923 公顷自由区的开发与经营。自由区基础设施已建设完毕，商务中心已投入使用，并于 2018 年 1 月 29 日举行了开园仪式。预计到 2055 年，瓜达尔港将成为巴基斯坦的最大港口。[1]

---

〔1〕 "Pakistan Economic Survey 2018-19", Finance Division of Government of Pakistan, http://www. finance. gov. pk/survey/chapters_ 19/Economic_ Survey_ 2018_ 19. pdf, March 20, 2021.

二、海洋事务主管部门及其职能

(一) 基本政治结构

1. 立法机关

巴基斯坦的最高立法机关为议会，由国民议会（National Assembly，即"下院"）和参议院（Senate，即"上院"）组成。其中，国民议会经普选产生，而参议院按每省议席均等的原则，由省议会和国民议会选出。

国民议会共有342席，其中，普通席位272个，女性席位60个，非穆斯林席位10个。国民议会议员任期5年，可连选连任。其主要职能包括：省议会的联席选举、罢免总统、通过总统对总理的提名、通过法律和法令、制定税收政策、审议提案、审批年度财政预算等。[1] 参议院共有104个议席，设主席、副主席各1名。参议员任期6年，每3年改选其中1/2。参议院有权通过自己提出的法律和法令或由国民议会转呈的法律和法令。参议院主席在总统不能履行其职责时代行总统职务。参议院每年至少召开3次会议，每次会期不得少于90天。[2]

2. 行政机关

巴基斯坦联邦的行政权力由其联邦政府以总统的名义执行。[3] 总统由议会及各省级议会成员选出，是国家元首、军队的最高指挥以及国家统一与荣誉的象征。非经总统同意，议会不得通过除财政法案外的其他立法提案。在议会休会期间如遇紧急事态，总统有权颁布"法令"（Ordinance）就相关事项立法。但该类"法令"将在6个月后失效，除非于期限届满时获议会通过成为"法案"（Act）。[4]

联邦政府由总理及联邦各部长组成。总理由国民议会多数选举产生，由

---

〔1〕 "Introduction", National Assembly of Pakistan, http：//www. na. gov. pk/en/index. php#, March 20, 2021.

〔2〕 "Overview", Senate of Pakistan, http：//senate. gov. pk/en/index. php? id = -1&cattitle = Home, March 20, 2021.

〔3〕 See Article 41, The Constitution of the Islamic Republic of Pakistan, The Pakistan Code, http：//pakistancode. gov. pk/english/UY2FqaJw1-apaUY2Fqa-apaUY2Fvbpw% 3D-sg-jjjjjjjjjjjjjj, March 20, 2021.

〔4〕 Omar Sial & Farah Khan, "UPDATE：A Legal Research Guide to Pakistan", https：//www. nyulawglobal. org/globalex/Pakistan1. html#President, March 20, 2021.

其带领内阁协助总统执行职权或向其提出建议。总统将在总理的建议下任命内阁成员，成员中 75% 来自国民议会，25% 来自参议院。内阁连同国务部长共同向参议院及国民议会负责。[1]

3. 司法机关

巴基斯坦司法机关由上级司法机构和下级司法机构组成。上级司法机构由最高法院、高级法院和伊斯兰教法院组成。下级司法机构由民事法院、刑事法院、行政法院和特殊法院组成。最高法院由 1 名首席法官和 16 名陪审法官组成，最高法院法官由司法委员会向议会委员会提名，议会委员会应将其确认的或视为已确认的提名人名单提交总统予以任命。最高法院是最高的司法权力机关，有权解释宪法和法律、审理政府和各省之间的争端。[2]

（二）海洋管理相关的行政机构

巴基斯坦中央政府下设 34 个政府部门，其中与海洋事务有关的政府部门主要包括：外交部（Ministry of Foreign Affairs）、国家粮食安全和研究部（Ministry of National Food Security and Research）、海事部（Ministry of Maritime Affairs）、能源部（Ministry of Energy）、科技部（Ministry of Science and Technology）等。

1. 外交部

外交部负责处理巴基斯坦的外交事务，推行外交政策。除推行前述宪法规定的巴基斯坦外交政策之外，外交部也负责维护国家驻外机构的外交和领事地位，承担相关国际条约的签署及参与事务，同时不断向国际社会申明和宣传巴基斯坦的海洋事务立场与政策目标。在外交部有效运行之下，巴基斯坦签署或参加了一系列的海洋相关条约，既包括联合国海洋法会议下相关条约、国际海事组织框架下系列条约、区域国际组织框架下相关条约等多边条约，也包括与周边国家划定管辖海域相关的双边条约；内容涉及海上主权、海上安全、海洋环境保护、渔业发展与管理、船舶及船员管理，等等。[3]

---

〔1〕　See Article 90-91, The Constitution of the Islamic Republic of Pakistan, The Pakistan Code, http://pakistancode. gov. pk/english/UY2FqaJw1-apaUY2Fqa-apaUY2Fvbpw% 3D-sg-jjjjjjjjjjjjj, March 20, 2021.

〔2〕　"Home", Ministry of Law and Justice of Government of Pakistan, http://www. molaw. gov. pk/, March 20, 2021.

〔3〕　"Profiles", Ministry of Foreign affairs of Government of Pakistan, http://www. mofa. gov. pk/contentlist. php, March 20, 2021.

2. 国家粮食安全和研究部

农业是巴基斯坦 62% 人口的主要生计来源，在巴基斯坦经济中起着至关重要的作用，其农业出口收入占总出口收入的 65%，占该国总附加值的 19.5%。巴基斯坦是一个农业多样化的国家，共有 12 个农业生态区，采用 35 种以上农作物和牲畜混合养殖的制度。[1] 实现国家粮食安全和营养充足是巴基斯坦自独立以来所有政策、规划、战略的核心目标之一。

国家粮食安全和研究部的前身是粮食和农业部 （Ministry of Food and Agriculture）。根据巴基斯坦《宪法第 18 次修正案》，自 2011 年 6 月 3 日起，有关粮食和农业部的职能被下放到各省。为了维持国家的粮食安全并更好地执行粮食和农业部未转移的职能，巴基斯坦政府于 2011 年 10 月 16 日成立了国家粮食安全和研究部。国家粮食安全和研究部的主要职能在于：第一，减轻国民贫困，消除国民的饥饿和营养不良情况，促进农业经济的可持续发展，通过升级农业技术增加农产品产量；第二，制定全面的农业领域规划，完善农产品的生产、加工、销售环节，向农民提供直接的技术援助，完善国家一级和省一级的农业政策；第三，对农产品的进出口进行检验和管制，制定农产品进出口的质量标准，对农产品的生产、消费、价格和进出口情况进行统计；第四，密切关注国内外市场的粮食价格，通过采购和发布行政命令来稳定粮食价格，对国内农产品进行补贴，防止粮食价格波动过大；第五，对土地资源和水资源进行充分有效的利用，确保在农业领域的科研投入，对畜牧业、渔业、养蜂业等领域的养殖方式进行改革创新；第六，制订粮食、化肥、农药的采购计划，为私营企业和外国企业对本国农业领域的投资创造有利环境，改善农业领域的基础设施，并致力于培养专业化的农业人才。[2]

国家粮食安全和研究部下属的渔业发展局 （Fisheries Development Board） 成立于 2007 年。进入 21 世纪以来，渔业和水产养殖业在巴基斯坦国家经济发展中逐渐受到重视，为了充分开发利用国家的渔业资源，国家粮食安全和研究部制定了《国家渔业政策》，并据此成立了渔业发展局。渔业发展局的主要职能包括：第一，管理与协调全国及各省的渔业和水产养殖活动，促进各方在国家鱼类养殖领域和虾类养殖领域的投资；第二，促进国内外投资者在渔业领域的合作，并与政府其他部门合作保护渔业领域的投资环境；第

---

〔1〕 "Introduction", Ministry of National Food Security and Research of Government of Pakistan, http: //www. mnfsr. gov. pk/, March 20, 2021.

〔2〕 "National Food Security Policy ", Ministry of National Food Security and Research of Government of Pakistan, http: //www. mnfsr. gov. pk/userfiles1/file/National% 20Food% 20Security% 20Policy% 20% 202018% 20 （1）. pdf, March 20, 2021.

三，完善市场基础设施并改善渔业产品的销售状况，为国家渔业产品探索出口市场；第四，加强对渔业产品的质量管理，并根据国际标准建立渔业部门的监管体系。[1]

3. 海事部

海事部本隶属于交通部。2004 年，港口和航运部（Ministry of Ports and Shipping）从交通部独立成为一个新兴部门。2017 年 10 月，港口和航运部更名为海事部。巴基斯坦在从中亚到世界其他地区的国际海上运输中具有至关重要的地位，航运是国家对外贸易和经济发展的支柱之一，海事部承担着支持国家航运发展的重任。海事部的主要职能包括：第一，按照国际标准建设和发展国家港口，制定实施符合国际实践的港口政策，使巴基斯坦港口转变为现代化国际转运中心，鼓励国内外各方在航运领域的投资，确保国家航运业的竞争力；第二，确保国家对航运业的后勤支持，建立并修缮沿海基础设施来保障船舶的安全航行；第三，确保可持续地利用和开发国家海洋渔业资源，根据国际海事组织相关公约制定符合国际要求的防污标准，积极采取措施保护和恢复海洋生态环境；第四，负责管理和监督巴基斯坦的港口运营，促进国家航运业的发展，提供政策指导以鼓励港口发展和航运业的增长，并制定相关安全标准；第五，对巴基斯坦海员进行培训和资质考核，确保巴基斯坦海员的资质水平符合《1978 年海员培训、发证和值班标准国际公约》。[2] 海事部中直接负责海洋事务的下属机构主要有八个部门。

（1）卡拉奇港口信托基金会

卡拉奇港口信托基金会（Karachi Port Trust）负责监督和管理卡拉奇港的日常事务。卡拉奇港由卡拉奇港口信托基金会的董事会管理，董事会由主席和 10 名受托人组成。其中，董事会主席由联邦政府任命，兼任卡拉奇港口信托基金会首席执行官；其余 10 名受托人名额在公共机构和私营机构平均分配，5 名公共部门受托人由联邦政府提名，5 名私营部门受托人的席位由各私营部门组织选出的代表填补。卡拉奇港是南亚最大、最繁忙的深水海港之一，也是巴基斯坦最大的港口，它靠近霍尔木兹海峡等主要航运线路，并处理巴基斯坦全国近 60% 的海运业务。卡拉奇港口有 2 个国际集装箱码头，分别为卡拉奇国际集装箱码头和巴基斯坦国际集装箱码头；有 30 个干货泊位，其中 17 个位于东码头，13 个位于西码头；有 3 个液体货物泊位。卡拉

---

[1] "About Us", Fisheries Development Bureau of Government of Pakistan, http://fdb. org. pk/, March 20, 2021.

[2] "About Us", Ministry of Maritime Affairs of Government of Pakistan, https://moma. gov. pk/? _ escaped_ fragment_ =, March 20, 2021.

奇港口每年可处理 65 万个集装箱和 2600 万吨货物。[1]

（2）卡西姆港务局

卡西姆港务局（Port Qasim Authority）于 1973 年 6 月 29 日建立，负责监督和管理卡西姆港的日常事务。卡西姆港由卡西姆港务局董事会管理，董事会由主席和 7 名成员组成，董事长是港口的首席执行官，7 名成员分别来自公共部门和私营部门。卡西姆港位于卡拉奇东南 28 海里处的印度河三角洲地区，处于阿拉伯海沿岸的贸易路线上。该港拥有 17 个泊位，包括 2 个边际码头、1 个钢铁和煤炭泊位、2 个集装箱码头。该港还拥有约 55.7 平方千米的土地用于发展港口工业和综合商业。该港口目前满足了巴基斯坦 40% 以上的海运贸易需求。[2]

（3）瓜达尔港务局

瓜达尔港由瓜达尔港务局（Gwadar Port Authority）董事会管理，董事会由 11 名成员组成。瓜达尔港位于巴基斯坦俾路支省西部的阿拉伯海沿岸，距卡拉奇约 533 公里，距伊朗约 120 公里。瓜达尔港位于霍尔木兹海峡外波斯湾入口，靠近进出波斯湾的主要航道。瓜达尔港被认为是中巴友谊的伟大纪念碑，港口的基石由中国前副总理吴邦国于 2002 年 3 月奠基。随着港口一期工程的完成，瓜达尔有望成为南亚和中东地区最重要的现代城市之一，瓜达尔港也有望成为南亚甚至全球的重要港口。该港建成后将与卡拉奇港、卡西姆港形成经济贸易和航运上的互补，进一步刺激巴基斯坦经济的发展。[3]

（4）政府船务办公室

政府船务办公室（Government Shipping Office）于 1948 年 5 月 15 日在卡拉奇港成立，该办公室原隶属于商务部，后转归交通部管辖，现隶属于海事部。政府船务办公室的主要职能有：第一，根据政府政策，为海员签发海员服务手册和海员身份证以供其在工作中使用，并在政府船务办公室内保存海员的服务记录。第二，根据《商船法令》（The Merchant Shipping Ordinance）和《商船规则》（The Merchant Shipping Rules），制定船员上船作业的规章制度，并监督和管理船员的上岗和退职。第三，为国内外船舶提供海员，在签发船舶卫生证时为海员安排体检，协调解决船员和雇主之间有关工资、津贴

---

[1] "About Us", Karachi Port Trust, https：//kpt. gov. pk/pages/38/about% 20-us, March 20, 2021.

[2] "Introduction", Port Qasim Authority, https：//www. pqa. gov. pk/en/about-us/introduction, March 20, 2021.

[3] "Vision and Mission", Gwadar Port Authority, http：//www. gwadarport. gov. pk/vision. aspx, March 20, 2021；Gwadar Port Authority, "Gwadar Port", http：//www. gwadarport. gov. pk/a-bout% 20us. aspx, March 20, 2021.

及衣食住行等生活方面的纠纷，并通过国家福利委员会提高海员的福利待遇。[1]

第四，审核船舶文件并批准船舶的入港申请，确保做好船舶维修工作。[1]

（5）商船局

商船局（Mercantile Marine Department）成立于1930年，负责各类船舶的安全检查和资格检验，对各类海员进行资格考核，依据国内法律法规和国际公约采取相关措施来确保海上人员的生命安全、船舶的航行安全，保护海洋环境免遭破坏。其主要职能包括：第一，根据《商船条例》和《港口法》（Port Act）等国内法为船舶进行注册，对商船、渔船等各类船舶进行法定检查并颁发相关证书，对各类海员进行资格考核并颁发证书。第二，检查进出港口的外国船舶是否符合国际安全标准并扣留不适合出海的船舶，为所有驶离巴基斯坦港口的船只签发港口许可证。第三，对计划装载危险货物的船舶进行审查和批准，并对可疑货物进行合法性检查。第四，负责安装和维护巴基斯坦海岸的助航设备，负责包括马克兰海岸（Makran Coast）和信德海岸（Sindh Coast）在内的巴基斯坦各海岸上的8座灯塔的运行和保养，为船舶航行提供便利。[2]

（6）卡拉奇港口运输部

卡拉奇港口运输部（Ports and Shipping Wing, Karachi）的主要职能包括：第一，根据国际公约和国际标准，制定和实施现代化、国际化的港口运输标准，为政府提供有关港口运输、海事培训及海事事务方面的专业性建议。第二，帮助海事部处理与港口及本部门相关的行政事务，负责推行有关港口事务和航运事务的政策，管理国家的商船并敦促其遵守国际海事公约和各项国内法规。第三，为船长、大副和工程师安排专业考试并为合格人员颁发证书，对所有船舶进行安全检验并颁发证书，批准其所认可的商船学校、机构所制定的培训大纲。[3]

（7）巴基斯坦海洋学院

巴基斯坦海洋学院（Pakistan Marine Academy）于1962年成立于现孟加拉国的吉大港，1971年东巴基斯坦独立后，该学院被转移到卡拉奇，并于1976年建造了新校园。1979年，海员训练中心也从交通部下属的哈吉营地（Haji Camp）转移到巴基斯坦海洋学院。2012年起，巴基斯坦海洋学院隶属

〔1〕 "Functions", Government Shipping Office of Pakistan, https：//shippingoffice. gov. pk/functions. aspx, March 20, 2021.

〔2〕 "Introduction & Objectives of the Department", Mercantile Marine Department, http：//mercantilemarine. gov. pk/, March 20, 2021.

〔3〕 "About Us", Directorate General Ports & Shipping, https：//dgps. gov. pk/, March 20, 2021.

于奈德工程技术大学（NED University of Engineering and Technology）。巴基斯坦海洋学院是巴基斯坦国内唯一的海员培训机构。该学院由海事部资助和管理，由高等教育委员会认定相关教育标准，并由巴基斯坦海军协助学院对学生进行体能训练。[1]

（8）巴基斯坦国家航运公司

巴基斯坦国家航运公司（Pakistan National Shipping Corporation）是一家大型国有公司，公司总部设在卡拉奇。巴基斯坦国家航运公司于1979年成立，1980年在卡拉奇证券交易所上市。巴基斯坦国家航运公司是一家独立法人（Autonomous Corporation），在海事部的全面控制下运作。该公司管理着由6艘邮轮和5艘散货船组成的船队，船队的总载重量超过81.3万吨，可承担全球范围的航运任务，为巴基斯坦的海外贸易提供了有力保障。[2]

4. 能源部

巴基斯坦是农业国家，为了使工业得到更好更快的发展，使水资源得到充分科学的开发利用，巴基斯坦前总理沙希德·哈坎·阿巴西（Shahid Khaqan Abbasi）于2017年将水电部（Ministry of Water & Power）解散，将其中的水利司（Water Wing）改建为水利部（Ministry of Water Resources），将其中的电力司（Electric Power Wing）与石油和自然资源部（Ministry of Petroleum and Natural Resources）合并为能源部。

巴基斯坦能源匮乏且能耗结构严重失衡，对石油和天然气产品依存度高达79%，且年需求量还将分别以5.7%和7.5%的速度增长。巴政府在《巴基斯坦2030远景展望》中指出，2030年巴基斯坦对石油和天然气产品需求量将分别达到68.4亿吨和1625.8亿吨油当量。油气资源开发情况和供应稳定与否对巴基斯坦社会经济发展有着重大影响。[3]

能源部负责确保石油和天然气供应的可持续性和安全性，以促进巴基斯坦的经济发展并满足国家的战略需求。同时，其也负责制定石油、天然气和其他矿产资源的开发规划。此外，能源部还致力于开发可再生资源，完善国家的能源结构，促进能源公平，提高能源负担能力，并制定合理的电力政策

---

〔1〕 See "Our Academy", Pakistan Marine Academy, https：//marineacademy. edu. pk/our-academy/, March 20, 2021; Pakistan Marine Academy, "Mission & Vision", https：//marineacademy. edu. pk/mission-and-vision/, March 20, 2021.

〔2〕 "Company Profile", Pakistan National Shipping Corporation, https：//pnsc. com. pk/about-us. html, March 20, 2021.

〔3〕 中华人民共和国驻巴基斯坦大使馆经济商务参赞处：《巴基斯坦概况》，载中华人民共和国商务部网站，http：//pk. mofcom. gov. cn/article/ddgk/，最后访问日期：2020年11月22日。

确保国家有稳定的能源供应。

能源部的下属机构有：替代能源开发委员会（Alternative Energy Development Board）、巴基斯坦国家工程服务局（National Engineering Services Pakistan）、私人电力和基础设施局（Private Power and Infrastructure Board）、全国电力输送公司（National Transmission & Despatch Company）、国家能源效率和节能局（National Energy Efficieny & Conservation Authority）、伊斯兰堡中央电力采购局（Central Power Purchasing Agency）等。能源部亦统辖众多国有石油公司，如巴基斯坦石油有限公司（Pakistan Petroleum Limited）、巴基斯坦国家石油天然气开发有限公司等。[1]

（1）巴基斯坦石油有限公司

巴基斯坦石油有限公司前身为一家股份有限公司，成立于 1950 年 6 月 5 日，由英国伯麦石油公司（Burmah Oil Company）控股。1997 年 9 月，伯麦石油公司将股权出售给巴基斯坦政府。截至 2019 年，巴基斯坦石油有限公司分别由巴基斯坦政府控股 67.51%、员工持股 7.35%、私人投资者持股 25.14%。

巴基斯坦石油有限公司是巴基斯坦能源工业的先驱，为巴基斯坦国内供应了 20% 的天然气份额并生产了相当规模的原油、液态天然气、液化石油气。该公司致力于为国家发现、开采油气以实现国家油气资源的自给自足，并为国家培训、培养能源方面的杰出人才。截至 2019 年 6 月 30 日，该公司已经探明天然气可采储量约为 518.6 亿立方米、石油 1480 万桶。该公司独资运营 28 个油气区块，与其他公司合作运营 19 个油气区块。其中合作经营的油气区块中有 3 个海上油气区块，分别是公司控股 40% 的 C2366-7 区块（Block 2366-7：Offshore Indus C），公司控股 30% 的 N2366-4 区块（Block 2366-4：Offshore Indus N）以及公司控股 25% 的 G2265-1 区块（Block 2265-1：Offshore Indus G）。[2]

（2）石油天然气开发有限公司

石油天然气开发有限公司前身为石油和天然气开发公司（Oil & Gas Development Corporation），于 1961 年 9 月 2 日成立，1997 年 10 月 23 日转化为股份有限公司，2003 年 11 月于巴基斯坦证券交易所上市，2006 年 12 月于伦敦证券交易所二次上市。截至 2019 年，巴基斯坦政府持有该公司 74.98% 的股份。该公司勘明的石油储量占全国总量的 23%，探明的天然气储量占全国

〔1〕 "Organizations", Ministry of Energy, http：//mowp. gov. pk/orgDetails. aspx, March 20, 2021.

〔2〕 "Overview", Pakistan Petroleum Limited, https：//www. ppl. com. pk/content/corporate-profile-overview, March 20, 2021.

总量的 38% ；同时，该公司的石油产量占全国总出产量的 47% ，天然气产量占全国总出产量的 30% 。该公司拥有 50 个油气田及 18 个石油和天然气加工工厂，石油的日产量可达 50000 桶。石油天然气开发有限公司和巴基斯坦石油有限公司以及埃克森美孚一起负责离岸印度洋 G2265-1 海上区块经营开发。[1]

5. 科技部

科学和技术研究部（Ministry of Science and Technology Research）成立于 1964 年，后于 1972 年更名为科技部（Ministry of Science and Technology）。科技部致力于发展科学技术以提升国家的工业水平，改善国家农业经济结构，提高自主创新能力并采取措施防止国家人才的流失。科技部共有专业人才 176 人，该部主要研究领域包括电子、海洋资源、新材料、生物技术、纺织、制药等。2019 年，科技部推出一项名为"未来怀想"（Think Future）的计划，表示科技部将从 3D 打印、人工智能、互联网、智能汽车、智能机器人等 7 个领域进行大力研发，以提升国家科研水平，改良国家的经济结构，从而提升国家经济增长率和提高人民生活水平。[2]

国家海洋研究所（National Institute of Oceanography）成立于 1981 年，总部位于卡拉奇，同时在瓜达尔、松米亚尼（Sonmiani）和戈拉巴里（Ghora Bari）设有分所。该所隶属于科技部，主要研究的海洋区域为北阿拉伯海及其周边地区。该所的研究资金由巴基斯坦中央政府提供，设施由信德省政府资助。该所共有 30 名杰出的海洋科学家，分别从事海洋生物学、海洋化学、海洋物理学、海洋地质学和海洋环境等方面的研究。该所为海洋学调查、水深测量、海洋勘探与地质工程测量、海洋污染与环境调查、虾类养殖、海洋学数据服务和海洋环境影响评估等提供研究和咨询服务。[3]

（三）海上武装执法机构

巴基斯坦的海洋武装执法单位主要集中于巴基斯坦国防部（Ministry of Defence）及与其执法职能关联的国防生产部（Ministry of Defence Production）。

---

〔1〕 "Facts and Figures", Oil and Gas Development Corporation Limited, https：//ogdcl. com/facts-and-figures, March 20, 2021.

〔2〕 "Introduction", Ministry of Science and Technology, https：//most. gov. pk/, March 20, 2021.

〔3〕 "NIO Introduction", National Institute of Oceanography Pakistan, http：//niopk. gov. pk/introduction. html, March 20, 2021.

1. 国防部

（1）巴基斯坦海事安全局

巴基斯坦海事安全局（Pakistan Maritime Security Agency）隶属于国防部。《公约》签署后，巴基斯坦政府获得约 62 万平方公里的专属经济区。为了维护国家海洋利益，巴基斯坦政府于 1983 年成立国家海事协调委员会（National Maritime Affairs Coordination Committee），由国家海事协调委员会对《公约》进行研究并探索维护国家海洋利益的途径，并首先于 1986 年 5 月促成国防部海事处（Maritime Affairs Wing）的设立。海事处即巴基斯坦海事安全局的前身。1987 年 1 月 1 日，巴基斯坦海事安全局成立，负责执行国内法律政策和国际公约。1994 年，议会通过了《巴基斯坦海事安全局法》（The Maritime Security Agency Act），为该机构执法提供了必要法律依据。[1] 2011 年 1 月 15 日，巴基斯坦海事安全局的新总部于卡拉奇建成并投入使用。

巴基斯坦海事安全局有 2500 名海军现役人员、22 艘船只和 3 架飞机。该局的 22 艘船只分别来自巴基斯坦国内的卡拉奇造船厂、中国的黄埔造船厂和西江造船厂以及美国海岸警卫队。该局共有 3 个船舶中队和 1 个飞机中队，分别是第 22 海上巡逻中队、第 23 海上巡逻中队、第 26 海上巡逻中队和第 93 飞机中队。

巴基斯坦海事安全局的主要职能包括：第一，执行国家法律和国际公约，防止国家管辖海域内的非法开采自然资源和非法捕捞行为，保护巴基斯坦的船舶和船员免受来自海域内的任何威胁。第二，对遇险船只进行救助，对海域内的海洋污染和船舶污染情况进行检查处理，协助国内外科研机构进行海洋和水文研究。第三，与其他机构配合做好海上设施的维护工作，为海域内的石油矿物勘探开采提供帮助，同时履行国家指派的其他相关工作，维护巴基斯坦的海洋利益。[2]

（2）巴基斯坦海军

隶属于国防部的巴基斯坦皇家海军（Royal Pakistan Navy）成立于 1947 年 8 月 14 日，于 1956 年改名为巴基斯坦海军（Pakistan Navy）。巴基斯坦海军设立之初只有包括 4 艘护卫舰、4 艘扫雷舰等在内的 16 只船舰。1948 年 4 月，海防炮台 "HMPS QASIM" 于马诺拉岛（Manora Island）建立。1949 年 9 月，巴基斯坦从英国购得两艘驱逐舰，分别为 "迪普·苏丹号"（Tip-

---

〔1〕 Maritime Security Agency Act, 1994, The Pakistan Code, http：//pakistancode. gov. pk/english/ UY2FqaJw1-apaUY2Fqa-apmdZw% 3D% 3D-sg-jjjjjjjjjjjjj, March 20, 2021.

〔2〕 "Pakistan Maritime Security Agency", Pakistan Maritime Security Agency, http：//www. pmsa. gov. pk/, March 20, 2021.

puSultanwas）和"塔里克"号（Tariq）。1949 年 12 月，海军机械培训机构（Mechanical Training Establishment）在马诺拉岛建立。1952 年 8 月，巴基斯坦皇家鱼雷发射场（Royal Pakistan Navy Torpedo Depot）正式投入使用。1953 年 3 月，巴基斯坦从美国购得第一艘扫雷舰守护者号（Muhafiz）。1969 年，巴基斯坦从法国购置了第一艘"达芙妮"（Daphne）级潜艇，并于 1970 年 12 月正式抵达巴基斯坦。1975 年 9 月，巴基斯坦从英国购入 7 架"威斯特兰海王"（Westland Sea King）直升机。2009 年 12 月 19 日，第二艘在中国建造完成的"剑"级护卫舰在巴基斯坦海军服役。

巴基斯坦海军总人数约有 37700 人，拥有 6 个水面舰队，包括第 9 辅助中队、第 25 驱逐舰中队、第 18 驱逐舰中队、第 10 护航艇中队、快速护卫舰中队和欧克斯龙（Auxron）21 中队。巴基斯坦海军拥有包括"达芙妮"级潜艇、"奥古斯塔90"级潜艇、"奥古斯塔70"级潜艇、"阿布杜兹"级潜艇等在内的 8 艘潜艇；同时拥有 6 个飞行中队，分别为 111ASW 飞行中队、222ASW 飞行中队、333AWS 飞行中队、27ASW 飞行中队、28 飞行中队和 29ASW 飞行中队。

巴基斯坦海军的主要目标是保障巴基斯坦的海上交通安全，维护巴基斯坦的海洋利益，防范和抵御来自海上的威胁和侵略，提供海上灾害援助，打击海上恐怖主义和沿海地区的走私犯罪。长期以来，巴基斯坦海军致力于提高自身在印度洋尤其是北阿拉伯海区域的威慑力，并为维持良好的国际海洋秩序作出贡献。[1]

2. 国防生产部

独立之初，巴基斯坦几乎没有任何工业基础。1949—1950 年，其工业部门对国民生产总值的贡献仅为 5.8%，其中小型工业占 4.8%。在几乎没有任何国防工业的情况下，武装部队的需求只能通过向国外购买来满足。为了满足武装部队的需求，巴基斯坦军械工厂（Pakistan Ordnance Factories）于 1951 年在瓦赫（Wah）成立，该工厂相继为巴基斯坦国内军队配备的英国武器系统和美国武器系统制造弹药，并在第二次印巴战争期间发挥了巨大作用。第二次印巴战争结束后，因为所有类型的军事援助都被停止，各种武器都被禁运，巴基斯坦越发认识到自力更生生产武器装备的重要性。1971 年第三次印巴战争结束后，政府决定启动一个自给自足的武器弹药生产计划，并

---

[1] See "PN History", Pakistan Navy, https://www.paknavy.gov.pk/history.html, March 20, 2021; "Vision & Mission", Pakistan Navy, https://www.paknavy.gov.pk/index.html, March 20, 2021; "PN Dimensions", Pakistan Navy, https://www.paknavy.gov.pk/fleet.html, March 20, 2021.

于 1972 年成立国防生产司（Defence Production Division），旨在制订军事采购计划，同时加速本土的军事技术发展，以本土的军火工厂和企业满足本国武器系统的需求。2004 年，国防生产司更名为国防生产部，成为一个独立的国家部门。国防生产部的主要职能为：第一，制定与国防工业有关的政策和准则，为武装部队采购枪支、弹药、设备等，促进国防工业的发展。第二，管理协调所有国防生产组织的生产活动，研发国防装备，与民间科研组织共同进行国防科学研究。第三，进行有关军事援助或军事合作的谈判，推动国防产品的出口，购买外国先进军事技术或进行本国军事技术的转让。[1]

卡拉奇造船厂（Karachi Shipyard & Engineering Works Limited）即隶属于国防生产部。该厂成立于 20 世纪 50 年代中期，于 1957 年注册上市，由专门董事会进行管理，以董事长为首席执行官。卡拉奇造船厂位于卡拉奇西码头，占地约 28.7 万平方米，拥有一个大型的造船厅、三个造船泊位、两个干船坞、一个设备齐全的机械车间、一套大型的喷漆设施以及一个起重能力为 7881 吨的升船转运系统。卡拉奇造船厂是巴基斯坦国内唯一的重型造船厂。该造船厂自成立以来已累计建造了 444 艘不同类型、不同尺寸的船舶，包括大型驱逐舰、快速攻击舰、后勤保障船、散货船、邮轮和远洋船等，其中最大吨位的船舶达 26000 吨。卡拉奇造船厂还与法国合作建造了“奥古斯塔90”级潜艇。目前，卡拉奇造船厂已累计修复了 5000 多艘船只，并定期为巴基斯坦海军、巴基斯坦海事安全局、卡拉奇港口信托基金会等国内机构和外国客户提供检修服务。卡拉奇造船厂还拥有设备完善的实验室，可对金属、矿石、矿物进行各类型的化学、物理及机械测试。多年来，卡拉奇造船厂为巴基斯坦的国防及造船技术发展作出积极贡献，并致力于协助海事部门和国防部门的发展和运行，为国防产品的自给自足和国防生产技术的本土化提供了有力支持。[2]

---

〔1〕 "Mission & Functions", Ministry of Defence Production, http：//www.modp.gov.pk/Detail/ZTliOWQzMjctZjgxNy00ZTZlLWExOTItZDY3OTU2ZDMzMzRm, March 20, 2021.

〔2〕 See "Company Profile", Karachi Shipyard & Engineering Works Limited, https：//www.karachishipyard.com.pk/company-profile/, March 20, 2021；Karachi Shipyard & Engineering Works Limited, "History", http：//www.karachishipyard.com.pk/category/history/, March 20, 2021.

三、国内海洋立法

与同源于古代印度次大陆的印度国内法历程相似，英国殖民统治的确立成为巴基斯坦法律演变进程的重要节点。但有别于以信奉印度教为主的印度，一方面，自莫卧儿帝国时起，伊斯兰法就成为巴基斯坦的至高法律，仅在属人法领域保留了印度教法的适用空间；另一方面，即使进入英国殖民时代，伊斯兰法仍然得到了殖民当局的官方承认，至少在穆斯林群体中延续其重要地位，并通过官方认可的穆斯林执法者对诸多法律领域产生影响。

至 1947 年独立，作为以伊斯兰教为国教的国家，巴基斯坦伊斯兰共和国建立的一个重要目标便是将其伊斯兰法中的殖民因素和印度教文化的影响消除。由此，1949 年，巴基斯坦制宪会议通过《目标决议》（The Objectives Resolution），启动对巴基斯坦国家法律的纯伊斯兰化。[1]

当前，巴基斯坦的国内法律渊源同时包含了制定法与判例法，而其制定法又有联邦立法层面与省级立法层面的两分结构。根据其宪法中相关解释，其现行法律包括法律（Law）、法令（Ordinance）、枢密令（Order-in Council）、命令（Order）、规则（Rule）、规章（Bye-law）、条例（Regulation）、高等法院管辖授权书（Letter Patent Constituting a High Court）、通告（Notification）及其他具有法律效力的立法文件。[2]

（一）划定管辖海域相关立法

1. 《1973 年巴基斯坦伊斯兰共和国宪法》

《巴基斯坦伊斯兰共和国宪法》（The Constitution of the Islamic Republic of Pakistan，以下简称《巴基斯坦宪法》）于 1973 年通过，并自 1974 年起出台了 25 份宪法修正案（最近一次为 2018 年 6 月）。根据该宪法第一部分第 1 条第 2 款，巴基斯坦的国家领土范围应包括：第一，俾路支省、开伯尔-普什图

---

〔1〕 该决议于 1956 年成为《巴基斯坦宪法》的序言，1985 年成为其宪法实质性条款的一部分，现被作为该宪法附件。See ANNEX（Article 2A），The Objectives Resolution，The Constitution of the Islamic Republic of Pakistan，The Pakistan Code，http：//pakistancode.gov.pk/english/UY2FqaJw1-apaUY2Fqa-apaUY2Fvbpw%3D-sg-jjjjjjjjjjjjj，March 20，2021. 同时参见王涛：《巴基斯坦法制的历史切变》，载《人民法院报》2019 年 6 月 7 日，第 8 版。

〔2〕 See Article 268，The Constitution of the Islamic Republic of Pakistan，The Pakistan Code，http：//pakistancode.gov.pk/english/UY2FqaJw1-apaUY2Fqa-apaUY2Fvbpw%3D-sg-jjjjjjjjjjjjj，March 20，2021.

赫瓦省、旁遮普省和信德省；第二，伊斯兰堡首都特区；第三，通过加入或以其他方式被纳入巴基斯坦的邦或领地。该条同时规定，联邦议会可根据法律，按照其认为适当的条件，将新的邦或地区纳入联邦。[1]

这一条款随后经 1974 年第一次修正案、2010 年第十八次修正案对相关序号、地名表述进行了调整，但未涉及实质改动。2018 年，为加强对邻接阿富汗的联邦直辖部落地区的管理与控制，巴基斯坦总统于该年 6 月签署《宪法（第 25 修正案）》[the Constitution（Twenty-fifth Amendment）Act, 2018]，将该区划并入开伯尔-普什图赫瓦省，原第 1 条第 2 款第 3 项的"联邦直辖的部落地区"（The Federally Administered Tribal Areas）一项由此从宪法领土条文中删去。[2]

显然，《巴基斯坦宪法》也未直接明确国家主权在海洋上的界限，这一状态在其加入《公约》后也未发生实质性变化。在这一领土条款之外，该宪法的涉海相关内容主要包括：第一，序言中的基本宣示。《巴基斯坦宪法》在其序言第 11 段宣示，共和国联邦的领土完整、独立及所有权利，包括其陆地、海洋及天空的主权权利应得以捍卫。[3] 第二，第 172 条中有关"无主财产"的部分规定。依第 172 条第 2 款，所有位于巴基斯坦大陆架或其领水以外海洋之下的陆地、矿产及其他有价值的物都应归属联邦政府。而第 3 款则规定，在遵守已有的相关承诺及义务的前提下，位于各省及其所邻接的领水中的矿物油及天然气应由省政府及联邦政府共同且平等享有。[4] 第三，附件中涉及联邦立法权限的关联内容。《巴基斯坦宪法》附表四的"联邦立法权清单"中，共有 5 项立法权限涉及海洋海事相关内容，分别包括：对口岸检疫，船员及海上医院，与口岸检疫相关医院的立法权（第 19 项）；对海上航运及航行，包括在潮汐水域的航运及航行的立法权，对海事管辖裁判的立法权（第 20 项）；对海上及空中客货运输的立法权（第 24 项）；对领水外捕鱼及渔业的立法权（第 36 项）；对经铁路、海上或空中运输客货的终端税种的

〔1〕 The Constitution of the Islamic Republic of Pakistan, The Pakistan Code, http：//pakistancode. gov. pk/english/UY2FqaJw1-apaUY2Fqa-apaUY2Fvbpw = -sg-jjjjjjjjjjjjj, March 12, 2020.

〔2〕 The Constitution（Twenty-fifth Amendment）Act, 2018, The Pakistan Code, http：//pakistancode. gov. pk/english/UY2FqaJw1-apaUY2Fqa-apaUY2Noa5s% 3D-sg-jjjjjjjjjjjjj, March 12, 2020.

〔3〕 "Preamble", The Constitution of the Islamic Republic of Pakistan, see The Pakistan Code, http：//pakistancode. gov. pk/english/UY2FqaJw1-apaUY2Fqa-apaUY2Fvbpw% 3D-sg-jjjjjjjjjjjjj, March 12, 2020.

〔4〕 See Article 172, The Constitution of the Islamic Republic of Pakistan, The Pakistan Code, http：// pakistancode. gov. pk/english/UY2FqaJw1-apaUY2Fqa-apaUY2Fvbpw% 3D-sg-jjjjjjjjjjjjj, March 12, 2020.

立法权（第 53 项）。[1]

2. 《1976 年领水及海域法》

巴基斯坦于 1976 年 12 月颁布《领水及海域法》（Territorial Waters and Maritime Zones Act，1976）。该法总计 14 条，分别就巴基斯坦的领水、毗连区、大陆架、专属经济区、历史性水域及与其海岸相向或相邻国家间的海洋划界原则作出规定。[2]

（1）关于领海及领海基线

巴基斯坦的主权延伸到巴基斯坦领水及其上空、海床和底土；而领水为陆地领土和内水以外从其基线量起 12 海里的区域。其基线向陆地一侧的水域构成巴基斯坦内水的一部分，该基线应由联邦政府在官方公报中确定。如果构成巴基斯坦领土一部分的某单个的岛屿、岩石或其组成的岛群位于主海岸之外，则该基线应沿着该岛屿、岩石或岛群向外海一面的界限进行绘制。

1996 年，巴基斯坦外交部依据《领水及海域法》相关规定发布政府公告，以直线基线划定巴基斯坦领海基线，并宣布将据此进一步划定与其海岸相邻国家（印度和伊朗）以及与其海岸相向国家（阿曼）的海洋边界。该公告所划定基点的坐标如第 Ⅱ 部分 表 1 所示。[3]

第 Ⅱ 部分 表 1　1996 年巴基斯坦外交部政府公告所确定的基点坐标[4]

序号	纬度（北）	经度（东）
a	25°02.20′	61°35.50′
b	25°00.95′	61°46.80′
c	25°05.30′	62°21.00′
d	25°06.30′	63°51.01′
e	25°09.00′	64°35.20′
f	25°18.20′	65°11.60′

---

[1] See Fourth Schedule, Federal Legislative List, The Constitution of the Islamic Republic of Pakistan, The Pakistan Code, http://pakistancode.gov.pk/english/UY2FqaJw1-apaUY2Fqa-apaUY2Fvbpw%3D-sg-jjjjjjjjjjjjj, March 12, 2020.

[2] Territorial Waters and Maritime Zones Act, 1976, The Pakistan Code, http://pakistancode.gov.pk/english/UY2FqaJw1-apaUY2Fqa-bpuUZGFs-sg-jjjjjjjjjjjjj, March 12, 2020.

[3] Division for Ocean Affairs and The Law of The Sea Office of Legal Affairs, "Pakistan Government Defines Territorial Maritime Boundaries", *The Law of the Sea Bulletins*, 34, United Nations, 1997, p. 45.

[4] 有关巴基斯坦 1996 年外交部政府公告所确定的直线基线示意图，参见 UN Office of Legal Affairs, "Illustrative map", https://www.un.org/Depts/los/LEGISLATIONANDTREATIES/PDF-FILES/MAPS/PAK_MZN27_1999_00ill.jpg, March 12, 2020。

续表

序号	纬度（北）	经度（东）
g	24°49.45′	66°40.00′
h	23°52.80′	67°26.80′
i	23°47.30′	67°35.90′
k	23°33.90′	68°07.80′

巴基斯坦于1999年5月向联合国秘书长提交了基于上述公告的基点声明及基线地图。此举随后引发印度的强烈反对。印度于2001年5月致信联合国秘书长，称不能接受巴基斯坦的基线声明及其所产生的海域划定效果，理由在于：第一，巴基斯坦的海岸线非常平滑，几乎不存在极为曲折或有系列岛屿的情形，应适用低潮线的正常基线，而非直线基线；第二，作为基点d的帆岩（Sail Rock）是不能维持人类定居及经济生活的岩礁，不能拥有领海，也不能被纳入基线体系之中；第三，基点a的设定违背国际法，因其为瓜达尔湾（Gwadar Bay）内陆地边界的终点。[1]

在领海的航行权方面，根据《领水及海域法》第3条，外国船舶在不损害巴基斯坦的和平、良好秩序或安全的情形下，可无害通过其领海，但特别规定：①外国军舰，包括潜艇及其他水下潜航器、外国军用飞机，须事先获得联邦政府许可方能通过巴基斯坦领海；②外国超级油轮、核动力船舶及载有核材料或其他有害或有毒物质或材料的船舶，须事先通知联邦政府方能通过巴基斯坦领海；③为了巴基斯坦全境或任何区域的和平、良好秩序或安全，联邦政府可在必要时通过政府公告暂停全部或任何一类外国船舶进入或通过其领海的资格。

（2）关于毗连区

按照《领水及海域法》，巴基斯坦的毗连区为在其领水之外邻接领水的区域，其宽度为从领海基线量起向海延伸的24海里。一方面，巴基斯坦基本接受了第三次联合国海洋法会议有关毗连区的一般成果，规定联邦政府可在毗连区内就"安全""移民和卫生""海关及其他财政事务"行使相应的权力和采取相应的措施。但另一方面，相较于《公约》中的基本制度，相关条款似又为政府扩大监管留下了余地，规定联邦政府可以通过政府公报将任何与巴基斯坦的安全、移民、卫生、海关及其他财政所涉事项有关的法律适用延伸至毗连区，并可在必要时就促进此类立法的实施作出规定。

---

[1] Division for Ocean Affairs and The Law of The Sea Office of Legal Affairs, "Statement by India", *The Law of the Sea Bulletins*, 46, United Nations, 2001, p. 90.

（3）关于专属经济区与大陆架

根据《领水及海域法》第6条，巴基斯坦专属经济区是领水以外且毗邻领水的区域，覆盖从领海基线量起200海里的区域。巴基斯坦在其专属经济区的海床、底土及上覆水域拥有如下权利：第一，对所有生物和非生物资源的勘探、开发、开采、养护和管理以及利用潮汐、风力、水流和太阳能生产能源的专属性主权权利；第二，为勘探和开发该区域资源或方便航运或任何其他目的而建造、维护或经营人工岛屿、离岸码头、设施及其他结构和装置的专属性权利与管辖权；第三，授权、规范和控制相关科学研究的专属性权利和管辖权；第四，养护海洋环境以及防止和控制海洋污染的专属性管辖权；第五，国际法承认的其他权利。同时，在巴基斯坦专属经济区内的捕鱼应受《1975年专属渔区（渔业监管）法》［Exclusive Fishery Zone（Regulation of Fishing）Act］的进一步管制。[1]

据《领水及海域法》第5条，巴基斯坦的大陆架应为巴基斯坦领水以外的海底区域的海床和底土，是巴基斯坦陆地领土大陆边外缘的自然延伸；若其自然延伸不足从领海基线量起的200海里，则延伸至从基线量起的200海里处。

巴基斯坦拥有对其大陆架的完全和专属的主权权利，包括：第一，就探测和开采矿物、海床和底土的其他非生物资源以及属于定居物种的生物体的专属主权权利；第二，授权、规范和控制相关科学研究的专属性权利和管辖权；第三，为方便航运或任何其他目的而建造、维护或营运人工岛屿、离岸码头设施及勘探和开发大陆架资源所需的其他结构和设备的专属性权利和管辖权；第四，养护海洋环境以及防止和控制海洋污染的专属管辖权。

为保护相关区域的海洋资源、人工岛屿及设施、海洋环境、海关及财政安全，联邦政府可以通过官方公报宣布大陆架或专属经济区的任何范围为指定区域（designated area），并通过建立沿海航线、海上航道、国际海事组织海上交通航线体系或以其他任何不损害巴基斯坦利益的方式，在确保航行自由的同时，就外国船只进入和通过大陆架和专属经济区的指定区域作出必要的管制规定。

《领水及海域法》第5条、第6条也都规定，在不影响巴基斯坦对其大陆架和专属经济区的主权权利以及为保护巴基斯坦利益所采取的相关措施的情况下，联邦政府不得阻碍外国铺设或维修大陆架或专属经济区海床上的电

---

〔1〕 Territorial Waters and Maritime Zones Act, 1976, The Pakistan Code, http：//pakistancode. gov. pk/english/UY2FqaJw1-apaUY2Fqa-bpuUZGFs-sg-jjjjjjjjjjjjjj, March 12, 2020.

缆或管道；但在划定铺设这种电缆或管道的路线时，相关方必须征得巴基斯坦联邦政府的同意。

巴基斯坦于2009年4月向联合国大陆架界限委员会提交了其200海里外大陆架的划界信息。该委员会于2015年3月通过了对其外大陆架划界的相关"建议"（Recommendation）。对于巴基斯坦的划界提案及相关信息，阿曼于2009年及2014年两次致信联合国大陆架界限委员会，要求保留其作为巴基斯坦海域邻接国的"国家权利"，允许其进一步收集相关数据及信息后再做判定，并不应影响其与巴基斯坦未来划定重叠海域大陆架界限的权利。[1]

2016年8月，巴基斯坦根据《公约》第76条第9款和第84条第2款向联合国秘书长提交其外大陆架界限案，并附随相关海图、地理坐标列表及其他关联信息。[2] 按照前述2015年3月通过的"建议"，从测算领海宽度的基线量起超过200海里的巴基斯坦北阿拉伯海大陆架的外部界限，是由一系列坐标点所连接的长度不超过60米的直线段所划定的，具体坐标点如第Ⅱ部分 表2所示：

第Ⅱ部分 表2　2016年巴基斯坦提交联合国秘书长的外大陆架界限坐标点[3]

外部界限各点序号	外部界限各点经度（东）	外部界限各点纬度（北）
7A	62.2730773	19.1801216
7	62.2806818	19.1806823
8	62.2901631	19.1813949
9	62.2996433	19.1821208
10	62.3091224	19.1828601
11	62.3186004	19.1836128
12	62.3280772	19.1843788
13	62.3375530	19.1851582

---

〔1〕 "Communication dated 7 August 2009", See UN Office of Legal Affairs, https：//www.un.org/depts/los/clcs_ new/submissions_ files/pak29_ 09/omn_ re_ pak_ 2009.pdf, March 12, 2020; "Communication dated 10 Novemberember 2014", UN Office of Legal Affairs, https：//www.un.org/depts/los/clcs_ new/submissions_ files/pak29_ 09/2014_ 11_ 10_ OMN_ NV_ UN_ 002.pdf, March 12, 2020.

〔2〕 "List of geographical coordinates of points", UN Office of Legal Affairs, https：//www.un.org/Depts/los/LEGISLATIONANDTREATIES/PDFFILES/DEPOSIT/pak_ mzn122_ 2016_ chart.pdf, March 12, 2020.

〔3〕 有关巴基斯坦2016年向联合国提交的外大陆架界限示意图，参见 UN Office of Legal Affairs, "Chart", https：//www.un.org/Depts/los/LEGISLATIONANDTREATIES/PDFFILES/MAPS/PAK_ MZN122_ 2016_ 00228.jpg, March 12, 2020。

续表

外部界限各点序号	外部界限各点经度（东）	外部界限各点纬度（北）
14	62. 3470275	19. 1859510
15	62. 3565009	19. 1867571
16	62. 3659731	19. 1875766
17	62. 3754440	19. 1884094
18	62. 3849137	19. 1892556
19	62. 3943821	19. 1901151
20	62. 4038493	19. 1909879
21	62. 4133151	19. 1918742
22	62. 4227796	19. 1927737
23	62. 4322427	19. 1936866
24	62. 4417045	19. 1946129
25	62. 4511649	19. 1955524
26	62. 4606239	19. 1965054
27	62. 4700814	19. 1974716
28	62. 4795375	19. 1984512
29	62. 4889921	19. 1994441
141A	63. 5334024	19. 2587332

阿曼政府随即于同年12月向联合国秘书长表达了反对立场。阿曼政府认为：第一，巴基斯坦政府无权就外大陆架界限作出"永久性划定"，也无权依据《公约》第76条第9款及第84条第2款提交这一信息；第二，巴基斯坦的外大陆架界限应立足于其与阿曼间的大陆架边界的划定，但当前两国已达成共识尚未划定这一边界；第三，依据联合国大陆架界限委员会"建议"所定的大陆架界限不应损害国家间的边界划分，而巴基斯坦的单边行为违背了这一原则，不应是"最终且有拘束力"的。[1]

（4）关于历史性水域

根据《领水及海域法》第7条，联邦政府可以通过政府公报明确与其陆地领土相邻的包括巴基斯坦的历史水域在内的水域界限。巴基斯坦的主权及

---

[1] "Communication dated 7 December 2016 concerning the Deposit by Pakistan of A Chart, including A List of Geographical Coordinates of Points and Relevant Information", UN Office of Legal Affairs, https: //www. un. org/Depts/los/LEGISLATIONANDTREATIES/PDFFILES/communications/omn_ re_ pak_ 07122016. pdf, March 12, 2020.

于且一直及于巴基斯坦历史性水域的海床和底土、水域上空以及水域本身。

（5）与海岸相向或相邻国家之间的海上边界问题

《领水及海域法》第 8 条还就巴基斯坦的海洋划界问题确立了初步原则。巴基斯坦与任何国家之间的领水边界的划定都应由巴基斯坦与该国之间通过协议确定。在此种协议达成之前，除非双方同意其他临时性安排，巴基斯坦与该国之间的领水范围不应超出基于巴基斯坦和该国家领海基线的等距离线。

而对于巴基斯坦和其他国家之间的毗连区、大陆架、专属经济区和其他海洋区域，相关分界线应根据公平原则并考虑所有相关情况后通过协议划定。在此类协议或解决方案议定之前，巴基斯坦与相关国家应根据上述毗连区、大陆架、专属经济区和其他海区的划界原则作出临时性安排。

3.《2014 年测绘法》

2014 年颁布的《测绘法》（The Surveying And Mapping Act，2014）共含八个部分，总计 25 条，分别就巴基斯坦测绘局（Survey of Pakistan）的组织机构、巴基斯坦测绘局的职能、地理空间数据的管理、地测数据的供应和安全、测绘标记的使用、地理名称的国家和国际提案、违反义务的相关惩罚等内容有所规范。

巴基斯坦测绘局依据该法而成立，总部设于拉瓦尔品第，并在联邦、省或区一级设有办事处。巴基斯坦测绘局局长（The Surveyor General of Pakistan）由联邦政府任命，由依本法规定及依本法订定之规则行使对测绘局的监督管理权，并向联邦政府负责。

作为巴基斯坦唯一的国家级地理测绘机构，巴基斯坦测绘局的职责主要包括：第一，利用最新的大地测量技术和手段，确认并更新巴基斯坦的大地测量基准及投影基准系统；第二，利用巴基斯坦测绘局、其他政府部门、相关注册机构或在巴基斯坦沿海设有此类设施的任何来源所获得的数据，确认并更新垂直基准；第三，划定和标定国家间边界，并重新定位界桩；第四，依据联邦政府及相关省政府的建议及授权，为巴基斯坦全国或特定地区提供地理空间数据、遥感和地理信息系统的应用与服务；第五，开展国家地图系列地形图的测绘、更新和印刷工作；等等[1]毫无疑问，无论是对于巴基斯坦的海洋划界的谈判进程，还是对其包括外大陆架界限在内的海洋权利主张的提出与实现，巴基斯坦测绘局都成为相关海洋地理、地质、地形数据资料

----

〔1〕 Surveying and Mapping Act，2014，The Pakistan Code，http：//pakistancode. gov. pk/english/ UY2FqaJw1-apaUY2Fqa-apaUY2FqZp4 = -sg-jjjjjjjjjjjjjj，March 16，2020.

与科学证据的最有力支撑。[1]

（二）海上安全相关立法

1.《1923 年海军军备法》

《1923 年海军军备法》（The Naval Armaments Act，1923）原为英印时期的国内立法，本意在于实施 1922 年于美国华盛顿签署的《限制海军军备条约》（Treaty for the Limitation of Naval Armament）。1936 年，面对即将到期的《限制海军军备条约》及 1930 年于伦敦签署的《限制与削减海军军备条约》（Treaty for the Limitation and Reduction of Naval Armament），美英法等国再次在英国伦敦召开海军大会，并通过了《1936 年限制海军军备和交换海军建设信息条约》（Treaty for the Limitation of Naval Armament and for the Exchange of Information concerning Naval Construction，1936，以下简称《1936 年条约》）。印度随之将《1923 年海军军备法》的立法目的更改为对该《1936 年条约》的执行。

印巴分治之后，巴基斯坦分别于 1949 年、1960 年、1975 年、1981 年通过国家法令或政府公报对《海军军备法》中的涉及印度的相关组织机构及表述进行了替换或删除。尽管《1936 年条约》已经于 1942 年 12 月失效[2]，但《1923 年海军军备法》仍是巴基斯坦的现行国内法之一。

《海军军备法》共计 14 条，主要涉及：（1）对建造或配备战船的限制；（2）战船许可证书的颁发主体、获取资格、申请程序及违法改造战船的一般义务；（3）对违反本法规定的个人及法人的民事及刑事责任认定；（4）对违法船舶的没收，包括没收船舶的司法程序、对利益相关人的权利保障以及对已没收船舶的处置方式与条件；（5）对违法战船的拿捕、扣押与搜查；（6）在有特殊证据或存在关联事实时对船舶性质的判断；（7）船舶被拿捕后，若未经合法释放或许可程序即再次出海时对船长及船东的处罚标准；（8）相关人员进入造船厂、修船厂等设施进行调查及搜查的权力；（9）有权对本法相关罪行进行审判的法院级别和条件；（10）对善意方的保护以及赔偿。[3]

---

[1] See "Map Showing Length of Borders With Neighbouring Countries & Coastal Line", Survey of Pakistan, http://surveyofpakistan. gov. pk/SiteImage/Downloads/pakistan _ showing _ border _ length. pdf, March 16, 2020.

[2] London Naval Treaty-1936, Naval Arms Control Archive, https://naval-arms-control-archive. site123. me/documents/london-naval-treaty-1936, March 16, 2020.

[3] Naval Armaments Act, 1923, The Pakistan Code, http://pakistancode. gov. pk/english/UY2FqaJw1-apaUY2Fqa-apyd-sg-jjjjjjjjjjjjjjjj, March 16, 2020.

2. 《1950 年巴基斯坦海军（延长服役）法》

《1950 年巴基斯坦海军（延长服役）法》［The Pakistan Navy（Extension of Service）Act，1950］是为在巴基斯坦海军服役人员保留服役资格、延长服役年限作出的专门性立法。该法案全文仅有两项条文，其核心规定在于：任何服役于巴基斯坦海军的人员，若因其入伍时所约定的服役期限届满而不再承担服役期相关义务的，应继续保持服役状态，并有责任继续为巴基斯坦海军服役，除非该服役期限由联邦政府通知决定，或经巴基斯坦海军总司令的命令解除。不过，该延长服役的最长时间，从其因其他原因中止之日算起，不得超过五年。[1]

3. 《1961 年巴基斯坦海军条例》

1961 年，《巴基斯坦海军条例》（The Pakistan Navy Ordinance）颁布，意在强化巴基斯坦海军纪律并修正相关政府职能。该法含十八章共 186 条及 1 个附表，所涉内容主要包括：（1）适用主体范围；（2）相关术语含义；（3）海军人员的入伍、任命、雇佣的条件与程序；（4）海军服役期间的相关权利，包括待遇、职责、时长、解职、终止服役等的要求与条件；（5）服役期间的特权，包括薪酬不受减损、遭受侵犯时的救济、相关行政强制措施及司法程序的豁免与优先权；（6）对相关违法违规行为的具体规定，包括军事行动时行为不端、通敌、玩忽职守、叛乱、擅离职守、违规航行或飞越等；（7）对上述违法违规行为的惩处，包括惩处的性质与方式、刑罚减免的情形、刑罚裁定主体、受审前的逮捕、军事法庭的专门程序、刑罚的执行等；（8）对死者、逃兵及精神失常者财产的处置在特定情形下适用的特别条款等。

根据该条例，巴基斯坦海军的所有现役军官、涉及特定职责或服役项目的已退役海军军官、处于训练及任务执行或军事服务中的巴基斯坦海军预备役人员、在一定情形及一定条件下适用本条例规定的巴基斯坦辅助部队人员，都为本条例的相应规范所约束的对象。作为以伊斯兰教为国教的国家，该条例明确规定，巴基斯坦海军各舰队和军事单位的指挥官应当为各自船舶及单位的军官、士官长和海员履行宗教职责提供合理的便利。[2]

---

〔1〕 Pakistan Navy（Extension of Service）Act，1950，The Pakistan Code，http：//pakistan-code. gov. pk/english/UY2FqaJw1-apaUY2Fqa-ap% 2BVaQ% 3D% 3D-sg-jjjjjjjjjjjjjj，March 16，2020.

〔2〕 Pakistan Navy Ordinance，1961，The Pakistan Code，http：//pakistancode. gov. pk/english/UY2FqaJw1-apaUY2Fqa-cJ2W-sg-jjjjjjjjjjjjjj，March 16，2020.

4.《1973 年巴基斯坦海岸警卫队法》

1973 年，巴基斯坦颁布《巴基斯坦海岸警卫队法》（The Pakistan Coast Guards Act），就巴基斯坦海岸警卫队的组建及运行作出规定，意图有效遏制以任何形式在阿拉伯海沿岸地区跨越巴基斯坦边界的走私行为，对任何在该区域损害巴基斯坦国防和安全的人员作出应对。该法共分三章 18 条及 3 个附表，分别就海岸警卫队的组建方式与程序、海岸警卫队的职能、海岸警卫队各级官员的任命、对其武装部队的指挥与监管、海岸警卫队军官及其他人员的薪酬待遇、对违法违规人员的惩处、对扣押货物的处置、《1952 年巴基斯坦军队法》对海岸警卫队的适用等作出规定。

根据该法第 3 条，海岸警卫队的职责主要在于：第一，防范走私；第二，防止向国内或国外的非法移民；第三，阻止敌方间谍或破坏者从沿岸区域向国内渗透；第四，作为战争防卫中的补充力量。根据附表 1 的说明，巴基斯坦海岸警卫队行动所及的"沿岸地区"（coastal area）包括俾路支省的南部地带邻接巴基斯坦与伊朗边界的部分地区与信德省南部至阿拉伯海的部分区域，但不包括上述区域内的港口。[1]

5.《1965 年巴基斯坦海军学院（授予学位）条例》

《巴基斯坦海军学院（授予学位）条例》［The Pakistan Naval Academy (Award of Degrees) Ordinance］于 1965 年 6 月生效，旨在授权巴基斯坦海军学院为成功修完与其专业方向相适应的规定课程的学院学员与外国士官生授予相应学位。根据这一条例，巴基斯坦海军学院可以授予三类学位，分别为：（海军）理学学士学位、（海军）文学学士学位以及海军管理学学士学位。[2]

（三）海洋渔业相关立法

1.《1897 年渔业法》

《1897 年渔业法》（The Fisheries Act，1897）同样为英印时期的立法，由巴基斯坦于 1949 年、1950 年、1952 年、1959 年、1960 年、1981 年就国家主体、监管机构及适用范围等进行了修订，但未触及其实质内容。

根据《1897 年通则法案》（The General Clauses Ac）第 4 条及第 26 条，

〔1〕 Pakistan Coast Guards Act, 1973, The Pakistan Code, http：//pakistancode. gov. pk/english/ UY2FqaJw1-apaUY2Fqa-bpuUY2hp-sg-jjjjjjjjjjjjj, March 16, 2020.
〔2〕 Pakistan Naval Academy (Award of Degrees) Ordinance, 1965, The Pakistan Code, http：//pakistancode. gov. pk/english/UY2FqaJw1-apaUY2Fqa-cJ%2Bc-sg-jjjjjjjjjjjjj, March 16, 2020.

该渔业立法将作为在巴基斯坦各地区所施行的任何其他渔业相关立法的补充。[1] 在其七项条款中，除对法律名称及适用范围的说明外，分别就鱼类及渔业设备的相关术语、在内陆水域和沿海使用爆炸物捕鱼或破坏渔业资源、向水中投毒方式捕鱼或破坏渔业资源、依省政府规章保护所选定水域鱼类等作出规定。同时，该法第 7 条规定，对违反上述规定的嫌疑人，若无法获知嫌疑人的姓名和地址，或嫌疑人拒绝提供其姓名和地址，或者有理由怀疑嫌疑人所提供的姓名和地址的真实性，则任何警务人员或经政府授权的人均可在未获地方治安官的指示和逮捕令的情况下直接逮捕相关嫌疑人。[2]

2. 《1975 年专属渔区（渔业监管）法》

为了有效监管专属经济区内的捕鱼活动，巴基斯坦于 1975 年颁布《专属渔区（渔业监管）法》[Exclusive Fishery Zone（Regulation Of Fishing）Act，以下简称《1975 年监管法》]，并经《1983 年专属渔区（渔业监管）（修订）条例》[Exclusive Fishery Zone（Regulation of Fishing）（Amdt.）Ordinance]及《1993 年专属渔区（渔业监管）（修订）法案》[The Exclusive Fishery Zone（Regulation of Fishing）（Amdt.）Act，1993]对其中七项条款进行了增补或修订。

根据第 2 条中的术语解释，《1975 年监管法》所谓的"专属渔区"即等同于《领水及海域法》中的"专属经济区"，适用于巴基斯坦全境此类水域、水域中的全部渔船以及渔船上的全部人员。该法对专属渔区中的捕鱼许可作出严格规定，进一步明确了渔船的航行规范，禁止爆破或投毒等捕鱼方式，划定休渔季与禁捕区域，对追捕和搜查违法船舶、处置没收船舶及鱼货等作出规定，并就相关违法行为的惩处、司法程序、责任承担及救济等作出规定。根据这一立法，巴基斯坦各有权管辖法院对专属渔区内的外国渔船及船上人员，拥有与对本国渔船及人员相同的管辖权。[3]

3. 《1997 年巴基斯坦鱼类检验与质量控制法》

为进一步管控渔业产品的质量，巴基斯坦于 1997 年颁布《巴基斯坦鱼类检验与质量控制法》（Pakistan Fish Inspection And Quality Control Act），以扩大本国的渔业出口规模，避免出口质量低于标准的鱼类及其他渔业产品。该

---

[1] General Clauses Act, 1897, The Pakistan Code, http：//pakistancode. gov. pk/english/UY2F qa-Jw1-apaUY2Fqa-cZ0% 3D-sg-jjjjjjjjjjjjj, March 16, 2020.

[2] Fisheries Act, 1897, The Pakistan Code, http：//pakistancode. gov. pk/english/UY2FqaJw1-apaUY2Fqa-cZs% 3D-sg-jjjjjjjjjjjjj, March 16, 2020.

[3] Exclusive Fishery Zone（Regulation of Fishing）Act, 1975, The Pakistan Code, http：//paki-stancode. gov. pk/english/UY2FqaJw1-apaUY2Fqa-bpuUZWNs-sg-jjjjjjjjjjjjj, March 16, 2020.

法共 18 条，内容主要包括：（1）鱼类加工厂、鱼类出口商的登记；（2）检验委员会的组成和职能；（3）渔业检验员对鱼类加工厂进行查验及惩处可能违法行为的相关特权；（4）禁止任何对腐烂、不卫生或被病原体污染的鱼类的加工出口；（5）鱼产品处理人员的健康要求；（6）鱼类及其他渔业产品的质量评估；（7）渔业官员的权力、职责和职能；（8）相关违法行为的认定与处罚，包括对渔业产品的没收与处置等。

依据该法所设立的核心机构"检验委员会"，由出口促进局、海洋渔业部及覆盖广泛的鱼类加工厂贸易协会各派一名代表组成。该检验委员会的职能为：第一，对各鱼类加工厂进行一项或多项调查，以确定它们是否符合登记要件；第二，就对渔业检验员的命令、决定、作为或不作为所提出的申诉举行听证；第三，就该行业的有效运作、消除其中的不法行为及扩大出口向联邦政府提出建议；第四，履行后续规则可能赋予的其他职能。[1]

（四）海洋能源相关立法

截至 2020 年 6 月，尚未发现巴基斯坦有涉及海洋传统或非传统能源的专门性立法行动。当前，其国内立法的官方数据库公布的能源相关立法共有 13 项，分别涉及煤炭、石油、天然气、可替代能源开发及外国石油公司（美国埃索东部石油公司）监管等相关事项。

1. 《1934 年石油法》

《1934 年石油法》（The Petroleum Act）经相应修订共同适用于今天的印度与巴基斯坦，其颁布的初衷在于对石油和其他易燃物质的进口、运输、储存、生产、提炼和混合相关法律进行整合与修订。全文共计四章 32 条，其中，第 32 条和附录已经由《1938 年废除法案》（The Repealing Act, 1938）废除。根据该法现行有效条款，其主要就石油进口、运输等环节的监管和控制，石油产品的检验和取样，以及在上述环节中的违法行为的惩处与相关程序分别作出规定。尽管该法没有直接涉及海洋区域，但是海洋石油产业在涉及相关环节时仍可能受到上述立法的调整和监管。[2]

2. 《1948 年矿山、油田及矿产开发监管（联邦控制）法》

1948 年，巴基斯坦颁布《矿山、油田及矿产开发监管（联邦控制）法》[The Regulation Of Mines And Oil Fields And Mineral Development（Federal Con-

---

〔1〕 Pakistan Fish Inspection and Quality Control Act, 1997, The Pakistan Code, http: //pakistan-code. gov. pk/english/UY2FqaJw1-apaUY2Fqa-apqaZg = = -sg-jjjjjjjjjjjjjj, March 16, 2020.

〔2〕 Petroleum Act, 1934, The Pakistan Code, http: //pakistancode. gov. pk/english/UY2FqaJw1-apaUY2Fqa-b56Y-sg-jjjjjjjjjjjjjj, March 16, 2020.

trol）Act］，以就巴基斯坦境内的矿山、油田及其矿产开发事项进行有效监管，并依 1949 年、1950 年、1953 年、1956 年、1960 年政府公报逐步扩展适用于随政局变动后的巴基斯坦全境。根据该法，相应政府可就以下事项制定具体规则：（1）勘探开发许可的颁发或续期、矿产协议或其他矿产特许的申请、在此类申请中需要缴纳的费用，规定申请的主管机关、申请的条件、申请被拒的情形、相应税率或费率；（2）厚矿石及矿物油的精炼；（3）矿产及矿物油从生产、储存到分配的管控；（4）矿产及矿物油产品的购销价格调整等。在这一立法授权之下，巴基斯坦于 1992 年通过了《压缩天然气（CNG）（生产与销售）规则》［Compressed Natural Gas（CNG）（Production and Marketing）Rules］，并于 2008 年、2009 年进行了三次修订。[1]

3. 《1961 年石油产品（开发附加费）条例》与《1967 年天然气（开发附加费）条例》

《1961 年石油产品（开发附加费）条例》［The Petroleum Products（Development Surcharge）Ordinance］共含 9 个条文及 4 个附表，就向石油产品征收石油税及其他关联事宜作出规定。根据该条例，任一公司、炼油厂及相关许可证持有人均应向联邦政府缴纳石油产品的石油税，税率由联邦政府通过政府公报予以公布。但该规定不适用于各炼油厂所生产的或公司所购买的用于出口的石油产品。所应纳税费如未能在联邦政府规定时间内或由其授权的任何官员所允许的时间内足额缴纳，将视为土地税的欠款被追缴。除此之外，该条例还对该项税费的豁免权、相关产品的最高销售价格、该项税费对企业所得税的抵扣等作出规定。该条例分别经《2009 年石油产品（石油开发税）（修订）条例》［Petroleum Products（Petroleum Development Levy）（Amendment）Ordinance］（分别于 2009 年 7 月及 10 月两次修订）及《2011 年石油产品（石油税）（修订）法》［Petroleum Products（Petroleum Levy）（Amendment）Act］围绕相关税费术语、缴税（费）主体及附表 5 中的税率等问题进行了修订。[2]

《1967 年天然气（开发附加费）条例》［The Natural Gas（Developments Surcharge）Ordinance］在动机与内容上都与上述《1961 年石油产品（开发附加费）条例》十分相似。全文共计 8 条，分别就天然气开发附加费征收的

---

〔1〕 Regulation of Mines and Oil Fields and Mineral Development（Federal Control）Act, 1948, The Pakistan Code, http：//pakistancode. gov. pk/english/UY2FqaJw1-apaUY2Fqa-ap + Uag = = -sg-jjjjjjjjjjjjjj, March 16, 2020.

〔2〕 Petroleum Products（Development Surcharge）Ordinance, 1961, The Pakistan Code, http：//pakistancode. gov. pk/english/UY2FqaJw1-apaUY2Fqa-cJyd-sg-jjjjjjjjjjjjjj, March 16, 2020.

对象、征收时间与费率、相关所得税抵扣、最高销售价格、相关犯罪行为的认定、进一步细则的制定权力、相关附表的颁布及修订权力等作出规定。[1]

4. 《2001 年石油天然气开发公司（重组）条例》

2001 年，巴基斯坦颁布《石油天然气开发公司（重组）条例》[The Oil And Gas Development Corporation（Reorganization）Ordinance]，将石油及天然气发展公司（Oil and Gas Development Corporation）重组为一个公共有限公司（public limited company），即石油及天然气发展有限公司（Oil and Gas Development Company Limited）。根据《1984 年公司条例》（Companies Ordinance）的规定，石油及天然气发展有限公司为股份公司，受巴基斯坦证券交易委员会监管，以巴基斯坦政府的名义由巴基斯坦联邦政府持股，但联邦政府可以在适当时机将股份移转给私人。该条例生效的同时，《1961 年油气开发公司条例》（The Oil and Gas Development Corporation Ordinance）随之废止。[2]

5. 《2002 年石油产品销售（联邦管制）（废止）条例》

为促进私营部门在本国油气行业的投资与经营，巴基斯坦于 2002 年颁布《石油产品销售（联邦管制）（废止）条例》[The Marketing of Petroleum Products（Federal Control）（Repeal）Ordinance]，旨在废除《1974 年石油产品销售（联邦管制）法》[The Marketing of Petroleum Product（Federal Control）Act，以下简称《1974 年石油条例》]。该条例明确，由联邦政府单独控制石油销售部门发展的做法不再是公共利益的必需；联邦政府正在解除对下游石油部门的管制，并鼓励私人投资这一部门，允许将其在下游石油部门的某些利益私有化。该条例适用于根据《1974 年石油条例》所组建的巴基斯坦国家石油有限公司（Pakistan State Oil Company Limited），并将依此条例减除国家在该公司所持股份，《1974 年石油条例》由此被废止。[3]

6. 《2002 年石油及天然气监管局条例》

《与 2002 年石油产品销售（联邦管制）（废止）条例》的背景相似，巴基斯坦于同年颁布《石油及天然气监管局条例》（The Oil And Gas Regulatory

---

[1] Natural Gas（Development Surcharge）Ordinance, 1967, The Pakistan Code, http：//pakistan-code. gov. pk/english/UY2FqaJw1-apaUY2Fqa-cZaa-sg-jjjjjjjjjjjjj, March 16, 2020.

[2] Oil And Gas Development Corporation（Re-Organization）Ordinance, 2001, The Pakistan Code, http：//pakistancode. gov. pk/english/UY2FqaJw1-apaUY2Fqa-cp + UY2Jq-sg-jjjjjjjjjjjjjj, March 16, 2020.

[3] Marketing Of Petroleum Products（Federal Control）（Repeal）Ordinance, 2002, The Pakistan Code, http：//pakistancode. gov. pk/english/UY2FqaJw1-apaUY2Fqa-apaUY2FtbZc%3D-sg-jjjjjjjjjjjjj, March 16, 2020.

Authority Ordinance)设立石油及天然气监管局,以促进竞争、增加中下游石油工业的私人投资和私人所有权比重,从而在尊重个人权利的同时保护公共利益,并为油气相关事项提供有用且高效的监管。该条例共有七章 47 条,主要涉及该油气监管机构的组建、政策准则、许可证的颁发、机构的权力与职能、政策准则、相关违法行为、技术标准、现行协议的适用、强制性土地征收、进一步细则制定权限等事项。[1]

7.《2006 年替代性能源开发局条例》

2006 年,巴基斯坦颁布《替代性能源开发局条例》(Alternative Energy Development Board Ordinance),就替代性能源开发局的设立作出相应规定。根据该条例,替代性能源开发局是施行替代性或可再生能源技术领域多种政策、规划及工程的自治性机构。该机构的宗旨在于,协助或促进替代性或可再生能源的开发及生产,通过多样化能源产出来完成基于本土科技发展的技术转化,从而实现可持续经济发展。

根据该条例第 8 条,替代性能源开发局主要包括:第一,为实现政府能源目标制定利用可替代或可再生能源的国家战略、政策及计划;第二,作为评估、监测及认证可替代或可再生能源项目或产品的判定方;第三,作为实现可替代或可再生技术商业应用的协调机构;第四,促进通过可替代或可再生能源资源的电力生产。其中,第四项职责中所指的可替代或可再生能源资源,在第 8 条中被特别指明包括潮汐能、海洋能。由此,该立法应可在巴基斯坦的海洋能源开发利用中得以直接适用。[2]

8.《2011 年天然气基础设施发展税法案》

2011 年,巴基斯坦颁布《天然气基础设施发展税法》(The Gas Infrastructure Development Cess Act)。根据该法,所谓"天然气基础设施发展税"是指由其附表 1 所列明的公司在固定销售价格之外向燃气消费者(国内部门消费者除外)所征收的燃气基础设施开发费用。该税费的征收将用于伊朗—巴基斯坦管道项目、土库曼斯坦—阿富汗—巴基斯坦—印度管道项目、液化天然气项目以及用于平抑进口能源价格的其他项目。[3]

---

[1] Oil and Gas Regulatory Authority Ordinance, 2002, The Pakistan Code, http://pakistancode. gov. pk/english/UY2FqaJw1-apaUY2Fqa-apaUY2Frbpg% 3D-sg-jjjjjjjjjjjjj, March 16, 2020.

[2] Alternative Energy Development Board Ordinance, 2006, The Pakistan Code, http://pakistancode. gov. pk/english/UY2FqaJw1-apaUY2Fqa-apaUY2FvbZ4% 3D-sg-jjjjjjjjjjjjj. March 20, 2021., March 16, 2020.

[3] Gas Infrastructure Development CESS Act, 2011, The Pakistan Code, http://pakistancode. gov. pk/english/UY2FqaJw1-apaUY2Fqa-apaUY2FsZ5g = -sg-jjjjjjjjjjjjj, March 16, 2020.

（五）海上运输相关立法

1. 船舶相关立法

（1）《1925 年海运法》

《1925 年海运法》原是英国殖民统治期间，印度对由英国主要推动的《1924 年海牙规则》作出的积极响应，同为巴基斯坦独立后被继承适用的立法之一，并经 1949 年、1960 年、1975 年的相关法案、条例作出修订。该法适用于巴基斯坦全境，其所附提单相关规则适用于从巴基斯坦任何港口至巴基斯坦境内或境外任何其他港口的海上货物运输。[1] 其法条正文及附表内容详见"印度海洋法律体系"中"海上运输相关立法"部分《1925 年印度海上货物运输法》。

（2）《2001 年商船运输条例》

2001 年，为就商船运输及其附带问题的相关在先立法进行整合并有所修订，巴基斯坦颁布了《商船运输条例》（The Merchant Shipping Ordinance）。根据该条例第 1 条，这一立法适用于巴基斯坦全境，除另有明文规定外，适用范围包括：第一，巴基斯坦的所有船舶，无论其位于何处；第二，被视为依该条例注册的所有船舶，无论其位于何处；第三，位于《领水及海域法》所划定的领水及专属经济区范围内任何港口或地点的其他船舶。该法生效后，《1838 年沿海船舶法》（The Coasting Vessels Act）、《1841 年船舶登记法》及其 1850 年修正案、《1923 年商船运输法》（The Merchant Shipping Ac）、《1946 年商船船员（诉讼）法》［The Merchant Seamen（Litigation）Act］、《1949 年商船运输（国家色彩）法》［The Merchant Shipping（National Colours）Act］、《1959 年航运控制条例》（The Control of Shipping Ordinance）等均随之废止。

作为彼时巴基斯坦商船航运相关在先立法的集大成者，《2001 年商船运输条例》内容极为庞杂，共含 16 个部分、45 章、610 条正文及 1 个附表。主要内容包括：①航海贸易部门的组建及特定职位的设立与职责；②各港口航运办公室的建立，涉及船长的职责、船员的雇佣和遣散费用及船员的待遇问题；③商船的登记条件、程序及国籍认定；④沿海运输的相关行为要求与监管规则；⑤不同类型的船员配备资格与要求、各类型船员的权利与救济；⑥旅客运输船舶的相关规则，包括客船设施的检验、特种客舱的营运、朝圣

---

[1] Carriage of Goods by Sea Act, 1925, The Pakistan Code, http：//pakistancode. gov. pk/english/UY2FqaJw1-apaUY2Fqa-ap6Y-sg-jjjjjjjjjjjjj, March 16, 2020.

船舶的开行等；⑦船舶建造与营运中的安全问题，包括安全设备的安装、无线电设备的安装使用、安全证书的颁发、载重线等安全标准的适用等；⑧船舶的航行、碰撞与其他海上事故相关应对与规则；⑨船舶日志等文书的记录、保管与使用；⑩适用于渔船、帆船及核动力船的专门性规则；⑪船难残骸的处置与海难救助的实施；⑫船东的责任相关规则，包括责任限制、抵押物权等；⑬防止来自船舶的污染；等等。同时，由于综合涵盖商船营运的多个环节，《2001 年商船运输条例》的适用需要与各环节关联的现行立法相配合，如，1898 年的《刑事诉讼法典》（Code of Criminal Procedure），1951 年的《巴基斯坦国籍法》（Pakistan Citizenship Act），1969 年的《关税法》（Customs Act），1976 年的《领水及海域法》，1984 年的《公司条例》（Companies Ordinance）等。[1] 2002 年，《商船运输（修订）条例》［Merchant Shipping（Amendment）Ordinance］颁布，对《2001 年商船运输条例》第 79 条第 A 款有关港口税费相关内容作出修订。[2]

2. 港口相关立法

（1）《1908 年港口法》

巴基斯坦于 1949 年将原《1908 年印度港口法》（Indian Ports Act，1908）更名为《1908 年港口法》（The Ports Act，1908），将其沿用于规范巴基斯坦国内港口及港口费用的相关事项。该法经 1953 年的《俾路支地方联邦（联邦法律）（延伸）命令》［Baluchistan States Union（Federal Laws）（Extension）Order］被延展适用于俾路支省相关地域；再经 1960 年的《瓜达尔（中央法律适用）条例》［the Gwadar（Application of Central Laws）Ordinance］被延展适用于瓜达尔地区。除在印巴分治前的修订外，《1908 年港口法》在巴基斯坦分别于 1949 年、1960 年、1961 年、1965 年、1975 年、1979 年、1981 年、1982 年就行政区域、机构名称、部分术语、不法行为范围、刑罚期限、罚金数额等规定作出了删改或修正。其中，依据《1981 年联邦法律（修订与声明）条例》［Federal Laws（Revision and Declaration）Ordinance］，有关东巴基斯坦的内容被全部删除。[3] 有关该法当前八章共 69 条规定的具体内容，详见"印度海洋法律体系"中"海上运输相关立法"部分《1908 年印度港

---

〔1〕　Merchant Shipping Ordinance，2001，The Pakistan Code，http：//pakistancode. gov. pk/english/UY2FqaJw1-apaUY2Fqa-cp％2BUY2Jv-sg-jjjjjjjjjjjjj，March 16，2020.

〔2〕　Merchant Shipping（Amendment）Ordinance，2002，The Pakistan Code，http：//pakistancode. gov. pk/english/UY2FqaJw1-apaUY2Fqa-apaUY2FvaJY％3D-sg-jjjjjjjjjjjjj，March 16，2020.

〔3〕　Ports Act，1908，The Pakistan Code，http：//pakistancode. gov. pk/english/UY2FqaJw1-apaUY2Fqa-apad-sg-jjjjjjjjjjjjj，March 16，2020.

口法》。

（2）《1948 年港口保护（特别措施）法》

《1948 年港口保护（特别措施）法》〔The Protection of Ports（Special Measures）Act〕旨在通过特别措施确保港口安全。该法所指的"港口"被界定为《1908 年港口法》中第 3 条第 8 款下的"主要港口"，但同时规定，联邦政府可以通过政府公报在任何时候将该法扩展适用于巴基斯坦的任何港口，无论其处于高潮线以内或以外。

为保护港口安全，该法所规定的特别措施主要围绕"保护区"的设立而展开。若联邦政府认为有必要对某港口的人员进入进行管制，即可通过发布命令，宣布某港口为"保护区"，并依相关命令通告划定这一"保护区"的范围。基于公共交通的便利、船舶的安全、港口设施的维护与良好管理，"保护区"的范围可包括任何码头、防波堤、防洪堤、泊位、登陆点，涵盖联邦政府认为必要的任何海岸及堤坝部分。联邦政府可以通过政府公报就"保护区"的人员进入许可、人员行为等制定相关规则，从而实现：第一，限制某些人员进入"保护区"；第二，将某些人员从"保护区"清离；第三，处置在"保护区"附近游荡的可疑人员。为强化保护效果，该法甚至规定，凡依该法行事或意图依该法善意行事的人，将免受刑事、民事诉讼及其他法律程序追究。[1]

（3）《1973 年卡西姆港务局法》及《1982 年科兰吉渔港管理局条例》

卡西姆港务局依《1973 年卡西姆港务局法》（The Port Qasim Authority Act）设立。依据该法，卡西姆港务局负责卡西姆港及其设施、行业相关的规划、发展和管理事宜，其成立方式、权力与职责、机构土地的收购、组织结构、财政管理、不当行为及惩处等均具体规定在该法的八章 72 项条文之中。[2] 根据该法，卡西姆港的覆盖范围由联邦政府通过政府公报确定或更改。基于公共交通的便利、船舶的安全、港口设施的维护与良好管理，这一范围可延伸至连接本港口区域的可通航航道的任何部分，包括任何码头、电车轨道、仓库、工棚及其他设施，无论其在高潮线以内或以外；同时，在不损害私人财产权利的情况下，还可包括高潮线约 46 米（50 码）以内海岸的

---

〔1〕 Protection of Ports（Special Measures）Act, 1948, The Pakistan Code, http：//pakistan-code. gov. pk/english/UY2FqaJw1-apaUY2Fqa-ap% 2BUZw% 3D% 3D-sg-jjjjjjjjjjjjj, March 16, 2020.

〔2〕 有关卡西姆港务局的基本职能及发展现状，参见本部分"二、海洋事务主管部门及职能"下"海事部"中"卡西姆港务局"一节。

任何部分。[1]

为了在卡西姆港范围内，就科兰吉渔港的规划、建造、营运、管理和维护作出安排，巴基斯坦于 1982 年颁布《科兰吉渔港管理局条例》（The Korangi Fisheries Harbour Authority Ordinance）。依据该条例，科兰吉渔港管理局正式成立，并在条例授权范围内落实条例宗旨及细则，以推进领水范围之外渔业资源的开发。作为服务于卡西姆港内的管理机构的下级立法，《科兰吉渔港管理局条例》的行文结构与《卡西姆港务局法》基本类似，其七章 33 项条文同样主要围绕机构的成立方式、机构的权力与职责、机构土地的收购、组织结构、财政管理、不当行为及惩处等内容而展开。[2]

3. 营运部门相关立法

（1）《1979 年巴基斯坦国家航运公司条例》

1979 年 3 月，《巴基斯坦国家航运公司条例》（Pakistan National Shipping Corporation Ordinance）颁布，旨在将国家航运公司和巴基斯坦航运公司合并设立为巴基斯坦国家航运公司，以便更好地服务于海上航行与交通，为海上运输行业的发展做好准备。根据该条例，巴基斯坦国家航运公司自 1979 年 1 月 1 日起正式成立，其职能主要在于：全面有效地担负起原国家航运公司和巴基斯坦航运公司根据本条例所移交并赋予的全部职责及全部业务，提供并进一步发展安全、高效、充足、经济和适当协调的沿海及国际航运服务，同时从事与航运相关的，或附随的，或有利于航运的一切形式的活动。[3]

（2）《1980 年巴基斯坦海运（管理机构移交）条例》

《1980 年巴基斯坦海运（管理机构移交）条例》［The Pakistan Maritime Shipping（Transfer of Managed Establishments）Ordinance，以下简称《1980 年条例》］意在为某些海运相关管理机构及设施的权益转让与功能移交提供法律依据。该条例应立足于《1974 年巴基斯坦海上运输（监管与控制）法》［Pakistan Maritime Shipping（Regulation and Control）Act，以下简称《1974 年海运法》］，推进相关海运管理设施的私人化进程。如该条例第 2 条规定，除主题或上下文相左的情形外，该条例中相关措施及表述的解释应与《1974 年

---

〔1〕　Port Qasim Authority Act, 1973, The Pakistan Code, http：//pakistancode. gov. pk/english/UY2FqaJw1-apaUY2Fqa-bpuUY2lr-sg-jjjjjjjjjjjjj, March 16, 2020.

〔2〕　Korangi Fisheries Harbour Authority Ordinance, 1982, The Pakistan Code, http：//pakistancode. gov. pk/english/UY2FqaJw1-apaUY2Fqa-bpeV-sg-jjjjjjjjjjjjj, March 16, 2020.

〔3〕　Pakistan National Shipping Corporation Ordinance, 1979, The Pakistan Code, http：//pakistancode. gov. pk/english/UY2FqaJw1-apaUY2Fqa-cZ6X-sg-jjjjjjjjjjjjj, March 16, 2020.

海运法》相一致。[1] 值得注意的是,《1974 年海运法》已于 1991 年经《巴基斯坦海上运输(监管与控制)(废止)法》 [Pakistan Maritime Shipping (Regulation and Control)(Repeal) Act] 明文废止,但《1980 年条例》仍然处于生效状态且未因《1974 年海运法》的废止作出相关修订。[2]

4. 争端解决相关立法

1980 年,巴基斯坦颁布的《高等法院海事管辖权条例》(The Admiralty Jurisdiction of High Courts Ordinance) 共有 9 条,意在通过划定高级法院的海事管辖权范围,明确海事管辖权的具体管辖事项与行使方式,判定船舶碰撞及其他类似案件的属人管辖权,设定船舶留置权的限制,明确上诉等相关程序及进一步规则的制定权等内容,对原海事法院相关立法有所整合和修订。依据这一条例,各高等法院之间的基本管辖范围划分为:第一,信德高等法院和俾路支高等法院应在各自的地域管辖范围内,拥有并行使本条例规定的海事管辖权;第二,拉合尔(Lahore)高等法院和白沙瓦(Peshawar)高等法院应在各自的地域管辖范围内,对涉及航空器的任何问题或索赔案件行使本条例所规定的管辖权。[3]

(六)海洋环境保护相关立法

《1997 年巴基斯坦环境保护法》 (The Pakistan Environmental Protection Act, 1997)旨在通过立法实现对环境的保护、养护、修复和改善,同时预防和控制污染,以促进国家的可持续发展。《1983 年巴基斯坦环境保护条例》(The Pakistan Environmental Protection Ordinance, 1983) 随该法的出台而被废除。作为巴基斯坦环境保护的基础性立法,该法为由巴基斯坦环境保护委员会、巴基斯坦环境保护署、省环境保护部门所组成的国家环保机构体系提供了法律依据。其中,前者主要负责环境保护工作的监督、协调和指导,而后二者主要负责对相关具体规则及环节的执行与落实。除上述三类机构的权力和职能相关事项外,该法的 34 项条文及 1 项附表还就可持续发展基金的管理、某些排放物的禁止、初步环境检查及环境影响评估、危险废物进口的禁

---

[1] Pakistan Maritime Shipping (Transfer of Managed Establishments) Ordinance, 1980, The Pakistan Code, http://pakistancode. gov. pk/english/UY2FqaJw1-apaUY2Fqa-cpuc-sg-jjjjjjjjjjjjj, March 16, 2020.

[2] Pakistan Maritime Shipping (Regulation and Control) (Repeal) Act, 1991, Josh and Mak International, https://joshandmakinternational. com/resources/laws-of-pakistan/admiralty-and-maritime-laws/the-pakistan-maritime-shipping-regulation-and-control-repeal-act-1991/, March 16, 2020.

[3] Admiralty Jurisdiction of High Courts Ordinance, 1980, The Pakistan Code, http://pakistan-code. gov. pk/english/UY2FqaJw1-apaUY2Fqa-cp2c-sg-jjjjjjjjjjjjj, March 16, 2020.

止、危险物质的处理、相关车辆管制、环境保护令的制定与发布、相关违法行为及处罚、环境法庭的设立与环境法官的选任等作出了规定。

尽管该法并未对海洋环境保护作出直接规定，但该法第1条明确规定其"适用于巴基斯坦全境"，而其第2条对"环境"一词的界定指明包括"空气、水、陆地"、"所有有机与无机组织及生物体"，以及"生态系统与生态关系"。同时，第31条规定，联邦政府可以通过政府公报制定旨在执行本法的相关规则，包括制定规则以实施附表中所列明的国际环境协定相关条款。其中，《联合国海洋法公约》《生物多样性公约》赫然在列。由此，该法也是可在巴基斯坦海洋环境保护中直接适用的重要法律文件。[1]

（七）海洋科研相关立法

为了保护和养护海洋环境，加强对相关海洋区域内海洋资源的勘探、开发和管理，巴基斯坦于2007年颁布《国家海洋研究所法》（The National Institute of Oceanography Act），宣布成立国家海洋研究所，以开展、协调和促进海洋学及海洋科学相关研究。

该研究所总部设在卡拉奇，并可在巴基斯坦各沿海地区设立分所。此前经联邦政府决议设立的其他研究所，应被视为根据该法设立的科研机构继续运行。根据该法第4条，国家海洋研究所的职能为：第一，在巴基斯坦海域内承担任务导向下有关物理、化学、生物及地质海洋学的跨学科研究；第二，在国家、国际、区域及次区域层级展开海洋调查；第三，在多个领域承担海洋学培训项目，以发展本土人力资源与相关专家；第四，建立国家海洋数据中心，作为巴基斯坦海域所有海洋数据或信息的国家资源库；第五，为政府提供必要建议，并在海洋活动中与其他国家机关合作；第六，与国际组织及机构保持联络，协同安排培训项目或提供专家服务，采购专用仪器设备，进行海洋技术转让，发展合作研究项目；第七，举办国家、国际、区域或次区域层级的研讨会、工作坊、讲习班等。国家海洋研究所的管理层由理事会、总干事、执行委员会组成。经联邦政府与理事会协商，应任命一名具有至少十年相关工作经验的著名科学家或工程师作为所长，研究所所长同时是技术咨询委员会主席。[2]

除此之外，《巴基斯坦水资源研究委员会法》（Pakistan Council of Re-

〔1〕 Pakistan Environmental Protection Act, 1997, The Pakistan Code, http：//pakistancode. gov. pk/english/UY2FqaJw1-apaUY2Fqa-apqaZQ＝＝-sg-jjjjjjjjjjjjj, March 16, 2020.
〔2〕 National Institute of Oceanography Act, 2007, The Pakistan Code, http：//pakistancode. gov. pk/english/UY2FqaJw1-apaUY2Fqa-apaUY2FsaJ4％3D-sg-jjjjjjjjjjjjj, March 16, 2020.

search in Water Resources Act）亦于 2007 年颁布。巴基斯坦水资源研究委员会的建立，旨在协调及促进水资源相关研究。尽管其第 2 条规定，该法所称"水资源"是指巴基斯坦内与水利学及水文力学相关的各个领域，包括供水、灌溉、排涝、围垦、防洪、内河航运及其他关联问题，似并未将海洋水域涵盖其中，但该法的适用对象仍可能涉及与海相通的水域或沿海水域，从而与海洋科学研究存在较密切关联。

四、缔结和加入的国际海洋法条约

（一）联合国框架下的海洋法公约

巴基斯坦于 1958 年 10 月 31 日签署了第一次联合国海洋法会议下的"日内瓦海洋法体系四公约"（《领海及毗连区公约》《公海公约》《捕鱼及养护公海生物资源公约》《大陆架公约》），但是其均未予批准。巴基斯坦随后于 1958 年 11 月 6 日对《关于强制争端解决的任择议定书》（Optional Protocol of Signature Concerning the Compulsory Settlement of Disputes）作出最终签署，表示对于其所签署的任何海洋法公约中之任何条款因解释或适用而发生涉及本国的一切争端，愿接受国际法院之强制管辖。[1]

巴基斯坦于 1982 年 12 月 10 日签署了由第三次联合国海洋法会议通过的《联合国海洋法公约》，并于 1997 年 2 月 26 日批准生效。1994 年 8 月 10 日，巴基斯坦签署了《关于执行 1982 年 12 月 10 日〈联合国海洋法公约〉第十一部分的协定》，并依照协定自 1994 年 11 月 16 日起开始对该协定临时适用，后于 1997 年 2 月 26 日予以正式批准。1996 年 2 月 15 日，巴基斯坦签署了《执行 1982 年 12 月 10 日〈联合国海洋法公约〉有关养护和管理跨界鱼类种群和高度洄游鱼类种群的规定的协定》；1999 年 9 月 9 日，巴基斯坦签署了《国际海底管理局特权与豁免议定书》；但巴基斯坦对以上公约均未作出批准。[2]

巴基斯坦在批准《公约》时提出三项声明。第一，巴基斯坦政府将在适当时就有关争端解决的第 287 条及第 298 条作出声明。第二，《公约》在处理从过境国领土的过境问题时，充分保障了过境国的主权。因此，内陆国依据第 125 条享有过境权利及便利，应确保不以任何方式损害过境国的主权与合法利益。因而，不同情况下有关过境自由的具体内容，必须由过境国与内陆国协议商定。在未能就过境权行使的条款及形式达成协议的情形下，在

---

[1] "Depository", United Nations Treaty Collection, https：//treaties. un. org/Pages/ViewDetails. aspx? src = TREATY&mtdsg_ no = XXI-1&chapter = 21&clang = _ en, March 20, 2020.

[2] See "Depository", United Nations Treaty Collection, https：//treaties. un. org/Pages/ViewDetailsI-II. aspx? src = TREATY&mtdsg_ no = XXI-6&chapter = 21&Temp = mtdsg3&clang = _ en, March 20, 2020; "Depository", United Nations Treaty Collection, https：//treaties. un. org/Pages/ViewDetails. aspx? src = TREATY&mtdsg_ no = XXI-6-a&chapter = 21&clang = _ en #6, March 20, 2020; "Depository", United Nations Treaty Collection, https：//treaties. un. org/Pages/ViewDetails. aspx? src = TREATY&mtdsg_ no = XXI-9&chapter = 21&clang = _ en, March 20, 2020.

巴基斯坦领土的通行行为将仅受巴基斯坦国内法律的约束。第三，巴基斯坦政府认为，除沿岸国同意外，《公约》并未授权他国在沿海国专属经济区及大陆架进行军事训练或演习，特别是在其间使用武器或爆炸物。[1]

（二）《国际海事组织公约》及相关修正案

巴基斯坦于 1958 年 11 月 21 日接受了 1948 年《国际海事组织公约》，成为国际海事组织的正式成员。其随后陆续接受了与国际海事组织框架相关的系列条约，包括：1964 年《〈国际海事组织公约〉第 17、第 18 条修正案》（Amendments to Articles 17 and 18 of the Convention on the International Maritime Organization），1965 年《〈国际海事组织公约〉第 28 条修正案》（Amendment to Article 28 of the Convention on the International Maritime Organization），1974 年《〈国际海事组织公约〉第 10、第 16、第 17、第 18、第 20、第 28、第 31、第 32 条修正案》（Amendment to Articles 10, 16, 17, 18, 20, 28, 31 and 32 of the Convention on the International Maritime Organization），1977 年《〈国际海事组织公约〉标题及实质性条款的修正案》（Amendment to the Title and Substantive Provisions of the Convention on the International Maritime Organization），1977 年《国际海事组织公约关于公约内技术合作委员会制度化的修正案》（Amendment to the Convention on the International Maritime Organization relating to the Institutionalization of the Committee on Technical Cooperation in the Convention），1979 年《〈国际海事公约〉第 17、第 18、第 20 和第 51 条修正案》（Amendment to Articles 17, 18, 20 and 51 of the Convention of the International Maritime Organization），1991 年《国际海事组织公约修正案（促进委员会的制度化)》［Amendment to the Convention on the International Maritime Organization (Institutionalization of the Facilitation Committee)]。[2]

（三）海上安全相关条约

为保障船舶在海上航行时的人命和财产安全，国际海事组织于 1974 年通过了《国际海上人命安全公约》。1985 年 4 月 10 日，巴基斯坦签署了该公约及《关于 1974 年〈国际海上人命安全公约〉1978 年议定书》（Protocol of

---

[1] "Declarations and Reservations", United Nations Treaty Collection, https：//treaties. un. org/Pages/ViewDetailsIII. aspx？src＝TREATY&mtdsg_ no＝XXI-6&chapter＝21&Temp＝mtdsg3&clang＝_ en #EndDec, March 20, 2020.

[2] "Depository", See United Nations Treaty Collection, https：//treaties. un. org/Pages/ViewDetails. aspx？src＝TREATY&mtdsg_ no＝XII-1-g&chapter＝12&clang＝_ en, March 20, 2020.

1978 relating to the International Convention for the Safety of Life at Sea, 1974, as amended)，并于 1985 年 7 月 10 日批准生效。2001 年 12 月 6 日，巴基斯坦加入了《1974 年国际海上人命安全公约 1988 年议定书》（Protocol of 1988 relating to the International Convention for the Safety of Life at Sea, 1974, as amended)，该议定书自 2002 年 3 月 6 日起对其生效。

为改善海上救险和救生安全通信、提高海陆空运输效率，国际海事组织于 1975 年推动召开建立国际海事卫星系统的国际会议并通过了一系列相关公约。巴基斯坦早在 1976 年 9 月 3 日就作为缔约国签署了《国际移动卫星组织业务协定》，其后于 2000 年 9 月 15 日批准了该协议的 1998 年修正案（1998 Amendments of Operating agreement on the International Mobile Satellite Organization)。巴基斯坦于 1985 年 2 月 6 日加入了经修正的 1976 年《国际移动卫星组织公约》，该公约自同日起对巴基斯坦生效。2000 年 9 月 15 日，巴基斯坦进一步接受了该公约的 1998 年修正案（1998 Amendments of the Convention on the International Mobile Satellite Organization)。

此外，巴基斯坦缔结和加入的与海上安全相关的公约还包括：《1971 年特种业务船客协定》、《1972 年国际海上避碰规则修正案》（Convention on the International Regulations for Preventing Collisions at Sea, 1972, as amended)、《1972 年国际集装箱安全公约》、经修订的《1979 年国际海上搜寻救助公约》、《1988 年制止危及海上航行安全非法行为公约》、《1988 年制止危及大陆架固定平台安全非法行为议定书》、《1988 年国际搜救卫星 COSPAS-SARSAT 系统计划协定》（The International COSPAS-SARSAT Programme Agreement) 等[1]。

（四）海洋环境保护相关条约

海洋环境保护问题一直是国际社会关注的重点之一，为此各国缔结了一系列公约，从不同层面促进在海洋环保领域的制度搭建与行动落实。为体现对海洋环境保护问题的关注和重视，巴基斯坦加入了多项海洋环境保护相关的条约，以表明其保护海洋环境的积极态度。

巴基斯坦于 1994 年 11 月 22 日加入《1973 年国际防止船舶造成污染公约的 1978 年议定书》（Protocol of 1978 relating to the International Convention for the Prevention of Pollution from Ships, 1973)，该条约自 1995 年 2 月 22 日起对巴基斯坦生效。此外，巴基斯坦在加入该公约修正案的同日（1994 年

---

[1]　See "Status of IMO Treaties", International Maritime Organization, https：//wwwcdn.imo.org/local-resources/en/About/Conventions/StatusOfConventions/Status% 20-% 202021.pdf, January 23, 2021.

11 月 22 日），接受了该公约的三个附件，分别是：《1973 年国际防止船舶造成污染公约附件三：以包装形式携带的有害物质》（International Convention for Prevention of Pollution from Ships，1973，Annex Ⅲ：Prevention of Pollution by Harmful Substances Carried by Sea in Packaged Form）、《1973 年国际防止船舶造成污染公约附件四：污水》（International Convention for Prevention of Pollution from Ships，1973，Annex Ⅳ：Sewage）以及《1973 年国际防止船舶造成污染公约附件五：垃圾排放》［International Convention for Prevention of Pollution from Ships（MARPOL），Annex Ⅴ（Optional）：Garbage］。其中，附件三与附件五自 1995 年 2 月 22 日起对巴基斯坦生效，附件Ⅳ自 2003 年 9 月 27 日起对巴基斯坦生效。

1995 年 3 月 9 日，巴基斯坦批准了《1972 年防止倾倒废物及其他物质污染海洋的公约》（Convention on the Prevention of Marine Pollution by Dumping of Wastes and other Matter，1972，as amended），该公约修正案于 1995 年 4 月 8 日对巴基斯坦生效。此外，巴基斯坦还加入了以下与海洋环境保护相关的公约：《1969 年国际干预公海油污事故公约》、《1973 年干预公海非油类物质污染公约》（Protocol relating to Intervention on the High Seas in Cases of Pollution by Substances other than Oil，1973，as amended）、《1990 年国际油污防备、反应和合作公约》以及《修正〈1969 年国际油污损害民事责任公约〉的 1992 年议定书》（Protocol of 1992 to Amend the International Convention on Civil Liability for Oil Pollution Damage，1969）。[1]

（五）船舶及船员相关条约

巴基斯坦共加入或接受了三部与船舶管理直接相关的条约，包括：第一，《1966 年国际载重线公约》。巴基斯坦于 1968 年 12 月 5 日接受该公约，该公约自 1969 年 3 月 5 日起对巴基斯坦生效。第二，《〈1966 年国际载重线公约〉1988 年议定书》［Protocol of 1988 relating to the International Convention on Load Lines，1996（LL PROT 1988）］。巴基斯坦于 2002 年 4 月 25 日加入该议定书，该议定书自 2002 年 7 月 25 日起对巴基斯坦生效。第三，《1969 年国际船舶吨位丈量公约》。巴基斯坦于 1994 年 10 月 17 日接受该公约，该公约于 1995 年 1 月 17 日起对巴基斯坦生效。[2]

---

〔1〕 See "Status of IMO Treaties"，International Maritime Organization，https：//wwwcdn. imo. org/local-resources/en/About/Conventions/StatusOfConventions/Status% 20-% 202021. pdf，January 23，2021.

〔2〕 See "Status of IMO Treaties"，International Maritime Organization，https：//wwwcdn. imo. org/local-resources/en/About/Conventions/StatusOfConventions/Status% 20-% 202021. pdf，January 23，2021.

另外，巴基斯坦于 1975 年 6 月 27 日签署了《联合国班轮公会行动守则公约》（Convention on A Code of Conduct for Liner Conference），[1] 于 2000 年 7 月 11 日签署了《1999 年国际扣押船舶公约》（International Convention on Arrest of Ships，1999），但后者尚未对巴基斯坦生效。[2] 巴基斯坦仅在 1985 年 4 月 10 日加入了一部与船员相关的条约，即《1978 年海员培训、发证和值班标准国际公约》，该公约于 1985 年 7 月 10 日对巴基斯坦生效。[3]

（六）渔业管理相关条约

渔业在巴基斯坦的国民经济发展中占重要地位，其海洋渔业资源较为丰富。在渔业管理方面，巴基斯坦主要接受了以下几个公约：《1948 年建立印度洋—太平洋渔业委员会协定》（Agreement for the Establishment of the Indo-Pacific Fisheries Council）[4]、《1992 年亚洲—太平洋水产养殖中心网协议》（Agreement on the Network of Aquaculture Centres in Asia and the Pacific）、《1993 年建立印度洋金枪鱼委员会协定》。其中，巴基斯坦于 1949 年 8 月 1 日接受了《建立印度洋—太平洋渔业委员会协定》，该协定于同日对巴基斯坦生效[5]；于 1990 年 1 月 28 日加入《亚洲—太平洋水产养殖中心网协议》，该协定于同日起对巴基斯坦生效[6]；于 1995 年 4 月 27 日接受了《建立印度洋金枪鱼委员会协定》，该协定自 1996 年 3 月 27 日起对巴基斯坦生效。[7]

---

[1] Convention on a Code of Conduct for Liner Conferences, United Nations Treaty Collection, https://treaties.un.org/Pages/ViewDetails.aspx? src = TREATY&mtdsg _ no = XII-6&chapter = 12&clang = _ en, March 20, 2020.

[2] International Convention on Arrest of Ships, 1999, United Nations Treaty Collection, https://treaties.un.org/pages/ViewDetails.aspx? src = IND&mtdsg_ no = XII-8&chapter = 12&clang = _ en, March 20, 2020.

[3] Status of IMO Treaties, International Maritime Organization, https://wwwcdn.imo.org/localresources/en/About/Conventions/StatusOfConventions/Status% 20-% 202021.pdf, January 23, 2021.

[4] 该委员会建立初期名为 "Indo-Pacific Fisheries Council"，于 1976 年更名为 "Indo-Pacific Fisheries Commission"，又于 1993 年更名为 "Asia-Pacific Fishery Commission"。 "Agreement for the Establishment of the Aisa-Pacific Fishery Commission", FAO, http://www.fao.org/fileadmin/user_ upload/legal/docs/001s-e.pdf, March 20, 2020.

[5] "Agreement for the Establishment of the Aisa-Pacific Fishery Commission", FAO, http://www.fao.org/fileadmin/user_ upload/legal/docs/001s-e.pdf, March 20, 2020.

[6] Agreement for the Establishment of the Network of Aquaculture Centres in Asia and the Pacific, Ecolex, https://www.ecolex.org/details/treaty/agreement-for-the-establishment-of-the-network-of-aquaculture-centres-in-asia-and-the-pacific-tre-001112/, March 20, 2020.

[7] Agreement for the Establishment of the Indian Ocean Tuna Commission, Ecolex, https://www.ecolex.org/details/treaty/agreement-for-the-establishment-of-the-indian-ocean-tuna-commission-tre-001227/, March 20, 2020.

五、海洋争端解决

（一）通过协议解决的海洋争端

1. 与阿曼之间的划界协定

《阿曼苏丹国与巴基斯坦伊斯兰共和国有关划定海洋边界的马斯喀特协定》（Muscat Agreement on the Delimitation of the Maritime Boundary between the Sultanate of Oman and the Islamic Republic of Pakistan，12 June，2000，以下简称《马斯喀特协定》）签署于 2000 年 6 月 12 日，并于 2000 年 11 月 21 日生效。该协定通过划定 146 海里的海上边界线将两国的专属经济区分隔开来。根据《马斯喀特协定》：第一，巴基斯坦和阿曼两国专属经济区之间的海上边界线应从基于《公约》所划定的基线量起；第二，两国专属经济区的界限应以符合《公约》的中间线原则为基础进行划定；第三，两国专属经济区的界限为连接一系列固定点的测地线（WGS84）。相关固定点的地理坐标如第 Ⅱ 部分 表 3 所示。

第Ⅱ部分 表 3　巴基斯坦与阿曼海洋边界坐标点

坐标点	纬度（北）	经度（东）
1	23°20′48″	61°25′00″
2	23°15′22″	61°32′48″
3	23°11′40″	61°38′11″
4	22°56′35″	62°00′51″
5	22°54′37″	62°03′50″
6	22°40′37″	62°25′17″
7	22°05′01″	63°08′23″
8	21°57′13″	63°14′21″
9	21°47′24″	63°22′13″

巴基斯坦与阿曼均承认对方在本协定划定范围内对包括底土及其上覆水域在内的海床所享有的主权权利。但对于跨越这一界限的任何地质石油构造、单独油气田、矿物或其他自然资源的延伸，若任何一方想以直接钻探方式从分界线一侧全部或部分地开发利用分界线另一侧的资源，应遵循以下限制：（1）上述资源的开发利用应根据普遍适用的国际法规则与习惯以及公正

公平的原则，在两国协商一致的情形下进行；（2）若非两国合意，任意一方均不能在所划定分界线两侧 125 米的区域内进行开采活动；（3）若在实施过程中发生争议，两国将尽最大努力达成协议以协调和统一其在分界线两侧的开发活动。[1]

值得注意的是，该协定并未涉及阿曼的大陆架外部界限。由于同属伊斯兰国家，阿曼和巴基斯坦之间一贯保持着良好的关系，阿曼亦在其官方声明中将两国定位为"拥有文化、科技及经济长期合作基础"而"拥有实质性的共同利益和广阔前景的友好邻邦"[2]。由此，尽管针对巴基斯坦向联合国大陆架界限委员会提交的外大陆架划界信息，阿曼向联合国表达了其"尚无提交划界案之意向，但保留日后提交的权利"的基本立场，但并未影响该协定在两国间的生效与后续适用。该协定签订后，巴阿双方始终严格遵守根据该协定划定的海上边界，为两国海上渔场和海产资源的开发和合理利用创造了良好环境。

2. 与伊朗之间的划界协定

巴基斯坦和伊朗间的友好关系可以追溯到巴基斯坦独立之初。1947 年 8 月巴基斯坦独立后，伊朗是第一个承认其主权地位的国家。[3] 1958 年 2 月 6 日，巴基斯坦和伊朗签署了两国的陆地边境划界协议，建立了相互信任的基础。但 1979 年伊朗伊斯兰革命的发生成为双方关系的转折点，对阿富汗地区的权力争夺及对待塔利班（Taliban）政权的态度分歧更使双方的紧张关系达到顶峰。[4] 虽然两国的双边交往一直在利益争夺的夹缝中前行，但是由于围绕波斯湾（Persian Bay）和阿曼海（Omen Sea）的地区外部压力日渐增加，双方仍然积极推动在海洋边界划定上的共识。

从 1992 年起，巴基斯坦和伊朗的政治和海洋专家就立足国际法围绕海床和底土资源的划分起草相关协议草案。经由该草案，两国外长于 1997 年 6 月在德黑兰签署了一项"海洋划界协定"。该协定界定了两国从阿曼所属的波

---

〔1〕 "Muscat Agreement on the Delimitation of the Maritime Boundary between the Sultanate of Oman and the Islamic Republic of Pakistan", UN Office of Legal Affairs, https：//www. un. org/Depts/los/LEGISLATIONANDTREATIES/PDFFILES/TREATIES/OMN-PAK2000MB. PDF, March 20, 2020.

〔2〕 Richard F. Nyrop et al. , *Area Handbook for the Persian Gulf States*, Cabin John, Wildside Press, 2008, pp. 360-361.

〔3〕 CIDOB, "Foreign Relations of Pakistan", https：//cn. bing. com/search? q = Pakistan + foreign + relations + Yearbook + 2003-2004&qs = n&form = QBLHCN&sp = -1&pq = pakistan + foreign + relations + yearbook + 2003-2004&sc = 0-, March 22, 2020.

〔4〕 Rizwan Hussain, *Pakistan and the Emergence of Islamic Militancy in Afghanistan*, Aldershot, Hampshire：Ashgate, 2005, p. 143.

斯湾向东北一直延伸至瓜达尔湾（Gwadar Bay）的大陆架界限，并且划定了两国间有关内水、领海、毗连区和专属经济区的海洋边界。根据该协定第 7 条的规定，这一协定于 1999 年 7 月 26 日生效，并成为两国海上合作的基本前提。由于该协定所划界限位于距巴基斯坦领海基线的 200 海里之内，因此，与确定巴基斯坦扩展大陆架的外部界限并没有关系。[1]

巴基斯坦和伊朗在国家交往中始终处于一种"和平共处下的竞争对手模式"。这种友好的竞争模式主要立足于双方共存的安全需要和相同的地缘政治利益。巴基斯坦扼守着世界各国通往波斯湾的海上要道，而伊朗则是西亚地区重要的产油国和海上贸易国，保持密切的战略合作关系符合两国作为南亚和西亚地区具有重要影响力国家的利益，两国共同努力使得巴伊关系在新世纪回暖的事实也印证了上述结论。由于在波斯湾和阿曼湾频繁发生的针对油轮的袭击事件，巴伊两国尤其在海上安全及海上搜救领域表现出强烈合作意愿。自 2016 年起，两国即就海上合作搜救相关协议草案展开积极协商。2019 年 5 月 29 日，巴基斯坦内阁审议并且通过了国防部所提出的与伊朗的合作备忘录。[2] 尽管由于伊朗方面实际推进措施的欠缺，相关合作协议的最终达成可能仍面临困难，但两国加强海洋上互利合作的共识不容否认。尊重前述划界协定下的海域疆界，维护具有重要价值的国际航运安全、平稳的海上运输要道，无论对于两国的海洋事业发展还是对于地区海洋秩序都作出了贡献。

（二）未决的海洋争端

1. 与印度间的划界争端

巴基斯坦同印度的海洋边界协定谈判至今尚未取得实质性进展。两国争议的焦点地区为巴基斯坦与印度西部的爵士湾及其所延伸相接的海上边界。爵士湾是位于北纬 23°58′、东经 68°48′的一片 96 公里的狭长水域，在地理上将巴基斯坦的信德省和印度的古吉拉特邦分隔开来。对于爵士湾相关区域的

---

〔1〕 See Syed Farooq Hasnat, *Pakistan*, California, ABC-CLIO, 2011, p. 27; Pirouz Mojtahed-Zadeh and Bahador Zarei, "Maritime Boundary Delimitations in the Persian Gulf", *International Studies Journal* 54, 2017, p. 18; "Submission by The Government of The Islamic Republic of Pakistan for Establishment of the Outer Limits of the Continental Shelf of Pakistan", UN Office of Legal Affairs, https: //www. un. org/Depts/los/clcs_ new/submissions _ files/pak29 _ 09/pak2009execut ive-summary. pdf, November 21, 2020.

〔2〕 "Pakistan, Iran to ink MoU on Maritime Search, Rescue Operations", Pakistan Today, https: // www. pakistantoday. com. pk/2019/07/02/pakistan-iran-to-ink-mou-on-maritime-search-rescue-oper-ations/, March 22, 2020.

海洋划界，印度方面坚持采用"航道中间线原则"，立足爵士湾航道中心线继而划定海上边界；巴基斯坦方面则强调公平原则，坚持两国的海上划界需以爵士湾右岸的"绿线"为前置要件[1]。

1969 年以来，巴基斯坦和印度就爵士湾划界举行了多轮会谈和讨论。两国还于 2005—2007 年，成立了联合调查队，通过对爵士湾有关区域进行的两轮联合调查确定了爵士湾近百年来的疆域变化，并据此绘制了新的区域地图。此后，巴印双方在 2011 年和 2012 年举行的双边会谈之中也都相继表达了和平解决有关爵士湾划界问题的意愿。虽然谈判意愿颇为强烈，但是由于双方都没有作出具体让步，爵士湾边界的划定问题仍然前景不明。如印度曾提议先行根据《公约》的技术方面的规定（Technical Aspects of the Law of the Sea）来划定海上边界，再行解决爵士湾的划界问题。但巴基斯坦回绝了该提议，认为应首先完成爵士湾的划界，再行解决海洋边界问题。同时，巴基斯坦曾提议通过国际仲裁解决划界争端，但同样为印度断然拒绝，其认为所有双边争端都应在没有第三方干预的情况下解决。自 2012 年 6 月以来，有关爵士湾的划界争议再未取得任何进展。

尽管爵士湾几乎没有军事价值，但其丰富的海底石油和天然气储藏赋予该区域巨大的经济价值，控制爵士湾就等于控制了大片潜在能源。作为两国海上边界的重要参照点，爵士湾的界限走向将在很大程度上决定印巴两国从领海到专属经济区直至大陆架的基本界域划分，从而决定两国相应海洋开发活动的范围。由于海上边界久拖不决，该海域的渔业争端时有发生，海上货运安全也难以保障。如何有效促成相关协议以调和并破解海上边界争端所带来的问题和矛盾，是关乎两国切身利益的迫切要求[2]。

2. 阿曼对巴基斯坦外大陆架划界的异议立场

2009 年 4 月 30 日，巴基斯坦正式向联合国大陆架界限委员会提出确认其 200 海里外大陆架划界信息的申请。作为与巴基斯坦海岸相向的国家，此举立即引发阿曼的高度关注。

巴基斯坦申请案所涉及的区域位于阿拉伯海穆雷山脊（Murray Ridge）的东边和南边。2009 年 5 月 4 日，联合国大陆架界限委员会秘书长根据《大陆架界限委员会议事规则》（Rules of Procedure of the Commission on the Limits

---

〔1〕　有关印巴爵士湾争端的背景、发展现状、具体主张等，详见本书"第 I 部分　印度海洋法体系"中"五、海洋争端解决"下"（三）未决的海洋争端"部分。

〔2〕　Young Bhartiya，"Sir Creek the Forgotten Dispute between India and Pakistan"，https：//www. youngbhartiya. com/article/sir-creek-the-forgotten-dispute-between-india-and-pakistan，March　22，2020.

of the Continental Shelf，以下简称《议事规则》）第 50 条将巴方提交的文件信息传阅至各缔约国，并根据传阅结果和《议事规则》第 51 条对该申请案进行了审议。

2009 年 8 月 7 日，阿曼宣称其正积极参与编制外大陆架延伸的相关申请，该申请所含的大陆架主张包括且不限于巴基斯坦所主张的同一区域。因此，阿曼向联合国大陆架界限委员会提出如下立场：第一，阿曼已于 2009 年 4 月 15 日提交了本国的外大陆架初步信息；第二，在完成并提出其大陆架延伸主张之前，阿曼不会考虑巴基斯坦 2009 年提交的外大陆架信息；第三，由于巴基斯坦的主张区域毗邻阿曼专属经济区，在缺乏进一步证据以核实的情形下，阿曼保留其主张专属经济区的权利。[1] 据此，经第 32 届联合国大陆架界限委员会讨论同意，于 2013 年 8 月 26 日正式成立了小组委员会（Sub-committee），对巴基斯坦 2009 年外大陆架申请案和阿曼的反对意见进行综合审议。

巴基斯坦随后与阿曼展开积极谈判，并促成双方对巴基斯坦外大陆架划界案的共识。双方确认：第一，若巴基斯坦的外大陆架主张与阿曼未来的主张海域存在重合，两国将通过双边方式划定界限；第二，巴基斯坦外大陆架申请中有关阿拉伯海的"潜在海洋边界"是巴基斯坦的单边主张，应以未来双方确定的界限为准；第三，巴基斯坦确认其当前的外大陆架申请将不损害阿曼未来的外大陆架申请或两国间最终的大陆架划界。[2] 由此，阿曼于 2014 年 11 月 10 日再次致信联合国大陆架界限委员会，表示撤回其 2009 年请求，不再反对该委员会就巴基斯坦划界申请的进一步审议程序。2015 年 3 月，联合国大陆架界限委员会通过了有关巴基斯坦申请案的最终建议。[3]

不过，在联合国大陆架界限委员会审议程序中的支持与配合，并不意味着阿曼对巴基斯坦大陆架主张的全盘接受，也未导向两国在大陆架划界问题上的彻底解决。2016 年 8 月，巴基斯坦根据《公约》第 76 条第 9 款和第 84 条第 2 款向联合国秘书长提交其外大陆架界限案，并附随相关海图、地理坐

---

〔1〕 "Communication dated 7 August 2009", UN Office of Legal Affairs, https：//www. un. org/depts/los/clcs_ new/submissions_ files/pak29_ 09/omn_ re_ pak_ 2009. pdf, March 22, 2020.

〔2〕 "Communication dated 10 Novemberember 2014", UN Office of Legal Affairs, https：//www. un. org/depts/los/clcs_ new/submissions_ files/pak29_ 09/2014_ 10_ 09_ PAK_ NV_ UN_ 003_ 14-00794. pdf, March 22, 2020.

〔3〕 "Summary of Recommendations of The Commission on The Limits of The Continental Shelf in Regard to The Submission Made by The Islamic Republic of Pakistan on 30 April 2009", UN Office of Legal Affairs, https：//www. un. org/depts/los/clcs_ new/submissions_ files/pak29_ 09/2015_ 03_ 13_ SC_ PAK. pdf, March 22, 2020.

标列表及相关信息。尽管在此前收获了巴基斯坦官方的褒扬与感谢，阿曼仍然迅速作出反应，于同年 12 月向联合国秘书长表达其反对立场。阿曼政府认为：第一，巴基斯坦政府无权就外大陆架界限作出"永久性划定"，也无权依据《公约》第 76 条第 9 款及第 84 条第 2 款提交这一信息；第二，巴基斯坦的外大陆架界限应立足于其与阿曼间大陆架边界的划定，而当前两国虽已达成共识但尚未划定这一边界；第三，依据联合国大陆架界限委员会"建议"所定的大陆架界限不应损害国家间的边界划分，而巴基斯坦的单边行为违背了这一原则，不应是"最终且有拘束力"的。[1] 可见，尽管巴基斯坦与阿曼间一直保持着较为积极的合作姿态，但"兄弟般"的情谊也无法超脱国家利益的激烈争夺，两国间的大陆架划界问题仍将多有波折。

---

〔1〕 "Communication dated 7 December 2016 concerning the Deposit by Pakistan of A Chart, including A List of Geographical Coordinates of Points and Relevant Information", UN Office of Legal Affairs, https：//www. un. org/Depts/los/LEGISLATIONANDTREATIES/PDFFILES/communications/omn_re_ pak_ 07122016. pdf, March 22, 2020.

六、国际海洋合作

（一）海洋防务合作

1. 与中国的合作

中巴友谊历久弥坚。2015 年，中国与巴基斯坦建立"全天候战略合作伙伴关系"。2018 年，两国进一步声明将加强这一关系，并"打造新时代更紧密中巴命运共同体"。中国与巴基斯坦一直有较为积极的国防合作意愿，也有意在航行安全、海洋经济、海洋资源开发利用、海洋科研和海洋环境保护方面保持紧密合作。20 世纪 70 年代起，中巴间即有海军及海上项目的合作。21 世纪以来，中巴两国在能源安全、海上通道、反恐等多个领域战略需求不断增强，两国海军人才交流得到了持续有效的开展。[1] 当前，两国已签署了多个军事合作项目协议和防务条约，巴基斯坦海军更意图立足紧密的海上防务合作，将中巴海上项目合作扩展至包括港口、渔业、海上经济区、造船、船坞建设等在内的更广阔空间。[2]

在高层对话与互访方面，中国与巴基斯坦分别于 2014 年、2016 年及 2018 年举行了三次"中巴海上合作对话"。巴方代表在第二轮对话中表示，海上合作是巴中关系的重要组成部分，双方应在海上互联互通、维护海上通道安全、海军和海警交流、海洋科技与渔业等领域加强合作，为地区稳定与经济繁荣作出贡献。而在第三轮对话中，双方就海上安全形势和两国各自海洋政策深入交换意见，回顾了近年来两国海上合作取得的进展，同意继续加强政策沟通与协调，拓展两国海军和海警交流以及港口建设、海洋科技、海上搜救等领域务实合作，加强在涉海多边事务上的协调配合。[3] 2018 年及

---

〔1〕 王小光：《中巴两国海军将继续携手为"和谐海洋"护航》，载中国网，http：//www.china.com.cn/military/txt/2010-08/26/content_ 20797851.htm，最后访问日期：2022 年 3 月 5 日。

〔2〕 "CPEC and Sino-Pak Military Cooperation"，Voice of Journalists，https：//www.voj.news/cpec-and-sino-pak-military-cooperation/，March 22，2020.

〔3〕 参见《首轮中巴海上合作对话联合新闻稿》，载中华人民共和国外交部网站，https：//www.mfa.gov.cn/web/gjhdq_ 676201/gj_ 676203/yz_ 676205/1206_ 676308/xgxw_ 676314/201407/t20140708_ 9288107.shtm，最后访问日期：2022 年 3 月 2 日；《中国与巴基斯坦举行第二轮海上合作对话》，载人民网，http：//world.people.com.cn/n1/2016/0203/c1002-28108409.html，最后访问日期：2022 年 3 月 2 日；《中国和巴基斯坦举行第三轮海上合作对话》，载中华人民共和国外交部网站，https：//www.mfa.gov.cn/web/gjhdq_ 676201/gj_ 676203/yz_ 676205/1206_ 676308/xgxw_ 676314/201808/t20180817_ 7971205.shtm，最后访问日期：2022 年 3 月 2 日。

2019年4月，中国国务委员兼国防部长魏凤和两度会见来访的巴基斯坦海军参谋长阿巴西。双方同意，中巴防务安全合作是两国关系的重要支柱，多年来中巴两军高层往来密切，各领域交流合作成效显著。阿巴西表示，愿与中方进一步密切高层交往和战略沟通，不断加强反恐及中巴经济走廊建设安保等领域的合作，不断深化两军在高层交往、实战化训练、装备技术等领域的交流，推动两国两军特别是两国海军关系的发展。[1]

在军备合作方面，中巴两国基础良好、势头蓬勃。2005年4月，中巴两国正式签署合同以建造4艘F-22P型护卫舰，其中3艘由上海沪东造船厂建造，最后1艘由卡拉奇造船及机械制造有限公司完成。2007年，巴基斯坦再次与中方签署合同追加4艘F-22P改进型导弹护卫舰的建造，并表示有意结合中国054A型护卫舰的特点研制更先进的舰艇。2015年，中巴两国签署了一份价值数十亿美元的协议，由中国帮助巴基斯坦海军建造8艘常规动力潜艇。这也成为中巴两国当时金额最大的军事合作协议。[2] 2016年7月，巴基斯坦内阁会议批准本国与中国议定长期防务协议。巴基斯坦内阁详细考虑了就巴基斯坦和中国在不同领域加强防务和安全合作的协议草案展开谈判的概要，以互相尊重主权和领土完整、互不侵犯、互不干涉内政、平等互利、和平共处为基础，寻求防务和安全方面的战略利益，包括武器和技术转让。[3] 2017年，巴军费增长7%，对外军购因此大幅增长，其中中国武器继续占据主要份额。巴空军在该年度增购14架中巴合作研发生产的FC-1"枭龙"战斗机，计划最终组建一支拥有150架"枭龙"的庞大战机编队。[4] 2018年7月，中国船舶工业集团为巴基斯坦建造的1500吨级海事巡逻舰PM-SA 143船在广州交付。中船集团与巴基斯坦海军有着长期的合作友谊，此前已经向巴基斯坦交付4艘反潜护卫艇和4艘400吨巡逻艇。PMSA 143船是巴基斯坦目前最大最先进的公务舰船，交付后将主要用于管辖海域巡逻执法、

---

〔1〕 参见欧阳浩：《魏凤和会见巴基斯坦海军参谋长》，载中华人民共和国国防部网站，http://www.mod.gov.cn/diplomacy/2018-04/18/content_4809783.htm，最后访问日期：2022年3月4日；欧阳浩：《魏凤和会见巴基斯坦海军参谋长》，载中华人民共和国国防部网站，http://www.mod.gov.cn/leaders/2019-04/21/content_4840174.htm，最后访问日期：2022年3月4日。

〔2〕 《巴基斯坦确认将从中国购2艘054A护卫舰3年内达4艘》，载观察者网，https://www.guancha.cn/military-affairs/2018_06_01_458662.shtml，最后访问日期：2022年3月5日。

〔3〕 《巴基斯坦批准与中国签订长期防务协议 含武器转让》，载观察者网，https://www.guancha.cn/global-news/2016_09_06_373533.shtml，最后访问日期：2022年3月5日。

〔4〕 李彦彬：《2017年南亚军情：巴铁涨军费 孟加拉国或买中国无人机》，载参考消息网，http://www.cankaoxiaoxi.com/mil/20180202/2254264.shtml，最后访问日期：2022年3月5日。

应对非对称袭击和威胁、专属经济区及渔场保护、海上搜索救援以及日常训练，承担起守卫瓜达尔港等的重任。[1] 同年 6 月，中巴还签署了 4 艘 054A/P 型护卫舰的建造合同。其首舰于 2020 年 8 月在上海下水，随后于 2021 年 11 月交付巴基斯坦海军。该舰也是我国迄今为止出口的吨位最大、技术最先进的水面战斗舰艇。巴基斯坦总统阿尔维盛赞 054A/P 型护卫舰项目是巴基斯坦与中国深厚友谊的又一典范，并宣布该型舰艇将被用于保卫中巴经济走廊海上通道的安全。除上述项目外，中巴重点海军防务合作还包括 F - 22P 型护卫舰、直-9 直升机、水文调查船、导弹攻击快艇、8 艘"汉果尔"级潜艇以及中空长航时无人机。[2]

在海上军事演习方面，至 2021 年 12 月，中国海军舰艇已先后 8 次赴巴基斯坦参加在阿拉伯海上的"和平"系列多国联合演习。2019 年 2 月，由两栖船坞登陆舰昆仑山舰、综合补给舰骆马湖舰组成的 998 舰艇编队，应邀前往巴基斯坦卡拉奇港参加"和平-19"演习。此次演习中，参演各国海军围绕编队快速离码头、航行补给、主炮对海实弹射击、营救落水人员、国际阅舰式、反海盗演练、海上拦截等内容展开联合演习。其间，中国海军还与其他参演国海军开展了舰艇开放参观、军事文化展示、体育比赛、军事研讨交流等活动，编队指挥员也在国际海事研讨会议上做了主旨交流发言。[3] 2021 年 2 月，中国海军 119 编队在结束执行亚丁湾护航任务后赴巴基斯坦参加"和平-21"多国海军联合演习。这是中国海军舰艇编队第 8 次参加由巴基斯坦海军组织的"和平"系列多边演习，再次加强了与相关国家海军的专业交流与友好互动。[4] 除"和平"系列的多国军演外，两国也以双边海上演习的方式进行海上防务合作交流与协同训练。2016 年 11 月，巴中两国海军举行了以中巴经济走廊为重点，旨在促进该地区海上安全与稳定的第四次联合

[1]《黄埔文冲交付巴基斯坦 1500 吨级海事巡逻船》，载国际船舶网，http://www. eworld-ship. com/html/2018/NewShipUnderConstrunction_ 0721/141324. html，最后访问日期：2022 年 3 月 2 日。

[2] 刘煊尊：《巴基斯坦首艘中国造 054A/P 护卫舰入列，巴总统：该舰将被用于保卫中巴经济走廊海上通道安全》，载环球网，https://baijiahao. baidu. com/s？ id = 1722878279215381151&wfr = spider&for = pc，最后访问日期：2022 年 3 月 2 日。

[3] 薛成清、顾亚根、崔晓洋：《中国海军 998 舰艇编队抵达巴基斯坦参加多国联合军演》，载中华人民共和国国防部网站，http://www. mod. gov. cn/shouye/2019-02/08/content_ 4835968. htm，最后访问日期：2022 年 3 月 4 日。

[4]《海军舰艇编队赴巴基斯坦参加"和平-21"多国海军联合演习》，载中华人民共和国国防部网站，http://www. mod. gov. cn/action/2021-02/11/content_ 4879040. htm，最后访问日期：2022 年 3 月 4 日。

演习。[1] 2020 年 1 月，代号为"海洋卫士 - 2020"（Sea Guardians-2020）的中巴第六次双边海军演习在阿拉伯海北部展开。为加强两国之间的安全合作，双方计划通过本次演习开展一系列训练活动，包括联合巡逻、防空、联合反潜、海上实弹射击和联合海上训练等。[2] 其中，第一阶段即"海洋卫士 - 2020"中巴海上联合演习港岸阶段圆满结束于 1 月 8 日结束；而第二阶段即海上实兵实弹演练阶段的演习于 1 月 10 日开始，中巴混合舰艇编队从巴基斯坦卡拉奇港解缆起航，前往位于北阿拉伯海的预定演习海域完成该阶段演练。[3]

2. 与俄罗斯的合作

巴俄的海上防务合作起步相对较晚。2013 年 3 月，俄罗斯作为观察员国参加了巴基斯坦"和平 - 13"（AMAN-13）的多国海军演习，此次海军演习的主要目标之一是展示各参加国联合打击恐怖主义和海上犯罪的决心。[4]

2014 年是两国防务合作的分水岭。2014 年 6 月，俄罗斯宣布解除对巴基斯坦的武器禁运。2014 年 11 月，俄罗斯国防部长在对伊斯兰堡访问期间与巴基斯坦签署了两国的第一份防务合作协议。依据该协议，两国将就政治军事问题交换情报，合作促进国际安全，加强反恐和军备控制活动，同时加强在教育、医学、历史、地理和文化等各个领域的合作，并分享两国维和行动的相关经验。[5]

2015 年 12 月，俄海军"乌达洛伊"级驱逐舰与巴基斯坦在阿拉伯海举行"季风 - 2015"（Monsoon-2015）联合反毒演习。俄罗斯海军、俄罗斯联邦缉毒局和特种部队与巴基斯坦海军的舰艇和直升机共同完成了本次在阿拉伯

---

〔1〕 Saima Ali, "Maritime Security Naval Cooperation China Pakistan", https：//foreignpolicynews. org/2016/11/25/maritime-security-naval-cooperation-china-pakistan/, March 22, 2020.

〔2〕 "Sea Guardians-2020：China, Pakistan Kick Off Major Naval Exercise on West Coast of India", Sputnik International, https：//sputniknews. com/military/202001061077958868-sea-guardians-2020-china-pakistan-kick-off-major-naval-exercise-on-west-coast-of-india/, March 22, 2020.

〔3〕 黎云、陈润楚：《"海洋卫士 - 2020"中巴海上联演转入海上实兵实弹演练》，载新华网，http：//www. xinhuanet. com/mil/2020-01/10/c_ 1210432353. htm，最后访问日期：2021 年 3 月 20 日。

〔4〕 "US, China take part in Pakistan naval drills", Dawn, https：//www. dawn. com/news/790930, March 22, 2020.

〔5〕 "Review of Russia-Pakistan Defence Cooperation：Reflection of Emerging Geo-Political Realities", Vivekananda International Foundation, https：//www. vifindia. org/article/2019/Februaryruary/02/review-of-russia-pakistan-defence-cooperation, March 22, 2020; "Pakistan, Russia sign landmark defence cooperation agreement", Dawn, https：//www. dawn. com/news/1145875, March 22, 2020.

海北部的演习。[1]

2017 年 2 月，俄罗斯正式参加巴基斯坦"和平"系列海军多国演习的第五次"和平－17"（AMAN-2017）军演。本次演习共有包括巴基斯坦在内的 37 个国家参加，其中俄罗斯派遣"塞韦罗莫斯克"号反潜舰（Severomorsk ASW）、"阿勒泰"号拖船（Altay tugboat）和"杜伯纳"号油轮（Dubna tanker）联合行动。俄罗斯与巴基斯坦均认为，各参演部队通过演练各种海军训练项目，增进了相互了解并有助于地区稳定。[2]

2018 年 8 月，巴基斯坦海军中将卡利姆·肖卡特（Kaleem Shaukat）访问俄罗斯期间，双方签署了有关双边海军合作问题的谅解备忘录。该谅解备忘录的重点是培训海军人员以及进行联合军事演习。随后，两国海军参加了在阿拉伯海举行的联合反毒演习，巴基斯坦又派遣了一艘军舰前往圣彼得堡参加俄罗斯海军日的大型阅兵式。[3] 同年 11 月，巴基斯坦和俄罗斯海军同意加强双边合作，以应对与海上安全相关的挑战。在圣彼得堡会晤期间，巴基斯坦海军参谋长阿巴西上将和俄罗斯海军总司令弗拉基米尔·科罗里奥夫（Vladimir Korolyov）上将决定加强"有效应对海洋领域跨国挑战和威胁的努力"。阿巴西上将还简要介绍了即将举行的"和平－19"（AMAN-19）多国海军演习。[4] 2018 年 12 月，俄罗斯海军舰艇访问卡拉奇，并与巴基斯坦海军在北阿拉伯海举行双边联合训练。[5]

2019 年 12 月，俄罗斯联邦海军总司令参观了海军总部并会见了巴基斯坦海军参谋长，双方讨论了有关海上安全、稳定和共同利益的问题，其中也涉及双边海军合作。巴基斯坦海军上将强调了巴基斯坦打击恐怖主义的承诺以及巴基斯坦海军为确保该地区的海上安全和和平所做的贡献。他对俄罗斯海军参加由巴基斯坦主办的"和平－19"多国海军演习表示感谢。俄罗斯指

〔1〕 "Russian, Pakistani Navies Commence Drills in Arabian Sea", Sputnik International, https：// sputniknews. com/military/201512071031370037-russia-pakistan-navy-drills-arabian-sea/, March 22, 2020.
〔2〕 "Multinational Naval Exercise Begins Today", Dawn, https：//www. dawn. com/news/1313937, March 22, 2020.
〔3〕 "Pakistan Inks Rare Military Cooperation Pact with Russia", Pakistan Today, https：//www. pakistantoday. com. pk/2018/08/09/pakistan-russia-ink-rare-historic-military-cooperation-pact/, March 22, 2020.
〔4〕 "Pakistan, Russia to Beef up Naval Cooperation", Dawn, https：//www. dawn. com/news/ 1444316/pakistan-russia-to-beef-up-naval-cooperation, March 22, 2020.
〔5〕 "Review of Russia-Pakistan Defence Cooperation：Reflection of Emerging Geo-Political Realities", Vivekananda International Foundation, https：//www. vifindia. org/article/2019/Februaryruary/02/ review-of-russia-pakistan-defence-cooperation, March 22, 2020.

挥官赞赏巴基斯坦海军在维护该地区和平与稳定以及成功进行"和平-19"演习方面所发挥的作用和作出的贡献。双方均同意进一步加强两国海军各领域的交流与合作。[1]

3. 与美国的合作

在军事援助方面，美国对巴基斯坦的经常性军事和经济援助始于1951年。根据美国国际开发署（USAID）的数据统计，截至2017年，美国对巴基斯坦双边援助中的军事援助总额为81亿美元。美巴在1954—1965年曾为最亲密的盟友，1966—1981年印巴战争导致美巴关系降温，1982—1990年美巴再次联合对抗苏联，1991—2000年巴基斯坦被美国再次"抛弃"，2001—2017年反恐合作成为美巴关系的重要主线，而特朗普时期美巴关系趋冷。美方的军事援助集中在1954—1965年、1982—1990年、2001—2011年以及2013年之后，阶段性差异较为显著，其中个别年份（1979—1981年、1992—1998年），美国曾暂停对巴基斯坦进行军事援助。[2]

基于2018年1月特朗普对美巴关系的表态，美国国防部表示美国对巴基斯坦安全方面的援助将继续暂停。此举被视为落实特朗普加强对巴基斯坦经济限制的承诺的第一步。巴基斯坦国防部长表示，在美国决定暂停对巴基斯坦的安全援助之后，巴基斯坦已经中止了与美国的军事和情报合作。[3]尽管局势紧张，美国和巴基斯坦官方仍然保持着一定渠道的军事联系。美国国防部长詹姆斯·马蒂斯（James Mattis）表示，即使在暂停军事援助之后，美国国防部仍在与巴基斯坦军方保持沟通。巴基斯坦外交部长特赫米纳·扬胡亚（Secre Tehmina Janjua）也表示，巴基斯坦将继续尽可能地与美国接触，因为美国不仅是一个全球大国，而且极具地区存在感，"对我们来说，它几乎是我们的邻国"。[4]

在海上军演方面，从2013年起，美国也开始参与在阿拉伯海的"和平"系列多国海上军演，以展示联合打击恐怖主义和海上犯罪的实力与信心。2013年3月，美国驱逐舰"威廉·P. 劳伦斯"号（USS William P. Lawrence）

〔1〕 "Pakistan, Russia Discuss Maritime Security", The Nation, https：//nation. com. pk/19-Dec-2019/pakistan-russia-discuss-maritime-security, March 22, 2020.

〔2〕 石培培：《美巴关系对中巴"一带一路"合作的影响》，载《学术探索》2019年第11期，第78—87页。

〔3〕 "Pakistan suspends 'wide field' of intelligence, defense cooperation with US-minister", The Defense Post, https：//thedefensepost. com/2018/01/09/pakistan-us-defense-cooperation/, March 22, 2020.

〔4〕 "Pakistan has Suspended Military and Intelligence Cooperation with US：Defence Minister", Dawn, https：//www. dawn. com/news/1381839, March 22, 2020.

参加了"和平-13"军演；2017年2月，美国海军"艾米莉亚·埃尔哈特"号油轮［USS Amelia Earhart（oiler）］、美国海军陆战队毛伊号（USCGS Maui）、美国海军陆战队"阿奎德涅克"号（USCGC Aquidneck）和美国"台风"号（USS Typhoon）参加巴基斯坦海军"和平-17"军演；2019年2月，美军再次派舰船参与了在巴基斯坦南部港口城市卡拉奇附近海域举行的"和平-19"军演。美国驻巴基斯坦领事馆的官员也参观了历次演习，认为军演有助于增进信息共享和相互理解，以便确定各方共同感兴趣的合作领域，从而制定海上风险应对策略，完善防止海上风险的技术和程序，并深化各国海军之间的合作。[1]

4. 与英国的合作

巴基斯坦有与英国进行军事合作的较长历史，包括情报共享、在全球反恐战争中使用巴基斯坦空军基地等。英国皇家海军和巴基斯坦海军曾多次举行双边联合演习，为两国打击海盗、反恐或任何可能面临的情况做好准备。英国皇家海军的"神龙"号（HMS Dragon）和"阿盖尔"号（HMS Argyll）都曾参与联合演习。[2] 2018年7月，为加强两国海军的双边合作，巴基斯坦海军"阿斯拉特"号（ASLAT）访问英国朴茨茅斯海军基地（Her Majesty's Portsmouth Naval Base），并在访问港口后参加了在英国海域内与英国皇家海军的双边演习。[3]

在多国演习方面，英国同样分别于2013年、2017年、2019年数次参加巴基斯坦"和平"系列海上军演，派遣皇家海军"达林"号（UK HMS DARING）等与多国海军参演部队联合演练，以增进相互了解、维护地区稳定，并加强对海盗、海上恐怖主义和海上走私犯罪的打击信心与潜力。[4]

---

［1］ See "US, China Take Part in Pakistan Naval Drills", Dawn, https：//www. dawn. com/news/790930, March 22, 2020; Dawn, "Multinational naval exercise begins today", https：//www. dawn. com/news/1313937, March 22, 2020; "US, 44 Other Nations Attend Pakistan Naval Exercise", Navy Times, https：//www. navytimes. com/news/your-navy/2019/02/08/us-44-other-nations-attend-pakistan-naval-exercise/, March 22, 2020.
［2］ "The Benefits of UK-Pakistani Military Cooperation", The Geopolitics, https：//thegeopolitics. com/the-benefits-of-uk-pakistani-military-cooperation/, March 22, 2020.
［3］ "Pakistan Navy Ship ASLAT Warmly Welcomed as It Arrived at Her Majesty's Portsmouth Naval Base", Pakchina News, http：//pakchinanews. pk/pakistan-navy-ship-aslat-warmly-welcomed-as-it-arrived-at-her-majestys-portsmouth-naval-base/, March 22, 2020.
［4］ See "Aman 2017 Naval Exercise", The News, https：//www. thenews. com. pk/print/185184-Aman-2017-naval-exercise, March 22, 2020; "US, 44 Other Nations Attend Pakistan Naval Exercise", Navy Times, https：//www. navytimes. com/news/your-navy/2019/02/08/us-44-other-nations-attend-pakistan-naval-exercise/, March 22, 2020.

5. 与日本的合作

自 2007 年以来，日本海上自卫队一直是巴基斯坦主办的"和平"系列多国海上军演的定期参与者，是在这一项目中较中国、俄罗斯、美国及英国都更早投入的推动方。[1] 除旨在增进相互了解和维护地区稳定外，这也体现了日本对在印度洋海域中保障船舶航行自由、维护海上贸易运输安全、促进海洋和平与稳定的持续关注与努力。[2]

在双边合作方面，2019 年 1 月，日本海军舰艇访问卡拉奇，与巴基斯坦海军举行双边演习。[3] 同年 7 月，巴基斯坦国防部长比尔格拉米（Owais Ahmed Bilgrami）少将与日本国防部国际事务司司长签署防务合作谅解备忘录。双方就加强和丰富双边合作交换了意见，同意加强海洋防务合作，共同促进国际和平与安全。[4]

6. 与土耳其的合作

巴基斯坦和土耳其是传统盟友。近年来，巴基斯坦与土耳其的防务合作有了显著发展，土耳其成为巴基斯坦重要的国防合作伙伴。在过去十年中，巴基斯坦与土耳其的防务合作不仅在于防务能力和防务产品，双方还通过双边军事教育交流项目使两国实现了军官的大规模频繁交流。巴基斯坦在土耳其驻有陆军、海军和空军三军武官，且全部安置在巴基斯坦驻安卡拉大使馆，这是巴基斯坦外交中非常罕见的做法。土耳其是巴基斯坦国际国防展览和研讨会（Pakistan's International Defence Exhibition and Seminar）的第二大（仅次于中国）参与方。土耳其和巴基斯坦之间建立了高级别合作委员会机制。通过这一机制，巴土两国签署了约 60 项防务合作协议。目前，这一合作机制已升格为高级别战略合作委员会。[5]

在军事演习方面，土耳其同样是"和平"系列海上军演的长期参加国，于 2013 年开始派遣"特奇利波卢"号（TCG Gelibolu）等海军舰船前往阿拉

〔1〕 "Japanese Navy Ship Visits Karachi, Conducted Bilateral Exercise With Pakistan Navy", Pakchina News, http://pakchinanews.pk/japanese-navy-ship-visits-karachi-conducted-bilateral-exercise-with-pakistan-navy/, March 22, 2020.

〔2〕 "US, China Take Part in Pakistan Naval Drills", Dawn, https://www.dawn.com/news/790930, March 22, 2020.

〔3〕 "Japanese Navy Ship Visits Karachi, Conducted Bilateral Exercise With Pakistan Navy", Pakchina News, http://pakchinanews.pk/japanese-navy-ship-visits-karachi-conducted-bilateral-exercise-with-pakistan-navy/, March 22, 2020.

〔4〕 "Pakistan, Japan Sign MoU on Defence Cooperation", Dawn, https://www.dawn.com/news/1489064/pakistan-japan-sign-mou-on-defence-cooperation, March 22, 2020.

〔5〕 "The Expanding Turkey-Pakistan Military Cooperation", IRAM, https://iramcenter.org/en/the-expanding-turkey-pakistan-military-cooperation/, March 22, 2020.

伯海参与联合行动。[1] 在军备合作方面,巴基斯坦的卡拉奇造船厂和土耳其工程厂于 2013 年签署了一份建造一艘补给油轮的协议,该油轮由土耳其技术和系统工程公司 (Savunma Teknolojileri Muhendislikve Ticaret) 设计。[2] 2018 年 4 月,由土耳其出口的巴基斯坦海军舰队 "PNS 莫阿温" 号 (PNS Moawin) 油轮在印度洋进行试航,并取得了巨大成功。这艘舰队油轮是土耳其国防工业有史以来出口的最大的单艘军舰,亦成为巴土两国之间军事合作的催化剂。[3]

(二) 海洋油气资源合作

据相关统计,巴基斯坦能源匮乏且能耗结构严重失衡,对石油和天然气产品的依赖度高达 79%。[4] 现已探明,巴基斯坦拥有约 166000 亿立方米天然气,其中约 30000 亿立方米技术上是可开采的;除了天然气储量,巴基斯坦还拥有 2270 亿桶石油储量,其中可开采量为 91 亿桶。美国能源信息管理局 (EIA) 的数据显示,由于巴基斯坦境内的勘探与开发技术以及炼油技术落后,其油气资源的对外依赖度颇高。[5]

巴基斯坦境内气多油少,油气资源主要分布在北部珀特瓦 (Potwar) 盆地、南部印度河盆地以及近海大陆架。[6] 根据巴基斯坦石油和自然资源部发布的《巴基斯坦上游油气行业机遇》(Opportunities in Pakistan's Upstream Oil & Gas Sector) 手册,可以得知巴基斯坦的油气资源分布主要以陆上为主,以

---

〔1〕 "Multinational Naval Exercise Begins Today", Dawn, https://www.dawn.com/news/1313937, March 22, 2020.

〔2〕 Burak Ege Bekdil, "Turkey, Pakistan Reach Their Largest-ever Defense Contract", https://www.defensenews.com/global/mideast-africa/2018/05/29/turkey-pakistan-reach-their-largest-ever-defense-contract/, March 22, 2020.

〔3〕 "Pakistan Navy Fleet Tanker PNS Moawin Conducts First Sea Trial in Indian Ocean", Navy Recognition, http://navyrecognition.com/index.php/news/defence-news/2018/april-2018-navy-naval-defense-news/6145-pakistan-navy-fleet-tanker-pns-moawin-conducts-first-sea-trial-in-indian-ocean.html, March 22, 2020.

〔4〕 《巴基斯坦油气资源状况和中巴合作前景》,载中华人民共和国商务部网站,http://shangwutousu.mofcom.gov.cn/aarticle/ddgk/zwjingji/cn/200803/200803054 06579.html,最后访问日期:2021 年 3 月 20 日。

〔5〕 中华人民共和国驻巴基斯坦伊斯兰共和国大使馆经济商务处:《巴基斯坦居 2017 年全球石油和天然气资源发现国前列》,载中华人民共和国商务部网站,http://pk.mofcom.gov.cn/article/jmxw/201806/20180602757125.shtml,最后访问日期:2021 年 3 月 20 日。

〔6〕 《巴基斯坦油气资源状况和中巴合作前景》,载中华人民共和国商务部网站,http://shangwutousu.mofcom.gov.cn/aarticle/ddgk/zwjingji/cn/200803/200803054 06579.html,最后访问日期:2021 年 3 月 20 日。

近海为辅。其境内的近海油气资源由两大区块组成：印度河盆地（Indus Basin）和马克兰盆地（Makran Basin）。当前，巴基斯坦已开发的油田主要为陆上油田，海上油气资源的勘探和开发集中在印度河盆地的近海区域。总体而言，巴基斯坦的海上油气资源勘探和开发仍有待进一步拓展。[1]

为加快实现国家能源领域自给自足，巴基斯坦出台了一系列的优惠政策以振兴油气行业。同时，巴基斯坦也推行积极的、激励性的油气合作政策，以期改善在巴基斯坦境内的外商投资合作勘探、开采、炼油等环境。目前，巴基斯坦境内设有多家从事上游勘探的外资石油公司，为勘探、开采巴基斯坦的油气资源以解决能源短缺问题提供了技术支持。

1. 与美国的合作

美国曾多次与巴基斯坦合作勘探开采海上油气资源，现已合作开发的海上油井区块，主要由美国的企业主导进行。1957 年，巴基斯坦政府与美国太阳石油公司（Sun Oil）签署了授予该公司在巴基斯坦南部和西南部区块的石油开采权及相关产品分成的协议。1961 年，美国太阳石油公司在地震勘测（seismic surveys）的基础上开始于印度河近海区域钻探近岸油井。这是巴基斯坦与外国公司合作勘探开发近海油井的最早尝试。美国太阳石油公司在此期间于该区域钻探了三口近岸井：1963 年的"达布湾 1 号"（Dabbo Creek-1）、1964 年的"帕提安尼湾 1 号"（Patiani Creek-1）和"戈伦吉湾 1 号"（Korangi Creek-1）。[2]

美国马拉松石油公司（Marathon Oil Company）于 1973 年与巴基斯坦政府签订协议，获得了马克兰海岸的石油勘探开发特许权，开采区域一半位于陆地，一半位于海上。[3] 1976 年，美国马拉松石油公司在马克兰近海进行了全面的地震勘测之后，钻探了油井"加尔巴里 1－A 号"（JalPari1-A），但是该油井由于超压无法控制而被废弃。[4]

---

〔1〕　Ministry of Petroleum & Natural Resources，"Opportunities in Pakistan's Upstream Oil & Gas Sector"，http：//www. ppisonline. com/gov-policy/@ dm！ n/uploadImage/63/InvestmentBrochure2013. pdf，March 22，2020.

〔2〕　Ministry of Petroleum & Natural Resources，"Investment Opportunities in Pakistan's Upstream OIL & GAS Sector"，http：//embassyofpakistanusa. org/wp-content/uploads/2017/05/Oil-and-Gas-Investment-Opportunities-in-Pakistan. pdf，March 22，2020.

〔3〕　"Exploration History"，Pakistan Association of Petroleum Geoscientists，https：//www. papg. org. pk/ehis. asp，March 22，2020.

〔4〕　Ministry of Petroleum & Natural Resources，"Investment Opportunities in Pakistan's Upstream OIL & GAS Sector"，http：//embassyofpakistanusa. org/wp-content/uploads/2017/05/Oil-and-Gas-Investment-Opportunities-in-Pakistan. pdf，March 22，2020.

美国赫斯基石油公司（Husky Oil Company）于 1978 年对位于巴基斯坦南部海岸、印度河三角洲的卡拉奇以南 40 公里的海底进行勘探，随后在该地区钻探近岸油井"卡拉奇南部 A－1 号"（Karachi South A-1）。[1]

西方石油公司与巴基斯坦合作的历史可以追溯到 1982 年 3 月，双方签署关于石油合作的谅解备忘录，约定合作开采巴基斯坦北部珀特瓦区块的石油，该区块约 1191 平方公里。西方石油公司先后在北部珀特瓦区块钻了两口陆上油井："图尔纳尔 1 号"（Dhurnal-1）和"图尔纳尔 2 号"（Dhurnal-2）。[2] 1989 年西方石油公司在进行现代地震勘测之后，在印度河近海区域钻了一口近岸油井"萨达夫 1 号"（Sadaf-1），但该油井很快枯竭。[3]

埃克森美孚公司于 2018 年在巴基斯坦伊斯兰堡开设了办事处，以推进该公司在巴基斯坦的商业活动。埃克森美孚公司与巴基斯坦政府在油气资源的勘探、开采以及产品的分销等方面均有合作。在天然气方面，埃克森美孚公司与巴基斯坦达成了协议，支持巴基斯坦开发建设第三个液化天然气进口码头并为其提供稳定的液化天然气供应。在近海油气资源勘探方面，埃克森美孚公司也与巴基斯坦政府建立了合作，通过持有由埃尼巴基斯坦有限公司经营的位于巴基斯坦近海 G 区块油气开发区域 25% 的股权，该公司与其他合作伙伴共同为这一海上区块的油气资源进行评估和勘探。该区块位于巴基斯坦海岸附近约 230 公里，水深为约 1.9 公里。[4]

2. 与意大利的合作

意大利埃尼集团自 2000 年起就与巴基斯坦合作，从事巴基斯坦境内陆地和海上油气资源勘探、开发等活动，是巴基斯坦石油产量最大的外资公司。截至 2018 年，埃尼集团在巴基斯坦的主要的天然气产量达 300 立方米/日，已开发和未开发的区块面积为 14876 平方公里。[5]

近年来，埃尼集团在巴基斯坦的海上区块采取了 2D 和 3D 模式的勘探手

〔1〕 Ministry of Petroleum & Natural Resources, "Opportunities in Pakistan's Upstream Oil & Gas Sector", http://www.ppisonline.com/gov-policy/@dm!n/uploadImage/63/InvestmentBrochure2013.pdf, March 22, 2020.

〔2〕 "Occidental Brings in New Pakistan Well", AP News, https://apnews.com/e26c95da74ff05f55f0cd9e8f4168d30, March 22, 2020.

〔3〕 Ministry of Petroleum & Natural Resources, "Opportunities in Pakistan's Upstream Oil & Gas Sector", http://www.ppisonline.com/gov-policy/@dm!n/uploadImage/63/InvestmentBrochure2013.pdf, March 22, 2020.

〔4〕 "Pakistan", Exxonmobil, https://corporate.exxonmobil.com/Locations/Pakistan, March 22, 2020.

〔5〕 "Our Work in Pakistan", Eni, https://www.eni.com/enipedia/en_IT/international-presence/asia-oceania/enis-activities-in-pakistan.page?lnkfrm=asknow, March 22, 2020.

段以推进开发进程。目前，埃尼集团在巴基斯坦获得了"印度河 M 号"（In-
dus-M）以及"N&C 号"区块的特许权，并已开始对"印度河 M 号"和
"印度河 C 号"（Indus-C）两口海上油井进行投资开发[1] 埃尼集团于 2010
年在巴基斯坦海上钻探了"鲨鱼 1 号"（Shark-1）油气井，深度达 3500 米，
但是该油气井很快枯竭。[2] 2012 年 12 月 13 日，埃尼集团与巴基斯坦政府和
巴基斯坦石油和天然气公司签署了合作协议，获得了位于巴基斯坦印度河盆
地的印度河 G 区块的勘探和开发的许可证。印度河 G 区块约 7500 平方公里，
位于巴基斯坦的近海超深水区（Ultra deep）。埃尼集团作为该区块的运营商，
享有 25% 的权益。此外，合作开发该区块的公司还有巴基斯坦石油和天然气
公司、巴基斯坦石油有限公司和联合能源巴基斯坦有限公司（United Energy
Pakistan Limited）等三家石油公司。[3] 随后，以埃尼集团为首的合资企业
（包括埃尼集团、埃克森美孚公司、巴基斯坦石油和天然气公司以及巴基斯
坦石油有限公司）于 2019 年 1 月开始在巴基斯坦印度河 G 区块钻探"克克
拉 1 号"（Kekra-1）油气井。但是此次钻探没有发现油气资源。[4]

3. 与其他国家的合作

由于巴基斯坦在油气开采方面缺乏成熟的技术，因而除美国和意大利
外，巴基斯坦还与多个国家合作进行油气资源的勘探与开采。但一如前述，
巴基斯坦目前已合作的油气开采项目中，陆上项目占比极高而近海项目偏
少，且多数已开发的近海油井储藏的油气资源不多。在已公开的资料中，仅
有少量的资料简单地对巴基斯坦近海油井的开发情况进行了记载。

除直接从事勘探活动外，多个国家以及世界银行都曾经对巴基斯坦的石
油勘探开发提供过资金援助。其中，加拿大曾在 1978 年为巴基斯坦提供了
5700 万美金的资金支持。在加拿大的帮助之下，巴基斯坦石油和天然气公司

[1] Ministry of Petroleum & Natural Resources, "Investment Opportunities in Pakistan's Upstream OIL & GAS Sector ", http：//embassyofpakistanusa. org/wp-content/uploads/2017/05/Oil-and-Gas-In-vestment-Opportunities-in-Pakistan. pdf, March 22, 2020.

[2] Ministry of Petroleum & Natural Resources, "Opportunities in Pakistan's Upstream Oil & Gas Sector", http：//www. ppisonline. com/gov-policy/@ dm! n/uploadImage/63/InvestmentBrochure2013. pdf, March 22, 2020.

[3] "Our Work in Pakistan", Eni, https：//www. eni. com/en_ IT/media/2012/12/eni-signs-agree-ment-for-the-acquisition-of-a-new-exploration-block-offshore-pakistan, March 22, 2020.

[4] Javed Mirza, "E&P Companies Plan Offshore Drilling in January 2019", https：//www. thenews. com. pk/print/334062-e-p-companies-plan-offshore-drilling-in-january-2019, March 22, 2020.

于 1986 年在印度河盆地区块开始钻探名为"帕克坎 1 号"(PakCan-1)的气井。[1]"帕克坎 1 号"是第一口在巴基斯坦的大陆架上发现的天然气井。[2]

20 世纪 70 年代,德国的温特沙尔(Wintershall)公司也在印度河近海区块先后钻探三口近岸油井,分别是 1972 年的"印度河海上 A-1 号"(Indus Marine A-1)、"印度河海上 B-1 号"(Indus Marine B-1)及 1975 年的"印度河海上 C-1 号"(Indus Marine C-1)。2004 年,法国道达尔石油公司(Total)在海底 2713 米深处对"帕克 G-2 号"(Pak G-2)井进行钻探,以测试渗透在火山高地上形成的碳酸盐岩。该井深达 4750 米,目前处于枯竭的状态。[3] 2007 年,荷兰皇家壳牌石油公司在巴基斯坦印度河盆地的深水区 1300 米处钻探了"安妮 1X 号"(Anne-1X)天然气井,井深 3250 米。但是由于该天然气井仅储有少量的天然气,后被壳牌石油公司封堵和废弃。[4]

2019 年 2 月,巴基斯坦与俄罗斯签署了海上石油勘探的双边协议。依据该协议,双方将共同在南亚国家海上进行石油和天然气勘探活动,并铺设一条长约 1500 公里的海上天然气管道。该天然气管道将由俄罗斯天然气工业股份有限公司(Gazprom)通过其在中东地区的天然气供应源向巴基斯坦输送天然气。[5] 据此,巴基斯坦省际天然气系统有限公司(ISGSL)与俄罗斯天然气工业股份有限公司的代表签署了企业间协议,该管道建设预计将在 3—4 年内完成。[6]

(三)海洋渔业合作

巴基斯坦的渔业资源十分丰富,但规模化经营却起步较晚,整体发展水

[1] Ministry of Petroleum & Natural Resources, "Investment Opportunities in Pakistan's Upstream OIL & GAS Sector", http://embassyofpakistanusa.org/wp-content/uploads/2017/05/Oil-and-Gas-Investment-Opportunities-in-Pakistan.pdf, March 22, 2020.

[2] "Exploration History", Pakistan Association of Petroleum Geoscientists, https://www.papg.org.pk/ehis.asp, March 22, 2020.

[3] Ministry of Petroleum & Natural Resources, "Investment Opportunities in Pakistan's Upstream OIL & GAS Sector", http://embassyofpakistanusa.org/wp-content/uploads/2017/05/Oil-and-Gas-Investment-Opportunities-in-Pakistan.pdf, March 22, 2020.

[4] Ministry of Petroleum & Natural Resources, "Opportunities in Pakistan's Upstream Oil & Gas Sector", http://www.ppisonline.com/gov-policy/@ dm!n/uploadImage/63/InvestmentBrochure2013.pdf, March 22, 2020.

[5] Mu Xuequan, "Pakistan, Russia Ink Accord for Offshore Oil Exploration", http://www.xinhuanet.com/english/2019-02/06/c_137803155.htm, March 22, 2020.

[6] Israr Khan, "Pakistan Signs $10 Bn Gas Pipeline Agreement with Russia", https://www.thenews.com.pk/print/428722-pakistan-signs-10-bn-gas-pipeline-agreement-with-russia, March 22, 2020.

平较低。巴基斯坦全国的渔业从业人员约 40 万人，其中直接从事渔业生产的约 21.9 万人；渔业产值约占巴基斯坦国内生产总值的 1%。[1] 巴基斯坦渔业产品出口的主要目的地包括美国、挪威、韩国、中国、日本和乌兹别克斯坦等国家和地区。为了规范渔业捕捞活动，促进渔业资源的开发，巴基斯坦与中国、韩国、美国和挪威等多个国家开展了渔业合作。

1. 与中国的合作

巴基斯坦与中国的海洋渔业合作始于 1998 年前后，中国渔业公司经巴基斯坦批准取得巴基斯坦的深海捕鱼证，在巴基斯坦指定海域（III 区）[2] 进行捕捞作业。2002 年，中国渔业公司采用与巴基斯坦本地公司合作的方式在巴基斯坦 II 区进行捕捞作业。近年来，巴中渔业领域交流逐渐频繁，合作前景十分广阔。[3]

2004 年 12 月 15 日，巴基斯坦和中国签订《中华人民共和国国家发展和改革委员会和巴基斯坦伊斯兰共和国食品、农业与畜牧业部关于农产品加工领域投资合作的谅解备忘录》，巴基斯坦表示巴中两国的农业合作对于两国关系非常重要，巴基斯坦将为中国投资者在渔业发展、冷藏设备等领域的投资提供便利条件和优惠政策。[4]

2006 年 2 月 19 日，巴基斯坦总统对中国进行国事访问。访问期间巴中两国签订了《中华人民共和国农业部与巴基斯坦伊斯兰共和国食品、农业与畜牧业部关于渔业合作的谅解备忘录》，巴中两国同意在有关地球、海洋和空间科学的学术机构之间开展更紧密的联系，推动相关技术在工农业领域的应用。[5]

---

〔1〕 "The Islamic Republic of Pakistan", FAO, http：//www. fao. org/fishery/facp/PAK/en, March 22, 2020.

〔2〕 巴基斯坦将捕捞作业范围按距陆地的远近划为三个区域，其中：距海岸 12 海里以内范围为近海区（I 区），12—20 海里范围为边界区（II 区），20—200 海里为深海区（III 区）。参见陈峰等：《巴基斯坦海洋渔业现状与合作开发对策分析》，载《海洋开发与管理》2016 年第 12 期，第 16 页。

〔3〕 中华人民共和国驻巴基斯坦使馆经商处：《巴基斯坦渔业发展现状及合作前景》，载中华人民共和国商务部官网，http：//template1. mofcom. gov. cn/article/co/cw/201110/2011100778077 27. shtml，最后访问日期：2020 年 4 月 2 日。

〔4〕 参见《中华人民共和国国家发展和改革委员会和巴基斯坦伊斯兰共和国食品、农业与畜牧业部关于农产品加工领域投资合作的谅解备忘录》，载中华人民共和国条约数据库，http：//treaty. mfa. gov. cn/tykfiles/20180718/1531876876455. pdf，最后访问日期：2020 年 2 月 16 日。

〔5〕 参见《中华人民共和国与巴基斯坦伊斯兰共和国联合声明》，载中国政府网，http：//www. gov. cn/gongbao/content/2006/content_ 253019. htm，最后访问日期：2020 年 4 月 2 日。

2009 年 8 月 24 日，巴基斯坦总统在访问中国期间专门到中国水产科学院南海水产研究所（以下简称"南海所"）和珠江水产研究所（以下简称"珠江所"）参观，并见证了南海所与巴基斯坦信德省海水与半咸水渔业研究所《关于海洋渔业及海水养殖技术合作谅解备忘录》、珠江所与巴基斯坦印度河淡水渔业研究院《关于种苗繁殖、饲料研发和生产、鱼类疾病防治、观赏鱼繁育等合作谅解备忘录》的签署，有力推动了两国在水产养殖领域的合作。[1]

2013 年 5 月 22 日，中国总理李克强对巴基斯坦进行正式访问。巴中两国签署了《中华人民共和国政府和巴基斯坦伊斯兰共和国政府海洋合作谅解备忘录》和《中国国家海洋局与巴基斯坦科技部海洋科技合作谅解备忘录》。双方表示将会深化两国在"蓝色经济"和海洋科研等领域的合作。[2]

2014 年 4 月 8 日，巴基斯坦驻广州总领事到中国水产科学研究院珠江所进行交流。双方围绕 2014 年珠江所与巴基斯坦旁遮普省拉合尔兽医与动物科学大学（University of Veterinary and Animal Sciences）签订的《关于开展淡水渔业及相关技术合作的谅解备忘录》拟开展以下合作：建立巴中渔业联合实验室及罗非鱼、龟鳖类增养殖技术示范基地；初步建立巴中共享鱼类种质资源数据库并进行水产种质资源引进；为双方开展水产新品种选育提供物质基础和标准化技术支持。[3]

2015 年 7 月 27 日，巴基斯坦拉合尔兽医和动物科学大学接待了中国珠江所的代表团。双方就渔业生态环境保护、水产品质量与安全、密集鱼类养殖以及鱼类遗传育种等领域进行了学术交流，双方也将致力于鱼类疾病的诊断和控制、鱼类的高产养殖等工作。此次会面，双方进一步讨论了渔业部门合作项目的进展，共同研究了现代集约化鱼类养殖的可能性，并同意开展专家互访交流，拉合尔兽医和动物科学大学将派两名教学人员赴中国进行博士

---

〔1〕 渔业渔政管理局：《巴基斯坦水资源与农业代表团访问水科院珠江所》，载中华人民共和国农业农村部，http://www.yyj.moa.gov.cn/kjzl/201904/t20190428_6221796.htm，最后访问日期：2020 年 4 月 2 日。

〔2〕 《中华人民共和国和巴基斯坦伊斯兰共和国关于深化两国全面战略合作的联合声明》，载新华网，http://www.xinhuanet.com/world/2013-05/24/c_124755934_3.htm，最后访问日期：2021 年 3 月 20 日。

〔3〕 《巴基斯坦驻穗总领事馆总领事巴伯·阿明到珠江所商谈合作事宜》，载中国水产科学研究院网站，https://www.prfri.ac.cn/info/1138/3248.htm，最后访问日期：2021 年 3 月 20 日。

后学习。[1]

2019年1月11日，中国驻巴基斯坦大使与巴基斯坦国家粮食安全和研究部部长进行了会晤。中国大使表示中国方面有兴趣在巴基斯坦网箱养鱼领域派遣专家并进行投资，以增进双方在渔业领域的互惠合作。中国还将为巴基斯坦渔业等领域的科研人员提供资金支持。[2]

2019年9月12日，巴基斯坦农业理事会（Pakistan Agricultural Research Council）和中国甘肃省水产研究所在伊斯兰堡联合举办了为期三天的"冷水渔业养殖"培训班。中国专家表示巴基斯坦北方拥有包括河流、湖泊等在内的丰富的淡水环境资源，十分适合渔业和水产养殖业的发展。中国表示愿意为巴基斯坦冷水渔业的发展提供技术和研究支持。巴基斯坦农业理事会和甘肃省水产研究所决定在吉尔吉特山区农业研究中心（Mountain Agriculture Research Centre）共同建立一个冷水鱼实验室。[3]

2019年11月1日，巴基斯坦国家粮食安全与研究部和中国农业部在伊斯兰堡举行第一次中巴联合工作组会议（China-Pakistan Joint Working Group），双方同意在互相理解的基础上，在渔业领域扩大合作，以增加巴基斯坦的渔业产值及出口产值。双方同意进行渔业领域的交流和学习，在研究机构之间建立技术联系，巴方表示愿意同中方科研人员共同建立国家渔业研究中心，就渔业经济、渔业资源开发利用、渔业科研和渔业环境保持紧密合作，实现互利共赢发展。[4]

2. 与韩国的合作

2009年8月7日，巴基斯坦驻韩国大使表示贸易信息的缺乏阻碍了韩国对巴基斯坦的投资，并表示：鉴于韩国在渔业、食品加工业等领域具有坚实的基础，而韩国也需要进口巴基斯坦的鱼类产品，双方可以借此加强渔业领域的合作，希望韩国可以鼓励本国大企业对巴基斯坦进行投资以及进行必要

---

〔1〕 "Fisheries Sector: Chinese Experts, UVAS Faculty Discuss Joint Ventures", The Express Tribune, https://tribune.com.pk/story/927011/fisheries-sector-chinese-experts-the-uvas-faculty-discuss-joint-ventures/, March 22, 2020.

〔2〕 "'We Want to Buy More (Potato, Cherry, Wheat), Invest More' Chinese Ambassador", Ministry of National Food Security & Research, http://www.mnfsr.gov.pk/frmDetails.aspx, April 3, 2020.

〔3〕 "PARC Organized Three (03) Days Training Course on Cold Water Fisheries (Trout Farming)", Pakistan Agricultural Research Council, http://www.parc.gov.pk/index.php/en/component/content/article/168-parc-flash-news-2018/1641-parc-organized-three-03-days-training-course-on-cold-water-fisheries-trout-farming, April 3, 2020.

〔4〕 "China-Pakistan Joint Working Group (JWG) Meeting between the Ministry of Agriculture and Rural Affairs of China and the Ministry of National Food Security and Research of Pakistan", Ministry of National Food Security & Research, http://www.mnfsr.gov.pk/frmDetails.aspx, April 3, 2020.

的技术转让。[1]

2012 年 1 月 27 日，韩国阿拉斯加公司（Alaska Inc）国际海鲜产品总裁带领公司团队访问了卡拉奇渔港。韩国来访者对信德省淡水区的泥蟹养殖和珍珠贝壳养殖表现出了极大的兴趣，表示愿意和当地养殖业展开合作并在两年后为当地渔民提供一种可溶解的塑料捕鱼网。巴基斯坦表示希望韩国在信德省建立渔业加工厂，并承诺将为韩国投资者提供便利。同时，巴基斯坦也提出希望与韩国展开技术交流，通过学习确保海鲜产品的新鲜卫生，并扩大高附加值产业的规模。[2]

2018 年 4 月 12 日，韩国国际农业计划（Korea Program on International Agriculture）代表团访问了巴基斯坦国家粮食安全与研究部。双方都认为，巴基斯坦有 1100 余公里的海岸线，具有巨大的渔业发展潜力。韩国表示愿意帮助巴基斯坦循序渐进地结束对他国鱼苗的依赖，并逐步培育巴基斯坦本国的鱼苗以增加网箱养殖的数量，扩大网箱养殖的规模。为此，韩国愿意按照国际标准为巴方提供网箱养殖所需的网箱材料、鱼种、贮存和运输设施，并愿意帮助巴基斯坦培训渔业领域的专家。巴基斯坦则宣称将在未来 5 年将渔业出口额提升到 10 亿美元。巴韩双方依据本次会议达成的共识签订了有关农业合作的谅解备忘录。[3]

2019 年 5 月 4 日，韩国驻巴基斯坦大使拜访了俾路支省首席部长（Chief Minister），讨论了韩国在俾路支省的投资计划。俾路支省首席部长向韩国大使介绍了俾路支省的矿业、渔业等领域的情况，指出瓜达尔港有能力将渔业产品快速通畅地运送到全世界，表示愿意尽一切可能为韩国投资者提供便利。韩国对在俾路支省进行投资展现出浓厚兴趣，表示愿意在俾路支省投资渔业加工和包装工厂，为俾路支省提供技术援助，并承诺俾路支省的学生可以通过巴韩联合教育项目前往韩国学习。[4]

3. 与美国的合作

2011 年 11 月，在美国农业部（United States Department of Agriculture）

---

[1] "Steps Urged to Promote Trade with S. Korea", Dawn, https：//www. dawn. com/news/960928/ steps-urged-to-promote-trade-with-s-korea, April 3, 2020.

[2] "Korean Experts Propose Technology for Crab Farming", The News, https：//www. thenews. com. pk/archive/print/343302-korean-experts-propose-technology-for-crab-farming, April 3, 2020.

[3] "Pakistan and Korea Move Ahead towards Establishing A Center of Excellence to Boost Agriculture", Ministry of National Food Security & Research, http：//www. mnfsr. gov. pk/frmDetails. aspx, A-pril 3, 2020.

[4] "South Korea Keen to Invest in Balochistan", The Express Tribune, https：//tribune. com. pk/sto-ry/1965376/1-south-korea-keen-invest-balochistan/, April 3, 2020.

的资金支持下，美国大豆协会（American Soybean Association）和巴基斯坦渔业发展局签署了一份谅解备忘录，以实施为期三年的水产养殖计划。该计划名为"供养巴基斯坦——一个聚焦水产养殖业的研究计划"（Feeding Pakistan—A Research Initiative Focusing on the Aquaculture Industry）。根据该计划，美国将向巴基斯坦出口由美国豆粕制成的鱼饲料，帮助巴基斯坦建设鱼饲料厂，并为巴基斯坦 6 名研究人员和 500 多名农民提供罗非鱼密集养殖培训。[1]

2013 年 3 月 15 日，美国政府表示，美国将继续支持巴基斯坦的发展，特别是支持重振斯瓦特山谷（Swat Valley）的地方产业。斯瓦特山谷的地方产业因遭遇洪水和地方武装冲突而被破坏，美国政府自 2010 年起发起斯瓦特地方产业恢复计划，向该山谷的 22 个渔场和 239 家酒店提供捐款，并进行技术援助和实物支持。截至 2013 年年底，当地渔业收入比实施该计划前增加 12 倍，当地酒店收入比实施该计划前增加 8 倍。[2]

2019 年 12 月 17 日，美国驻巴基斯坦大使与巴基斯坦国家粮食安全和研究部部长举行会晤，双方表示两国在渔业、畜牧业等领域有极大的合作潜力，并鼓励两国渔业、畜牧业等领域的专家进行交流和学习。巴基斯坦表示将优先考虑和美国开展广泛的农业合作。[3]

4. 与挪威的合作

2011 年 12 月 10 日，挪威代表团访问卡拉奇港。为了达到欧盟的鱼类产品标准，巴基斯坦已经改装了近 500 艘渔船并采购了大量鱼类保鲜设备。巴基斯坦和挪威正在执行一项名为《Pak - 3004 机构合作计划框架协议》（Pak-3004 Framework Agreement for Institutional Cooperation Program）的双边协定。在此协定下，挪威将帮助巴基斯坦加强巴基斯坦渔业机构的能力建设，并协助巴基斯坦进行海洋渔业的资源调查。[4]

2017 年 12 月 1 日，巴基斯坦规划委员会（Planning Commission）副主席

〔1〕 Banrie，"Feeding Pakistan Aquaculture Project：Potential to Develop Modern Aquaculture Industry"，https：//thefishsite. com/articles/feeding-pakistan-aquaculture-project-potential-to-develop-modern-aquaculture-industry，April 3，2020.

〔2〕 "Growth Projections：Washington to Help Revive Tourism in Swat，Olson"，The Express Tribune，https：//tribune. com. pk/story/521138/growth-projections-washington-to-help-revive-tourism-in-swat-olson/，April 3，2020.

〔3〕 "Khusro Bakhtiar Solicited USAID Interventions for Locust Control，Access to Halal Meat Market and Value Addition"，Ministry of National Food Security & Research，http：//www. mnfsr. gov. pk/frmDetails. aspx，April 3，2020.

〔4〕 "Norwegian Mission Visits Karachi Fish Harbour"，The News，https：//www. thenews. com. pk/archive/print/335227-norwegian-mission-visits-karachi-fish-harbour，April 3，2020.

在研讨会上致辞，祝贺巴基斯坦和挪威两国科学机构之间的合作圆满结束。巴基斯坦对挪威政府提供 6 亿卢比的财政拨款表示感谢，并表示两国的合作帮助巴方在海洋渔业、海啸建模等 17 个领域取得长足发展。[1]

2019 年 4 月 4 日，巴基斯坦和挪威之间的第十轮双边政治磋商（The 10th Round of Bilateral Political Consultation）在伊斯兰堡举行，双方全面评估了两国关系。巴基斯坦表示挪威是个资源丰富、渔业产业成熟的国家，而巴基斯坦有着巨大的发展和投资潜力，两国可以在能源、渔业等领域展开积极合作。巴基斯坦邀请挪威在巴基斯坦渔业、农业、清洁能源等领域进行投资，巴基斯坦承诺将制定有利于挪威的投资政策。[2]

5. 与泰国的合作

2002 年 8 月 17 日，巴基斯坦—泰国联合经济委员会（Joint Economic Commission）第二届会议在曼谷举行。巴基斯坦代表团团长在会议中表达了巴基斯坦希望扩大和泰国的双边关系的强烈愿望，并指出两国在水产养殖业、渔业等领域具有极大的合作潜力。为进一步加强两国间的投资关系，双方就投资促进事宜签署了谅解备忘录。[3]

2019 年 3 月 30 日，泰国代表和信德省拖网渔船船东和渔民协会（Sindh Trawlers Owners & Fishermen Association）举行会议。巴基斯坦方面表示，其 80% 的水产品出口到泰国，而泰国则出口捕鱼设备到巴基斯坦，两国在渔业领域具有良好的合作前景。巴基斯坦邀请泰国对巴基斯坦的沿海渔业和水产养殖业进行调查和投资，并表示希望泰国能协助巴基斯坦升级现有的海洋产品加工厂。巴基斯坦希望两国的合作可以从金枪鱼的捕捞、冷冻和加工开始，并承诺考虑取消两国鱼类和海鲜产品的进口关税。[4]

6. 与日本的合作

2018 年 2 月 27 日，日本驻巴基斯坦大使宣布日本政府已经向巴基斯坦

[1] "'Pak Institutes' Collaboration with Norway Crucial in Promoting Capacity Building", Pakistan Today, https://www.pakistantoday.com.pk/2017/12/01/pak-institutes-collaboration-with-norway-crucial-in-promoting-capacity-building/, April 3, 2020.

[2] "10th Round of Pakistan-Norway Bilateral Political Consultation", Ministry of Foreign Affairs of Government of Pakistan, http://mofa.gov.pk/10th-round-of-pakistan-norway-bilateral-political-consultation/, April 3, 2020.

[3] "Two MoUs Signed Pakistan, Thailand to Expand Trade", Dawn, https://www.dawn.com/news/52811, April 3, 2020.

[4] Royal Thai Consulate-General, "Discussion between CG and Sindh Trawlers Owners & Amp: Fishermen Association (STOFA)", https://karachi.thaiembassy.org/th/content/101529-discussion-between-cg-and-sindh-trawlers-owners-fishermen-association-(stofa)?page=5d761e4e15e39c4534004b77&menu=5d761e4e15e39c4534004bed, April 3, 2020.

的联邦直辖部落区（Federally Administered Tribal Areas）提供了770万美元的捐款。巴日两国共同表示该笔赠款将用于发展联邦直辖部落区的渔业、畜牧业等产业，以改善当地粮食安全状况，促进当地农业经济的发展。[1]

2019年12月23日，巴基斯坦陆军总司令和日本首相的外交事务特别顾问举行会晤。巴日双方表示两国将进一步加强双边关系，继续为巴基斯坦的和平与安全作出努力。日本还同巴基斯坦签署了一份有关人力引进的谅解备忘录，以引进巴基斯坦捕鱼业、水产养殖业、船舶业等14个领域的技术工人。[2]

7. 与毛里求斯的合作

2007年1月11日，巴基斯坦和毛里求斯在巴基斯坦举行了第五次联合工作会议，并在会议期间签订了双边优惠贸易协议。根据该协议，毛里求斯的鱼、茶叶等产品进入巴基斯坦市场将享受关税减免待遇。巴基斯坦和毛里求斯表示两国期望进一步在渔业、软件开发等领域签署备忘录。[3]

2009年10月，巴基斯坦和毛里求斯签订《巴基斯坦与毛里求斯有关双边渔业合作的谅解备忘录》（MoU on Bilateral Cooperation in Fishing between Mauritius and the Republic of Pakistan），以促进两国渔业领域的合作和贸易往来。[4]

2019年9月14日，卡拉奇工商联合会（Karachi Chamber of Commerce and Industry）和毛里求斯联合工会（Mauritius Chamber of Commerce and Industry）签署了一项谅解备忘录，代表两国的相关行业同意加强双边贸易。巴基斯坦表示，毛里求斯是通往非洲47个国家的门户，两国将在渔业、旅游等领域开展业务合作。[5]

---

[1] "Japan Grants ＄7.7 Million for Development Projects in FATA", The Express Tribune, https://tribune.com.pk/story/1646168/1-japan-grants-us7-7-million-development-projects-fata/, April 3, 2020.

[2] "Pakistan, Japan Vow to Enhance Efforts for Regional Peace", The Express Tribune, https://tribune.com.pk/story/2123390/1-pakistan-japan-vow-enhance-efforts-regional-peace/, April 3, 2020.

[3] 中华人民共和国商务部：《巴基斯坦与毛里求斯签署双边贸易协定》，载中华人民共和国商务部网站，http://mu.mofcom.gov.cn/sys/print.shtml?/jmxw/200701/20070104299076，最后访问日期：2020年2月16日。

[4] Ministry of Agro Industry and Food Security of Mauritius, "Status of Memoranda of Understanding on The Agricultural/ Fisheries Sector Signed between Mauritius and Other Countries", https://agriculture.govmu.org/Pages/Legislation/MoUs.aspx, April 3, 2020.

[5] "MoU Inked to Strengthen Pakistan-Mauritius Trade", Daily Times, https://dailytimes.com.pk/117014/mou-inked-to-strengthen-pakistan-mauritius-trade/, April 3, 2020.

8. 与其他国家的合作

2013 年 3 月 16 日，巴基斯坦和越南发表共同声明，表示将简化两国间的签证程序，通过定期互派贸易代表团、交换商业信息来促进两国的双边贸易。卡拉奇工商联合会主席表示，巴越两国在 20 世纪 70 年代就保持着经济联系，2004 年两国签订了有关避免双重征税的双边协定，2011 年 5 月两国签署了贸易协定。巴越两国在渔业、海鲜、皮革等领域有极大的贸易潜力，巴越将在种植业和渔业等领域扩大投资，深化合作。[1]

2017 年 10 月 17 日，巴基斯坦和菲律宾签署了有关农业领域合作的谅解备忘录，强调双方将加强渔业、能源等领域的研究和交流，深化渔业、家禽养殖等领域的合作。巴基斯坦表示愿意同菲律宾建立合资公司，共同开拓在渔业、种植业等领域的合作。[2]

（四）海洋科研合作

巴基斯坦拥有 1046 公里的海岸线，南临阿拉伯海和阿曼湾，东北与中国毗邻，东连印度，西临阿富汗和伊朗。由于其得天独厚的地理位置，巴基斯坦的港口成为其本国甚至周边国家对外贸易的交通枢纽。积极加强和周边国家的海事科学技术交流，也成为巴基斯坦促进商业贸易交往、维护国家海洋安全的重要推动力之一。

1. 与中国的合作

巴基斯坦与中国在科学领域的合作由来已久，近年来更是随着双方友好关系的持续发展而不断深化。2010 年，在"大洋一号"的远洋考察中，中国就对巴基斯坦海洋研究所的科技人员进行了技能培训。2012 年 3 月 8 日，中国国家海洋局第二海洋研究所所长及相关人员，访问巴基斯坦国家海洋研究所。访问主要就该两所海洋研究机构开展海洋地质与天然气水合物资源、印度河三角洲地区地面沉降检测与海水倒灌灾害防治、海水低氧区变化等研究的合作确立初步意向。第二海洋研究所还与巴基斯坦海洋研究所在伊斯兰堡共同签署了《中国国家海洋局第二海洋研究所与巴基斯坦海洋研究所海洋科技合作框架协议》。这是巴基斯坦和中国在海洋领域签署的第一份合作协议，

---

〔1〕 "KCCI, Vietnamese Commercial Consular", The News, https：//www. thenews. com. pk/archive/print/418472-kcci-vietnamese-commercial-consular, April 3, 2020.

〔2〕 "Philippines Bilateral Relations", Ministry of Foreign Affairs of Government of Pakistan, http：//mofa. gov. pk/philippines-bilateral-relations, April 3, 2020.

受到巴中双方的高度重视。[1]

2013 年 5 月 22 日，中国国家海洋局与巴基斯坦科技部共同签署了《中华人民共和国国家海洋局与巴基斯坦伊斯兰共和国科技部海洋科技合作谅解备忘录》（以下简称《备忘录》）。根据《备忘录》，双方将进一步加强在海洋科学研究与调查、气候变化与海平面上升、海岸综合治理及相关研究培训、海洋环境保护、海洋观测与海洋防灾减灾、海洋卫星遥感与运用、海洋资料与数据交换、海洋能开发与研究、海洋政策与海洋法等领域的合作。[2]此外，双方还将通过对最新海洋领域研究成果的交流，开展项目合作、人员交流、举办论坛、研讨会、能力培训等活动，促进两国专家、学者、政府官员的交流，推动两国在海洋科技领域的务实合作。2013 年 6 月 24—30 日，华东师范大学与巴基斯坦国家海洋研究所河口与海岸重点实验室（State Key Laboratory of Estuarine Coastal Research，SKLEC）举办的双边研讨会就是对该《备忘录》的积极践行。[3] 2013 年 12 月，中国国家海洋局第二海洋研究所与巴基斯坦国家海洋研究所在交流了双方的海洋科技发展需求和设立海域遥感卫星的细化意见后，决定建立"中巴海洋合作研究中心"，标志着巴基斯坦与中国的海洋科技合作进入了一个新时代。[4]

在此后的数年里，巴基斯坦和中国的官方和学界组织也多次进行海洋科技领域的交流。2014 年 2 月 20 日，巴基斯坦科工委主任到中国海洋科学与工程学院进行访问合作。双方就海洋船舶制造与设计和海洋结构物新材料研究展开了积极的交流和讨论，确立了进一步交流合作的意向。[5] 2015 年 4 月 20 日，习近平主席抵达巴基斯坦首都伊斯兰堡进行国事访问。双方在坚持积极参与"一带一路"建设的基础上，同意进一步加强海上合作。在习近平主席与谢里夫总理的见证下，中国国家海洋局局长与巴基斯坦科技部常任秘书互换了《中华人民共和国国家海洋局与巴基斯坦伊斯兰共和国关于共建中

---

〔1〕 朱永灵：《我所与巴基斯坦海洋研究所签订海洋科技合作框架协议》，载自然资源部第二海洋研究所网站，http：//www. sio. org. cn/redir. php? catalog_ id =84&object_ id =7419，最后访问日期：2021 年 3 月 20 日。

〔2〕 董冠洋：《中国—巴基斯坦签署海洋科技合作备忘录》，载中国新闻网，http：//www. chinanews. com/gn/2013/05-22/4846550. shtml，最后访问日期：2021 年 3 月 20 日。

〔3〕 "China-Pak First Research Expedition Completes"，National Institute of Oceanography Pakistan，http：//www. niopk. gov. pk/Events. html，April 3，2020.

〔4〕 傅斌、丁巍伟：《郑玉龙副所长一行访问巴基斯坦国家海洋研究所》，载自然资源部第二海洋研究所网站，http：//www. china. com. cn/haiyang/2013-01/09/content_ 27628877. htm，最后访问日期：2021 年 3 月 20 日。

〔5〕 《巴基斯坦科工委主任访问海洋科学与工程学院》，载上海海事大学网站，https：//immse. shmtu. edu. cn/2014/0220/c6904a55618/page. htm，最后访问日期：2020 年 2 月 16 日。

巴联合海洋研究中心的议定书》。双方同意两国在巴基斯坦卡拉奇建设联合海洋科学研究中心，共同申请"丝路基金支持"。该研究中心致力于海洋科学研究，包括海洋卫星遥感技术应用、海洋灾害预防与管理、海洋环境与生态保护等方面。中方还于 2015 年为南亚国家举办海洋科技研讨班，巴基斯坦方面对此表示欢迎并积极参与。[1]

2014—2018 年，巴基斯坦和中国分别在北京和伊斯兰堡举行了巴中第一轮、第二轮和第三轮海上合作对话。双方相关政府部门参加了历次对话，共同回顾了总体的海事形势，并就进一步加强海上科学技术合作、反海盗合作、海上抢险救灾等活动达成了共识。[2]

2018 年 10 月 31 日，中船重工总经理助理、中国船贸党委书记徐子秋在北京会见了到访的巴基斯坦海事部部长，双方肯定了之前两国围绕海军装备、船厂升级改造、人员培训、技术转让等领域所开展的全方位合作和丰硕的合作成果，重新确立了进一步深化多领域多层次的精诚合作，营造国际经济技术合作新平台，共谱巴中海洋科技合作新篇章的寄望。[3] 2018 年 11 月 5 日，巴基斯坦卡拉奇大学海洋生物卓越中心（Centre of Excellence in Marine Biology，University of Karachi）以及拉斯贝拉农业、水和海洋科学大学（Lasbela University of Agriculture，Water and Marine Sciences）的数位教授应邀到中国水产科学研究院南海水产研究所进行访问交流，并与中方签署了海洋渔业科技合作备忘录。双方均希望以签署备忘录为契机，不断开展海洋渔业科技方面的合作。此次访问中，双方还就南海渔业资源状况和可捕量评估、在阿拉伯海的科研情况和成果等问题做了学术报告并进行热烈讨论。[4]

在联合科学考察方面，巴基斯坦和中国的共同行动最早可以追溯到 20 世纪 90 年代在南大洋进行的一系列合作，并在近年来数次完成了两国间的正式海洋联合科考实践。2018 年 1 月，巴基斯坦与中国首次在北印度洋联合开展海洋地质等多学科科学考察。在这次由巴基斯坦国家海洋研究所与中国科学院南海海洋研究所进行的联合考察中，两国科学家在卡拉奇港口乘坐"实验 3"号科考船航行至北印度洋马克兰海沟（Makran Trench），重点研究

〔1〕《中国将与巴基斯坦合作建立联合海洋研究中心》，载环球网，https：//mil. huanqiu. com/article/9CaKrnJKeYm，最后访问日期：2020 年 2 月 16 日。

〔2〕 "Pakistan，China Hold Maritime Cooperation Dialogue"，Ecns，http：//www. ecns. cn/2016/02-03/198147. shtml,，April 3，2020.

〔3〕《徐子秋会见巴基斯坦海事部部长》，载中国船贸网站，http：//www. csoc. cn/show/news/774. html，最后访问日期：2021 年 3 月 20 日。

〔4〕《南海所积极推进与巴基斯坦开展海洋渔业科技务实合作》，载中国水产科学研究院网站，https：//www. cafs. ac. cn/info/1032/30771. htm，最后访问日期：2021 年 3 月 20 日。

马克兰海沟的大尺度地质构造以及邻近地区的地震海啸等海洋地质灾害，并利用先进的科学手段，首次开展了跨越马克兰俯冲带的高精度海底地震实验，更清晰地揭示了板块内部结构与地震断层特征。考察中测量到的高精度海底地形反映出马克兰海底大断层与滑坡分布；所获取的深海沉积样品，也用于识别重大古地震与海啸引起的浊流沉积事件，从而为巴基斯坦海上安全与减灾提供科学依据，也将服务于"一带一路"的沿线建设。联合考察还促进了马克兰海沟与南海天然气水合物形成机制的对比研究，丰富了两国科学家的海上合作经验，为进一步推动巴中双方海洋科技合作奠定了坚实的基础。[1]

2. 与伊朗的合作

巴基斯坦与伊朗分别于2002年和2007年签署了有关科技领域合作计划的谅解备忘录。其后，伊朗与巴基斯坦关于科学、技术和教育的专家委员会于2016年5月在伊斯兰堡举行了第一次会议。双方就加强两国之间的科技合作提出了许多具体的建议，例如通过联合项目进行合作研究，定期组织联合会议、研讨会、特别会议和专家交流等。[2] 此外，双方提出以下两项倡议：第一，根据巴基斯坦与伊朗科学技术研究部（Ministry of Science，Research and Technology，MSRT）签署的合作计划，持续开展相应的联合活动；第二，巴基斯坦和伊朗科学技术研究部应于2016年11月15日—2017年1月25日启动联合倡议。该倡议主要涉及海洋资源的经济利用、水域生物技术与基因工程、水资源短缺等自然资源工程领域，例如从水域和生物样品中提取药物成分、水体中砷（Ⅴ）的高选择性传感器（highly selective sensor）的开发以及如何合作开发周边海域资源等科学技术问题。[3] 巴基斯坦和伊朗两国在海洋资源开采和海洋技术开发方面都具有较大的提升空间，通过加强该领域的合作和信息共享，两国海洋实力势必会获得显著提升。

巴基斯坦和伊朗的合作并不停留在政府层面上，民间和学界也有相应的交流。2007年1月，巴基斯坦巴利亚大学（Bahria University）国家海事政策研究中心（National Center of Maritime Policy Research，NCMPR）成立，为研究人员和相关学者提供了一个就海事问题展开研究工作的平台。该研究中心与伊朗恰巴哈海事大学（Chabahar Maritime University）在巴利亚大学伊斯兰

---

〔1〕　张建松、岑志连：《中巴首次北印度洋联合考察圆满结束》，载《河北日报》2018年2月4日，第4版。

〔2〕　"Pakistan Science Foundation（PSF）International Relations with Iran"，Pakistan Science Foundation，http：//psf. gov. pk/iran_ linkage. aspx，April 3，2020.

〔3〕　"General Guidelines for Application of Joint Research Projects between Pakistan and Iran"，Pakistan Science Foundation，http：//psf. gov. pk/call-for-proposals-msrt-February-2018. aspx，April3，2020.

堡校区签署了谅解备忘录。依据该备忘录,巴利亚大学和恰巴哈海事大学同意通过双方的共同努力,促进巴基斯坦和伊朗在海洋研究方面的合作,合作领域包括师生交流、研究人员交流、联合研究项目、联合会议和研讨会、共享并交换信息和资源、共同开发课程以及其他可能互利互惠的领域。[1]

3. 与美国的合作

2020 年 1 月,巴基斯坦海事研究论坛(Maritime Study Forum)与美国国家海事研究所(National Institute of Maritime Affairs,NIMA)、美国国家海事政策研究中心(National Centre for Maritime Policy Research,NCMPR)共同在卡拉奇巴利亚大学举办了第三期"寒假海事学校"(Maritime Winter School 2020)。该学校的主旨在于,帮助学生"了解海洋和沿海社区、海洋经济与政策、海洋资源与水文、海洋安全与外交",从而更好地为巴基斯坦培养海洋研究领域的专业人才。在本期寒假学校的最后一天,学校举行了一场以"透过主流媒体和另类媒体预测巴基斯坦的海上潜力"(Projecting Pakistan's Maritime Potential through Mainstream & Alternative Media)为主题的研讨会,与会者包括媒体及海事科研专家,具体讨论了媒体在促进巴基斯坦海事部门发展之中所起的作用。[2]

(五)区域性国际合作

1. 南亚区域合作联盟

南亚区域合作联盟(South Asian Association for Regional Cooperation,SAARC,以下简称"南盟"),成立于 1985 年 12 月 7 日,是南亚国家共同建立的互助合作组织。南盟共有 8 个成员国:巴基斯坦、孟加拉国、不丹、印度、尼泊尔、斯里兰卡、马尔代夫和阿富汗。

2014 年,各成员国在第 18 届南盟首脑会议上阐明了其对于海洋蓝色经济的立场。首脑会议通过宣言表明,各成员国"已经认识到海洋蓝色经济对于该地区南盟国家的多方面贡献,以及在这方面进行合作、建立友好伙伴关系的必要性"。2016 年 3 月,在尼泊尔举行的第 37 届南盟部长理事会议上,与会人员又再次强调了包括生物与非生物资源在内的海上资源开发的潜力,指明南盟国家对海洋环境和海洋资源进行合作保护势在必行。作为南盟的重要成员,巴基斯坦拥有广阔的海洋疆界和重要的海洋利益,与南盟进行更广泛更全

〔1〕 "Bahria University Signed An MoU with Chabahar Maritime University",International Office,https://sites. google. com/site/internationalofficebu/mouwithchabaharmaritimeuniversity,April3,2020.

〔2〕 "Maritime Winter School-2020 Ends",Pakobserver,https://pakobserver. net/maritime-winter-school-2020-ends/,April 3,2020.

面的海洋合作既符合其国家利益，亦是大势所趋。[1] 总体而言，巴基斯坦在南盟框架下的海洋领域合作主要体现在海洋环境保护和海洋生物技术方面。

1997 年 10 月 15 日，南盟环境部长会议在马累（Male）通过了第一个南盟环境行动计划（SAARC Environmentation Plan），并在 2005 年印度洋海啸后形成了灾害区域合作框架。该计划和框架旨在通过各会员国之间的气候和海洋数据等专业知识的分享以及专业技能的培训，应对气候变化所引起的海平面上升、海洋灾害防治等方面的环境问题，并制定适应气候变化的战略和举措。南盟环境部长还将按照第九次南盟首脑会议的决定每年举行相关环境会议的磋商，审议南盟区域的环境状况。[2] 2004 年 12 月的印度洋海啸所造成的损失给巴基斯坦带来了现实紧迫感，促进了巴基斯坦在南盟框架下的海洋环境灾害方面的合作。

南盟设立之初，就将生物技术领域的合作写入联盟主要合作领域的规章之中，而海洋生物技术的合作就是生物技术领域重要的组成部分。2019 年 4 月，南盟在尼泊尔博卡拉（Pokhara）举行了"在水塘、湖泊、河流和海水中使用网箱和围栏饲养以促进南亚水产养殖多样化的区域磋商"（Regional Consultation on Fish Culture in Cages and Pens in Reservoirs, Lakes, Rivers and Marine Waters for Aquaculture Diversification in South Asia）。该磋商会谈的目标在于确保南亚地区的粮食供应，以解决拥有全球四分之一人口的南亚地区的粮食安全问题。随着全球人口的快速增长，各地区对渔业产品的食用及营养需求也大大增加，南盟举办这一磋商为参与者分享水产养殖经验提供了宝贵的机会。对于渔业在农业中占有较大比重的巴基斯坦而言，在该磋商机制中的积极参与无疑有助于给其国家粮食安全带来更多的保障。[3]

2. 南亚环境合作计划

南亚环境合作计划（South Asia Co-operative Environmental Programme, SACEP）是南亚第一个政府间的环境保护合作机制。[4] 该组织由南亚各国政府于 1982 年建立，成员国包括巴基斯坦、阿富汗、孟加拉国、不丹、印度、

---

〔1〕 "The Maritime Dimension in SAARC: Redefining Relations", Maritimeindia, http://www. mar-itimeindia. org/View%20Profile/636183051598989395. pdf, April 3, 2020.

〔2〕 "Index for the South Asian Association for Regional Cooperation (SAARC): Comparison of The Pro-visions of The Draft Global Pact for The Environment", IUCN, https://www. iucn. org/sites/dev/files/content/documents/2018/globalpactsaarcFebruary2018. pdf, April 3, 2020.

〔3〕 "Press Release-Secretary General of SAARC", SAARC, https://www. saarc-sec. org/index. php/press-release/267-press-release-secretary-general-of-saarc-addressed-the-inaugural-session-of-the-re-gional-consultation-on-fish-culture-in-cages-and-pens, April 3, 2020.

〔4〕 "Asian Countries Agree to Tackle Environmental Issues", Nation, https://nation. com. pk/09-Dec-2013/s-asian-countries-agree-to-tackle-environmental-issues, April 3, 2020.

马尔代夫、尼泊尔和斯里兰卡，为一个独立的法律实体。该组织旨在支持和促进该地区的环境保护，推行管理和改善环境的区域性举措。[1]

南亚环境合作计划自成立以来实施过多项海洋环境保护项目。1984 年，该组织的国家联络点会议在泰国曼谷举行，区域内的五个海洋国家：巴基斯坦、印度、斯里兰卡、孟加拉国和马尔代夫同意采取有效行动以进一步促进南亚海洋地区环境保护事业的发展，并制定了一项保护和管理南亚海域环境的行动计划。其后，南亚环境合作计划多次组织国家联络点会议，通过会议推进多方交流、作出多项决议。1986 年 12 月 2—5 日，该组织在曼谷通过了建立南亚区域海洋专家会议的协议，进一步促进了五个国家之间的海洋合作与交流。除各项重大的海洋合作会议和举措之外，该组织自 1990 年至今还为南亚五个海洋国家各部门的 724 名与会者举办了 32 次培训和能力建设讲习班。如，1993 年在斯里兰卡科伦坡举办的关于保护南亚海洋区域沿海和海洋环境的管理策略讲习班（ESCAP/UNEP/SACEP Workshop on Management Strategies for the Protection of the Coastal and Marine Environment in the South Asian Seas Region），2006 年在科伦坡举行的关于南亚海洋和沿海保护区的长期管理和保护的区域资源协调与动员探讨会（Regional Resource Co-ordination and Mobilisation Workshop on Long term Management and Conservation of Marine and Coastal Protected Areas in South Asia），等等。[2]

巴基斯坦作为区域内的主要海洋国家，在这一过程中积极作为，致力于增进与域内其他海洋国家的协作水平。1999 年，南亚环境合作计划在巴基斯坦伊斯兰堡举行了第一届南亚海洋政府间部长会议，巴基斯坦作为东道主，积极响应了南亚海洋环境保护的倡议。通过政府间部长会议，各项海洋保护的举措得以有效落实。2010 年 7 月 22 日，南亚环境合作计划与巴基斯坦政府签署了《合作应对南亚海域溢油化学污染的谅解备忘录》（MoU on Co-operation on the Response to Oil Spill and Chemical Pollution in the South Asia Seas Region）。同年 10 月，巴基斯坦海洋专家与该组织合作将南亚章节编入《区域海洋公约》（Regional Seas Conventions）以及"海洋生物多样性评估和展望系列丛书"（Action Plans for the Marine Biodiversity Assessment and Outlook Series）。2013 年，第五届南亚海洋部长级政府间会议在巴基斯坦伊斯兰堡举行。2014 年，南亚环境合作计划为南亚区域制定了"区域海洋和沿海生物多

---

〔1〕 "About Us", SACEP, http：//sacep. org/about-us, April 3, 2020.

〔2〕 UN Office of Legal Affairs, "South Asia Co-operative Environment Programme", https：//www. un. org/Depts/los/general_ assembly/contributions_ 2010/SACEP. pdf,, April 3, 2020.

样性战略"（Regional Marine and Coastal Biodiversity Strategy，MCBS）。[1]

同时，南亚海洋计划（The South Asian Seas Programme，SASP）也是巴基斯坦积极参与的南亚环境合作计划框架下的合作计划之一。南亚海洋计划于 1984 年 3 月由南亚五个海洋国家——巴基斯坦、印度、斯里兰卡、马尔代夫和孟加拉国共同商定。1995 年 3 月，《南亚海洋行动计划》（The South Asian Seas Action Plan，SASAP）通过，以更有针对性地保护南亚地区广泛的河流三角洲系统以及多样化的海洋和沿海生态环境，尤其是红树林、海草床和珊瑚礁等。巴基斯坦就保护其沿海大量的红树林片区与南亚海洋计划展开了合作。[2] 巴基斯坦科技部部长扎西德·哈米德（Zahid Hamid）在该计划第五次政府间部长级会议上的主题演讲中表示，"区域合作和协作方法是克服我们所面临的共同挑战的前进之路"，南亚海洋计划的推行将有助于"加强区域共同合作的努力，集中一系列的应对方案和手段，以应对因环境退化和气候变化引发灾害（例如南亚地区频发的洪水、海啸）而带来的挑战"[3]。

3. 上海合作组织

上海合作组织（The Shanghai Cooperation Organization，以下简称"上合组织"），是中国、哈萨克斯坦、吉尔吉斯斯坦、俄罗斯、塔吉克斯坦和乌兹别克斯坦六国于 2001 年 6 月 15 日在中国上海宣布成立的永久性政府间国际组织。巴基斯坦和印度于 2017 年成为上合组织的正式成员。上合组织是全球安全治理的重要机构，而海上安全是全球安全治理不可或缺的组成部分。巴基斯坦面临着严峻的海上非法移民、毒品贩卖、海盗袭击与海上恐怖主义等非传统安全威胁，在上合组织框架下开展更为紧密的海上安全合作已是刻不容缓。巴基斯坦在上合组织框架下的重点合作领域为海上警务合作和海上反恐合作，旨在全球化进一步发展的当前情势下，为海外贸易营造更加安全的海上环境。[4] 同时，在上合组织首脑理事会会议精神的倡导下，巴基斯坦能源部、国家海洋研究所与中国地质调查局于 2018 年 10 月举行会谈，以推动落实双方的海洋地学合作，加快双方开展巴中海洋地质调查。[5]

---

〔1〕 "Milestones"，SACEP，http：//sacep. org/milestones，April 3，2020.

〔2〕 "About SASP"，SACEP，http：//www. sacep. org/programmes/south-asian-seas/about，April 3，2020.

〔3〕 "Asian Countries Agree to Tackle Environmental Issues"，Nation，https：//nation. com. pk/09-Dec-2013/s-asian-countries-agree-to-tackle-environmental-issues，April 3，2020.

〔4〕 贺鉴、王璐：《海上安全：上海合作组织合作的新领域?》，载《国际问题研究》2018 年第 3 期，第 69—79 页。

〔5〕 白冰：《钟自然率团访问巴基斯坦、土耳其和塔吉克斯坦加强地质矿产与海洋地学合作》，载中国地质调查局网站，https：//www. cgs. gov. cn/xwl/ddyw/201811/t20181106_ 470615. html，最后访问日期：2021 年 3 月 20 日。

4.《亚洲地区反海盗及武装劫船合作协定》

《亚洲地区反海盗及武装劫船合作协定》（ReCAAP）是亚洲地区第一个政府间共同促进打击海盗和武装劫船的区域性合作协定。该协定由日本于2006年首倡，成员覆盖包括东盟各国、巴基斯坦、孟加拉国、澳大利亚、中国、斯里兰卡、日本、韩国、美国等在内的20个亚太国家。根据该协定相关条款，成员国有义务采取措施共同对抗海盗，也有义务同其他成员国分享知晓的海盗活动信息，以更有效地通过合作建立具体防范机制，并在海盗事件发生时采取更加有效的应对措施。

该协定成员国在新加坡建立了永久的信息交流中心（ReCAAP ISC），作为其主要执行机构，使合作协议得以体制化。该信息中心24小时运作，可以搜集、整理分析并分享整个亚太区域内海盗和武装劫船的相关信息，并及时发出海盗袭击警告，从而有效降低了巴基斯坦海域内的海盗风险，也强化了巴基斯坦与其他成员国之间的海上安全合作，积累了海盗犯罪的治理经验。[1]

5. 印度洋海洋事务合作组织

印度洋海洋事务合作组织（Indian Ocean Marine Affairs Cooperation，IO-MAC）的成立理念是将管理学相关工具融合到指定领域内，尝试将相关的国家、地区和全球机构要素整合到区域管理框架之下，从而实现印度洋区域内的一体化海洋管理活动。印度洋海洋事务合作组织的进程也是该地区国家发起的先锋性海洋管理运动发展的过程。在该组织中，印度洋被视为统一的整体，而不是以差别性的视角来看待。该组织不仅强调促进印度洋国家与该区域外的实体（包括技术先进的国家和国际组织）之间的合作，也注重为印度洋国家之间的区域合作开辟新视野，提升区域内国家之间的合作水平与密切度，从而实现区域海洋的整体性监管。当前，印度洋海洋事务合作组织中所涉及的"海洋事务"主要包括海洋科学技术和海洋服务、生物资源、非生物资源、海洋法与海洋政策及管理、海洋运输和通信、海洋环境等方面。

巴基斯坦作为印度洋海洋事务合作组织的主要成员国，于1990年与印度尼西亚、伊朗、肯尼亚、毛里求斯等国共同通过并签署了《有关印度洋海洋事务合作组织的阿鲁沙协定》（Arusha Agreement on the Organization for Indian Ocean Marine Affairs Cooperation，以下简称《阿鲁沙协定》）。虽然该协定最终因未得到足够的批准书而未能生效，但是印度洋海洋事务合作组织的技术合作小组（Technical Cooperation Group，TCG）仍根据《阿鲁沙协定》而启

---

[1] "About ReCAAP Information Sharing Centre | Combating Maritime Robbery, Sea Piracy", Re-CAAP, http://www.recaap.org/about_ReCAAP-ISC, April 3, 2020.

动。技术合作小组的建立是为了实现印度洋海洋事务合作组织与印度洋地区以外的发达国家之间的交流合作。该小组正在推行或实施包括同国际海洋研究所（International Ocean Institute）合作开展的 IOMAC-IOI 海事培训计划在内的诸多活动。到目前为止，印度洋海洋事务合作组织已经与多个国际组织开展了广泛的海洋合作活动，这些组织包括但不限于：国际海洋研究所、国际海事组织、海洋法研究所（Law of the Sea Institute，LSI）、联合国印度洋和平区特设委员会（UN Ad hoc Committee of the Indian Ocean Peace Zone）、联合国海洋事务和海洋法司（UN Division of Ocean Affairs and the Law of the Sea）。巴基斯坦是技术合作小组的积极推动及参加者之一。[1]

6. 其他区域性合作

除了与特定区域性组织之间进行合作，巴基斯坦还多次举行与海洋科技学术相关的论坛和国际研讨会，积极与周边国家展开交流合作。2014 年 11 月 18—19 日，巴基斯坦在伊斯兰堡政策研究所（Institute for Policy Studies）举办了主题为"大国在印度洋的利益：巴基斯坦面临的挑战和选择"的国际学术研讨会。来自巴基斯坦、印度、伊朗、马来西亚和中国等 12 个国家的海洋科研专家在会上发言，主要涉及海洋法律、政策以及海洋科技合作等问题。[2] 2019 年 2 月 9—11 日，巴基斯坦在卡拉奇举办了主题为"全球地缘政治格局转变：重新思考印度洋区域的海洋动因"的第八届国际海事会议。该会议由巴基斯坦国家海洋研究所主办，是拉开"和平-19"多国海上军演帷幕的重要活动。会议内容涵盖了印度洋地区和中国"一带一路"倡议等多项议题。[3] 同年 3 月 5—7 日，巴基斯坦在卡拉奇举办了"亚洲海事暨海滨展"，展会面积 15000 平方米，展商数量为 350 家，主要有三个国际馆，观众人数约为 35000 人。该展会以展出最前沿的海洋技术和设备为特色，为全世界行业参展商、技术与设备购买商提供了面对面交流的合作平台。多项区域性合作实践表明，巴基斯坦政府极为重视港口和海上商业合作，注重吸引外来投资、增加货物往来，致力于蓝色经济与海洋科技的发展。[4]

---

[1] "The Indian Ocean Marine Affairs Cooperation", United Nations University, http：//archive. unu. edu/unupress/unupbooks/uu15oe/uu15oe0n. htm，April 3, 2020.

[2] 中国社会科学院法学研究所：《王翰灵赴巴基斯坦参加国际研讨会》，载中国法学网，http：//iolaw. cssn. cn/xzxz/201412/t20141201_ 4631497. shtml，最后访问日期：2021 年 3 月 20 日。

[3] 《我院研究人员在卡拉奇出席第八届国际海事会议》，载中国南海研究院网站，http：//www. nanhai. org. cn/dynamic-detail/35/7424. html，最后访问日期：2021 年 3 月 20 日。

[4] 《巴基斯坦海事海滨展览会》，载新丝路网，http：//www. me360. com/convention/3998，最后访问日期：2021 年 3 月 20 日。

（六）全球性国际组织框架下的合作

1. 国际海事组织

国际海事组织成立于 1959 年 1 月 6 日，现已有 173 个正式成员。国际海事组织的目标可以概括为"在干净的海洋上安全、可靠和高效地运输"，其主要目标在于创建一个公平合理的航运业框架，并保障在此框架内的船舶设计、设备安装、货物卸载、人员施工等实践操作的顺利进行，同时通过合理监督，确保整个过程有效、快捷、安全、节能、环保地运作。国际海事组织还涉及与航运有关的法律问题，例如在航海事故中各方所应承担的赔偿责任和赔偿事宜，包括实体案件和相关程序。国际海事组织下设海上安全委员会（The Maritime Safety Committee）、海洋环境保护委员会（The Marine Environment Protection Committee）、法律委员会（The Legal Committee）、技术合作委员会（The Technical Cooperation Committee）、促进委员会（The Facilitation Committee）。

早在 2004 年，国际海事组织秘书长就对巴基斯坦政府发展海事大学的愿望和举措表示了支持和赞赏。秘书长表示会积极协调从而使巴基斯坦有更多机会参与该组织的工作，并且同意考虑让巴基斯坦加入世界海洋大学（World Maritime University，WMU）理事会。除此之外，在捐助巴基斯坦的海事学院建设方面，国际海事组织虽然不能为基本的建设项目提供资金，但同意在收到需求评估的建议后，以任何可行的方式向巴基斯坦提供援助。[1]

巴基斯坦已经批准了在国际海事组织框架下的众多国际条约，这些条约可以分为船舶管理、海上航行安全、海员海务管理、海洋污染防治等方面。具体公约及其对巴基斯坦的生效时间详见本书第 Ⅱ 部分"四、缔结和加入的国际海洋法条约"下相关内容。

2. 政府间海洋学委员会

政府间海洋学委员会（Intergovernmental Oceanographic Commission，IOC）成立于 1960 年，是联合国教科文组织的一个下属机构。其建立的目的在于促进国际海洋领域的合作并强化各成员国之间的海洋研究和海洋服务，增强各成员国预防和治理海洋灾害的能力，了解并有效管理海洋和沿海地区的资源，从而促进海洋环境的可持续发展，特别是在发展中国家之中实现这一目标。[2] 政府间海洋学委员会由大会（General Conference）、执行理事会（Ex-

---

[1] "IMO Welcomes Pakistan's Move to Set Up Maritime University", Business Rocorder, https://fp. brecorder. com/2004/12/2004122592195/, April 3, 2020.

[2] "About the Intergovernmental Oceanographic Commission", UNESCO, http://www. unesco. org/ new/en/natural-sciences/ioc-oceans/about-us/, April 3, 2020.

ecutive Board)、秘书处（Secretariat）和一些附属机构组成。其中，秘书处是常设机构，设在巴黎的联合国教科文组织总部，负责实施大会、执行理事会及其下各附属机构的决议。1969 年委员会第六届大会通过的"海洋勘探与研究长期扩大方案"，是该组织活动的总体规划。据此，委员会的活动可以大致分为三个方面：海洋科学、海洋服务以及培训、教育和互援。

巴基斯坦于 1961 年加入了该组织，并参与了该组织发起的国际印度洋考察，扩充了委员会的海洋科学探测信息。1994 年 10 月 10—14 日，政府间海洋学委员会和巴基斯坦科学技术部国家海洋研究所联合组织了"海岸带管理国际研讨会"（International Workshop on Integrated Coastal Zone Management, ICZM)[1]。由于巴基斯坦所具备的完善的基础设施和积极的参与热情，1994 年 11 月 12—26 日，政府间海洋学委员会和印度洋海洋事务合作组织在巴基斯坦卡拉奇联合举办了巴基斯坦近海海洋地质学和地球物理学的高级培训课程（IOC-IOMAC Advanced Training Course on Marine Geology and Geophysics of Pakistan）。这门培训课程旨在培养印度洋国家在海洋地质学和地球物理学领域的科学家。[2]

---

〔1〕 "International Workshop on Integrated Coastal Zone Management", JODC, https：//www.jodc. go. jp/info/ioc_ doc/Workshop/w114. pdf, April 10, 2020.

〔2〕 "IOC-IOMAC Advanced Training Course on Marine Geology and Geophysics of Pakistan", JODC, https：//www.jodc. go. jp/info/ioc_ doc/Training/tc033. pdf, April 10, 2020.

七、对中国海洋法主张的态度

（一）对"南海仲裁案"的态度

作为中国"全天候"的合作伙伴，巴基斯坦坚决支持中国关于"南海仲裁案"的立场。2016 年 4 月 28 日，巴基斯坦总理外事顾问同中国外交部长王毅在亚洲相互协作与信任措施会议第五次外长会议期间举行会晤，就南海问题达成三大共识：第一，双方认为南海有关争议应由直接当事国根据双边协议及《南海各方行为宣言》通过磋商和谈判以和平方式加以解决。双方反对任何形式的将一国单边意志强加给他国的做法。第二，双方认为域外国家应充分尊重中国和东盟国家为维护南海地区和平稳定所做的努力，并发挥建设性作用。第三，巴方表示尊重中国根据《公约》第 298 条作出的排除性声明。[1]

"南海仲裁案"裁决作出后，巴基斯坦外交部发言人表示，南海争端应依据双边协议和《南海各方行为宣言》，通过对话和协商和平解决。巴基斯坦反对任何形式的将一国单边意志强加给他国的做法，并尊重中国依据《公约》第 298 条规定作出的排除性声明。[2]

可以看到，由于南海并非巴基斯坦的国家战略利益所在地，更基于与中国的密切关系，巴基斯坦对"南海仲裁案"的立场始终与中国保持一致。在"南海仲裁案"裁决作出前，巴基斯坦即在正式外交场合公开表达对中国立场的支持。在裁决作出后，巴基斯坦亦在第一时间重申了本国立场，继续支持中国依据《公约》的有关规定行使法定权利，以维护在南海的合法权益。

（二）对《南海各方行为宣言》的态度

虽然巴基斯坦并非南海争端的直接当事国，亦非东盟成员国，更不是《南海各方行为宣言》的签署国，但其对《南海各方行为宣言》表示支持，

---

〔1〕《中国同巴基斯坦就南海问题达成共识》，载中华人民共和国驻巴基斯坦共和国大使馆网站，http：//pk. chineseembassy. org/chn/zgxw/t1359374. htm，最后访问日期：2020 年 4 月 10 日。

〔2〕 Indiatimes，"South China Sea：India，US Say'Accept Ruling'While Pakistan Backs China"，ht-tps：//timesofindia. indiatimes. com/india/South-China-Sea-India-US-say-accept-ruling-while-Paki-stan-backs-China/articleshow/53178722. cms，April 10，2020.

并多次在涉及南海问题的国际场合提及或呼吁有关各方遵守《南海各方行为宣言》，尽快落实《南海行为准则》。

在 2012 年 7 月举行的第 19 次东盟地区论坛（ASEAN Regional Forum）上，巴基斯坦前外长在发言中充分支持中国在南海问题上的立场，强调南海当事各方应该按照《南海各方行为宣言》中的承诺和平解决所有争端。

2015 年 8 月 6 日，巴基斯坦总理外事顾问在吉隆坡举行的第 22 届东盟地区论坛部长级会议上表示，南海地区的所有国家都应遵守国际法原则，并有效地执行《南海各方行为宣言》，为和平解决南海问题作出贡献。[1]

2016 年 4 月 28 日，巴基斯坦总理外事顾问同中国外交部长王毅在亚洲相互协作与信任措施会议第五次外长会议期间举行会晤，就南海问题达成共识：双方认为南海有关争议应由直接当事国根据双边协议及《南海各方行为宣言》通过磋商和谈判以和平方式加以解决。双方反对任何形式的将一国单边意志强加给他国的做法。[2]

2016 年 7 月 26 日，在第 23 届东盟地区论坛部长级会议上，巴基斯坦代表表示：巴方认为南海争端应由直接相关各方按照有关双边协议和《南海各方行为宣言》以谈判和协商的方式和平解决。[3]

可以看到，在巴基斯坦方面看来，《南海各方行为宣言》既是明晰南海各方权利义务的重要依据，也是和平解决南海各方争议的有效手段，南海问题的最终和平解决，有赖于争议各方对《南海各方行为宣言》的尊重和遵守。

（三）在"一带一路"框架下与中国合作的态度

巴基斯坦既是"丝绸之路经济带"的重要支点国家，也是"海上丝绸之路"的沿岸国家。基于这种特殊的区域历史格局和巴中传统友好关系，巴基斯坦在"一带一路"建设的实施过程中起着独特的作用。"一带一路"倡议让巴中关系不再局限于以政治和安全合作为主，而是在政治、经济、文化多

---

〔1〕 "South China Sea Conflict: Far Off? No Pakistani Position Is Important", Global village space, ht-tps://www.globalvillagespace.com/south-china-sea-conflict-far-off-no-pakistani-position-is-impor-tant/, April 10, 2020.

〔2〕 Permanent Mission of The People's Republic of China to The United Nations Office at Geneva And Other International Organizations in Switzerland, "China and Pakistan Reach Consensus on South China Sea Issue", http://www.china-un.ch/eng/wjyw/t1360240.htm, April 10, 2020.

〔3〕 "South China Sea Conflict: Far Off? No Pakistani Position Is Important", Global village space, ht-tps://www.globalvillagespace.com/south-china-sea-conflict-far-off-no-pakistani-position-is-impor-tant/, April 10, 2020.

层面、多维度的全面合作。因此，"一带一路"倡议一经提出，就迅速得到了巴基斯坦方面的积极响应。

2013 年 5 月 23 日，李克强总理在巴基斯坦参议院发表演讲，指出"中国愿与巴方一道，加快推进喀喇昆仑公路升级改造项目，并积极探索和制定中巴经济走廊远景规划，促进南亚、东亚互联互通，带动周边经济发展和民生改善，不断拉紧中巴利益纽带，为本地区国家间开展合作提供示范。我们愿与巴方共同努力，以大项目合作为契机，继续加强金融和投资合作，继续集中力量推进在基础设施建设、互联互通、海洋、能源、农业、防务等领域的合作"。[1] 随后，巴中两国发表《中华人民共和国和巴基斯坦伊斯兰共和国关于深化两国全面战略合作的联合声明》，该声明第三部分提出："双方将共同努力，不断提升中巴互联互通水平……推进喀喇昆仑公路升级改造和巴国道公路网修复项目，加强交通基础设施建设合作。双方同意，在充分论证的基础上，共同研究制订中巴经济走廊远景规划，推动中巴互联互通建设，促进中巴投资经贸合作取得更大发展。"[2]

2015 年 4 月 20 日，巴中两国发表《中华人民共和国和巴基斯坦伊斯兰共和国关于建立全天候战略合作伙伴关系的联合声明》。该声明第 6 条明确："双方高度评价将中巴经济走廊打造成丝绸之路经济带和 21 世纪海上丝绸之路倡议重大项目所取得的进展。巴方欢迎中方设立丝路基金并将该基金用于中巴经济走廊相关项目。巴方将坚定支持并积极参与'一带一路'建设。丝路基金宣布入股三峡南亚公司，与长江三峡集团等机构联合开发巴基斯坦卡洛特水电站等清洁能源项目，这是丝路基金成立后的首个投资项目。丝路基金愿积极扩展中巴经济走廊框架下的其他项目投融资机会，为'一带一路'建设发挥助推作用。双方认为，'一带一路'倡议是区域合作和南南合作的新模式，将为实现亚洲整体振兴和各国共同繁荣带来新机遇。"该声明第 7 条提出："双方对中巴经济走廊建设取得的进展表示满意，强调走廊规划发展将覆盖巴全国各地区，造福巴全体人民，促进中巴两国及本地区各国共同发展繁荣。双方同意，以中巴经济走廊为引领，以瓜达尔港、能源、交通基础设施和产业合作为重点，形成'1+4'经济合作布局。双方欢迎中巴经济走廊联委会第四次会议成功举行，同意尽快完成《中巴经济走廊远景规划》。

---

〔1〕《国务院总理李克强在巴基斯坦参议院的演讲（全文）》，载中国政府网，http://www.gov.cn/ldhd/2013-05/24/content_ 2410141. htm，最后访问日期：2020 年 4 月 20 日。

〔2〕《中华人民共和国和巴基斯坦伊斯兰共和国关于深化两国全面战略合作的联合声明》，载中国政府网，http://www.xinhuanet.com/world/2013-05/24/c_ 124755934_ 3.htm，最后访问日期：2020 年 4 月 20 日。

双方将积极推进喀喇昆仑公路升级改造二期（塔科特至哈维连段）、瓜达尔港东湾快速路、新国际机场、卡拉奇至拉合尔高速公路（木尔坦至苏库尔段）、拉合尔轨道交通橙线、海尔－鲁巴经济区、中巴跨境光缆、在巴实行地面数字电视传输标准等重点合作项目及一批基础设施和能源电力项目。"该声明第 10 条更强调："双方同意进一步加强海上合作，切实用好中巴海上合作对话机制，就海上问题加强政策对话和战略沟通，在维护航行安全、发展海洋经济、开发利用海洋资源、开展海洋科研、保护环境等领域深入开展合作。双方同意两国在巴基斯坦建设联合海洋科学研究中心。中方将于 2015 年为南亚国家举办海洋科技研讨班，巴方表示将积极参与。"[1]

2017 年 5 月 14—15 日，巴基斯坦积极参加首届"一带一路"国际合作高峰论坛，并与中国在"一带一路"建设框架下达成多项新的合作，如巴基斯坦规划发展和改革部与中国国家发展和改革委员会签署了关于中巴经济走廊项下开展巴基斯坦 1 号铁路干线升级改造和新建哈维连陆港项目合作的谅解备忘录，巴基斯坦铁道部与中国国家铁路局签署了关于实施巴基斯坦 1 号铁路干线升级改造和哈维连陆港项目建设的框架协议，巴基斯坦各相关机构还分别与中国国家开发银行签署了港口、电力、工业园区等领域基础设施融资合作协议。[2] 论坛最后，巴基斯坦还与各与会方一道发表了《"一带一路"国际合作高峰论坛圆桌峰会联合公报》。[3]

2017 年 12 月 18 日，巴基斯坦发布了《中巴经济走廊远景规划》，将"巴基斯坦 2025 发展愿景"（Pakistan Vision 2025）与中国"一带一路"倡议深入对接，指导规划走廊建设，推动两国协同发展。规划明确了走廊建设的指导思想和基本原则、重点合作领域以及投融资机制和保障措施。巴基斯坦规划发展和改革部部长兼内政部长阿赫桑·伊克巴尔（Ahsan Iqbal）在发布仪式上说，中巴经济走廊是两国全天候战略合作的重要体现，帮助巴基斯坦经济发展步入快速增长轨道，社会各领域进步显著。[4]

---

〔1〕《中华人民共和国和巴基斯坦伊斯兰共和国关于建立全天候战略合作伙伴关系的联合声明（全文）》，载新华网，http：//www. xinhuanet. com/world/2015-04/21/c_ 127711924. htm，最后访问日期：2020 年 4 月 20 日。

〔2〕《"一带一路"国际合作高峰论坛成果清单》，载中国政府网，http：//www. gov. cn/xinwen/2017-05/16/content_ 5194255. htm? gs_ ws = tsina_ 6363053233487 16746，最后访问日期：2020 年 4 月 20 日。

〔3〕《"一带一路"国际合作高峰论坛圆桌峰会联合公报（全文）》，载中国政府网，http：//www. gov. cn/xinwen/2017-05/15/content_ 5194232. htm，最后访问日期：2020 年 4 月 20 日。

〔4〕刘天：《〈中巴经济走廊远景规划〉在巴基斯坦发布》，载中国一带一路网，https：//www. yidaiyilu. gov. cn/xwzx/hwxw/40239. htm，最后访问日期：2020 年 4 月 20 日。

2018 年 11 月 4 日，巴中两国发表《中华人民共和国和巴基斯坦伊斯兰共和国关于加强中巴全天候战略合作伙伴关系、打造新时代更紧密中巴命运共同体的联合声明》，该声明第二部分从六大角度论述了巴基斯坦对"一带一路"倡议的立场：第一，"伊姆兰·汗总理赞赏习近平主席提出的旨在加强地区和国际互联互通的'一带一路'倡议。双方重申，'一带一路'倡议提供了一种共赢的国际合作模式，为所有国家经济发展和繁荣带来新的机遇。作为'一带一路'的标志性项目，中巴经济走廊的快速发展，为'一带一路'合作发挥了重要作用"。第二，"双方回顾了中巴经济走廊早期收获项目进展，对各领域特别是能源领域的建设成果感到满意。双方对中巴经济走廊未来发展方向有高度共识，一致同意及时完成在建项目，聚焦经济社会发展、创造就业和改善民生，加快产业及园区和农业领域的合作，争取早日释放中巴经济走廊全部潜力"。第三，"双方同意责成中巴经济走廊联合合作委员会继续探索新的合作领域，决定今年年底前在北京召开第 8 次联合合作委员会会议。为进一步拓展在中巴经济走廊框架内合作，双方宣布增设社会民生工作组，以便更好地利用援助合作支持巴方改善民生"。第四，"双方重申致力于中巴经济走廊建设，一致认为中巴经济走廊是合作共赢的项目，将促进地区互联互通，给整个地区带来繁荣和发展。双方同意，通过现有机制和渠道，包括中巴战略对话、外交磋商和中巴经济走廊联委会等，就推动中巴经济走廊建设进行探讨"。第五，"双方一致认为，瓜达尔港是跨区域互联互通的重要节点和中巴经济走廊的支柱。双方同意加快瓜达尔港港口和配套项目建设"。第六，"双方反对针对中巴经济走廊的负面宣传，坚决保护中巴经济走廊建设安全。巴方赞赏参与巴基斯坦境内经济项目的中方人员作出的巨大贡献。中方感谢巴方为保护在巴基斯坦的中国人员和项目安全所采取的措施"。[1]

2019 年 4 月，巴基斯坦出席第二届"一带一路"国际合作高峰论坛并与中国和其他国家达成多项新的合作，如巴基斯坦邮政局与中国国家邮政局、伊朗邮政局和匈牙利国际发展部签署了《响应"一带一路"倡议加强邮政和快递领域合作的谅解备忘录》，巴基斯坦食品与农业部与中国、孟加拉国、柬埔寨等国的农业部门共同发布了《促进"一带一路"合作共同推动建立农药产品质量标准的合作意向声明》，巴基斯坦与中国、沙特阿拉伯、老挝等

---

〔1〕《中华人民共和国和巴基斯坦伊斯兰共和国关于加强中巴全天候战略合作伙伴关系、打造新时代更紧密中巴命运共同体的联合声明（全文）》，载中国政府网，http://www.gov.cn/xin-wen/2018-11/04/content_ 5337407. htm，最后访问日期：2020 年 4 月 20 日。

国政府签署交通运输领域合作文件。[1] 论坛最后，巴基斯坦与各与会方共同发表了《共建"一带一路" 开创美好未来——第二届"一带一路"国际合作高峰论坛圆桌峰会联合公报》，强调各方将加强发展政策对接，加强基础设施互联互通，加强务实合作，加强人文交流，推动可持续发展。[2]

2019 年 9 月 7 日，中国、巴基斯坦和阿富汗三国外长在伊斯兰堡举行第三次中国—阿富汗—巴基斯坦三方外长对话并发表《第三次中国—阿富汗—巴基斯坦外长对话联合声明》。三方在《联合声明》中重申，三国将"共同致力于加强关系，探讨深化合作的新路径，包括在'一带一路'、阿富汗区域经济合作会议和其他地区经济倡议框架内推进互联互通建设"。三国还决定将于 2020 年在北京举行第四次三方外长对话。[3]

2020 年 1 月 2 日，中国驻巴基斯坦大使姚敬在巴基斯坦《新闻报》《国民报》《今日巴基斯坦报》《每日时报》《观察家报》等主流媒体上发表题为《深化互信合作开启中巴关系新篇章》的署名文章。文章指出，2019 年是中巴关系深入发展的一年，伊姆兰·汗总理两度访华、三次与习近平主席会面，双方围绕打造新时代更紧密的中巴命运共同体、高质量共建"一带一路"交流智慧经验，达成一系列重要成果和共识，将"一带一路"倡议同"新巴基斯坦"发展战略良好对接，中巴经济走廊顺利推进。双方将社会民生、产业园区和农业作为合作重点，在走廊框架下确定了 27 个社会民生优先项目，其中 17 个计划在 2020 年上半年全面启动。[4]

可以看到，巴中友好关系的历史渊源，为"一带一路"倡议在巴基斯坦的顺利开展和落实奠定了良好的政治和外交基础。"中巴经济走廊"作为"一带一路"倡议的旗舰项目，连同"一带一路"倡议下的其他合作项目一道得到了巴基斯坦的大力支持和积极推进。积极响应顺应时代发展新要求的"一带一路"倡议，促进经济要素有序自由流动、资源高效配置和市场深度融合，实现欧亚非大陆及附近海洋的互联互通，既是巴基斯坦在"一带一

---

〔1〕 《第二届"一带一路"国际合作高峰论坛成果清单》，载中华人民共和国外交部网站，ht-tps：//www. fmprc. gov. cn/web/ziliao_ 674904/zt_ 674979/dnzt_ 674981/qtzt/ydyl_ 675049/zyxw_ 675051/t1658760. shtml，最后访问日期：2020 年 4 月 20 日。

〔2〕 《第二届"一带一路"国际合作高峰论坛圆桌峰会联合公报（全文）》，载新华网，http：//www. xinhuanet. com/world/2019-04/27/c_ 1124425237. htm，最后访问日期：2020 年 4 月 20 日。

〔3〕 《第三次中国—阿富汗—巴基斯坦外长对话联合声明》，载中华人民共和国外交部网站，ht-tp：//new. fmprc. gov. cn/web/wjbzhd/t1695752. shtml，最后访问日期：2020 年 4 月 20 日。

〔4〕 《驻巴基斯坦大使姚敬在巴主流媒体发表新年署名文章》，载中华人民共和国驻巴基斯坦共和国大使馆网站，http：//pk. chineseembassy. org/chn/zbgx/t1729318. htm，最后访问日期：2020 年 1 月 20 日。

路"框架下与中国合作的态度，也是新时期巴中关系的发展目标。

结 语

相较于域内其他海洋国家，巴基斯坦的海洋面积并不广阔，却在地区及世界的海洋地理结构中有着独特的枢纽地位与关隘价值。总体而言，巴基斯坦表现出对海洋的持续关注，并努力在全球海洋秩序中体现本国的海洋地位、扩张本国海洋权益。

在海洋管理机构体系的建设方面，巴基斯坦并无专门性海洋事务管理机构，但已经在较宽泛的意义上建成了涉及海上航行、海洋渔业、海洋能源、海上安全的涉海事务的基本监管体系。在国内海洋立法方面，巴基斯坦同样已经初步实现从管辖海域、海上安全、海上航行到海洋渔业、海上油气、海洋科研的综合海洋法律体系的构建。但相较于区域第一大国印度，巴基斯坦在海上能源开发、海上环境保护等领域相关专门性立法的更新进度与完善程度仍显滞后与迟缓。在国际海洋立法方面，巴基斯坦一方面签署大量条约，表现出参与国际海洋秩序建设的正面姿态；另一方面，除因复杂的历史与现实纠葛而与印度间的遗留争议外，巴基斯坦也积极利用相关国际海洋法律框架解决海洋争端，并取得较好的效果。同时，作为中国的亲密外交伙伴，巴基斯坦不但在"南海仲裁案"等问题上坚定地站在中国一方，在"一带一路"倡议的建设过程中，巴基斯坦也积极发挥自己"支点"的作用，努力将"一带一路"与本国政策和发展战略相对接，借"一带一路"之风，助推本国更好更快发展。

参考文献

一、中文文献

1. 孙士海、葛维钧主编：《印度》，社会科学文献出版社 2010 年版。

2. 厉以宁、王武龙主编：《中国企业投资分析报告》，经济科学出版社 2006 年版。

3. 时光慧、祁艺主编：《能源工业 中国石油天然气集团公司发展概况》，载中华人民共和国年鉴编辑部主编：《中华人民共和国年鉴》，中华人民共和国年鉴社 2017 年版。

4. 黄素奕、林一歆：《能源与节能技术》（第三版），中国电力出版社 2016 年版。

5. 朱华荣：《试论法律体系及其科学分类》，载《法学》1983 年第 3 卷。

6. 陆德山、孙育玮：《关于我国法律体系的几个问题》，载《求是学刊》1984 年第 6 期。

7. E. B. 库马尼：《政治体系与法律体系的相互作用》，徐晓晴译，载《现代法学》1988 年第 1 卷。

8. 赵长生：《法律体系的哲学思考》，载《法学》1991 年第 6 卷。

9. 杨思灵：《印度与其"大周边"地区的能源合作》，载《亚非纵横》2009 年第 3 期。

10. 易传剑：《我国海洋法律体系的重构——以海权为中心》，载《广东海洋大学学报》2010 年第 2 期。

11. 汤喆峰、司玉琢：《论中国海法体系及其建构》，载《中国海商法研究》2013 年第 3 期。

12. 张湘兰、叶泉：《建设海洋强国的法律保障：中国海洋法体系的完善》，载《武大国际法评论》2013 年第 1 期。

13. 龚大明：《印度莫迪政府的南海政策》，载《东南亚南亚研究》2015 年第 4 期。

14. 初北平、曹兴国：《海法概念的国际认同》，载《中国海商法研究》2015 年第 3 卷。

15. 徐祥民：《走出国际法范畴的海洋法——服务于我国海洋基本法建设的思考》，载《山东大学学报》（哲学社会科学版）2015 年第 1 期。

16. 曹兴国、初北平：《我国涉海法律的体系化完善路径》，载《太平洋学报》2016 年第 9 卷。

17. 刘仝保、王志飞：《引领国际海洋游戏规则——访国家课题〈完善我国海洋法律体系研究〉首席专家赵劲松》，载《经济》2016 年第 1 期。

18. 刘磊、寇鹏程：《析莫迪执政以来印度与美国海上安全合作》，载《国际关系研究》2018 年第 5 期。

19. 张帅、任欣霖：《印度能源外交的现状与特点》，载《国际石油经济》2018 年第 3 期。

20. 梅冠群：《印度对"一带一路"倡议的态度及成因》，载《东南亚南亚研究》2018 年第 1 期。

21. 贺鉴、王璐：《海上安全：上海合作组织合作的新领域?》，载《国际问题研究》2018 年第 3 期。

22. 邵建平：《"东进"遇上"西看"：印越海洋合作新态势及前景》，载《国际问题研究》2019 年第 4 期。

23. 石培培：《美巴关系对中巴"一带一路"合作的影响》，载《学术探索》2019 年第 11 期。

24. 徐惠喜：《"一带一路"释放中国与南亚合作潜力》，载《经济日报》2017 年 6 月 22 日，第 9 版。

25. 张建松、岑志连：《中巴首次北印度洋联合考察圆满结束》，载《河北日报》2018 年 2 月 4 日，第 4 版。

26. 王涛：《巴基斯坦法制的历史切变》，载《人民法院报》2019 年 6 月 7 日，第 8 版。

二、外文文献

1. Richard F. Nyrop et al. , *Area Handbook for the Persian Gulf States*, Cabin John, Wildside Press, 2008.

2. Rizwan Hussain, *Pakistan and the Emergence of Islamic Militancy in Afghanistan*, Aldershot, Hampshire：Ashgate, 2005.

3. Syed Farooq Hasnat, *Pakistan*, California, ABC-CLIO, 2011.

4. Pirouz Mojtahed-Zadeh and Bahador Zarei, "Maritime Boundary Delimitations in the Persian Gulf", *International Studies Journal* 54, 2017.

5. Yoshifumi Tanaka, *Predictability and Flexibility in the Law of Maritime Delimitation* (*Second Edition*), Oxford, Hart Publishing, 2019.

6. M. Hassan Shetol et al. , "Present Status of Bangladesh Gas Fields and Fu-

ture Development：A Review"，*Journal of Natural Gas Geoscience* 6，2019.

三、数据库和网站

（一）中文数据库和网站

1. 中华人民共和国条约数据库，http：//treaty. mfa. gov. cn。

2. 中华人民共和国外交部网站，https：//www. fmprc. gov. cn。

3. 中华人民共和国驻印度大使馆网站，https：//www. fmprc. gov. cn。

4. 中华人民共和国驻巴基斯坦共和国大使馆网站，http：//pk. chineseembassy. org。

5. 中华人民共和国驻塞尔维亚共和国大使馆网站，http：//rs. chineseembassy. org。

6. 中华人民共和国驻巴基斯坦大使馆经济商务参赞处网站，http：//pk. mofcom. gov. cn。

7. 中华人民共和国商务部网站，http：//www. mofcom. gov. cn。

8. 中华人民共和国商务部对外投资和经济合作司网站，http：//fec. mofcom. gov. cn。

9. 中华人民共和国商务部亚洲司网站，http：//template1. mofcom. gov. cn。

10. 中华人民共和国商务部中国企业境外商务投诉服务中心网站，http：//shangwutousu. mofcom. gov. cn。

11. 中华人民共和国农业农村部渔业渔政管理局网站，http：//www. yyj. moa. gov. cn。

12. 中国政府网，http：//www. gov. cn。

13. 中共中央对外联络部网站，https：//www. idcpc. gov. cn。

14. 中国地质调查局网站，https：//www. cgs. gov. cn/。

15. 中国一带一路网，https：//www. yidaiyilu. gov. cn。

16. 新华网，http：//www. xinhuanet. com/。

17. 新华财经网，http：//world. xinhua08. com/。

18. 人民网时政频道，http：//politics. people. com. cn/。

19. 人民网国际频道，http：//world. people. com. cn/。

20. 环球网国际新闻频道，http：//world. huanqiu. com/。

21. 环球网国内新闻频道，https：//china. huanqiu. com/。

22. 环球网军事频道，https：//mil. huanqiu. com/。

23. 腾讯新闻网，https：//news. qq. com/。

24. 搜狐网，http：//www. sohu. com/。

25. 中国网，http：//www. china. com. cn/。

26. 央广网，http：//www. cnr. cn/。

27. 新浪新闻网，http：//news. sina. com. cn/。

28. 新浪军事网，http：//mil. news. sina. com. cn/。

29. 中国新闻网，http：//www. chinanews. com/。

30. 观察者网，https：//www. guancha. cn/。

31. 中国自然资源部第二海洋研究所网站，http：//www. sio. org. cn/。

32. 中国自然资源部第三海洋研究所网站，http：//www. tio. org. cn/。

33. 中国水产科学研究院网站，http：//www. cafs. ac. cn/。

34. 中国水产科学研究院珠江水产研究所网站，https：//www. prfri. ac. cn/。

35. 中国水产科学研究院黄海水产研究所网站，http：//www. ysfri. ac. cn/。

36. 中国南海研究院网站，http：//www. nanhai. org. cn/。

37. 青岛海洋科学与技术试点国家实验室网站，http：//www. qnlm. ac/。

38. 中国水产养殖网，http：//www. shuichan. cc/。

39. 国际船舶网，http：//www. eworldship. com/。

40. 中国船贸网站，http：//www. csoc. cn/。

41. 上海海事大学网站，https：//immse. shmtu. edu. cn/。

42. 中国科学院网站，http：//www. cas. cn/。

43. 中国法学网，http：//iolaw. cssn. cn/。

44. 中国教育在线网，https：//www. eol. cn/。

45. 新丝路网，http：//www. me360. com/。

46. 国防信息网，http：//www. dsti. net/。

47. 国际在线网，http：//news. cri. cn/。

48. 亚太日报网站，https：//cn. apdnews. com/。

49. 印度世界广播网，http：//airworldservice. org/。

50. 石油圈网，http：//www. oilsns. com/。

51. 海峡风，http：//www. fishexpo. cn/。

52. 腾氏水产网，http：//www. tensfish. com/。

（二）外文数据库和网站

1. Oceans & Law of The Sea（United Nations），https：//www. un. org/ Depts/los/index. htm.

2. UN Treaty Collection，https：//treaties. un. org/.

3. International Seabed Authority，https：//www. isa. org. jm/.

4. International Maritime Organization，http：//www. imo. org/.

5. World Bank，https：//databank. worldbank. org/.

6. International Whale Comission，https：//iwc. int/home.

7. Commission for the Conservation of Antarctic Marine Living Resources，https：//www. ccamlr. org/.

8. Global Ocean Data Assimilation Experiment，https：//www. godae. org/.

9. International Collective in Support of Fishworkers，https：//indianlegal. icsf. net/.

10. Indian Ocean Tuna Commission，https：//www. iotc. org/.

11. The Network of Aquaculture Centres in Asia and the Pacific，https：//enaca. org/.

12. ECOLEX，https：//www. ecolex. org/.

13. The Indian Rim Association，https：//www. iora. int/.

14. Bay of Bengal Initiative for Multi-Sectoral Technical and Economic Cooperation，https：//bimstec. org/.

15. ReCAAP，http：//www. recaap. org/.

16. Globe Environment Facility，https：//www. thegef. org/.

17. FAO，http：//www. fao. org/home/en/.

18. United Nations University，http：//archive. unu. edu/.

19. UNESCO，http：//www. unesco. org/.

20. InfoFish，http：//infofish. org/.

21. Asian Infrastructure Investment Bank，https：//www. aiib. org/en/index. html.

22. The Commonwealth，https：//thecommonwealth. org/.

23. International Union for Conservation of Nature，https：//www. iucn. org/.

24. IRAM，https：//iramcenter. org/.

25. SAARC，https：//www. saarc-sec. org/.

26. SACEP，http：//sacep. org/.

27. IEA，https：//www. iea. org/.

28. Permanent Court of Arbitration，https：//pca-cpa. org/.

29. Convention on the Conservation of Migratory Species of Wild Animals，https：//www. cms. int/.

30. National Portal of India，https：//www. india. gov. in/.

31. Ministry of Earth Sciences of India，https：//moes. gov. in/.

32. Ministry of Ports，Shipping and Waterways of India，http：//sagarma-

la. gov. in/.

33. India Code, https：//www. india. gov. in/.

34. Depatrment of Agriculture Cooperation & Farmers Welfare of India, http：//agricoop. nic. in/.

35. Fishery Survey of India, http：//fsi. gov. in/.

36. Ministry of Environment, Forest and Climate Change of India, http：//moef. gov. in.

37. National Centre for Polar and Ocean Research of India, http：//www. ncaor. gov. in/.

38. Ministry of Shipping of India, http：//shipmin. gov. in.

39. Department of Science & Technology of India, https：//dst. gov. in/.

40. The Council of Scientific & Industrial Research of India, https：//www. csir. res. in/.

41. National Institute of Oceanography of India, http：// www. nio. org.

42. Directorate General of Hydrocarbons of India, http：//dghindia. gov. in/.

43. Ministry of New & Renewable Energy of India, https：//mnre. gov. in/.

44. Ministry of Petroleum and Natural Gas of India, http：//petroleum. nic. in/.

45. Offshore Technology, https：//www. offshore-technology. com/.

46. Indian Coast Guard, https：//www. indiancoastguard. gov. in/.

47. Indian Navy, https：//www. indiannavy. nic. in/.

48. Hauser Global Law School Program, https：//www. nyulawglobal. org/.

49. Central Marine Fisheries Research Institute, http：//eprints. cmfri. org. in/.

50. Directorate General of Shipping of India, https：//www. dgshipping. gov. in/.

51. Indian Kanoon, https：//indiankanoon. org/.

52. Law Teacher, https：//www. lawteacher. net/.

53. Ministry of External Affairs of India, https：//www. mea. gov. in/.

54. Department of Government Information of Sri Lanka, https：//www. dgi. gov. lk/.

55. Livemint, https：//www. livemint. com/.

56. ACADEMIA, https：//www. academia. edu/.

57. Carnegie Endowment for International Peace, https：//carnegieendowment. org/.

58. Carnegieindia, https：//carnegieindia. org/.

59. United States Department of State, https：//www. state. gov/.

60. American School of International Law, https：//www. asil. org/.

61. History PAK. COM, https：//historypak. com/.

62. India Today, https：//www. indiatoday. in/.

63. India Times, https：//www. indiatimes. com/.

64. The Economist, https：//www. economist. com/.

65. The AsiaN, http：//www. theasian. asia/.

66. Sun Media Group, https：//en. sun. mv/.

67. Gk Today, https：//www. gktoday. in/.

68. Telly Updates, https：//www. tellyupdates. com/.

69. IAS Preparation Online, https：//www. iaspreparationonline. com/.

70. ONLANKA, https：//www. onlanka. com.

71. Galedialogue, http：//galledialogue. lk.

72. SSBCrack, https：//www. ssbcrack. com/.

73. FORCE, http：//forceindia. net/.

74. Indo-Pacific Defense Forum, https：//ipdefenseforum. com/.

75. Hindustan Times, https：//www. hindustantimes. com/.

76. Sandia National Laboratories, https：//www. sandia. gov/.

77. The Economic Times, https：//economictimes. indiatimes. com/.

78. India. com, https：//www. india. com/.

79. Jatin Verma's IAS Academy, https：//www. jatinverma. org/.

80. U. S. Department of Defense, https：//dod. defense. gov/.

81. Navaltoday, https：//navaltoday. com/.

82. US Embassy and Consulate in Japan, https：//jp. usembassy. gov/.

83. The Russian International Affairs Council, https：//russiancouncil. ru/en/.

84. Navy Recogniton, http：//navyrecognition. com/.

85. The Defense Post, https：//thedefensepost. com.

86. Australian Institute of International Affairs, https：//www. internationalaffairs. org. au/.

87. Financial Express, https：//www. financialexpress. com/.

88. The Hindu, https：//www. thehindu. com.

89. U. S. Energy Information Administration, https：//www. eia. gov.

90. India Brand Equity Foundation, https：//www. ibef. org/.

91. National Data Repository, https：//www. ndrdgh. gov. in/.

92. India Brand Equity Foundation, https：//www. ibef. org/.

93. Jagran Josh, https：//www. jagranjosh. com/.

94. Bar and Bench, https：//www. barandbench. com/.

95. Prime Minister's Citizen Assistance and Relief in Emergency Situations Fund, https：//www. pmindia. gov. in/.

96. The London School of Economics and Political Science, https：//blogs. lse. ac. uk/.

97. Deparment of Fisheries of India, http：//dof. gov. in/.

98. Press Information Bureau of India, https：//pib. gov. in/.

99. The Norwegian Agency for Development Cooperation, https：//www. norad. no/en/front/.

100. Embassy of India in Moscow, https：//www. indianembassy-moscow. gov. in/.

101. Embassy of India in Tokyo, https：//www. indembassy-tokyo. gov. in/.

102. India Bioscience, https：//indiabioscience. org/.

103. The Diplomat, https：//thediplomat. com/.

104. Institute for Security & Development Policy, http：//isdp. eu/.

105. Embassy of the Islamic Republic of Pakistan Beijing, http：//www. pakbj. org/.

106. Ministry of Foreign Affairs of Pakistan, http：//www. mofa. gov. pk/.

107. Finance Division of Government of Pakistan, http：//www. finance. gov. pk/.

108. National Assembly of Pakistan, http：//www. na. gov. pk/.

109. Senate of Pakistan, http：//senate. gov. pk/.

110. The Pakistan Code, http：//pakistancode. gov. pk/.

111. Ministry of Law and Justice of Government of Pakistan, http：//www. molaw. gov. pk/.

112. Ministry of Foreign affairs of Government of Pakistan, http：//www. mofa. gov. pk/.

113. Ministry of National Food Security and Research of Government of Pakistan, http：//www. mnfsr. gov. pk/.

114. Ministry of Maritime Affairs of Government of Pakistan, https：//moma. gov. pk/.

115. Fisheries Development Bureau of Government of Pakistan, http：//fdb. org. pk/.

116. Karachi Port Trust, https：//kpt. gov. pk/.

117. Port Qasim Authority, https: //www. pqa. gov. pk/.

118. Gwadar Port Authority, http: //www. gwadarport. gov. pk/.

119. Government Shipping Office of Pakistan, https: //shippingoffice. gov. pk/.

120. Mercantile Marine Department of Pakistan, http: //mercantilemar-ine. gov. pk/.

121. Directorate General Ports & Shipping of Pakistan, https: //dgps. gov. pk/.

122. Pakistan Marine Academy, https: //marineacademy. edu. pk/.

123. Pakistan National Shipping Corporation, https: //pnsc. com. pk/.

124. Ministry of Energy of Pakistan, http: //mowp. gov. pk/.

125. Pakistan Petroleum Limited, https: //www. ppl. com. pk/.

126. Oil and Gas Development Corporation Limited, https: //ogdcl. com/.

127. Ministry of Science and Technology, https: //most. gov. pk/.

128. National Institute of Oceanography Pakistan, http: //niopk. gov. pk/.

129. Pakistan Maritime Security Agency, http: //www. pmsa. gov. pk/.

130. Pakistan Navy, https: //www. paknavy. gov. pk/.

131. Ministry of Defence Production of Pakistan, http: //www. modp. gov. pk/.

132. Karachi Shipyard & Engineering Works Limited, https: //www. kara-chishipyard. com. pk/.

133. Survey of Pakistan, http: //surveyofpakistan. gov. pk/.

134. Josh and Mak International, https: //joshandmakinternational. com/.

135. Pakistan Today, https: //www. pakistantoday. com. pk.

136. Pakchina News, http: //pakchinanews. pk/.

137. Dawn, https: //www. dawn. com/.

138. Foreign Policy News, https: //foreignpolicynews. org/.

139. VivekanandaInternational Foundation, https: //www. vifindia. org/.

140. Ministry of Petroleum & Natural Resources, http: //www. ppisonline. com/.

141. Embassy of Pakistan, Washington D. C. , http: //embassyofpakista-nusa. org/.

142. Pakistan Association of Petroleum Geoscientists, https: //www. papg. org. pk/.

143. Pakistan Agricultural Research Council, http: //www. parc. gov. pk/.

144. Ministry of Agro Industry and Food Security of Mauritius, https: //agri-culture. govmu. org/.

145. Royal Thai Consulate-General, Karachi, Pakistan, https: //karachi. thaiembassy. org/.

146. Pakistan Science Foundation, http: //psf. gov. pk/.

147. Permanent Mission of The People's Republic of China to The United Nations Office at Geneva And Other International Organizations in Switzerland, http: //www. china-un. ch/.

148. Ministry of Agriculture and Rural Development of Vietnam, https: //www. mard. gov. vn/.

149. Royal Norwegian Embassy in Colombo, https: //www. norway. no/.

150. Indian legal. icsf, https: //indianlegal. icsf. net/.

151. Air World Service, http: //airworldservice. org/.

152. Sputnik International, https: //sputniknews. com/.

153. ADA Derana, http: //www. adaderana. lk/.

154. Arabnews, https: //www. arabnews. com.

155. Gulfnews, https: //gulfnews. com.

156. Heinonline, https: //heinonline. org.

157. Voice of Journalists, https: //www. voj. news.

158. The Express Tribune, https: //tribune. com. pk.

159. Pakchina News, http: //pakchinanews. pk.

160. The Geopolitics, https: //thegeopolitics. com.

161. Theindubusinessline, https: //www. thehindubusinessline. com/.

162. Thefishsite, https: //thefishsite. com/.

163. Navy Times, https: //www. navytimes. com/.

164. JODC, https: //www. jodc. go. jp/.

165. Pakobserver, https: //pakobserver. net/.

附　录

附录 1　印度《1976 年领海、大陆架、
专属经济区及其他海洋区域法》[1]

THE TERRITORIAL WATERS, CONTINENTAL SHELF, EXCLUSIVE ECONOMIC ZONE
AND OTHER MARITIME ZONES ACT, 1976

ARRANGEMENT OF SECTIONS

---

[1]　See "The Territorial Waters, Continental Shelf, Exclusive Economic Zone and Other Maritime Zones Act, 1976", India Code, https：//www. indiacode. nic. in/handle/123456789/1484？ view＿ type = browse&sam＿ handle = 123456789/1362#. , March 20, 2021.

THE TERRITORIAL WATERS, CONTINENTAL SHELF, EXCLUSIVE ECONOMIC ZONE
AND OTHER MARITIME ZONES ACT, 1976

ACT No. 80 OF 1976

[25th August, 1976.]

An Act to provide for certain matters relating to the territorial waters continental shelf, exclusive economic zone and other maritime zones of India.

BE it enacted by Parliament in the Twenty-seventh Year of the Republic of India as follows:—

1. Short title and commencement.—(1) This Act may be called the Territorial Waters, Continental Shelf, Exclusive Economic Zone and Other Maritime Zones Act, 1976.

(2) Sections 5 and 7 shall come into force on such date or on such different dates as the Central Government may, by notification in the Official Gazette, appoint; and the remaining provisions of this Act shall come into force at once.

2. Definition.—In this Act, "limit", in relation to the territorial waters, the continental shelf, the exclusive economic zone or any other maritime zone of India, means the limit of such waters, shelf or zone with reference to the mainland of India as well as the individual or composite group or groups of islands constituting part of the territory of India.

3. Sovereignty over, and limits of, territorial waters.—(1) The sovereignty of India extends and has always extended to the territorial waters of India (hereinafter referred to as the territorial waters) and to the seabed and subsoil underlying, and the air space over, such waters.

(2) The limit of the territorial waters is the line every point of which is at a distance of twelve nautical miles from the nearest point of the appropriate baseline.

(3) Notwithstanding anything contained in sub-section (2), the Central Government may, whenever it considers necessary so to do having regard to International Law and State practice, alter, by notification in the Official Gazette, the limit of the territorial waters.

(4) No notification shall be issued under sub-section (3) unless resolutions approving the issue of such notification are passed by both Houses of Parliament.

4. Use of territorial waters by foreign ships.—(1) Without prejudice to the provisions of any other law for the time being in force, all foreign ships (other than warships including sub-marines and other underwater vehicles) shall enjoy the right of innocent passage through the territorial waters.

Explanation.—For the purposes of this section, passage is innocent so long as it is not prejudicial to the peace, good order or security of India.

(2) Foreign warships including submarines and other underwater vehicles may enter or pass through the territorial waters after giving prior notice to the Central Government:

Provided that submarines and other underwater vehicles shall navigate on the surface and show their flag while passing through such waters.

(3) The Central Government may, if satisfied that it is necessary so to do in the interests of the peace, good order or security of India or any part thereof, suspend, by notification in the Official Gazette, whether absolutely or subject to such exceptions and qualifications as may be specified in the notification, the entry of all or any class of foreign ships into such area of the territorial waters as may be specified in the notification.

---

1. 15th January, 1977, *vide* notification No. G.S.R. 16(E), dated 15th January, 1977, *see* Gazette of India, Extraordinary, Part II, sec. 3(*i*).

5. Contiguous zone of India.—(*1*) The contiguous zone of India (hereinafter referred to as the contiguous zone) is an area beyond and adjacent to the territorial waters and the limit of the contiguous zone is the line every point of which is at a distance of twenty-four nautical miles from the nearest point of the baseline referred to in sub-section (*2*) of section 3.

(*2*) Notwithstanding anything contained in sub-section (*1*), the Central Government may, whenever it considers necessary so to do having regard to International Law and State practice, alter, by notification in the Official Gazette, the limit of the contiguous zone.

(*3*) No notification shall be issued under sub-section (*2*) unless resolutions approving the issue of such notification are passed by both Houses of Parliament.

(*4*) The Central Government may exercise such powers and take such measures in or in relation to the contiguous zone as it may consider necessary with respect to,—

(*a*) the security of India, and

(*b*) immigration, sanitation, customs and other fiscal matters.

(*5*) The Central Government may, by notification in the Official Gazette,—

(*a*) extend with such restrictions and modifications as it thinks fit, any enactment, relating to any matter referred to in clause (*a*) or clause (*b*) of sub-section (*4*), for the time being in force in India or any part thereof, to the contiguous zone, and

(*b*) make such provisions as it may consider necessary in such notification for facilitating the enforcement of such enactment,

and any enactment so extended shall have effect as if the contiguous zone is a part of the territory of India.

6. Continental shelf.—(*1*) The continental shelf of India (hereinafter referred to as the continental shelf) comprises the seabed and subsoil of the submarine areas that extend beyond the limit of its territorial waters throughout the natural prolongation of its land territory to the outer edge of the continental margin or to a distance of two hundred nautical miles from the baseline referred to in sub-section (*2*) of section 3 where the outer edge of the continental margin does not extend up to that distance.

(*2*) India has, and always had, full and exclusive sovereign rights in respect of its continental shelf.

(*3*) Without prejudice to the generality of the provisions of sub-section (*2*), the Union has in the continental shelf,—

(*a*) sovereign rights for the purposes of exploration, exploitation, conservation and management of all resources;

(*b*) exclusive rights and jurisdiction for the construction, maintenance or operation of artificial islands, off-shore terminals, installations and other structures and devices necessary for the exploration and exploitation of the resources of the continental shelf or for the convenience of shipping or for any other purpose;

(*c*) exclusive jurisdiction to authorise, regulate and control scientific research; and

(*d*) exclusive jurisdiction to preserve and protect the marine environment and to prevent and control marine pollution.

(*4*) No person (including a foreign Government) shall, except under, and in accordance with, the terms of a licence or a letter of authority granted by the Central Government, explore the continental shelf or exploit its resources or carry out any search or excavation or conduct any research within the continental shelf or drill therein or construct, maintain or operate any artificial island, off-shore terminal, installation or other structure or device therein for any purpose whatsoever.

(*5*) The Central Government may, by notification in the Official Gazette,—

(*a*) declare any area of the continental shelf and its superjacent waters to be a designated area; and

(*b*) make such provisions as it may deem necessary with respect to,—

(*i*) the exploration, exploitation and protection of the resources of the continental shelf within such designated area; or

(*ii*) the safety and protection of artificial islands, off-shore terminals, installations and other structures and devices in such designated area; or

(*iii*) the protection of marine environment of such designated area; or

(*iv*) customs and other fiscal matters in relation to such designated area.

Explanation.—A notification issued under this sub-section may provide for the regulation of entry into and passage through the designated area of foreign ships by the establishment of fairways, sealanes, traffic separation schemes or any other mode of ensuring freedom of navigation which is not prejudicial to the interests of India.

(*6*) The Central Government may, by notification in the Official Gazette,—

(*a*) extend with such restrictions and modifications as it thinks fit, any enactment for the time being in force in India or any part thereof to the continental shelf or any part [including any designated area under sub-section (*5*)] thereof; and

(*b*) make such provisions as it may consider necessary for facilitating the enforcement of such enactment,

and any enactment so extended shall have effect as if the continental shelf or the part [including, as the case may be, any designated area under sub-section (*5*)] thereof to which it has been extended is a part of the territory of India.

(*7*) Without prejudice to the provisions of sub-section (*2*) and subject to any measures that may be necessary for protecting the interests of India, the Central Government may not impede the laying or maintenance of submarine cables or pipelines on the continental shelf by foreign States:

Provided that the consent of the Central Government shall be necessary for the delineation of the course for the laying of such cables or pipelines.

7. Exclusive economic zone.—(*1*) The exclusive economic zone of India (hereinafter referred to as the exclusive economic zone) is an area beyond and adjacent to the territorial waters, and the limit of such zone is two hundred nautical miles from the baseline referred to in sub-section (*2*) of section 3.

(*2*) Notwithstanding anything contained in sub-section (*1*), the Central Government may, whenever it considers necessary so to do having regard to International Law and State practice, alter, by notification in the Official Gazette, the Limit of the exclusive economic zone.

(*3*) No notification shall be issued under sub-section (*2*) unless resolutions approving the issue of such notification are passed by both Houses of Parliament.

(*4*) In the exclusive economic zone, the Union has,—

(*a*) sovereign rights for the purpose of exploration, exploitation, conservation and management of the natural resources, both living and non-living as well as for producing energy from tides, winds and currents;

(*b*) exclusive rights and jurisdiction for the construction, maintenance or operation of artificial islands, off-shore terminals, installations and other structures and devices necessary for the exploration and exploitation of the resources of the zone or for the convenience of shipping or for any other purpose;

(*c*) exclusive jurisdiction to authorise, regulate and control scientific research;

(*d*) exclusive jurisdiction to preserve and protect the marine environment and to prevent and control marine pollution; and (*e*) such other rights as are recognised by International Law.

(*5*) No person (including a foreign Government) shall, except under, and in accordance with, the terms of any agreement with the Central Government or of a licence or a letter of authority granted by the Central Government, explore or exploit any resources of the exclusive economic zone or carry out any search or excavation or conduct any research within the exclusive economic zone or drill therein or construct, maintain or operate any artificial island, off-shore terminal, installation or other structure or device therein for any purpose whatsoever:

Provided that nothing in this sub-section shall apply in relation to fishing by a citizen of India.

(*6*) The Central Government may, by notification in the Official Gazette,—

(*a*) declare any area of the exclusive economic zone to be a designated area; and

(*b*) make such provisions as it may deem necessary with respect to,—

(*i*) the exploration, exploitation and protection of the resources of such designated area; or

(*ii*) other activities for the economic exploitation and exploration of such designated area such as the production of energy from tides, winds and currents; or

(*iii*) the safety and protection of artificial islands, off-shore terminals, installations and other structures and devices in such designated area; or

(*iv*) the protection of marine environment of such designated area; or

(*v*) customs and other fiscal matters in relation to such designated area.

Explanation.—A notification issued under this sub-section may provide for the regulation of entry into and passage through the designated area of foreign ships by the establishment of fairways, sealanes, traffic separation schemes or any other mode of ensuring freedom of navigation which is not prejudicial to the interests of India.

(*7*) The Central Government may, by notification in the official Gazette,—

(*a*) extend, with such restrictions and modifications as it thinks fit, any enactment for the time being in force in India or any part thereof to the exclusive economic zone or any part thereof; and

(*b*) make such provisions as it may consider necessary for facilitating the enforcement of such enactment,

and any enactment so extended shall have effect as if the exclusive economic zone or the part thereof to which it has been extended is a part of the territory of India.

(*8*) The provisions of sub-section (*7*) of section 6 shall apply in relation to the laying or maintenance of submarine cables or pipelines on the seabed of the exclusive economic zone as they apply in relation to the laying or maintenance of submarine cables or pipelines on the seabed of the continental shelf.

(*9*) In the exclusive economic zone and the air space over the zone, ships and aircraft of all States shall, subject to the exercise by India of its rights within the zone, enjoy freedom of navigation and over flight.

8. Historic waters.—(*1*) The Central Government may, by notification in the Official Gazette, specify the limits of such waters adjacent to its land territory as are the historic waters of India.

(*2*) The sovereignty of India extends, and has always extended, to the historic waters of India and to the seabed and subsoil underlying, and the air space over, such waters.

9. Maritime boundaries between India and States having coasts opposite or adjacent to those of India.—(*1*) The maritime boundaries between India and any State whose coast is opposite or adjacent to that of India in regard to their respective territorial waters, contiguous zones, continental shelves, exclusive economic zones and other maritime zones shall be as determined by agreement (whether entered into before or after the commencement of this section) between India and such State and pending such agreement between India and any such State, and unless any other provisional arrangements are agreed to between them, the maritime boundaries between India and such State shall not extend beyond the line every point of which is equidistant from the nearest point from which the breadth of the territorial waters of India and of such State are measured.

(2) Every agreement referred to in sub-section (1) shall, as soon as may be after it is entered into, be published in the Official Gazette.

(3) The provisions of sub-section (1) shall have effect notwithstanding anything contained in any other provision of this Act.

10. Publication of charts.—The Central Government may cause the baseline referred to in sub-section (2) of section 3, the limits of the territorial waters, the contiguous zone, the continental shelf, the exclusive economic zone and the historic waters of India and the maritime boundaries as settled by agreements referred to in section 9 to be published in charts.

11. Offences.—Whoever contravenes any provision of this Act or of any notification thereunder shall (without prejudice to any other action which may be taken against such person under any other provision of this or of any other enactment) be punishable with imprisonment which may extend to three years, or with fine, or with both.

12. Offences by companies.—(1) Where an offence under this Act or the rules made thereunder has been committed by a company, every person who at the time the offence was committed was in charge of, and was responsible to the company for the conduct of the business of the company, as well as the company shall be deemed to be guilty of the offence and shall be liable to be proceeded against and punished accordingly.

Provided that nothing contained in this sub-section shall render any such person liable to any punishment provided in this Act if he proves that the offence was committed without his knowledge or that he exercised all due diligence to prevent the commission of such offence.

(2) Notwithstanding anything contained in sub-section (1) where an offence under this Act or the rules made thereunder has been committed by a company and it is proved that the offence has been committed with the consent or the connivance of, or is attributable to any neglect on the part of, any director, manager, secretary or other officer of the company, such director, manager, secretary or other officer shall also be deemed to be guilty of that offence and shall be liable to be proceeded against and punished accordingly.

Explanation.—For the purposes of this section,—

(a) "company" means any body corporate and includes a firm or other association of individuals; and

(b) "director", in relation to a firm, means a partner in the firm.

13. Place of trial.—Any person committing an offence under this Act or any rules made thereunder or under any of the enactments extended under this Act or under the rules made thereunder may be tried for the offence in any place in which he may be found or in such other place as the Central Government may, by general or special order, published in the Official Gazette, direct in this behalf.

14. Previous sanction of the Central Government for prosecution.—No prosecution shall be instituted against any person in respect of any offence under this Act or the rules made thereunder without the previous sanction of the Central Government or such officer or authority as may be authorised by that Government by order in writing in this behalf.

15. Power to make rules.—(1) The Central Government may, by notification in the Official Gazette, make rules for carrying out the purposes of this Act.

(*2*) In particular and without prejudice to the generality of the foregoing power, such rules may provide for all or any of the following matters, namely:—

(*a*) regulation of the conduct of any person in the territorial waters, the contiguous zone, the continental shelf, the exclusive economic zone or any other maritime zone of India;

(*b*) regulation of the exploration and exploitation, conservation and management of the resources of the continental shelf;

(*c*) regulation of the exploration, exploitation, conservation and management of the resources of the exclusive economic zone;

(*d*) regulation of the construction, maintenance and operation of artificial islands, off-shore terminals, installations and other structures and devices referred to in sections 6 and 7;

(*e*) preservation and protection of the marine environment and prevention and control of marine pollution for the purposes of this Act;

(*f*) authorisation, regulation and control of the conduct of scientific research for the purposes of this Act;

(*g*) fees in relation to licences and letters of authority referred to in sub-section (*4*) of section 6 and sub-section (*5*) of section 7 or for any other purpose; or

(*h*) any matter incidental to any of the matters specified in clauses (*a*) to (*g*).

(*3*) In making any rule under this section, the Central Government may provide that a contravention thereof shall be punishable with imprisonment which may extend to three years, or with fine which may extend to any amount, or with both.

(*4*) Every rule made under this Act and every notification issued under sub-section (*5*) of section 6 or sub-section (*6*) of section 7 shall be laid, as soon as may be after it is made or issued, before each House of Parliament while it is in session for a total period of thirty days which may be comprised in one session or in two or more successive sessions and if, before the expiry of the session immediately following the session or the successive sessions aforesaid both Houses agree in making any modification in the rule or the notification or both Houses agree that the rule or notification should not be issued, the rule or notification shall, thereafter, have effect only in such modified form or be of no effect, as the case may be; so, however, that any such modification or annulment shall be without prejudice to the validity of anything previously done under that rule or notification.

16. Removal of difficulties.—(*1*) If any difficulty arises in giving effect to the provisions of this Act or of any of the enactments extended under this Act, the Central Government may, by order published in the Official Gazette, make such provisions not inconsistent with the provisions of this Act or, as the case may be, of such enactment, as may appear to it to be necessary or expedient for removing the difficulty:

Provided that no order shall be made under this section—

(*a*) in the case of any difficulty arising in giving effect to any provision of this Act, after the expiry of three years from the commencement of such provision;

(*b*) in the case of any difficulty arising in giving effect to the provisions of any enactment extended under this Act, after the expiry of three years from the extension of such enactment.

(*2*) Every order made under this section shall be laid, as soon as may be after it is made, before each House of Parliament.

附录 2　印度关于《1976 年领海、大陆架、专属经济区及其他海洋区域法》的 2002 年政府公告（S. O. 189E)[1]

2002 Notification on The Territorial Waters, Continental Shelf,
Exclusive Economic Zone and Other Maritime Zones Act, 1976
New Delhi, the 7th February, 2002

S. O. 189 （E）. —In exercise of the powers conferred by clause （a） of Sub-section （6） of Section 6 and clause （a） of sub-section （7） of Section 7 of the Territorial Waters, Continental Shelf, Exclusive Economic Zone and other Maritime Zones Act, 1976 （80 of 1976）, the Central Government hereby extends the Customs Act1962 （51 of 1962） and Customs Tariff Act 1975 （51 of 1975） to the continental shelf of India and the exclusive economic zone of India with effect from the date of publication of this publication in the Official Gazette, for the for the following purposes, namely—

（a） the prospecting for extraction of production of mineral oils in the continental shelf of India or the exclusive economic zone of India, and

（b） the supply of any goods [as defined in clause （22） of Section 2 of the Customs Act 1962] in connection with any of theactivities referred to in clause （a）.

Explanation: For the purposes of this notification "mineral oils" include petroleum and natural gas.

[No. L - 111/3/2002]
Dr. P. S. RAO, Addl. Secy. and the Legal Adviser.

---

[1]　See "2002 Notification on The Territorial Waters, Continental Shelf, Exclusive Economic Zone and Other Maritime Zones Act, 1976 （07. 02. 2002 ）", India Code, https: //upload. india-code. nic. in/showfile? actid = AC_ CEN_ 10_ 10_ 00002_ 197680_ 1517807318455&type = notification&filename = 2002% 20Notification% 20on% 20The% 20Territorial% 20Waters,% 20Continental% 20Shelf,% 20Exclusive% 20Economic% 20Zone% 20and% 20Other% 20Maritime% 20Zones% 20Act,% 201976. pdf, March 20, 2021.

附录3　印度关于扩展规定适用范围的 S. O. 2168 号公告[1]

SO2168 Extension of Application of Provisions （22. 12. 2006）
New Delhi，the 22nd December，2006

S. O. 2168 （E）—In exercise of the powers conferred by clause （a） of Sub-section （7） of Section 7of the Territorial Waters，Continental Shelf，Exclusive Economic Zone and other Maritime Zones Act，1976 （80 of 1976），the Central Government hereby extends the application of the provisions under Section 497 and clause 2 of section 3 of the Merchant Shipping Act，1958 to the Exclusive Economic Zone of India with effect from the date of the publication of this notification in the Official Gazette.

［No. L‐111/04/2006］
NARINDER SINGH，Jt. Secy. &Legal Adviser

---

［1］　See "SO2168 Extension of Application of Provisions （22. 12. 2006）"，India Code，https：//upload. indiacode. nic. in/showfile? actid = AC_ CEN_ 10_ 10_ 00002_ 197680_ 1517807318455& type = notification&filename = SO2168% 20Extension% 20of% 20application% 20of% 20provisions% 20 （22. 12. 2006） . pdf，March 20，2021.

附录4　印度关于领海基线地理坐标的
2009 年政府公告（S. O. 1197E）[1]

[फा. स. यूआइ/251.1/04/20

दिनेश पटनायक, संयुक्त स]

MINISTRY OF EXTERNAL AFFAIRS
NOTIFICATION

New Delhi, the 11th May, 2009

S.O. 1197(E).—In exercise of the powers conferred by section 10, read with sub-section (2) of section 3, of the Territorial Waters, Continental Shelf, Exclusive Economic Zone and Other Maritime Zones Act, 1976 (80 of 1976) (hereinafter referred to as the said Act), the Central Government hereby notifies the following baseline system from which the limits of the territorial waters, the contiguous zone, the continental shelf, the exclusive economic zone and the maritime boundaries shall be measured seaward, namely:—

(a) the list of geographical coordinates (in Everest Spheroid) of the points set out in the Schedules I to IV annexed to this notification shall be the baseline system for the Republic of India and this baseline system consists of normal and straight baselines that join the outermost points to the coast, low-water line, low-water reefs and islands, as marked on the larger scale charts published or, as the case may be, notified, from time to time, by the Chief Hydrographer to the Government of India;

(b) the limits of the historic waters of India already notified, before the publication of this notification, in pursuance of the maritime boundary agreement between India and Sri Lanka for Palk Strait and Palk Bay and Gulf of Mannar, in the Gazette of India, Extraordinary, *vide* notification of the Government of India in the Ministry of External Affairs, number G.S.R.17 (E), dated the 15th January, 1977 shall remain unchanged;

(c) the sea-area enclosed within the normal and straight baseline system referred to in paragraph (a) and limits of the historic waters of India referred to in paragraph (b) shall form the internal waters of the Republic of India.

---

[1] See " SO1197E List of Geographical Coordinates (11.05.2009)", India Code, https://upload. indiacode. nic. in/showfile? actid = AC _ CEN _ 10 _ 10 _ 00002 _ 197680 _ 1517807318455&type = notification&filename = SO1197% 20List% 20of% 20Geographical% 20Coordinates% 20 (11.05.2009) .pdf, March 20, 2021.

SCHEDULE I
[See paragraph (a)]

BASELINE SYSTEM-WEST COAST

Baseline Point	Geographical Name	Geographical Coordinates (Approx)	
		Latitude (N)	Longitude (E)
(1)	(2)	(3)	(4)
1	Sir Mouth N.	23° 40' 20.80"	68° 04' 31.20"
2	Sir Mouth S.	23° 36' 30.30"	68° 07' 00.90"
3	Pir Sanai Creek	23° 36' 15.20"	68° 07' 28.50"
4	Kori Creek	23° 24' 14"	68° 20' 49
5	Veraya Thar	23° 18' 24"	68° 27' 48"
6	Kharo Creek	23° 15' 40"	68° 30' 50"
7	Bari Bn.	23° 11' 03"	68° 36' 33"
8	Kachchigad (Thence following low water line to baseline point 9)	22° 18' 36"	68° 55' 58"
9	Diu Head W.	20° 41' 24"	70° 49' 18"
10	Tarapur Pt.	19° 50' 32"	72° 38' 13"
11	Mahim Cr.	19° 37' 40"	72° 41' 16"
12	Ussapur Rk.	19° 32' 26"	72° 42' 00"
13	Poshpir Is.	19° 20' 15"	72° 44' 58"
14	Outer Is.	19° 15' 52"	72° 45' 36"
15	Mehti Khada	19° 08' 00"	72° 46' 27"
16	Outer Rf. Back Bay	18° 55' 21"	72° 47' 21"
17	Prongs Rf.	18° 52' 33"	72° 47' 42"
18	Kanhoji Angre	18° 42' 12"	72° 48' 48"
19	Whale Rf.	18° 16' 16"	72° 54' 53"

续表

(1)	(2)	(3)	(4)
20	Kumbaru Pt.	18° 13' 01"	72° 55' 55"
21	Srivardhan Lt.	18° 03' 14"	72° 59' 28"
22	Srivardhan Pt.	18° 01' 12"	73° 00' 09"
23	Bankot	17° 58' 08"	73° 01' 10"
24	Dighi	17° 56' 31"	73° 01' 50"
25	Ranvi Pt.	17° 33' 20"	73° 08' 16"
26	Boria Pt	17° 24' 18"	73° 10' 00"
27	Jaigarh Lt.	17° 17' 53"	73° 11' 27"
28	Miria Head	17° 01' 36"	73° 15' 12"
29	Mushroom Rk.	16° 32' 17"	73° 18' 36"
30	Girye Bay	16° 30' 40"	73° 18' 59"
31	Burnt Is.	15° 53' 18"	73° 27' 21"
32	Saint George Is. (Sail rock)	15° 20' 38"	73° 45' 40"
33	Cape Rama	15° 05' 00"	73° 54' 46"
34	Mangalgudda Is	14° 48' 54"	74° 03' 18"
35	Basavarajadurg Is	14° 18' 43"	74° 23' 54"
36	Netrani Is	14° 00' 37"	74° 19' 22"
37	Coconut Is (North)	13° 24' 06"	74° 38' 57"
38	Mulki Rks.	13° 11' 54"	74° 40' 18"
39	Mangalore S	12° 50' 58"	74° 49' 32"
40	Bekal	12° 24' 30"	75° 00' 32"
41	Kotte Kunnu	12° 00' 20"	75° 12' 04"
42	Sacrifice Rk.	11° 29' 30"	75° 31' 40"

(1)	(2)	(3)	(4)
43	Ponnani N.	10° 47' 24"	75° 54' 36"
44	Chetwai	10° 31' 30"	76° 01' 42"
45	Sand Patch (off Kochi)	09° 58' 27"	76° 13' 18"
46	Alleppey. Thence following low water line including offlying islands to baseline point 47.	09° 30' 22"	76° 18' 48"
47	Vivekananda Memorial	08° 04' 24"	77° 33' 24"
48	Idindakarai	08° 10' 33"	77° 44' 48"
49	Manappad Pt.	08° 22' 24"	78° 04' 12"
50	Tiruchchendur Pt.	08° 29' 44"	78° 07' 54"
51	Tuticorin Jetty Lt. House	08° 44' 48"	78° 13' 48"
52	Nalla Tanni Is	09° 06' 03"	78° 34' 48"
53	Musal Tivu	09° 11' 24"	79° 05' 18"
54	Adam's Bridge (Thence join by straight line on East Coast to baseline point 55)	09° 05' 36"	79° 31' 48"

SCHEDULE II
[See paragraph (a)]

BASELINE SYSTEM-EAST COAST

(1)	(2)	(3)	(4)
55	Adam's Bridge N.	09° 06' 24"	79° 31' 36"
56	Devils Point (Thence following low water line to baseline point 57)	09° 19' 00"	79° 20' 12"
57	Pt. Calimere W	10° 17' 30"	79° 52' 42"
58	Pt. Calimere NE	10° 18' 30"	79° 53' 20"

(1)	(2)	(3)	(4)
59	Pt. Calimere N. (Thence following low water line to baseline point 60)	10° 19' 30"	79° 52' 50"
60	Caverippattinam N	11° 11' 50"	79° 51' 30"
61	Coleroon S.	11° 21' 00"	79° 50' 45"
62	Cuddalore	11° 42' 22"	79° 47' 00"
63	Malakkanam	12° 13' 15"	79° 59' 37"
64	Palar R.	12° 26' 48"	80° 08' 45"
65	Mamallapuram	12° 36' 24"	80° 12' 30"
66	Covelong Pt.	12° 46' 54"	80° 15' 24"
67	Ennur N	13° 16' 36"	80° 20' 48"
68	Kattupalli	13° 18' 25"	80° 20' 56"
69	Tangal	13° 20' 36"	80° 20' 36"
70	Pulicat	13° 26' 36"	80° 19' 36"
71	Point Pudi	13° 46' 54"	80° 15' 20"
72	Penner R.	14° 34' 40"	80° 11' 50"
73	Motumala	15° 29' 45"	80° 12' 45"
74	False Divi E.	15° 43' 25"	80° 56' 30"
75	Golumuttapaya R.	15° 46' 00"	81° 00' 40"
76	Divi Pt.	15° 58' 00"	81° 09' 24"
77	Narsapur Pt.	16° 17' 40"	81° 42' 00"
78	Bandamurlanka	16° 23' 40"	81° 57' 30"
79	Karakutippa	16° 34' 15"	82° 19' 20"
80	Jonnala Konda	17° 35' 24"	83° 12' 54"
81	Kalingapatnam	18° 19' 00"	84° 08' 03"

(1)	(2)	(3)	(4)
82	Bavana Padu S.	18° 33' 22"	84° 21' 32"
83	Ganguvada. Thence following low water line to baseline point 84.	18° 47' 40"	84° 33' 30"
84	Devi Pt.	19° 57' 00"	86° 22' 30"
85	Dowdeswell Is.	20° 20' 30"	86° 47' 33"
86	Wheeler Is.	20° 44' 30"	87° 06' 06"
87	West Spit	21° 22' 42"	88° 43' 30"
88	New Moore Is. S	21° 33' 54"	89° 08' 45"
89	New Moore Is. E	21° 34' 37"	89° 12' 23"

SCHEDULE III
[See paragraph (a)]

BASELINE SYSTEM-ANDAMAN & NICOBAR ISLANDS (WEST)

(1)	(2)	(3)	(4)
90	Cape Land Fall E	13° 40' 29"	93° 01' 12"
91	Cape Land Fall W	13° 40' 30"	93° 00' 52"
92	Landfall Is NE	13° 39' 57"	92° 59' 03"
93	Land Fall Island W	13° 39' 44"	92° 58' 39"
94	West Is N	13° 35' 50"	92° 53' 28"
95	West Is S	13° 34' 46"	92° 52' 58"
96	Point Is. N	13° 25' 27"	92° 48' 32"
97	North Reef Is.	13° 05' 12"	92° 41' 10"
98	Interview Is.	12° 51' 40"	92° 39' 00"
99	Flat Is.	12° 32' 00"	92° 40' 12"

(1)	(2)	(3)	(4)
100	North Sentinel Is.	11° 35' 06"	92° 11' 50"
101	South Sentinel Is.	10° 58' 36"	92° 12' 36"
102	Little Andaman Is. (Sandy Pt.)	10° 32' 15"	92° 23' 10"
103	Car Nicobar Is.	09° 09' 28"	92° 43' 02"
104	Teressa Island	08° 16' 24"	93° 04' 48"
105	Great Nicobar Is.(Teesta Pt)	07° 00' 18"	93° 39' 32"
106	Great Nicobar Is. SW. Thence following low water line to baseline point 107.	06° 45' 33"	93° 48' 16"
107	Indira Pt.	06° 45' 16"	93° 50' 15"

SCHEDULE IV
[See paragraph (a)]

BASELINE SYSTEM-LAKSHADWEEP ISLANDS

(1)	(2)	(3)	(4)
121	Cherbaniani Reef	12° 23' 15"	71° 51' 48"
122	Byramgore Reef NW	11° 57' 48"	71° 43' 20"
123	Byramgore Reef SW	11° 52' 30"	71° 45' 00"
124	Peremul Par	11° 10' 30"	71° 59' 50"
125	Suheli Par	10° 01' 00"	72° 14' 00"
126	Viringili Is. (Minicoy) NW. Thence following low water line to baseline point 127.	08° 16' 34"	73° 00' 36"
127	Kodi Pt.	08° 19' 27"	73° 04' 52"
128	Kalpeni Is.	10° 03' 30"	73° 38' 56"
129	Cheriyan Is.	10° 08' 15"	73° 39' 55"
130	Androth Is.	10° 48' 47"	73° 42' 10"

(1)	(2)	(3)	(4)
131	Kiltan Is.	11° 29' 14"	73° 00' 38"
132	Cherbaniani	12° 23' 50"	71° 53' 10"
133	Cherbaniani North Pt. Thence join by straight line to baseline point 121.	12° 24' 00"	71° 52' 30"

[F. No. UI/251.1/04/2009]

DINESH PATNAIK, Jt. Secy.

附录5 印度关于修订 S. O. 1197E 公告的 2009 年政府公告（S. O. 2962E）[1]

MINISTRY OF EXTERNAL AFFAIRS
CORRIGENDUM

New Delhi, the 20th November, 2009

S.O. 2962(E).—In exercise of the powers conferred by Section 10, read with sub-section (2) of Section 3, of the Territorial waters, Continental shelf, Exclusive Economic Zone and other Maritime Zones Act, 1976 (80 of 1976) (hereinafter referred to as the said Act), the Central Government on being satisfied that it is necessary in the public interest so to do, hereby makes the following amendments in the notification of the Government of India in the Ministry of External Affairs, No. [F. No. UI/251.1/04/2009] dated the 11th May, 2009 which was published in the Gazette of India, Extraordinary, Part II, Section 3, Sub-section (ii) *vide* number S.O. 1197(E) dated the 11th May, 2009, namely:—

In the said notification,

(i) in the first line of sub-paragraph (a), the phrase "(in Everest Spheroid)" shall be replaced by "[Indian Geodetic Datum (Everest Ellipsoid 1956)];

(ii) the word "Approx." shall be deleted in the table heading "Geographic Coordinates" in Schedule I; and

(iii) in Schedule III, a new row shall be inserted after serial number 107, as follows:—

108-120	To be notified separately

Except the amendments as detailed above, the contents of the aforesaid Gazette Notification of May 11, 2009 shall remain unchanged.

[F. No. UI/251.1/04/2009]

RAJIVA MISRA, Jt. Secy.

---

[1] See "SO2962E （20. 11. 2009） Amendment to SO1197E of 11. 05. 2009", India Code, https://upload. indiacode. nic. in/showfile? actid = AC _ CEN _ 10 _ 10 _ 00002 _ 197680 _ 1517807318455&type = notification&filename = SO2962E% 20 （20. 11. 2009）% 20Amendment% 20to% 20SO1197% 20of% 2011. 05. 2009. pdf, March 20, 2021.

附录6　印度《海洋渔业（监管和管理）草案》（2019）[1]

THE MARINE FISHERIES（REGULATION AND MANAGEMENT）BILL, 2019

	A **BILL**	
	to provide for regulation and management of fisheries in the Exclusive Economic Zone of India and the high seas and for conservation and sustainable use of marine fisheries resources; maintenance of law and order in the maritime zones of India (for fishing and fishing related activities); supporting the social security, livelihoods and safety at sea of fishers and fish-workers, in particular the traditional and small-scale fishers; and for matters connected therewith and incidental thereto.	
	Be it enacted by Parliament in the Seventieth Year of the Republic of India as follows:	
	CHAPTER I **PRELIMINARY**	
Short title and commencement.	1. (1) This Act may be called the Marine Fisheries (Regulation and Management) Act, 2019. (2) It shall come into force on such date as the Central Government may, by notification, in the Official Gazette, appoint: Provided that different dates may be appointed for different provisions of this Act, and any reference in any such provision to the commencement of this Act shall be construed as a reference to the coming into force of that provision.	
Definitions.	2.In this Act, unless the context otherwise requires, (a) "authorized officer" means any officer or subordinate officer of the Indian Coast Guard constituted under the Coast Guard Act, 1978, or such other officer of Government as may be authorized by the Central Government. (b) "code of conduct for responsible fisheries" means establishment of guiding principles and standards applicable for conservation, management and development of fisheries in the maritime zones of India and to provide a necessary framework for sustainable exploitation of aquatic living resources in harmony with the environment. (c) "company" means a company as defined in the Companies Act, 2013; (d) "ecosystem approach to fisheries management" means a practical way to implement sustainable development and sustainably maximize the ecosystem benefits of a fishery system, including: 　(i) Ecological well-being (e.g. healthy habitats, food webs, and sustainable fishing); 　(ii) Human well-being (e.g. Increased & equitable wealth, food security and sustainable livelihoods); and 　(iii) Good governance (e.g. effective institutions and arrangements for setting and implementing rules and regulations). (e) "endangered, threatened and protected species" include forms of marine animals that are endangered or threatened and need protection by national legislations or applicable international instruments or in need of a protected status, and *inter alia* include sea turtles, marine mammals and some species of sharks and rays. (f) "exclusive economic zone" means the exclusive economic zone of India as defined under section 7 of the Territorial Waters, Continental Shelf, Exclusive Economic Zone and Other Maritime Zones of India Act, 1976; (g) "fish" means finfish, molluscs, crustaceans, and all other forms of marine animals and plant life other than marine mammals, reptiles and birds.	80 of 1976

---

[1]　See "Marine Fisheries（Regulation and Management）Bill, 2019", Indian legal. icsf, https：// indianlegal. icsf. net/images/resources/externalNews/docs/legal ＿ india/documents/65005543. pdf, Feburary 11, 2020.

(h) "fisheries" means all activities related to fishing, harvesting, conservation and management of marine living resources;
 	
(i) "fisheries management plan" means any document issued by the Central Government in relation to sustainable use and development of fisheries; management and conservation, including monitoring, control and surveillance of fishing and fishing related activities; and maintenance of law and order in the maritime zones of India;
 	
(j) "fishing" and "fishing related activities" include-
   (i) searching for or tracking or trailing or pursuing fish;
   (ii) catching or taking or harvesting of fish by any method;
   (iii) engaging in any other activity that *inter alia* includes landing, packaging, processing, transshipping, or transporting of fish that have not been previously landed at a port;
   (iv) any operations at sea directly in support of or linked to or in preparation of any activity described in this definition or for processing of or preservation of any fish;
 	
(k) "fishing vessel" as defined in the Merchant Shipping Act, 1958;
 	
(l) "foreign fishing vessel" means any fishing vessel other than an Indian fishing vessel;
 	
(m) "high seas" means the waters that are outside the outer limits of the exclusive economic zone of India, and which do not fall within the exclusive economic zone of any other country;
 	
(n) "illegal, unreported and unregulated fishing" includes following activities:
 	
(A) Illegal fishing:
   (i) conducted by Indian fishing vessels in the Exclusive Economic Zone of India without the permit issued under this Act;
   (ii) conducted by foreign vessels in the maritime zones of India;
   (iii) conducted by Indian flag vessels in contravention of the conservation and management measures adopted by Regional Fisheries Management Organization to which India is a party, or relevant provisions of the applicable international law;
(B) Unreported fishing:
   (i) which have not been reported, or have been misreported to the authority notified under this Act, in contravention of this Act and the Rules and Regulations framed thereunder;
(C) Unregulated fishing:
   (i) by an Indian fishing vessel, in a manner that is not consistent with or contravenes the conservation and management measures of regional fisheries management organization in its area of application; or
   (ii) in areas or for fish stocks in relation to which there are no applicable conservation or management measures and where such fishing activities are conducted in a manner inconsistent with India's responsibilities for the conservation of living marine resources under international law.
 	
(o) "Indian fishing vessel" means a fishing vessel registered under the Merchant Shipping Act, 1958 and is owned by:
 	
(i) the Government of India or by the Government of any State, or by a corporation established by a Central Act or a State Act; or
 	
(ii) by persons to each of whom any of the following descriptions apply, namely-
   (a) a citizen of India; or
   (b) a company in which the entire share capital is held by Indian citizen(s); or
   (c) a duly registered firm wherein every partner whereof is a citizen of India;
	44 of 1958
	
	44 of 1958

	or	
	(d) a fisher organization/association registered under the Societies Registration Act, 1890 or any other such Law enacted by the coastal States/UTs and every member whereof is a citizen of India; or	..... Act of 1890
	(e) a registered co-operative society, every member whereof is a citizen of India or where any other cooperative society is a member thereof, every individual member of such other cooperative society is a citizen of India; or	
	(f) any boat or craft of any type other than those specified as above, which the Central Government may, by notification in the Official Gazette, specify to be an Indian fishing vessel.	
	(p) "maritime zones of India" means the territorial waters, contiguous zone, continental shelf, exclusive economic zone and other maritime zones determined in accordance with the Territorial Waters, Continental Shelf, Exclusive Economic Zone and Other Maritime Zones Act, 1976;	80 of 1976
	(q) "master" in relation to a vessel, means any person having command, or charge of the vessel;	
	(r) "notification" means notification published in the Official Gazette and the expression 'notified' shall be construed accordingly;	
	(s) "owner" in relation to a vessel means the owner of the vessel as well as any other person, including any organization or association of persons, whether incorporated or not, by whom the vessel or a share in the vessel is owned, or who has assumed the legal responsibility for the operation of the vessel;	
	(t) "permit" means a permission granted under this Act for fishing and fishing related activities.	
	(u) "prescribed" means prescribed by Rules made under this Act;	
	(v) "processing" in relation to fishing, includes cleaning, cutting and removal of spines, fins, shells, viscera (guts and other internal soft parts), beheading, bleeding, filleting, peeling, icing, freezing, canning, salting, smoking, cooking, pickling, drying and otherwise preparing or preserving fish by any other method;	
	(w) "specified ports" means such ports as the Central Government may, by notification in the Official Gazette, specify for the purpose of this Act;	
	(x) "territorial waters of India" means the territorial waters of India in accordance with the provisions of section 3 of the Territorial Waters, Continental Shelf, Exclusive Economic Zone and other Maritime Zones of India Act, 1976;	80 of 1976
	(y) "vessel" includes any ship, or craft or vessel, sailing vessel, chase boats, pilot boats, transport, or carrier vessels, or any craft or vessel used for research on fisheries or any other vessel of any other description that is capable of fishing, stocking or storing or processing or transporting fish, fuel or other supplies from or to a fishing vessel or is otherwise capable of providing logistical or any other support to fishing vessels.	
	CHAPTER II **REGULATION OF FISHERIES IN THE EXCLUSIVE ECONOMIC ZONE AND HIGH SEAS**	
Prohibition of fishing without permit.	3.(1)　No Indian fishing vessel shall engage in any fishing or fishing related activity within the exclusive economic zone of India or the high seas, except with a permit issued by the Central Government or any authority notified under this Act for fishing, and shall be subject such conditions and restrictions as prescribed.	
Levy of Fee, charges and exemptions	(2)　Permit issued under this Act shall be subject to levy of fee and charges for fishing	

thereof	and fishing related activities and in such manner as prescribed.	
	Provided that Central Government may exempt any person, entity or category or class of vessel(s) from the requirement of payment of fee and charges as prescribed.	
	(3) No permit shall be issued unless the fishing vessel is registered under the Merchant Shipping Act, 1958.	44 of 1958
	(4) No permit shall be granted under this Act to foreign fishing vessel for fishing and fishing related activities within the exclusive economic zone of India.	
	(5) A permit granted under this Act shall be non-transferrable, and shall not be assigned to, or create interest in favour of any third party.	
	(6) No fishing vessel granted permit under this Act shall indulge in any form of Illegal, Unreported and Unregulated fishing activity in the maritime zones of India, the high seas and in the waters under national jurisdictions of other countries without authorization.	
	(7) The Central Government may deny or withhold the issuance of permit, to a vessel or a class of vessels, having regard to matters related to national security of India and maintenance of law and order in the maritime zones of India.	
	(8) Every order of accepting or rejecting an application for the grant of permit shall be in writing.	
	(9) The Central Government may, by notification in this regard, exempt a Government entity, or corporation or any category or class of vessel(s) from the requirement of a permit under sub-section (1) of this section 3, and from the application of any other provision of this Act.	
Fisheries Management Plan.	4. (1) The Central Government may, from time to time, after consultation, notify one or more plans for management of one or more fisheries or fishing related activities in such area(s) of the maritime zones of India as may be prescribed.	
	Provided that if a fisheries management plan is being made in relation to any area within the territorial waters of India, then such plan shall be formulated by the Central Government in consultation with the Government of the State or Union Territory under whose jurisdiction the relevant area of the territorial waters falls.	
	(2) All permits granted under this Act, shall be subject to fisheries management plan(s) as may be notified by the Central Government and in the event of any inconsistency between a permit so granted and a fisheries management plan, all such permits shall be deemed amended in consonance with such fisheries management plan.	
	(3) Fisheries management plan(s) shall follow the Code of Conduct for Responsible Fisheries and the Ecosystem Approach to Fisheries Management and other relevant instruments as may be prescribed.	
	(4) Fisheries management plan(s) will ensure protection of endangered, threatened and protected species as prescribed.	
	(5) Fisheries management plan(s) will ensure that the ecological integrity of the maritime zones of India, including prevention, control and mitigation of any form of pollution arising through fishing and fishing related activities is maintained.	
	(6) Fisheries management plan(s) shall also ensure that they are consistent with the implementation of international or regional conventions/obligations/ agreements/ arrangements for fisheries and fishing related activities to which India is a signatory.	
	(7) Any other matter which the Central Government may determine to be relevant for achieving any of the objectives of regulation and management of marine fisheries	

	under this Act.	
Cancellation or Suspension of a permit.	5. (1) The Central Government may cancel or suspend a permit granted under this Act, if there is reasonable cause to believe that- (a) there has been a violation of any of the provisions of the Act; or (b) there has occurred a contravention of the provisions in the permit or any conditions or restrictions specified in the permit, or of any Rules made under this Act, or of any fisheries management plan; or engaged in fishing in 'no fishing zone', or (c) the permit or any renewal thereof has been issued on false or erroneous information. Provided that no permit shall be cancelled or suspended under sub-section (1), unless the holder of the permit shall be given reasonable opportunity of showing cause why the permit should not be cancelled or suspended, as the case may be. Provided further that nothing in this sub-section shall apply where the Central Government is satisfied that, for reasons to be recorded in writing, it is not reasonably practicable to give to the holder of the permit an opportunity for showing cause. (2) Every person whose permit has been cancelled or suspended under sub-section (1) above shall, immediately after such suspension or cancellation, stop fishing or undertaking any fishing related activity in respect of which the permit had been given, and shall not resume such fishing or fishing related activity, as the case may be, until such order has been revoked in writing. (3) The Central Government may also cancel a permit issued under this Act, having regard to matters relating to protection of national security of India, maintenance of law and order in the maritime zones of India or any other matter relating to public interest.	
Notification of transit.	6. Every foreign fishing vessel that transits through the Maritime Zones of India according to their entitlements to this effect under the applicable international law shall follow the procedure as prescribed.	
Regulation of scientific research and recreational fishing.	7. The Central Government may, through a special permit to be issued in writing, allow a vessel to carry out any scientific research, survey or investigation relating to fisheries or for any experimental or recreational fishing in accordance with such terms and conditions as may be prescribed.	
	CHAPTER III **POWERS TO BOARD, SEARCH AND SEIZURE**	
Powers of authorized officers.	8. (1) Any authorized officer may, to ensure compliance with this Act, either with or without a warrant may board, search and seize a fishing vessel in any maritime zone of India, and or in the high seas as may be prescribed for foreign vessels (2) In taking any action under sub-section (1), the Authorized Officer may use such force as may be reasonably necessary. (3) The seized vessel shall be provided with docking facility by the port notified for the purpose and charges towards docking, maintenance and other related costs of the seized vessel shall be made as prescribed. (4) Where any vessel or other things are seized under sub-section (1), the same, as soon as possible, be produced before a Magistrate competent to try an offence under this Act and the Magistrate shall make such order as prescribed. (5) Where, in pursuance of the commission of any offence under this Act, any vessel is	

	pursued beyond the limits of the exclusive economic zone of India, the powers conferred on an Authorized Officer by this section may be exercised beyond such limits in the circumstances and to the extent recognized by international law and applicable laws of India.	
	CHAPTER IV **OFFENCES AND PENALTIES**	
Penalty for fishing without a permit issued under section 3.	9. (1) Where any Indian fishing vessel is fishing in the exclusive economic zone of India and or the high seas without obtaining a permit granted under sub-section (1) of section 3, such vessel shall be impounded and the owner or master of such vessel shall be punishable with a fine as prescribed.	
	(2) Where any foreign fishing vessel is fishing in the Maritime Zones of India, such vessel shall be impounded and the owner or master of such vessel shall be punishable with a fine as prescribed.	
Penalty for contravention of permit Granted under Section 3. **Composition of certain offences.**	(3) Where any Indian fishing vessel is used in contravention of the permit granted under the provisions of sub-section (1) of section 3, the owner and or master of such vessel shall be punishable with a fine as prescribed.	
	(4) Any person who fails to comply with an order made by the officer referred to in sub-section (1), in respect of compounding the offence, shall be punishable with imprisonment for a term which may extend to six months, or with fine as prescribed, or with both.	
Penalty for IUU fishing	(5) Any fishing vessel violates the provisions of sub-section (5) of section 3 shall be punishable with fine as prescribed.	
Penalty for foreign fishing vessels.	(6) Where any foreign fishing vessel contravenes the provisions of section 6, the owner and or master of such vessel shall be punishable with [imprisonment for a term not exceeding three years] and/or with fine as prescribed.	
Penalty for contravention of section 7.	(7) Whoever contravenes the provisions of section 7, shall be punishable for imprisonment not exceeding five years and/or with fine as prescribed.	
Penalty for obstruction of authorized officers.	(8) If any person intentionally obstructs any authorised officer in the exercise of any powers conferred under this Act or in the discharge of the duties of the authorised officer, he/she shall be punishable with imprisonment for a term which may extend to one year or with fine as prescribed or with both.	
Offence by companies.	(9) Where an offence under this Act has been committed by a company, every person who, at the time the offence was committed, was in charge of, and was responsible to, the company for the conduct of the business of the company, as well as the company, shall be deemed to be guilty of the offence and shall be liable to be proceeded against and punished as prescribed.	
	Provided that nothing contained in this sub-section shall render any such person liable to any such punishment provided in this Act if he proves that the offence was committed without his knowledge or that he had exercised all due diligence to prevent the occurrence of such offence.	
	(10) Notwithstanding anything contained in sub-section (1), where an offence under this Act has been committed by a company and it is proved that the offence has been committed with the consent or connivance of, or is attributable to any neglect on the part of any director, manager, secretary or other officer, such person shall also be deemed to be guilty of that offence and shall be liable to be proceeded against and punished as prescribed.	

	CHAPTER V	
	MISCELLANEOUS	
General Power to create agencies to discharge functions	10. The Central Government may by notification in the Official Gazette, designate one or more Central Government or State Government agencies or officials or create a new government agency to discharge any one or more of its powers and functions under this Act.	✓
Offences to be cognizable.	11. Notwithstanding anything contained in the Code of Criminal Procedure, 1973, every offence punishable under this Act shall be cognizable.	
Cognizance and trial of offences.	12. (1) No Court shall take cognizance of any offence punishable under this Act except on a report in writing of the facts constituting such offence made by an authorised officer.	
	(2) No Court inferior to that of a Metropolitan Magistrate or a Judicial Magistrate of the first class shall try any offence under this Act.	
Magistrate's power to impose enhanced penalties.	13. Notwithstanding anything contained in section 29 of the Code of Criminal Procedure, 1973, it shall be lawful for any Metropolitan Magistrate or any Judicial Magistrate of the first class specially empowered by the State Government in this behalf to pass any sentence authorised by this Act.	
Appeals.	14. Any person aggrieved by the decision of the Central Government appointing any agency under this Act may prefer an appeal to the High Court which has jurisdiction over such matters.	
Protection of action taken in good faith.	15. (1) No suit, prosecution or other legal proceeding shall lie against authorized officer or any person for anything which is in good faith done or intended to be done in pursuance of the provisions of this Act.	of 1974
	(2) No suit or other legal proceeding shall lie against the Government for any damage caused or likely to be caused for anything which is in good faith done or intended to be done in pursuance of the provisions of this Act.	80 of 1976.
Co-operation between Central and State Governments.	16. (1) The Central Government shall ensure co-ordination with the Governments of the coastal States/Union Territories in relation to the effective implementation of this Act, especially in so far as such implementation has impact on the territorial waters of India.	42 of 1981.
	(2) The Governments of the coastal States/Union Territories shall extend full co-operation and assistance at all times to the Central Government to ensure effective implementation of this Act.	
Safety nets and good working conditions for fishers	17. The Central Government may ensure provision of safety nets for fishers and fish workers, including protection of their life at sea, during weathers of severe intensities and other forms of natural calamities.	
	18. The Central Government may make provisions for securing sustainable small-scale fisheries in the context of food security and poverty eradication.	
	19. The Central Government in coordination with the coastal States/Union Territories shall ensure good conditions onboard fishing vessels.	
Power to make rules.	20. (1) The Central Government may, by notification in the Official Gazette, make rules to carry out the provisions of this Act.	
	(2) In particular, and without prejudice to the generality of the foregoing powers, such rules may provide for all or any of the following matters, namely:	
	(a) the manner, form, payment of fees for permit, and conditions and restrictions for fishing and fishing activity under sub-section (1) of section 3;	

International co-operation & compliance Presumptions.	(b) provisions to prevent, deter and eliminate all forms of IUU fishing in the maritime zones of India, the high seas and the waters under national jurisdiction of other countries without authorization under sub-section (5) of section 3; (c) the conditions under which the permit may be exempted under sub-section (8) of section 3; (d) the details of one or more plans for management of one or more fishing activities in relation to any such area of the maritime zones of India under sub-section (1) of section 4; (e) formulation of fisheries management plan(s) following the Code of Conduct for Responsible Fisheries and Ecosystem Approach to Fisheries Management under sub-section (3) of section 4; (f) form and manner for implementation of measures to protect endangered, threatened and protected species as per sub-section (4) of section 4; (g) formulation of plan(s) to prevent, control and mitigate any form of pollution, whether originating from the land or at sea as per sub-section (5) of section 4; (h) the manner and form for implementation or compliance of any international or regional conventions/obligations/agreements for fisheries, fishing and fishing related activities as per sub-section (6) of section 4; (i)any other matter which is to be or may be prescribed by the Central Government to be relevant for achieving any of the objectives of regulation and management of marine fisheries under this Act as per sub-section (7) of section 4; (j) declaration of 'no fishing zone(s)' by the Central Government as per sub-section (1) (b) of section 5; (k) the manner of keeping fishing gear, other paraphernalia and matters relating to movement of the vessels through the maritime zone of India as per section 6; (l) the forms and conditions for which special permit may be issued to vessel to carry out scientific research, survey or investigation, experimental fishing, or for recreational fishing as per section 7; (m) the form and manner in which the Central Government may notify the authorized officer(s) under sub-section (1), (2) and (3) of section 8; (n) the form and manner in which the matter will be produced before a Magistrate competent to try an offence under this Act as per sub-section (4) of section 8; (o) describe the offence and penalty for each category of fishing vessels as per sub-section (1) of section 9; (p) describe the offences and their corresponding penalties for each category of fishing vessels as per sub-section (2) of section 9; (q) the payment of sum for compounding of offence under sub-section (3) of section 9; (r) describe offences and corresponding penalties for foreign fishing vessel including owner and or master of such vessel as per sub-section (4) of section 9; (s) describe the quantum of fine and penalties for Indian and foreign vessels as per sub-section (5) of section 9; (t) describe the quantum of fine for Indian and foreign vessels in cases of obstructions to authorised officer as per sub-section (6) of section 9; (u) describe the offences and penalties for violations committed by companies as per	

	sub-sections (7) and (8) of section 9;
	(v) provisions to provide safety nets for fishers and fish workers, including protection of their life at sea during weathers of severe intensities and other forms of natural calamities as per section 17.
	(w) provisions for securing sustainable small-scale fisheries in the context of food security and poverty eradicationas per section 18.
	(x) measures to ensure good conditions onboard fishing vessels as per section 19.
	(y) any other matter which is to be or may be prescribed by, or provided for by Rules under, this Act, and any matter, which in its opinion is expedient for proper control over fishing and any fishing activity and for ensuring law and order.
	(3)　Every rule made under this section shall be laid, as soon as may be after it is made, before each House of Parliament, while it is in session, for a total period of thirty days which may be comprised in one session or in two or more successive sessions, and if, before the expiry of the session immediately following the session or the successive session aforesaid, both Houses agree in making any modification in the rule or both Houses agree that the rule should not be made, the rule shall thereafter have effect only in such modified form or be of no effect, as the case may be; so, however, that any such modification or annulment shall be without prejudice to the
Proviso to sub-section (5) of section 7 of Act No. 80 of 1976 not to apply.	validity of anything previously done under that rule.
	21. The proviso to sub-section (5) of section 7 of the Territorial Waters, Continental Shelf, Exclusive Economic Zone and Other Maritime Zones Act, 1976 shall not apply to requirements for a permit and other requirements specified under this Act.
Removal of difficulties.	22. (1)　If any difficulty arises in giving effect to the provisions of this Act, the Central Government may, by order published in the Official Gazette, make such provisions not inconsistent with the provisions of this Act as may appear to it to be necessary for removing the difficulty.
	Provided that no such order shall be made after expiry of a period of three years from the commencement of this Act.
Repeal and savings.	(2)　Provided that no such order shall be made after the expiry of a period of three years from the date of commencement of this Act.
	23. (1) The Maritime Zones of India (Regulation of Fishing by Foreign Vessels) Act, 1981, is hereby repealed.
	(2) Notwithstanding such repeal, anything done or any action taken under the Act so repealed (including any notification, order, appointment, certificate, notice, or receipt issued, application made, or permit granted) which is not inconsistent with the provisions of this Act shall be deemed to have been done or taken under the corresponding provisions of this Act.

附录7 《1978 年泰王国政府与印度共和国政府间
关于划定两国在安达曼海海床边界的协定》[1]

Agreement between the Government of the Kingdom of Thailand and
the Government of the Republic of India on the Delimitation of Seabed
Boundary between the two Countries in the Andaman Sea, 22 June 1978

THE GOVERNMENT OF THE KINGDOM OF THAILAND AND THE GOVERN-
MENT OF THE REPUBLIC OFINDIA,

DESIRING to strengthen the existing bonds of friendship between the two countries,
and DESIRING to establish seabed boundary between the two countries in the Andaman
Sea, and to settle permanently the limits of the areas within which the respective Governments shall exercise sovereign rights,

HAVE AGREED as follows:

Article 1

1. The seabed boundary between Thailand and India in the Andaman Sea comprises the
straight lines connecting Points 1 and 2, 2 and 3, 3 and 4, 4 and 5, 5 and 6 and 6
and 7.

2. The co-ordinates of these points are specified below:

	Latitude	Longitude
Point 1	07°48′00″N,	95°32′48″E
Point 2	07°57′30″N,	95°41′48″E
Point 3	08°09′54″N,	95°39′16″E
Point 4	08°13′47″N,	95°39′11″E
Point 5	08°45′11″N,	95°37′42″E
Point 6	08°48′04″N,	95°37′40″E
Point 7	09°17′18″N,	95°36′31″E

3. The extension of the boundary in either direction up to the trijunction points between
Thailand, India and Indonesia on the one hand and Thailand, India and Burma on the oth-

---

[1] See "Agreement between the Government of the Kingdom of Thailand and the Government of the Re-
public of India on the Delimitation of Seabed Boundary between the two Countries in the Andaman
Sea, 22 June 1978", UN Office of Legal Affairs, https://www.un.org/Depts/los/LEGISLATIO-
NANDTREATIES/PDFFILES/TREATIES/THA - IND1978SB. PDF, March 20, 2021.

er will be done subsequently.

Article 2

1. The co-ordinates of the points specified in Article 1 are geographical co-ordinates and the straight lines joining them are indicated on the chart attached as Annexure "A" to this Agreement.

2. The actual location of these points at sea and of the lines joining them shall be determined by a method to be mutually agreed upon by the competent authorities of the two Governments.

3. For the purpose of paragraph 2 of this Article, the term "competent authorities" in relation to the Kingdom of Thailand shall mean Chaokrom Uthokkasat (Director of Hydrographic Department) and include any person authorised by him, and in relation to the Republic of India shall mean the Chief Hydrographer to the Government of India and include any person authorised by him.

Article 3

The Government of the Kingdom of Thailand and the Government of the Republic of India recognise and acknowledge the sovereign rights of the respective Governments over the seabed, including the subsoil thereof, within the limits established by this Agreement.

Article 4

If any single geological petroleum or natural gas structure or field, or other mineral deposit of whatever character, extends across the boundary referred to in Article 1, the two Governments shall communicate to each other all information in this regard and shall seek to reach agreement as to the manner in which the structure, field or deposit will be most effectively exploited and the benefits arising from such exploitation equitably shared.

Article 5

Any dispute between the two Governments relating to the interpretation or implementation of this Agreement shall be settled peacefully by consultation or negotiation.

Article 6

This Agreement shall be ratified in accordance with the constitutional requirements of each country. It shall enter into force on the date of exchange of the Instruments of Ratification which will take place at Bangkok as soon as possible.

IN WITNESS THEREOF the undersigned, being duly authorised thereto by their respective Governments, have signed this Agreement.

DONE in duplicate at New Delhi, on the Twenty-Second day of June, One Thousand Nine hundred and Seventy-eight, in the Thai, Hindi and English languages. In the event of any conflict between the texts, the English text shall prevail.

附录8 《1974年印度共和国政府与印度尼西亚共和国政府关于两国间大陆架划界的协定》[1]

Agreement between the Government of the Republic of India and the
Government of the Republic of Indonesia relating to the Delimitation of the
Continental Shelf Boundary between the two Countries 8 August 1974

THE GOVERNMENT OF THE REPUBLIC OF INDIA AND

THE GOVERNMENT OF THE REPUBLIC OF INDONESIA

DESIRING to strengthen the existing historical bonds of friendship between the two countries,

AND DESIRING to establish the continental shelf boundary between the two countries,

HAVE AGREED AS FOLLOWS:

Article 1

(1) The boundary of the Indian and the Indonesian continental shelf in the area between Great Nicobar (India) and Sumatra (Indonesia) is the straight lines connecting Points 1 and 2, 2 and 3, and 3 and 4. The coordinates of these Points are specified below:

Point 1: 06°38'.5 N, 94°38'.0 E

Point 2: 06°30'.0 N, 94°32'.4 E

Point 3: 06°16'.2 N, 94°24'.2 E

Point 4: 06°00'.0 N, 94°10'.3 E

(2) The coordinates of the Points specified in clause (1) are geographical coordinates and the straight lines connecting them are indicated on the chart attached as Annexure "A" to this Agreement.

(3) The actual location of the above – mentioned Points at sea shall be determined by a method to be mutually agreed upon by the competent authorities of the two Governments.

(4) For the purpose of clause (3), "competent authorities" in relation to the Republic of India means the Chief Hydrographer to the Government of India and includes any person authorised by him, and in relation to the Republic of Indonesia means the Direktur

---

[1] See "Agreement between the Government of the Republic of India and the Government of the Republic of Indonesia relating to the Delimitation of the Continental Shelf Boundary between the two Countries 8 August 1974", UN Office of Legal Affairs, https://www.un.org/Depts/los/LEGISLATIONANDTREATIES/PDFFILES/TREATIES/IND – IDN1974CS. PDF, March 20, 2021.

Badan Koordinasi Survey dan Pametaan National (Director of Coordinating Body for National Survey and Mapping) and includes any person authorised by him.

Article 2

Each Government hereby undertakes to ensure that all the necessary steps shall be taken at the domestic level to comply with the terms of this Agreement.

Article 3

If any single geological petroleum or natural gas structure or field, or other mineral deposit of whatever character, extends across the boundary line referred to in Article I, the two Governments shall communicate to each other all information in this regard and shall seek to reach agreement as to the manner in which the structure, field or deposit will be most effectively exploited and the benefits arising from such exploitation will be equitably shared.

Article 4

Any dispute between the two Governments relating to the interpretation or implementation of this Agreement shall be settled peacefully by consultation or negotiation.

Article 5

This Agreement shall be ratified in accordance with the constitutional requirements of each country. It shall enter into force on the date of the exchange of the Instruments of Ratification which will take place at Delhi as soon as possible.

IN WITNESS WHEREOF the undersigned, being duly authorised thereto by the irrespective Governments, have signed this Agreement.

DONE IN DUPLICATE at Jakarta on the eighth day of August 1974, in the Hindi, Indonesian and English languages. In the event of any conflict between the texts, the English text shall prevail.

附录9　《1977 年印度共和国政府与印度尼西亚共和国政府关于延伸两国 1974 年在安达曼海与印度洋的大陆架边界的协定》[1]

Agreement between the Government of the Republic of India and the
Government of the Republic of Indonesia on the Extension of the 1974
Continental Shelf Boundary between the two Countries in the
Andaman Sea and the Indian Ocean14 January 1977

THE GOVERNMENT OF THE REPUBLIC OF INDIA AND THE GOVERNMENT OF THE REPUBLIC OFINDONESIA,

RECALLING the Agreement between the Republic of India and the Republic of Indonesia relating to the Delimitation of the Continental Shelf Boundary between the two countries signed on 8th August, 1974 which, upon the exchange of instruments of ratification in New Delhi on 17th December, 1974 entered into force with effect from that date,

DESIRING to extend this boundary between the two countries in the Andaman Sea and the Indian Ocean in areas not covered by the aforementioned Agreement,

AND RESOLVING, as good neighbours and in a spirit of cooperation and friendship, to settle permanently the limits of the areas referred to in the preceding paragraph within which the respective Governments shall exercise sovereign rights,

HAVE AGREED as follows:

Article 1

In the area of the Andaman Sea:

The boundary of the seabed between India and Indonesia in the Andaman Sea is the straight lines connecting points land K, points K and N, and points N and O.

The co-ordinates of these points are specified below:

Point 1: 06°38′. 5 N, 94°38′. 0 E

Point K: 07°02′24″N, 94°55′37″E

---

[1] See "Agreement between the Government of the Republic of India and the Government of the Republic of Indonesia on the Extension of the 1974 Continental Shelf Boundary between the Two Countries in the Andaman Sea and the Indian Ocean 14 January 1977", UN Office of Legal Affairs, https://www. un. org/Depts/los/LEGISLATIONANDTREATIES/PDFFILES/TREATIES/IND – IDN1977CS. PDF, March 20, 2021.

Point N: 07°40′06″N, 95°25′45″E

Point O: 07°46′06″N, 95°31′12″E

Article 2

In the area of the Indian Ocean:

The boundary of the seabed between India and Indonesia in the Indian Ocean is the straight lines connecting points 4 and R, points R and S, points S and T and points T and U.

The co-ordinates of these points are specified below:

Point 4: 06°00′. 0 N, 94°10′. 3 E

Point R: 05°25′20″N, 93°41′12″E

Point S: 04°27′34″N, 92°51′17″E

Point T: 04°18′31″N, 92°43′31″E

Point U: 04°01′40″N, 92°23′55″E

Article 3

1. The co-ordinates of the points specified in Articles 1 and 2 are geographical co-ordinates and the straight lines joining them are indicated on the chart attached as Annexure "B" to this Agreement.

2. The actual location of these points at sea and of the lines joining them shall be determined by a method to be mutually agreed upon by the competent authorities of the two Governments.

3. For the purpose of paragraph 2 of this Article, the "competent authorities" in relation to the Republic of India shall be the Chief Hydrographer to the Government of India and includes any person authorised by him, and in relation to the Republic of Indonesia shall be the Ketua Badan Koordinasi Survey dan Pemetaan Nasional (Chief of the Co-ordinating Body for National Survey and Mapping) and includes any person authorised by him.

Article 4

The Government of the Republic of India and the Government of the Republic of Indonesia recognize and acknowledge the sovereign rights of the respective Governments in and over the seabed areas, including the subsoil thereof, within the limits established by this Agreement.

Article 5

If any single geological petroleum or natural gas structure or field, or other mineral deposit of whatever character, extends across the boundary line referred to in Articles 1 and 2, the two Governments shall communicate to each other all information in this regard and shall seek to reach agreement as to the manner in which the structure, field or deposit will be most effectively exploited and the benefits arising from such exploitation will be equitably shared.

Article 6

Any dispute between the two Governments relating to the interpretation or implementation of this Agreement shall be settled peacefully by consultation or negotiation.

Article 7

This Agreement shall be ratified in accordance with the constitutional requirements of each country. It shall enter into force on the date of the exchange of the Instruments of Ratification which will take place at Jakarta as soon as possible.

IN WITNESS WHEREOF the undersigned, being duly authorized by their respective Governments, have signed this Agreement.

DONE IN DUPLICATE at New Delhi on the 14th January, 1977, in the Hindi, Indonesian and English languages. In the event of any conflict between the texts, the English text shall prevail.

附录 10　《1986 年缅甸联邦社会主义共和国与印度共和国间关于在安达曼海、科科海峡与孟加拉湾划定海上边界的协定》[1]

Agreement between the Socialist Republic of the Union of Burma and
the Republic of India on the Delimitation of the Maritime
Boundary in the Andaman Sea, in the Coco Channel and
in the Bay of Bengal, 23 December 1986

THE SOCIALIST REPUBLIC OF THE UNION OF BURMA AND THE REPUBLIC OF INDIA,

DESIRING TO strengthen the existing historical bonds of friendship between the two countries,

DESIRING to delimit by mutual agreement the maritime boundary between the two countries in the Andaman Sea, in the Coco Channel and in the Bay of Bengal,

HAVE AGREED as follows:

Article 1

The maritime boundary between Burma and India in the Andaman Sea and in the Coco Channel is the straight lines connecting points 1 to 14, the geographical co-ordinates of which are in the sequence given below:

Points	Latitude North	Longitude East
1	09°38′00″	95°35′25″
2	09°53′14″	95°28′00″
3	10°18′42″	95°16′02″
4	10°28′00″	95°15′58″
5	10°44′53″	95°22′00″
6	11°43′17″	95°26′00″
7	12°19′43″	95°30′00″
8	12°54′07″	95°41′00″

---

[1]　See "Agreement between the Socialist Republic of the Union of Burma and the Republic of India on the Delimitation of the Maritime Boundary in the Andaman Sea, in the Coco Channel and in the Bay of Bengal, 23 December 1986", UN Office of Legal Affairs, https://www. un. org/Depts/los/ LEGISLATIONANDTREATIES/PDFFILES/TREATIES/MMR – IND1986MB, March 20, 2021.

9	13°48′00″	95°02′00″
10	13°48′00″	93°50′00″
11	13°34′18″	93°40′59″
12	13°49′11″	93°08′05″
13	13°57′29″	92°54′50″
14	14°00′59″	92°50′02″

The extension of the maritime boundary beyond point 1 up to the maritime boundary trijunction point between Burma, India and Thailand will be done subsequently after the trijunction point is established by agreement between the three countries.

Article 2

The Maritime Boundary between Burma and India in the Bay of Bengal is the straight lines connecting points 14 to 16, the geographical co-ordinates of which are in the sequence given below:

Points	Latitude North	Longitude East
14	14°00′59″	92°50′02″
15	14°17′42″	92°24′17″
16	15°42′50″	90°14′01″

The extension of the maritime boundary beyond point 16 in the Bay of Bengal will be done subsequently.

Article 3

The co-ordinates of the points specified in articles I and II are the geographical co-ordinates and the straight lines connecting them are as indicated in Indian Chart No. 41 of 1 December 1979 (Andaman Sea) and Indian Chart No. 31 of 1 November 1976 (Bay of Bengal) annexed hereto, which form an integral part of this Agreement and which have been signed by the competent authorities of the two Parties.

Article 4

The actual location at sea and on the sea-bed and on the continental shelf of the points specified in articles I and II shall be determined by a method to be mutually agreed upon by the Hydrographic Surveyors authorized for the purpose by the two Parties.

Article 5

Each Party has sovereignty over the existing islands and any islands that may emerge, falling on its side of the maritime boundary.

Article 6

Each Party has sovereignty, sovereign rights and jurisdictions in its respective maritime zones, falling on its side of the maritime boundary, in accordance with the relevant provisions of the United Nations Convention on the Law of the Sea, 1982.

Article 7

Any dispute concerning the interpretation or implementation of this Agreement shall be settled peacefully by consultation or negotiation between the two Parties.

Article 8

This Agreement shall be ratified in accordance with the constitutional requirements of each Party. It shall enter into force on the date of the exchange of the instruments of ratification, which will take place at New Delhi as soon as possible.

IN WITNESS WHEREOF the undersigned, being duly authorized thereto by their respective Governments, have signed this Agreement.

DONE at Rangoon, this twenty-third day of December, one thousand nine hundred and eighty-six, in duplicate, each being drawn up in three authentic texts in the Burmese, Hindi and English languages. In the event of any conflict between the texts the English text shall prevail.

附录 11　2001 年印度致联合国秘书长照会[1]

With reference to the deposit by Pakistan of the list of geographical coordinates of points for the drawing of the straight baselines, established by Notification of 29 August 1996, with an illustrative map (see M. Z. N. 27. 1999. LOS of 4 June 1999), it needs to be noted that the Secretary-General received, on 22 May 2001, the following statement by India:

The Permanent Mission of India to the United Nations . . . , in continuation of its note No. NY/PM/444/3/97 dated 24 February 1997 on Pakistan's notification specifying baselines, has the honour to state the following:

1. The Government of India is of the view that certain baseline points notified by the Government of the Islamic Republic of Pakistan are inconsistent with international law and the relevant provisions of the United Nations Convention on the Law of the Sea (UNCLOS), 1982. The Government of India reserves its rights and rights of its nationals in that regard.

2. The Government of India wishes to recall that, according to article 5 of UNCLOS, except where otherwise provided in the Convention, the normal baseline for measuring the breadth of the territorial sea is the low-water line along the coast as marked on large-scale charts officially recognized by the coastal States. Only in localities where the coastline is deeply indented and cut into, or if there is a fringe of islands along the coast in its immediate vicinity, may the coastal State elect to use the method of straight baselines joining appropriate points in drawing the baseline from which the breadth of the territorial sea is measured.

3. The Government of India notes that, not withstanding the fact that the Pakistani coastline is quite smooth, is rarely deeply indented or fringed by islands, Pakistan has employed straight baselines along its entire coastline. The appropriate baseline for all of Pakistan's coast should be the normal baseline. i. e. , the low-water line.

4. Further, under UNCLOS, rocks which cannot sustain human habitation or economic life of their own cannot have a territorial sea, exclusive economic zone or continental shelf. Sail Rock, which forms basepoint (d) 25°06. 30′N, 63°51. 01′E of Pakistan's notification, cannot thus be a part of any baseline system as contemplated under UNCLOS.

---

[1]　See Division for Ocean Affairs and The Law of The Sea Office of Legal Affairs, "Statement by India", *The Law of the Sea Bulletins*, 46, United Nations, 2001, p. 90.

5. The Government of India also wishes to note that the basepoint (a) 25°02. 20'N, 61°35. 50'E is violative of international law. As per international law, the basepoint (a) should have been the terminal point of land boundary inside the Gwatar Bay.

6. In view of the above, the Government of India does not recognize the arbitrary method of drawing straight baselines. Any claim Pakistan makes on the basis of this notification to extend its sovereignty/jurisdiction on Indian waters or extend its internal waters, territorial sea, exclusive economic zone and continental shelf is rejected by India as the same does not have any sanction under international law.

附录 12　2017 年印度致联合国秘书长照会[1]

संयुक्त राष्ट्र स्थित भारत का स्थायी मिशन
न्यूयॉर्क
PERMANENT MISSION OF INDIA TO THE UNITED NATIONS
NEW YORK

PM/ NY/443/1/2017   3 August 2017

　　The Permanent Mission of India to the United Nations has the honour to refer to the Secretary General's communication dated 7 April 2016 regarding the deposit by Bangladesh, pursuant to Article 16(2) of the 1982 United Nations Convention on the Law of the Sea, of a list of geographical coordinates of points concerning the Straight Baselines for measuring the breadth of the territorial sea of Bangladesh, as contained in notification S.R.O. No.328-Law/2015/MOFA/UNCLOS/113/2/15, dated 4 November 2015.

　　The Government of the Republic of India has noted that the Base points used by Bangladesh for drawing the straight baselines are at variance with the Base points used in the Award dated 7 July 2014 by the Arbitral Tribunal in the Matter of Bay of Bengal Maritime Boundary Arbitration between the People's Republic of Bangladesh and the Republic of India.

　　The Government of the Republic of India is of the view that the Exclusive Economic Zone of Bangladesh measured from baselines using Base point 2 (21^0 36' 39.2"N; $89^0$22'14.0"E) and Base point 5 (Southern end of St Martin's Island – Coordinates not defined) results in seaward shift of Bangladesh's Exclusive Economic Zone and consequently encroaches into the Indian Exclusive Economic Zone in the Grey Area recognised by the Tribunal. Within this Grey Area, India's sovereign rights prevail in the Exclusive Economic Zone.

　　The Government of the Republic of India, therefore, objects to the use of the new Base points 2 and 5 by Bangladesh for determining its straight baselines and the resultant seaward shift of Bangladesh's Exclusive Economic Zone that encroaches into India's Exclusive Economic Zone in the Grey Area and thereby alters and violates the Award.

---

[1]　See "Communication from the Permanent Mission of India Dated 3 August 2017 with Respect to the Deposit by Bangladesh (M. Z. N. 118. 2016. LOS of 7 April 2016) of a List of Geographical Coordinates", UN Office of Legal Affairs, https: //www. un. org/Depts/los/LEGISLATIONANDTREATIES/ PDFFILES/2017_ 08_ 03_ IND_ UN. pdf. , March 20, 2021.

The Government of the Republic of India wishes to recall that under Article 11 of Annex VII of the 1982 United Nations Convention on the Law of the Sea, the Award is final and to be complied with by both Parties.

The Government of the Republic of India therefore reiterates/reasserts all its rights and those of its nationals in the waters in question.

The Permanent Mission of India to the United Nations avails of this opportunity to renew to the Secretary General of the United Nations the assurances of its highest consideration.

The Secretary General of the United Nations
(Attn: Division for Ocean Affairs and
the Law of the Sea)
Room no. DC2-0450
Fax: (212) 963 5847

附录 13　印度缔结和加入的国际海洋法条约

（一）联合国海洋法公约及其相关条约

序号	条约名称	签署日期 （年/月/日）	批准日期 （年/月/日）
1	《联合国海洋法公约》 United Nations Convention on the Law of the Sea	1982/12/10	1995/6/29
2	《关于执行 1982 年 12 月 10 日〈联合国海洋法公约〉第十一部分的协定》 Agreement relating to The Implementation of Part XI of The United Nations Conventions on the Law of the Sea，10 December 1982	1994/11/16	1995/6/29
3	《执行 1982 年 12 月 10 日〈联合国海洋法公约〉有关养护和管理跨界鱼类种群和高度洄游鱼类种群的规定的协定》 Agreement for the Implementation of the Provisions of the United Nations Convention on the Law of the Sea of 10 December 1982 relating to the Conservation and Management of Straddling Fish Stocks and Highly Migratory Fish Stocks		2003/8/19
4	《国际海底管理局特权和豁免议定书》 Protocol on the Privileges and Immunities of the International Seabed Authority		2005/11/14
5	《国际海洋法法庭特权和豁免协定》 Agreement on the Privileges and Immunities of the International Tribunal for the Law of the Sea		2005/11/14

（二）缔结与加入的其他海洋海事条约

类别	条约名称	签署/批准/加入/ 接受日期 （年/月/日）	对印度生 效的日期
与海上航行安全相关的条约	《制止危及海上航行安全非法行为公约》 Convention for the Suppression of Unlawful Acts against the Safety of Maritime Navigation	1999/10/15	2000/1/13
	《制止危及大陆架固定平台安全非法行为议定书》 Protocol for the Suppression of Unlawful Acts against the Safety of Fixed Platforms Located on the Continental Shelf	1999/10/15	2000/1/13

类别	条约名称	签署/批准/加入/接受日期（年/月/日）	对印度生效的日期
与海上航行安全相关的条约	《1974 年国际海上人命安全公约》 International Convention for the Safety of Life at Sea, 1974	1976/6/16	1980/5/25
	《1974 年国际海上人命安全公约 1978 年议定书》 Protocol of 1978 relating to the International Convention for the Safety of Life at Sea, 1974, as Amended	1986/4/3	1980/7/3
	《1974 年国际海上人命安全公约 1988 年议定书》 Proctocol of 1988 Relating to the International Convention for the Safety of Life at Sea, 1974	2000/8/22	2000/11/22
	《1972 年国际海上避碰规则公约》 Convention on the International Regulations for Preventing Collisions at Sea, 1972	1973/5/30	1977/7/15
	《国际海事卫星组织公约》 Convention on the International Mobile Satellite Organization	1978/6/16	1979/7/16
	《国际海事卫星组织业务协定》 Operating Agreement on the International Mobile Satellite Organization	1976/9/3	1993/9/10 （1989 Amendments） 1999/5/14 （1994 Amendments） 2000/1/5 （1998 Amendments）
	《1989 年国际救助公约》 International Convention on Salvage, 1989	1995/10/18	1996/10/18
	《1979 年国际海上搜寻救助公约》 International Convention on Maritime Search and Rescue, 1979	2001/4/17	2001/5/17
	《1972 年国际集装箱安全公约》 International Convention for Safe Containers, 1972	1978/1/27	1979/1/27
	《2007 年内罗毕国际船舶残骸清除公约》 Nairobi International Convention of Removal of Wrecks, 2007	2011/3/23	2015/4/24
	《1971 年特种业务客船协定》 Special Trade Passenger Ships Agreement, 1971	1976/9/1	1976/12/1
	《1971 年特种业务客船协定 1973 年议定书》 Protocol on Space Requirements for Special Trade Passenger Ships, 1973	1976/12/1	1977/6/2

续表

类别	条约名称	签署/批准/加入/接受日期（年/月/日）	对印度生效的日期
与船舶及船员管理相关的条约	《1966 年国际船舶载重线公约》 International Convention on Load Lines, 1966	1968/4/19	1968/7/21
	《1965 年便利国际海上运输公约》 Convention on Facilitation of International Maritime Traffic, 1965	1976/5/25	1976/7/24
	《1969 年国际船舶吨位丈量公约》 International Convention on Tonnage Measurement of Ships, 1969	1977/5/26	1982/7/18
	《1978 年海员培训、发证和值班标准国际公约》 International Convention on Standards of Training, Certification and Watchkeeping for Seafarers, 1978	1984/11/16	1985/2/16
与防治海洋污染相关的条约	《1969 年国际油污损害民事责任公约》 International Convention on Civil Liability for Oil Pollution Damage, 1969	1987/5/1	1987/7/30 (2001/6/21 退出)
	《1990 年国际油污防备、反应与合作公约》 International Convention on Oil Pollution Preparedness, Response and Co-operation, 1990	1997/11/17	1998/12/17
	《1973 年国际防止船舶造成污染公约的 1978 年议定书》附则一及附则二 International Convention for the Prevention of Pollution from Ships, 1973 as modified by the Protocol of 1978 relating thereto, Annex I, II	1986/9/24	1986/12/24
	《经 1978 年议定书修订的〈1973 年国际防止船舶造成污染公约〉》1997 年议定书 Protocol of 1997 to amend the International Convention for the Prevention of Pollution from Ships, 1973, as modified by the Protocol of 1978 relating thereto	2011/11/23	2012/2/23
	《1969 年国际干预公海油污事故公约》 International Convention relating to Intervention on the High Seas in Cases of Oil Pollution Casualties, 1969	2000/6/16	2000/9/14
	《控制船舶有害防污底系统国际公约》 International Convention on the Control of Harmful Anti-Fouling Systems On Ships	2015/4/24	2015/7/24

类别	条约名称	签署/批准/加入/接受日期（年/月/日）	对印度生效的日期
与防治海洋污染相关的条约	《修正〈1971年设立国际油污损害赔偿基金国际公约〉的1992年议定书》 Protocol of 1992 to Amend the International Convention on the Establishment of an International Fund for Compensation for Oil Pollution Damage, 1971	2000/6/21	2001/6/21
	《1976年海事索赔责任限制公约》 Convention on Limitation of Liability for Maritime Claims, 1976	2002/8/20	2002/12/1
	《修订1976年海事索赔责任限制公约的1996年议定书》 Protocol of 1996 to Amend the Convention on Limitation of Liability for Maritime Claims, 1976	2011/3/23	2011/6/21
与渔业资源相关的条约	《鲸鱼管制国际公约》 International Convention for the Regulation of Whaling	1981/3/9	1981/3/9
	《保护南极海洋生物资源公约》 Convention for the Conservation of Antarctic Marine Living Resources	1985/6/17	1985/7/17
	《建立印度洋金枪鱼委员会协定》 The Agreement for the Establishment of the Indian Ocean Tuna Commission	1995/3/13	1996/3/17
	《建立亚洲及太平洋水产养殖中心网络的协定》 Agreement for the Establishment of the Network of Aquaculture Centres in Asia and the Pacific	1992/6/4	1992/6/4
	《建立亚太地区渔业产品市场信息及科技咨询服务政府间组织的协定》 Agreement for the Establishment of the Intergovernmental Organization for Marketing Information and Technical Advisory Services for Fishery Products in the Asia and Pacific Region	1986/9/19	1987/3/3 （2019/5/14 退出）

附录 14　巴基斯坦《1976 年领水及海域法》[1]

The Territorial Waters and Maritime Zones Act, 1976
31st December, 1976

An Act to provide for the declaration of the territorial waters and maritime zones of Pakistan.

WHEREAS it is expedient to provide for the declaration of the territorial waters and maritime zones of Pakistan and for matters connected therewith;

It is hereby enacted as follows:

1. Short title and commencement.

(1) This Act may be called the Territorial Waters and Maritime Zones Act, 1976.

(2) It shall come into force at once.

2. Territorial waters.

(1) The sovereignty of Pakistan extends and has always extended to the territorial waters of Pakistan, hereinafter referred to as the territorial waters, as well as to the airspace over, and the bed and sub soil of, such waters.

(2) The limit of the territorial waters is twelve nautical miles beyond the land territory and internal waters of Pakistan measured from the baseline.

(3) The baseline from which such limit shall be measured and the waters on the landward side of which shall form part of the internal waters of Pakistan shall be specified by the Federal Government by notification in the official Gazette.

(4) Where a single island, rock or a composite group thereof constituting a part of the territory of Pakistan is situated off the main coast, the baseline referred to in sub-section (3) shall be drawn along the outer seaward limits of such island, rock of composite group.

3. Use of territorial waters by foreign ships.

(1) Without prejudice to the provisions of any other law for the time being in force and subject to the provisions of sub-section (2) and sub-section (3), all foreign ships shall enjoy the right of innocent passage through the territorial waters.

Explanation: For the purposes of this section, passage is innocent so long as it is not prejudicial to the peace, good order or security of Pakistan.

---

[1] See "The Territorial Waters and Maritime Zones Act, 1976", The Pakistan Code, http://pakistancode.gov.pk/english/UY2FqaJw1-apaUY2Fqa-bpuUZGFs-sg-jjjjjjjjjjjj, March 20, 2021.

(2) Foreign warships, including submarines and other under water vehicles and Foreign Military Aircraft may enter or pass through the territorial waters and the air space over such waters with the prior permission of the Federal Government:

Provided that submarines and other under water vehicles shall navigate on the surface and show their flag while passing through such waters.

(3) Foreign super ankers, nuclear powered ships and ships carrying nuclear or other inherently dangerous or noxious substances or materials may enter or pass through the territorial waters after giving prior notice to the Federal Government.

(4) The Federal Government may, if satisfied that it is necessary so to do in the interest of the peace, good order or security of Pakistan or any part thereof, suspend, by notification in the official Gazette, subject to such exceptions and qualifications, if any, as may be specified in the notification, the entry of all or any class of foreign ships into such area of the territorial waters as may be specified in the notification.

4. Contiguous Zone.

(1) The Contiguous Zone of Pakistan, hereinafter referred to as the Contiguous Zone, is an area adjacent to and beyond the territorial waters and extending seawards to aline twenty-four nautical miles measured from the baseline declared under sub-section (3) of section2.

(2) The Federal Government may exercise such powers and take such measures in or in respect of the Contiguous Zone as it may consider necessary to prevent and punish the contravention of, and an attempt to contravene, any law in force in Pakistan relating to—

(a) the security of Pakistan;

(b) immigration and sanitation; and

(c) customs and other fiscal matters.

(3) The Federal Government may, by notification in the official Gazette, —

(a) extend to the Contiguous Zone any law relating to any matter referred to in clause (a) or clause (b) or clause (c) of sub-section (2), for the time being in force in Pakistan or any part thereof, with such modifications, if any, as may be specified in the notification; and

(b) make such provisions as it may consider necessary for facilitating the enforcement of such law and any law so extended shall have effect as if the Contiguous Zone formed part of the territory of Pakistan.

5. Continental Shelf.

(1) The Continental Shelf of Pakistan, hereinafter referred to as the Continental Shelf, shall comprise the seabed and sub-soil of the submarine areas that extend beyond the limit of the territorial waters of Pakistan throughout the natural prolongation of the land terri-

tory of Pakistan to the outer edge of the continental margin or, where the outer edge of the continental margin does not extend up to a distance of two hundred nautical miles from the baseline declared under sub-section (3) of section 2, up to that distance.

(2) Pakistan has, and always had, full and exclusive sovereign rights in respect of its Continental Shelf including

[(a) exclusive sovereign rights for the purpose of exploring and exploiting minerals and other non-living resources of the bed and sub-soil together with living organisms belonging to the sedentary species;] [Subs. by the T erritorial Waters and Maritime Zones Act, 1977 (5 of 1977), s. 2, for cl. (a) .]

(b) exclusive rights and jurisdiction to authorize, regulate and control scientific research;

(c) exclusive rights and jurisdiction for the construction, maintenance or operation of artificial islands, off-shore terminals installations and other structures and devices necessary for the exploration and exploitation of the resources of the Continental Shelf, for the convenience of shipping or for any other purpose; and

(d) exclusive jurisdiction to preserve and protect the marine environment and to prevent and control marine pollution.

[Explanation: For the purpose of this sub-section, the expression "living organisms" shall mean those organisms which, at the harv estable stage, are either immobile under the sea-bed or are unable to move except in constant physical contact with the sea-bed or the sub-soil.]

(3) No person, including a foreign Government shall, except under, and in accordance with the terms of, any agreement with the Federal Government of a licence or letter of authority granted by the Federal Government, explore the Continental Shelf or exploit its resources or carry out any search or excavation or conduct any research within the Continental Shelf or drill therein or construct, maintain or operate therein for any purpose whatsoever any artificial islands, off shore terminal, installation or other structure or device.

(4) The Federal Government may, by notification in the official Gazette,

(a) declare any area of the Continental Shelf 1 [∗ ∗ ∗] to be a designated area; and

(b) make such provisions as it may deem necessary with respect to all or any of the following matters, namely —

(i) the exploration, development, exploitation and protection of the resources of the Continental Shelf within such designated area;

(ii) the safety and protection of artificial islands, off-shore terminals, installations and other structures and devices in such designated area;

(iii) the protection of marine environment of such designated area;

(iv) customs and other fiscal matters in relation to such designated area; and

(v) the regulation of entry into and passage through the designated area of foreign ship by the establishment of fairways, sealanes, traffic separation schemes or any other mode of ensuring freedom of navigation which is not prejudicial to the interests of Pakistan.

(5) The Federal Government may, by notification in the official Gazette,

(a) extend to the whole or any part of the Continental Shelf any law for the time being inforce in Pakistan or any part thereof, with such modifications, if any, as may be specified in the notification; and

(b) make such provisions as it may consider necessary for facilitating the enforcement of such law; and any law so extended shall have effect as if the Continental Shelf or, as the case may be, the part thereof to which it has been extended formed part of the territory of Pakistan.

(6) Subject to any measures that may be necessary for protecting the interests of Pakistan, and without prejudice to the provisions of sub-section (2), the Federal Government may not impede the laying or maintenance of submarine cables or pipelines on the seabed of the Continental Shelf by foreign States:

Provided that the consent of the Federal Government shall be necessary for the delineation of the course for the laying of such cables or pipelines.

6. Exclusive Economic Zone.

(1) The Exclusive Economic Zone of Pakistan, hereinafter referred to as the Exclusive Economic Zone, is an area beyond and adjacent to the territorial waters the limit of which is two hundred nautical miles from the baseline declared under sub-section (3) ofsection 2.

(2) In the Exclusive Economic Zone, its bed and subsoil and the superjacent waters, Pakistan has—

(a) exclusive sovereign rights for the purpose of exploration, development, exploitation, conservation and management of all resources, both living and non-living, as well as for producing energy from tides, winds, currents and the sun.

(b) exclusive rights and jurisdiction for the construction, maintenance or operation of artificial islands, offshore terminals, installations and other structures and devices necessary for the exploration and exploitation of the resources of the Zone or for the convenience ofshipping or for any other purpose;

(c) exclusive rights and jurisdiction to authorize, regulate and control scientific research;

(d) exclusive jurisdiction to preserve and protect the marine environment and to prevent and control marine pollution; and

(e) such other rights as are recognized by international law.

(3) No person, including a foreign Government, shall, except under, and in accordance with the terms of, any agreement, with the Federal Government or a licence or letter of authority granted by the Federal Government, explore or exploit any resources of the Exclusive Economic Zone or carry out any search or excavation or conduct any research within the Exclusive Economic Zone or drill therein or construct, maintain or operate, therein for any purpose whatsoever any artificial island off-shore terminal, intallation or other structure or device:

Provided that fishing in the Exclusive Economic Zone shall be regulated by the provisions of the Exclusive Fishery Zone (Regulation of Fishing) Act, 1975 (XXII of 1975) .

(4) The Federal Government may, by notification in the official Gazette, —

(a) declare any area of the Exclusive Economic Zone to be a designated area; and

(b) make such provisions as it may deem necessary with respect to all or any of the following matters, namely,

(i) the exploration, development, exploitation and protection of the resources of such designated area;

(ii) other activities for the economic exploitation and exploration of such designated area, such as the production of energy from tides, winds, currents and the sun;

(iii) the safety and protection of artificial islands, off-shore terminals, installations and other structures and devices in such designated area;

(iv) the protection of marine environment of such designated area;

(v) customs and other fiscal matters in relation to such designated area; and

(vi) the regulation of entry into and passage through the designated area of foreign ships by the establishment of fairways, sealanes, traffic separation schemes or any other-mode of ensuring freedom of navigation which is not prejudicial to the interest of Pakistan.

(5) The Federal Government may, by notification in the official Gazette, —

(a) extend to the whole or any part of the Exclusive Economic Zone any law for the time being in force in Pakistan or any part thereof subject to such modifications as may be-specified in the notification; and

(b) make such provisions as it may consider necessary for facilitating the enforcement of such law, and any law so extended shall have effect as if the Exclusive Economic Zone or, as the case may be, the part thereof to which it has been extended formed part of the territory of Pakistan.

(6) The provisions of sub-section (6) of section 5 shall apply in relation to the laying or maintenance of submarine cables or pipelines on the seabed of the Exclusive Econom-

ic Zone as they apply in relation to the laying or maintenance of submarine cables or pipelines on the seabed of the Continental Shelf.

(7) In the Exclusive Economic Zone and the air space over the Zone, ships and aircraft of all States shall, subject to the exercise by Pakistan of its rights within the Zone, enjoy freedom of navigation and over-flight.

7. Historic waters.

(1) The Federal Government may, by notification in the official Gazette, specify the limits of such waters adjacent to its land territory as are the historic waters of Pakistan.

(2) The sovereignty of Pakistan extends, and has always extended, to the historic maters of Pakistan and to the seabed and subsoil underlying, and the air space over, such waters.

8. Maritime boundaries between Pakistan and States having coasts opposite or adjacent to those of Pakistan.

(1) Notwithstanding anything contained in any other provision of this Act,

(a) the delimitation of the territorial waters between Pakistan and any other State whose coast is opposite or adjacent to that of Pakistan shall be determined by agreement between Pakistan and such state and pending such agreement and unless any other provisional arrangements are agreed to between them, the boundary with regard to the territorial waters between Pakistan and such State shall not extend beyond the line every point of which is equidistant from the baseline from which the breadth of the territorial waters of Pakistan and of such state is measured; and

(b) the delimitation of the Contiguous Zone, the Continental Shelf, the Exclusive Economic Zone and other maritime zones between Pakistan and any other state whose coast is opposite or adjacent to that of Pakistan shall be effected by agreement in accordance with equitable principles and taking account of all the relevant circumstances, and pending such agreement or a settlement Pakistan and such state shall make provisional arrangements taking into account the said principles for delimitation of the Contiguous Zone, the Continental Shelf, the Exclusive Economic Zone and other maritime zones.

(2) Every agreement referred to in clauses (a) and (b) of sub-section (1) shall, as soon as may be after it is entered into, be published in the official Gazette.

9. Publication of charts. The Federal Government may cause the baseline referred to in subsection (3) of section 2, the limits of the Territorial Waters, the Contiguous Zone, the Continental Shelf and the Exclusive Economic Zone and the maritime boundaries as settled by agreements referred to in section 8 to be published in charts.

10. Offences. Whoever contravenes any provision of this Act or of any rule or notification made or issued thereunder shall, without prejudice to any other action which may be taken against such person under any other provision of this or of any other law, be punishable with imprisonment for a term which may extend to three years, or with fine, or with both.

11. Offences by companies.

(1) Where an offence punishable under section 10 has been committed by a company, every person who, at the time the offence was committed, was in charge of, and was responsible to the company for, the conduct of the business of the company, as well as the company, shall be deemed to be guilty of the offence and shall be liable to be proceeded against and punished accordingly:

Provided that nothing contained in this subsection shall render any such person liable to any punishment provided in this Act if he proves that the offence was committed without his knowledge or that he exercised all due diligence to prevent the commission of such offence.

(2) Notwithstanding anything contained in sub-section (1), where an offence punishable under section 10 has been committed by a company and it is proved that the offence has been committed with the consent or connivance of, or is attributable to any neglect on the part of, any director, manager, secretary or other officer of the company, such director, manager, secretary or other officer shall also be deemed to be guilty of that offence and shall be liable to be proceeded against and punished accordingly.

Explanation: —For the purpose of this section, —

(a) "company" means anybody corporate and includes a firm or other association of individuals; and

(b) "director", in relation to a firm, means a partner in the firm.

12. Place of trial. Any person committing an offence punishable under section 10 or under any of the laws extended under this Act may be tried for the offence in such place or places as the Federal Government may, by general or special order published in the official Gazette, direct in this behalf.

13. Previous sanction of the Federal Government for Prosecution. No prosecution shall be instituted against any person in respect of any offence punishable under section 10 or under any of the laws extended under this Act without the previous sanction of the Federal Government or such officer or authority as may be authorised by that Government by order in writing in this behalf.

14. Power to make rules.

(1) The Federal Government may, by notification in the official Gazette, make rules for carrying out the purposes of this Act.

(2) In particular and without prejudice to the generality of the fore going power, such

rules may provide for all or any of the following matters, namely: —

(a) regulation of the conduct of any person in the Territorial Waters, the Contiguous Zone, the Continental Shelf, the Exclusive Economic Zone or any other maritime zone of Pakistan;

(b) regulation of the exploration, development, exploitation, conservation and management of the resources of the Continental Shelf;

(c) regulation of the exploration, development, exploitation, conservation and management of the resources of the Exclusive Economic Zone;

(d) regulation of the construction, maintenance and operation of artificial islands, off-shore terminals, installations and other structures and devices referred to in section 5 and section 6;

(e) preservation and protection of the marine environment and prevention and control of marine pollution;

(f) authorisation, regulation and control of the conduct of scientific research;

(g) fees in relation to licences and letters of authority referred to in subsection (3) of section 5and sub-section (3) of section 6 or for any other purpose; or

(h) any matter incidental to any of the matters specified in clauses (a) to (g) .

附录 15　巴基斯坦《1897 年渔业法》[1]

The Fisheries Act, 1897
4th February, 1897

WHEREAS it is expedient to provide for certain matters relating to fisheries in [Pakistan]; It is hereby enacted as follows:

1. Title and extent.

(1) This Act may be called the Fisheries Act, 1897.

[(2) It extends to the whole of Pakistan.]

2. Act to be read as supplemental to other Fisheries Laws. Subject to the provisions of sections [4 and 26 of the General Clauses Act, 1897 (X of 1897)], this Act shall be read as supplemental to any other enactment for the time being in force relating to fisheries in any part [Pakistan].

3. Definitions. In this Act, unless there is anything repugnant in the subject or context, ——

(1) "fish" includes shellfish;

(2) "fixed engine" means any net, cage, trap or other contrivance for taking fish, fixed in the soil or made stationary in any other way; and

(3) "private water" means water which is the exclusive property of any person or in which any person has for the time being an exclusive right of fishery whether as owner, lessee or in any other capacity.

Explanation. —Water shall not cease to be "private water" within the meaning of this definition by reason only that other persons may have by custom a right of fishery therein.

4. Destruction of fish by explosives in inland waters and on coasts.

(1) If any person uses any dynamite or other explosive substance in any water with intent thereby to catch or destroy any of the fish that may be therein, he shall be punishable with imprisonment for a term which may extend to two months, or with fine which may extend to two hundred rupees.

(2) In subsection (1) the word "water" includes the sea within a distance of one marine league of the seacoast: and an offence committed under that subsection in such sea

---

[1] See "The Fisheries Act, 1897", The Pakistan Code, http://pakistancode. gov. pk/english/UY2FqaJw1-apaUY2Fqa-cZs% 3D-sg-jjjjjjjjjjjjjj, March 20, 2021.

may be tried, punished and in all respects dealt with as if it had been committed on the land abutting on such coast.

5. Destruction of fish by poising waters.

(1) If any person puts any poison, lime or noxious material into any water with intent thereby to catch or destroy any fish, he shall be punishable with imprisonment for a term which may extend to two months, or with fine which may extend to two hundred rupees.

(2) The [Provincial Government] may, by notification in the official Gazette, suspend the operation of this section in any specified area, and may in like manner modify or cancel any such notification.

6. Protection of fish in selected waters by rules of Provincial Government.

(1) The [Provincial Government] may make rules for the purposes hereinafter in this section mentioned, and may by notification in the official Gazette apply all or any of such rules to such waters, not being private waters, as the [Provincial Government] may specify in the said notification.

(2) The [Provincial Government] may also, by a like notification, apply such rules or any of them to any private water with the consent in writing of the owner thereof and of all persons having for the time being any exclusive right of fishery therein.

(3) Such rules may prohibit or regulate all or any of the following matters, that is to say—

(a) the erection and use of fixed engines;

(b) the construction of weirs; and

(c) the dimension and kind of the nets to be used and the modes of using them.

(4) Such rules may also prohibit all fishing in any specified water for a period not exceeding two years.

(5) In making any rule under this section the [Provincial Government] may

(a) direct that a breach of it shall be punishable with fine which may extend to one hundred rupees, and, when the breach is a continuing breach, with a further fine which may extend to ten rupees for every day after the date of the first conviction during which the breach is proved to have been persisted in; and

(b) provide for—

(i) the seizure, forefeiture and removal of fixed engines, erected, or used, or nets used, in contravention of the rule, and

(ii) the forfeiture of any fish taken by means of any such fixed engine or net.

(6) The power to make rules under this section is subject to the condition that they shall be made after previous publication.

7. Arrest without warrant for offences under this Act.

(1) Any policeofficer, or other person specially empowered by the [provincial Government] in this behalf, either by name or as holding any office, for the time being, may, without an order from a Magistrate and without warrant, arrest any person committing in his view any offence punishable under section 4 or 5 or under any rule under section 6—

(a) if the name and address of the person are unknown to him, and

(b) if the person declines to give his name and address, or if there is reason to doubt the accuracy of the name and address if given.

(2) A person arrested under this section may be detained until his name and address have been correctly ascertained:

Provided that no person so arrested shall be detained longer than may be necessary for bringing him before a Magistrate, except under the order of a [Judicial Magistrate] for his detention.

附录 16　巴基斯坦《1975 年专属渔区（渔业监管）法》[1]

The Exclusive Fishery Zone（Regulation of Fishing）Act，1975
1st March，1975

An Act to provide for the regulation of fishing within the exclusive fishery zone of Pakistan.

WHEREAS it is expedient to provide for the regulation of fishing within the exclusive fishery zone of Pakistan and for matters ancillary thereto；

It is hereby enacted as follows：—

1. Short title，extent，application and commencement.

（1）This Act may be called the Exclusive Fishery Zone（Regulation of Fishing）Act，1975.

［（2）It extends to the whole of Pakistan and to waters within the zone］.

（3）It applies to all fishing crafts within the Zone and to all persons on board such fishing crafts.

（4）It shall come into force at once.

2. Definitions. In this Act，unless there is anything repugnant in the subject or context，

（a）"fish" includes molluscs，crustaceans，kelp and other marine animals；

（b）"Fishery Officer" means any person who is authorised by the Federal Government，by notification in the official Gazette，to exercise or perform any of the powers or functions of Fishery Officer under this Act；

（c）"fishing" means taking or catching of fish within the Zone by any means；

（d）"fishing craft" includes every vessel of whatever description and size and in whatever way propelled or moved which is used in fishing or the transport or processing thereof；

（e）"fishing gear" includes all appliances used for fishing；

（f）"licencing authority" means any person authorized by the Federal Government，by notification in the official Gazette，to issue licenses under this Act；

---

［1］　See "The Exclusive Fishery Zone（Regulation Of Fishing）Act，1975"，The Pakistan Code，http：//pakistancode. gov. pk/english/UY2FqaJw1-apaUY2Fqa-bpuUZWNs-sg-jjjjjjjjjjjjj，March 20，2021.

(g) "prescribed" means prescribed by rules;

(h) "rules" means rules made under this Act; [and]

(i) "Zone" means the Exclusive Economic Zone specified in section 6 of the Territorial Waters and Maritime Zones Act, 1976 (LXXXII OF 1976).

3. Fishing without licence prohibited. No person shall, for the purpose of fishing, operate a fishing craft or use any kind of fishing gear within the Zone except under the authority of a licence granted by the licencing authority nor otherwise than in accordance with the terms and conditions of such licence.

4. Fishing craft subject to navigational regulations.

(1) Every fishing craft shall be subject to any law relating to navigation for the time being in force.

(2) The location of nets and traps set by a fishing craft shall be prominently displayed by such means as may be prescribed.

(3) Every fishing gear shall be clear of the navigation channel and specified routes of commercial vessels.

5. Dynamiting and poisoning prohibited. No person shall use dynamite or any other explosive substance or poison, lime or noxious material for fishing or destroying fish in the Zone.

6. Closed season and prohibited area. Notwithstanding anything contained in this Act, the Federal Government may, by notification in the official Gazette, declare any period to be period during which, and any area to be an area within which, fishing of all or any specified description of fish shall be prohibited in the Zone.

7. Power to search. Any Fishery Officer may search any fishing craft or landing ground in or on which he has reason to believe to be concealed any fish caught or taken, or anything used, in contravention of any provision of this Act or the rules.

8. Seizure and disposal.

(1) If any Fishery Officer has reason to believe that any fish has been caught or taken in contravention of any provision of this Act or the rules, or that any fishing craft and fishing gear has been used for such fishing, he may arrest without warrant the owner or the person in charge of the vessel and seize such fish.

(2) Every officer making an arrest under subsection (1) shall, without unnecessary delay, take or send the person arrested before a Magistrate having jurisdiction in the case or before the officer in charge of the nearest policestation; and thereupon the provisions of the Code of Criminal Procedure, 1898 (Act V of 1898) applicable in respect of a person who, having been arrested without warrant, has been taken or sent before a Magistrate or an officer in charge of a police-station shall apply to him.

（3）Any fish seized under subsection（1）shall be disposed of in accordance with the decision of the court before which the owner or person in charge of the fishing craft is prosecuted under subsection（2）:

Provided that, if the fish seized is such as is likely to perish unless preserved or processed without delay, it may be sold or otherwise disposed of and, if it is sold, its value shall be treated as seized property for the purpose of this subsection.

9. Penalty [and procedure] .

（1）Whoever contravenes any provision of this Act or the rules shall be punishable with [rigorous imprisonment for a term which may extend to five years, or with fine which may extend to ten million rupees, or with both] .

（2）Any court convicting any person under subsection（1）may order that any fish caught or taken 3 [and any fishing craft and fishing gear used,] in contravention of the provisions of this Act or the rules, shall be forfeited to the Federal Government.

（3）Where the person contravening any provision of this Act or the rules is a company or other body corporate, every director, manager, secretary or other officer or agent thereof shall, unless he proves that the contravention was committed without his knowledge or that he exercised all due diligence to prevent such contravention, be deemed to be guilty of such contravention.

（4）Whoever, attempts to contravene, or abets the contravention of, any provision of this Act or the rules shall be deemed to have contravened the provisions of this Act or the rules.

（5）No court inferior to that of a Magistrate of the first class shall try any offence punishable under this Act.

（6）Notwithstanding anything contained in the Code of Criminal Procedure, 1898 (Act V of 1898) it shall be lawful for any Magistrate of the first class specially empowered by the Provincial Government in this behalf to pass any sentence authorised by this Act or by any of the laws extended under this Act.

10. False statement. Whoever, upon being so required by a police officer not below the rank of Sub-Inspector or a Fishery Officer, makes any statement or furnishes any information which is false in any material particulars and which he knows or has reason to believe to be false, or does not believe to be true, or makes any such statement as aforesaid in any book, account, record, declaration, or any document which he is required to maintain, shall be punishable with imprisonment for a term which may extend to one month, or with fine which may extend to five thousand rupees, or with both.

11. Burden of proof. Where any person is prosecuted for doing any act or being in possession of anything without lawful authority or licence, the burden of proving that he has such authority or licence shall lie on that person.

12. Liability of the owner etc. The owner or the person in charge of any fishing craft carrying anything in contravention of any provision of this Act or the rules shall be deemed to have contravened the provisions of this Act or the rules, as the case may be, if –

(i) such carriage is part of the transaction involving the contravention; and

(ii) if the owner or person in charge knew or had reason to believe that a contravention was being committed;

and shall be punishable under section 9.

13. Indemnity. No suit or other legal proceeding shall lie against the Federal Government or any Fishery Officer for anything in good faith done or intended to be done under this Act or any rule.

14. Delegation of Powers. The Federal Government may, by notification in the official Gazette, delegate all or any of its powers under this Act or the rules to any officer.

15. Jurisdiction of courts. For the purpose of giving jurisdiction to courts under this Act, a fishing craft shall be deemed to be a ship within the meaning of any enactment for the time being in force relating to offences committed on board a ship, and every court shall have the same jurisdiction over a foreign fishing craft within the Zone and persons belonging to such fishing craft as such court would have if such fishing craft were a Pakistan fishing craft.

16. Power to make rules.

(1) The Federal Government may, by notification in the official Gazette, make rules for carrying out the purposes of this Act.

(2) In particular and without prejudice to the generality of the foregoing power, such rules may provide for all or any of the following matters, namely: —

(a) the sizes of meshes and the sizes and types of nets;

(b) the size and the quantity of fish which may be caught by any fishing gear or processed at any time;

(c) the terms and conditions to which licences for fishing shall be subject;

(d) the registration of fishing craft and fishing gear;

(e) the regulation of operations of fishing craft;

(f) registration fee, licence fee and royalties on catches, and other dues of the Federal Government;

(g) specification of the area for landing of fish taken or caught in the Zone; and

(h) regulation of landing and inspection of fish taken or caught in the Zone.

附录 17　巴基斯坦《2014 年测绘法》[1]

The Surveying and Mapping Act, 2014
14th May, 2014

An Act to provide for constitution and regulation of Survey of Pakistan.

WHEREAS in the view of prevailing circumstances it is expedient to constitute Survey of Pakistan to provide for the regulation of surveying and mapping activities and for the matters connected therewith orancillary thereto;

AND WHEREAS it is necessary to provide for speedy disposal of such cases and execution in matters connected therein or ancillary thereto;

It is hereby enacted as follows:

PART I
PRELIMINARY

1. Short title, extent and commencement.

(1) This Act may called the Surveying and Mapping Act, 2014.

(2) It extends to the whole of Pakistan.

(3) It shall come into force at once.

2. Definitions. In this Act, unless there is anything repugnant in the subject or context, —

(i) "aerial photography" means the act of taking photographs of any portion of the earth with the help of cameras installed in an aircraft or any sort of air borne vehicle;

(ii) "datum" means an arbitrarily selected reference point, plane or surface to which all measurements are referred including geodetic, vertical and gravimetric datum;

(iii) "deposit works" mean extra departmental jobs carried out on payment basis;

(iv) "digital maps" mean geographic maps produced through satellite images, GPS, total station data or digitized using mapping software;

(v) "engineering maps" mean the large-scale topographical maps on which engineering works, of development projects are planned and designed, generally their scale is equivalent or larger than 1 : 10000;

(vi) "gravity datum" means the point to which all gravity measurements are referred;

---

[1] See "The Surveying and Mapping Act, 2014", The Pakistan Code, http://pakistancode.gov.pk/english/UY2FqaJw1-apaUY2Fqa-apaUY2FqZp4 = -sg-jjjjjjjjjjjjj, March 20, 2021.

（vii）"Government department" means a department controlled by Federal or a Provincial Government and includes any autonomous body, authority or organization established by or under the Federal or a Provincial law or which is owned or controlled or administered by the Federal or a Provincial Government or in which the Federal or a Provincial Government have controlling share or interest and also includes any local Government;

（viii）"geodetic datum" means the origin or a point to which all horizontal measurements are referred;

（ix）"geographical maps" mean maps that show general configuration of physical features of acertain area on a reference plane;

（x）"geospatial data" means information collected in hard copy format or in digital format or any other format for the purposes of preparation of geographical or topographical data and its attributes, its processing and analysis;

（xi）"imagery" means remotely sensed image of any resolution depicting any part of the earth and acquired or obtained using optical or, as the case may be, non-optical sensor;

（xii）"local plane coordinate system" means a rectangular coordinate system generally used for large-scale mapping;

（xiii）"mapping" means the art of map-making using specific datum, projection and scale and includes digital mapping;

（xiv）"national co-ordinate system" means a plane coordinate system as notified by the Federal Government;

（xv）"National Naming Authority" means the National Naming Authority established under section 19;

（xvi）"National Spatial Data Infrastructure" means a system of geospatial databases handling facilities capable of interacting with each other for effective use of geospatial data and include set of standards, specifications and policies defining a framework for collecting, sharing, disseminating, processing and carrying out analysis on geospatial data in the most cost effective manner with the key features to allow unrestricted yet controlled sharing of data for decision support system at strategic, tactical and operational levels;

（xviii）"prescribed" means prescribed by rules made under this act.

（xviii）"photogrammetry" means the art of taking measurements and mapmaking by using mono or, as the case may be, stereo image of the photographs taken by an aircraft or airborne vehicle or a satellite;

（xix）"public survey" means a survey in respect of which details are included in the register of public surveys;

（xx）"registered surveyor" means a person who is registered with the Survey of Pakistan as a land survey or under this Act and competent to carry out authorized type of survey work, processing and analysis;

(xxi) "remote sensing" means the method and art by which characteristics of the objects of interest can be identified, classified, measured or analyzed without physical contact;

(xxii) "registered organization" means any organization or authority or agency of the Government, a private firm or organization duly registered with the Survey of Pakistan under this Act and competent to carry out authorized type of survey work, processing and analysis;

(xxiii) "survey" means the act of taking topographic surveying measurements and collection of spatial and non-spatial data for preparing geospatial database, its processing and analysis;

(xxiv) "satellite" means an artificial body revolving around the earth at some distance;

(xxv) "Survey of Pakistan" means the department of Survey of Pakistan, which is the national surveying and mapping organization of Pakistan;

(xxvi) "Survey or General of Pakistan" means head of the department of Survey of Pakistan;

(xxvii) "survey mark" means benchmark pillar, iron bolt fixed in rock, a mark engraved on any building, a mark engraved on an in situ rock or a stone embedded in ground, atriangulation point protected by a cairn, a gravity pillar, a leveling benchmark, a fixedmark, hill station, monument or any other station or mark created by the Survey of Pakistan for the purpose of surveying and mapping;

(xxviii) "sub-standard work" means any survey work which does not conform to the approved specifications and standards as may be prescribed by the Survey of Pakistan;

(xxix) "topographical data" means data, which shows detailed information about shape, size and relationship of all features and abstract information of the earth, including but not limited to natural and man-made objects or features, geographical names, administrative boundaries and information like elevation, hydrology, vegetation, population and others; and

(xxx) "vertical datum" means the surface to which all vertical measurements are referred and mean sea level is taken as vertical datum of a country.

PART II

CONSTITUTION OF SURVEY OF PAKISTAN

3. Constitution of Survey of Pakistan.

(1) Notwithstanding anything contained in any other law for the time being in force, the Survey of Pakistan shall be deemed to have been established under this Act.

(2) For efficient administration of Survey of Pakistan, there shall be a Survey or General of Pakistan who shall be appointed by the Federal Government and there shall be other officers and staff as may be appointed by the Federal Government in the prescribed manner.

4. Offices of Survey of Pakistan. Survey of Pakistan shall have its head office at Rawalpindi or Islamabad and shall have offices at Federal, Provincial or district level and such other offices as the Survey of Pakistan may, by notification in the Official Gazette, establish.

5. Administration of Survey of Pakistan. Under this Act, —

(a) superintendence of Survey of Pakistan shall vest in the Federal Government; and

(b) administration of Survey of Pakistan shall vest in, and be exercised by, the Surveyor General of Pakistan in accordance with the provisions of this Act and the rules made thereunder.

6. Functions of Survey of Pakistan. For carrying out the purposes of this Act, Survey of Pakistan shall—

(a) be the sole national surveying and mapping organization of Pakistan;

(b) determine and update geodetic datum and projection system of Pakistan using latest geodetic techniques and technologies;

(c) determine and update vertical datum using data captured by Survey of Pakistan and obtained from Government departments, registered organizations or any other source having such installations along the coastal line of Pakistan;

(d) delineate and demarcate international borders and relocate boundary pillars;

(e) provide geodetic control, heights and geographical positions all over Pakistan;

(f) advise Federal Government on the practices to be followed in the production of geospatial data as well as surveying and mapping practices and as the case may be in the collection and dissemination of this kind of information needed for geographical information systems (GIS) applications;

(g) prepare geospatial data, remote sensing and geographical information system applications of the entire country on various scales as advised by the Federal Government and provide above services as a deposit work for a specific area with predefined specifications to the Provincial Governments, district and local governments and other clients from public as well as private sector;

(h) carry out topographic survey, its updation and printing of topographic maps of national map series;

(i) compile derived maps on various scales as required by the Federal Government;

(j) generate maps on any scale through aerial photography and remote sensing using analytical and digital methods;

(k) be responsible to prepare and print guide maps, provincial maps, district maps, road maps, tehsil maps and miscellaneous geographical maps for the whole of Pakistan;

(l) establish and maintain National Spatial Data Infrastructure (NSDI) of Pakistan;

(m) be responsible to survey and prepare cantonment areas maps:

(n) train departmental employees and potential candidates from private sector in various disciplines of surveying, geographical and mapping in the Survey Training Institute at various levels;

(o) control and coordinate surveying and mapping activities done by registered organizations and individuals and their registration process;

(p) carry out magnetic survey of entire country in a cyclic order as prescribed by Survey of Pakistan for the purpose of magnetic declination;

(q) have such other functions as are conferred or imposed on it by or under this Act or any other law; and

(r) perform such other functions as may be assigned by the Federal Government.

7. Research and development activities.

(1) Survey of Pakistan shall encourage and collaborate research activities in the field of surveying and mapping, remote sensing, GIS and other fields related to the discipline of surveying and mapping, cartography, instrument development and database with national and international organizations.

(2) Survey of Pakistan shall endeavor to upgrade scientific and technology level in this field and encourage and support any registered organizations and individuals that produce outstanding work in any field of surveying and mapping and related scientific or technological research.

8. Surveys and demarcation, etc.

(1) Survey of Pakistan shall be responsible for the delineation and demarcation of international land boundaries of Pakistan, jointly with the national mapping organizations or other organizations as authorized by the neighboring countries, in accordance with mutually agreed protocol and the plans drawn in the light of such protocol before taking up actual demarcation work.

(2) Survey of Pakistan shall carry out surveying and mapping of the provinces, districts and other administrative boundaries of Pakistan on receipt of requests there for after the alignment thereof has been agreed upon.

(3) Survey of Pakistan may also take up demarcation of land or state boundaries as a deposit work on mutual agreement of the parties consisting of Federal Government, Provincial Governments, district Governments, semigovernment departments, autonomous

bodies, private parties or individuals or as ordered by a court of law.

(4) Fifty per cent of the money received against the deposit shall be utilized for capacity building of the Survey of Pakistan in accordance with the prescribed procedure.

9. Authorization to enter into any land.

(1) Any person authorized by Survey of Pakistan for the purpose of this section may, in accordance with the applicable law, —

(a) enter into any land and public building, office or structure for the purpose of carrying out assigned task of collection of spatial or nonspatial data or information subject to applicable laws;

(b) take measurements in or from any such land from survey mark;

(c) search for and, if necessary, uncover any existing survey marks in or on any such land; and

(d) insert new survey marks in or on any such land for the purpose of carrying out any survey under this Act or for the purpose of maintaining or repairing any permanent survey marks.

(2) This section does not entitle any person so authorized to enter any building or structure on land, other than a building or structure referred to in clause (a) of subsection (1).

10. Datum, projection and standards.

(1) Survey of Pakistan shall establish and adopt geodetic, vertical and gravimetric datum at national level. This datum shall be adopted in all national activities of surveying and mapping, including those carried out by the armed forces of Pakistan and the Geological Survey of Pakistan (GSP).

(2) Survey of Pakistan shall define a unified projection system and system of geodetic coordinates and plane coordinates and shall define classification, order and accuracies of these coordinate systems as may be prescribed.

(3) For the purpose of this section, Survey of Pakistan shall establish independent local plane coordinate systems to meet the needs of construction work, urban planning and scientific research activities, which systems may be connected with the national coordinate system and shall be kept and maintained as classified information.

11. Registration.

(1) No public or private organization, private firm or individual, national or international, shall undertake any geospatial data collection, production or analysis work and surveying and mapping activities unless they are registered with Survey of Pakistan for such purpose as may be prescribed. The qualifications of staff and suitability for such work shall also be certified by Survey of Pakistan in the prescribed manner.

(2) Before registration, Survey of Pakistan shall obtain clearance of such firms, organizations and individuals in accordance with such procedure as may be prescribed.

(3) Subsections (1) and (2) shall not apply to operations of geospatial data production, analysis, surveying and mapping carried out by—

(a) any student of surveying, studying in a public educational institution or a university; and

(b) any person who produces geospatial data under immediate supervision of a registered organization, firm or individual.

12. Register.

(1) Survey of Pakistan shall maintain a register for the purpose of geospatial data of public surveys which shall contain details about—

(a) surveys carried out by Survey of Pakistan; and

(b) surveys for which details have been forwarded to Survey of Pakistan by any registered organization or individual.

(2) Survey of Pakistan may ensure that public survey conforms with the prescribed standards.

13. Joint survey and mapping and geospatial data production work with foreign companies. No work related to surveying and mapping, collection and production of geospatial data within Pakistan shall be undertaken by any individual, private firm or Government organization in collaboration with any foreign company or firm or nongovernmental organization unless prior written approval is obtained from the Federal Government, observing the requisite channels.

14. Correction of erroneous data.

(1) Where it comes to knowledge of Survey of Pakistan that erroneous data is being or was produced by a registered individual, firm or organization, it—

(a) may nominate an authorized official to inform by notice in writing requiring such data producer to correct the same within the time specified in the notice; and

(b) shall have the authority to engage another registered surveyor to make the correction if data producer does not comply with the notice. The defaulting data producer shall be informed to this effect through a written notice.

(2) The data specified in subsection (1), if not corrected within the time specified therein, shall immediately be forfeited by Survey of Pakistan and shall not be used for any purpose whatsoever.

(3) Any costs or expenses incurred on work mentioned in subsection (1) shall, as a debt due to the Government, be recoverable through a court of competent jurisdiction from the registered individual, firm or organization surveyor.

PART III
MANAGEMENT OF GEOSPATIAL DATA

15. Management of geospatial data.

(1) Survey of Pakistan shall establish and maintain National Spatial Data Infrastructure (NSDI) with support of key stakeholders to ensure consistent mechanism of maintenance, dissemination and sharing geospatial data among all users by reducing duplication in collection and maintenance of aforesaid data and to enhance and improve objective decision making.

(2) NSDI established and maintained under subsection (1) shall, for development of a system of geospatial databases and data handling facilities, be capable of interacting a-mongst all stakeholders and ensure putting in place design, implementation and mainte-nance mechanisms for facilitating, sharing, access and responsible for effective use of geo-spatial data at an affordable cost.

(3) All basic data or information comprising geodetic data, gravity data, magnetic data, topographical or geographical data, aerial photographs and all relevant records, both analogue and digital, prepared and possessed by Survey of Pakistan shall be maintained in the form of a national geospatial database. Any registered organization, developing geospa-tial data, shall, in accordance with the procedure prescribed, forward a copy of the data to Survey of Pakistan free of cost for inclusion in the national geospatial database, except the classified data collected by army survey group engineers, Geological Survey of Pakistan or strategic organizations.

(4) Survey of Pakistan shall regularly update geospatial data in the national spatial data infrastructure and supply the same to various users on demand as may be prescribed.

PART IV
SUPPLY AND SECURITY OF GEOSPATIAL DATA

16. Supply and use of geospatial data.

(1) All geospatial data, aerial photographs and satellite imageries may be supplied in the manner and on payment to any individual or organization, as may bepre-scribed. Classified data shall be provided in the manner prescribed and the same shall be re-turned to Survey of Pakistan after the specified period.

(2) No classified maps and data shall be allowed to be used by foreign consultants, firms or organizations without prior written approval of the Federal Government.

(3) Without prior written approval of the Surveyor General of Pakistan, no individu-al, company, firm, private or Government agency shall copy, digitize or print a map or aerial photograph or a part thereof prepared by Survey of Pakistan except digitization by ar-my survey group engineers for operational requirement of armed forces of Pakistan.

(4) Any map which is top secret, secret or restricted shall not be exported out of Pakistan in any format or by any means.

（5）Except as provided under this Act, any act of copying, digitizing or printing any geographic map or photograph or satellite imagery shall be prohibited.

17. Classified data. The use and maintenance of all data or maps categorized as top secret, secret and restricted shall be in accordance with rules.

PART V

USE OF SURVEY MARKERS

18. Protection, use and maintenance of survey marks.

（1）Nobody shall damage, destroy or remove any survey mark or seize or occupy the land used for permanent surveying marks. In case the marks are established on private property, compensation thereof shall be paid by the Federal Government under applicable law.

（2）No quarrying, demolition, soil gathering or removing or mining activities shall be carried out on, near or over any survey mark, which may damage or endanger its safety and effective utilization.

（3）No individual or organization shall carry out any type of construction within a radius of ten metres of a survey mark, except with prior permission of Survey of Pakistan and such individual or organization shall bear all expenses incurred on removal or reestablishment of the survey mark.

（4）Every surveyor or user of survey marks shall ensure its proper safety during the course of taking observations.

（5）The local administration shall be responsible for protection of all survey marks under its area of jurisdiction and shall send to Survey of Pakistan annual report on prescribed form about condition of the survey marks.

PART VI

NATIONAL AND INTERNATIONAL INITIATIVES

19. Geographical names.

（1）Notwithstanding anything contained in any other law for the time being in force, the Federal Government shall establish, by notification in the official Gazette, a National Naming Authority which shall consist of not more than ten members and shall be chaired by the Surveyor General of Pakistan.

（2）The functions of the National Naming Authority shall be to appropriately name particular geographical locations and it shall have such powers to enable it to carry out the said functions as may be prescribed.

PART VII

OFFENCES AND PENALITIES

20. Offences. Any organization, firm, individual or group of individuals engaged in any unauthorized activity within the meanings of this Act shall render itself an accused of illegal practices and

(a) shall be asked by Survey of Pakistan to immediately suspend all such activities;

(b) Survey of Pakistan shall ask concerned police to register a criminal case on such activities;

(c) depending upon nature of such violations, the accused shall be asked by Survey of Pakistan or its designated official to deposit with the department of Survey of Pakistan the entire received money and a penalty up to fifty thousand rupees; and

(d) in case Survey of Pakistan is convinced of major offence on part of the accused then his case shall be referred to a court of law and shall be tried for the following, namely:

(i) any individual or group causing hindrance and obstruction to the work being done by Survey of Pakistan and a registered surveyor shall be liable to be imprisoned for a term which may extend upto one month and a fine upto fifty thousand rupees;

(ii) any individual or group causing damage to survey mark shall be liable to be imprisoned for a term which may extend upto three months and a fine upto one hundred thousand rupees;

(iii) an individual who engages in geospatial data production, analysis and surveying and mapping activities in violation of the provisions of this Act shall be liable to be imprisoned for a term which may extend upto one year and a fine upto one million rupees;

(iv) every act of damaging, destroying, removing, seizing, occupying or establishing a mark resembling a permanent survey mark of Survey of Pakistan shall be an offence under this Act, punishable with imprisonment for a term which may extend upto one month and a fine upto fifty thousand rupee; and

(v) the owners, directors or managers whosoever of any accused organization, firm, individual or group of individuals, which engages in geospatial data production, analysis, surveying and mapping activities or any related activities in violation of the provisions of this Act, shall, if it is proved that such activities have been committed with the consent or connivance on the part of the owner, director or manager, as the case be, be liable to be imprisoned for a term which may extend up to one year and a fine upto five million rupees.

21. Jurisdiction of courts.

(1) Notwithstanding anything contained in the Code of Criminal Procedure, 1898 (Act V of 1898), no court other than a court of Magistrate of the First Class shall have jurisdiction to try an offence under this Act.

(2) The offences under this Act shall be noncognizable and bailable.

PART VIII
MISCELLANEOUS

22. Printing and publishing of maps and geospatial data.

(1) Any of the maps and geospatial data, whole or part thereof, falling in the responsibility of Survey of Pakistan, shall not be printed and published by any firm, individual or organization.

(2) During an emergency, selected printing presses of Pakistan shall come under command of Survey of Pakistan on required basis. A list of selected printing presses shall be prepared and updated, on annual basis, by Survey of Pakistan and notified by the Government of Pakistan.

23. Power to make rules. The Federal Government may, by notification in the official Gazette, make rules for carrying out the purposes of this Act.

24. Indemnity. No suit, prosecution or other legal proceedings shall lie against any person in respect of anything which is in good faith done or intended to be done under this Act.

25. Employees to be Civil Servants. The terms and conditions of service under Survey of Pakistan shall be governed by the Civil Servants Act, 1973 (LXXI of 1973) and the rules made thereunder.

附录 18 巴基斯坦关于领海基线的 1996 年政府公告[1]

Statutory Notification of 29 August 1996, Specifying The Baseline from Which The Limits of The Territorial Waters, The Contiguous Zone, The Exclusive Economic Zone and The Continental Shelf Shall Be Measured

ISLAMABAD, Thursday, 29 August 1996

Government of Pakistan

MINISTRY OF FOREIGN AFFAIRS

Notification

S. R. O. 714 (I) 96. In exercise of the powers conferred by sub-section (3) of section 2 of the Territorial Waters and Maritime Zones Act, 1976 (LXXXII of 1976), the Federal Government is pleased to specify below the baseline from which the limits of the Territorial Waters, the Contiguous Zone, the Exclusive Economic Zone and the Continental Shelf shall be measured namely:

(a) 25°02. 20′N, 61°35. 50′E

(b) 25°00. 95′N, 61°46. 80′E

(c) 25°05. 30′N, 62°21. 00′E

(d) 25°06. 30′N, 63°51. 01′E

(e) 25°09. 00′N, 64°35. 20′E

(f) 25°18. 20′N, 65°11. 60′E

(g) 24°49. 45′N, 66°40. 00′E

(h) 23°52. 80′N, 67°26. 80′E

(i) 23°47. 30′N, 67°35. 90′E

(j) 23°33. 90′N, 68°07. 80′E

The waters within the aforesaid straight baselines shall form the internal waters of Pakistan.

---

[1] See "Statutory Notification of 29 August 1996", UN Office of Legal Affairs, https://www. un. org/ Depts/los/LEGISLATIONANDTREATIES/PDFFILES/PAK_ 1996_ Notification. pdf, March 20, 2021.

附录19　2011 年巴基斯坦致联合国秘书长照会[1]

PAKISTAN MISSION TO THE UNITED NATIONS
PAKISTAN HOUSE
8 EAST 65TH STREET, NEW YORK, NY 10065
TEL: (212) 879-8600 FAX: (212) 744-7348

No. Sixth/LS/7/2011　　　　　　　　　　　　　　　6 December 2011

The Permanent Mission of the Islamic Republic of Pakistan to the United Nations presents its compliments to the Secretary-General of the United Nations and with reference to Government of India's Notifications No. S.O.1197(E) dated 11 May 2009 and S.O. 2962(E) dated 20 November 2009, specifying list of geographical coordinates of base points defining Baseline System of India to measure its maritime boundaries, posted on the website of Division for Ocean Affairs and the Law of the Sea (UN circular No. M.Z.N. 76.2010.LOS of 17 February 2010) and published in Law of the Sea Bulletins No. 71& 72 has the honour to state the following:-

    a. The Government of Pakistan is of the view that the following sections of the baseline points notified by India are inconsistent with international law, including the relevant provisions of 1982 United Nations Convention on the Law of the Sea (UNCLOS). The Government of Pakistan therefore, reserves its rights and those of its nationals in this regard.

    b. India's Base Points 1 to 3 of Schedule-I of India Notification (coordinates mentioned below), impinge upon Pakistan's territorial limits in Sir Greek area and encroach upon its territorial waters, which are within its sovereign jurisdiction. This encroachment by India in Pakistan's limits is a grave violation of international principles and established practices and clear violation of UNCLOS-82 Article 7(6) which states that system of straight baseline may not be applied by a State in such a manner as to cut off the territorial sea of another state from the high seas or EEZ.

i)	Sir Mouth N.	-	23° 40' 20.80" N, 68° 04' 31.20" E
ii)	Sir Mouth S.	-	23° 36' 30.30" N, 68° 07' 00.90" E
iii)	Pir Sanai Creek	-	23° 36' 15.20" N, 68° 07' 28.50" E

    c. The Government of Pakistan notes that disregarding the provisions of UNCLOS 82 Article 5, straight baseline segments joining base points No.24-25, 27-28, & 18-19 have been drawn by India on relatively smooth coast which is not indented

---

[1] See "Communication from the Government of Pakistan dated 6 December 2011", UN Office of Legal Affairs, https://www. un. org/Depts/los/LEGISLATIONANDTREATIES/PDFFILES/DEPOSIT/ communicationsredeposit/mzn76_ 2011_ pak. pdf, March 20, 2021.

or fringed by islands. India should have used normal baseline, the low water line, as required by UNCLOS 82. Pakistan is of the view that this creeping appropriation of sea due to excessive baselines have infringed the rights of international community as a whole being part of res communis in international Seabed Area and Pakistan in particular being adjacent Coastal State.

d. The Government of Pakistan further notes that straight baselines have been drawn by India to and from low-tide elevations in West/East Coast of India, which do not have lighthouses or similar installations on them or any international recognition, contravening Article 7(4) of UNCLOS-82.

e. Coordinates of normal baseline segments have not been given in the Notification.

f. Lengthy segments of straight baseline, which is against the spirit and practices of UNCLOS have been used to maximize the area of internal waters.

In view of the above, the Government of Pakistan does not recognize the Baseline System promulgated by India. While the Government of Pakistan reserves its right to seek suitable revision of this notification, any claim India makes on the basis of above cited Indian Notification to extend its sovereignty/jurisdiction on Pakistani waters or extend its internal waters, territorial sea, Exclusive Economic Zone and Continental Shelf is therefore, not acceptable to Pakistan being in contravention to the provisions of UNLCOS 1982.

The Permanent Mission of the Islamic Republic of Pakistan to the United Nations avails itself of this opportunity to renew to the Secretariat of the United Nations the assurances of its highest consideration.

The United Nation Secretariat,
Ms. Patricia O'Brien -
Under Secretary-General/Legal Counsel,
Office of Legal Affairs,
New York. N.Y. 10017.

附录20　2014年阿曼致联合国秘书长照会[1]

Permanent Mission of Oman
to the United Nations
New York

5223/25220/2212/290

The Permanent Mission of the Sultanate of Oman to the United Nations presents its compliments to the Executive Office of the Secretary-General to the United Nations and has the honour to refer to the submission made by the Islamic Republic of Pakistan regarding the outer limits of its continental shelf submitted to the Commission on the Limits of the Continental Shelf on 30 April 2009.

The Sultanate of Oman acknowledges that the area of the continental shelf contained in Pakistan's submission may overlap with the area of Oman's continental shelf submission. The Sultanate of Oman further confirms that it is actively involved in the preparation of a continental shelf submission and plans to present its submission as detailed in its "Preliminary Information" submitted to the Commission on the Limits of the Continental Shelf on 15 April 2009. The overlapping area, if any, would be subject to the delimitation of a Continental Shelf boundary between Oman and Pakistan.

Without prejudice to any future delimitation or any Continental Shelf Submission to be made by Oman, the "Potential Maritime Boundaries" in the Arabian Sea published in Pakistan's submission were ascertained unilaterally, and may, therefore be subject to future delimitation.

The Sultanate of Oman notes the statement made by the Islamic Republic of Pakistan in its note no. Sixth/LS/7/2014 of 9th October 2014 that, consistent with Article 76, paragraph 10, of the United Nations Convention on the Law of the Sea, its submission has been made without prejudice to any future submission to be made by Oman or to any eventual future delimitation of the continental shelf between Pakistan and Oman that may be required. On that basis, the Sultanate of Oman withdraws the request contained in its note on 7th of August 2009, and confirms that it has no objection to the Commission considering and making recommendations on Pakistan's Submission.

The Permanent Mission of the Sultanate of Oman to the United Nations avails itself of this opportunity to renew to the Executive Office of the Secretary-General to the United Nations the assurances of its highest consideration.

New York, 10 November 2014

Executive Office of the Secretary-General
To the United Nations
New York

---

[1]　See "Communication Dated 10 November 2014 concerning The Submission by Pakistan regarding The Outer Limits of Continental Shelf", UN Office of Legal Affairs, https：//www. un. org/Depts/los/ LEGISLATIONANDTREATIES/PDFFILES/communications/omn_ re_ pak_ 07122016. pdf. , March 20, 2021.

附录21 2016年阿曼致联合国秘书长照会[1]

Permanent Mission of Oman
to the United Nations
New York

5223/25220/2212/368

The Permanent Mission of the Sultanate of Oman to the United Nations presents its compliments to the Office of the Secretary-General of the United Nations and has the honour to refer to the United Nations Maritime Zone Notification M.Z.N.122.2016.LOS dated 08 September 2016 regarding the deposit by Pakistan on 30 August 2016 of a chart including a list of geographical coordinates of points and relevant information "permanently describing the outer limits of its continental shelf". Such deposit was purported to be made under Articles 76(9) and 84(2) of the United Nations Convention on the Law of the Sea.

It is the view of the Government of Oman that the Government of Pakistan is not in a position in accordance with international law to "permanently describe" the outer limits of its continental shelf at this time, nor to deposit such information pursuant to Articles 76(9) or 84(2) of the Convention.

The Government of Oman wishes to recall that the outer limits of the continental shelf of Pakistan remain subject to the delimitation of a continental shelf boundary with Oman in accordance with the principles in Article 83 of the Convention. The need for such delimitation was acknowledged by the Government of Pakistan in its diplomatic note Sixth/LS/7/2014 to the Executive Office of the Secretary-General dated 09 October 2014. No such continental Shelf boundary has yet been delimited, although the Government of Oman remains willing to work with the Government of Pakistan towards the delimitation boundary at the mutual convenience of both parties.

As provided by Articles 76(10) and Article 9 of Annex II of the Convention, the recommendations of the Commission on the Limits of the Continental Shelf in respect of the outer limits of the continental shelf of Pakistan, shall not be prejudiced in matters relating to the delimitation of boundaries between States. The Government of Pakistan therefore may not act on the recommendation of the Commission if doing so would prejudice matters relating to the delimitation of the continental shelf boundary with Oman.

3 DAG HAMMARSKJÖLD PLAZA, 305 EAST 47TH ST, 12TH FL. NEW YORK, NY 10017 - TEL (212) 355-1505 FAX (212) 644-0070

---

[1] See "Communication Dated 7 December 2016 concerning The Deposit by Pakistan of A Chart, including A List of Geographical Coordinates of Points and Relevant Information", UN Office of Legal Affairs, https：//www. un. org/Depts/los/LEGISLATIONANDTREATIES/PDFFILES/communications/omn_re_ pak_ 07122016. pdf. , March 20, 2021.

The Government of Oman is of the view that the deposit by the Government of Pakistan on 30 August 2016 of charts and information purporting to "permanently describe" the outer limits of the continental shelf is inconsistent with that principle. Any outer limits unilaterally described by the Government of Pakistan in such circumstances thus cannot be regarded as "final and binding" on other States, including Oman, under Article 76(8) of the Convention.

The Government of Oman requests the Secretary-General to give due publicity to this communication and to circulate a copy to member states of the United Nations.

The Permanent Mission of the Sultanate of Oman avails itself of this opportunity to renew to the Office of the Secretary-General to the United Nations the assurances of its highest consideration.

New York, December 2016

The Office of the Secretary-General
United Nations
New York

附录 22 《阿曼苏丹国与巴基斯坦伊斯兰共和国 有关划定海洋边界的马斯喀特协定》[1]

Muscat Agreement on the Delimitation of the Maritime Boundary between the Sultanate of Oman and the Islamic Republic of Pakistan, 12 June 2000

The Government and people of the Sultanate of Oman and the Government and people of the Islamic Republic of Pakistan,

Recalling the bonds of friendship and good-neighbourly relations existing between them,

Expressing their wish to delimit the maritime boundary between the two countries permanently, equitably and definitively in conformity with international law and relevant international conventions,

Have agreed as follows:

Article 1

The maritime boundary between the exclusive economic zones of the Sultanate of Oman and the Islamic Republic of Pakistan shall be measured from baselines established in conformity with the United Nations Convention on the Law of the Sea of 1982.

Article 2

The delimitation of the maritime boundary between the exclusive economic zones of the Sultanate of Oman and the Islamic Republic of Pakistan shall be based on the median line principle, in conformity with the United Nations Convention on the Law of the Sea of 1982.

Article 3

The delimitation line between the exclusive economic zones of the Sultanate of Oman and the Islamic Republic of Pakistan shall be the geodesic lines, referred to the World Geodetic System 1984 (WGS 84) joining a series of fixed points whose geographical coordinates, referred to WGS 84, are as follows:

---

[1] See UN Office of Legal Affairs, "Muscat Agreement on the Delimitation of the Maritime Boundary between the Sultanate of Oman and the Islamic Republic of Pakistan, 12 June 2000", https://www.un.org/Depts/los/LEGISLATIONANDTREATIES/PDFFILES/TREATIES/MMR-IND1986MB, March 20, 2021.

Point No.	Latitude (N)	Longitude (E)
1	23°20′48″	61°25′00″
2	23°15′22″	61°32′48″
3	23°11′40″	61°38′11″
4	22°56′35″	62°00′51″
5	22°54′37″	62°03′50″
6	22°40′37″	62°25′17″
7	22°05′01″	63°08′23″
8	21°57′13″	63°14′21″
9	21°47′24″	63°22′13″

Article 4

The delimitation line between the exclusive economic zones of the Sultanate of Oman and the Islamic Republic of Pakistan defined in article 3 of this Agreement is illustrated on United Kingdom Admiralty Chart BA 38 (edition dated 6 March1992) and United Kingdom Admiralty Chart BA 707 (edition dated 2 January 1997), a copy of each of which is attached hereto. (2)

Article 5

The Government of the Sultanate of Oman and the Government of the Islamic Republic of Pakistan recognize and acknowledge the sovereign rights of their respective States over the seabed, including the subsoil and superjacent waters, within the limits established pursuant to this Agreement.

Article 6

In the event of the discovery of an extension of any geological petroleum structure, individual oil or gas field, mineral or other natural resources that cross the delimitation line defined in article 3 of this Agreement, and the partial or full exploitation of the oil or gas field, mineral or other natural resources on one side of the delimitation line by means of directional drilling from the other side thereof, the following provisions shall apply:

(1) Exploitation of the aforementioned resources shall be undertaken by mutual agreement of the two States Parties. These resources shall be divided according to the then prevailing rules and customs of international law as well as the principles of justice and equity.

(2) A zone of 125 metres width on either side of the delimitation line defined in article 3 of this Agreement shall not be exploited by either State Party except by mutual consent.

(3) In the event of any dispute arising during the implementation of this article, the two States Parties shall do their utmost to reach agreement regarding the best ways of coordinating and unifying their operations on both sides of the delimitation line defined in article 3

of this Agreement.

Article 7

The delimitation line defined in article 3 of this Agreement is illustrated on the two charts mentioned in article 4 of this Agreement. The delimitation line has been drawn on these charts as precisely as is practical within the limitations imposed by their scale. These charts form an integral part of the Agreement, and have the same legal validity as the A-greement. The charts have been prepared in duplicate, and the two States Parties shall sign both sets and shall retain one set each.

Article 8

This Agreement shall be subject to ratification in accordance with the respective legal procedures of the two countries and shall come into force following the exchange of the instruments of ratification between them. A copy of the Agreement shall be deposited with the Secretariat of the United Nations.

Article 9

DONE at Muscat on this 12th day of June 2000, in duplicate, in the Arabic and English languages, both texts being legally authentic. However, in the event of any divergence in the interpretation of the texts, the English version shall prevail.

附录 23　巴基斯坦缔结和加入的国际海洋法条约

（一）联合国海洋法公约及其相关条约

序号	条约名称	签署日期 （年/月/日）	批准日期 （年/月/日）
1	《联合国海洋法公约》 United Nations Conventionon the Law of the Sea, 1982	1982/12/10	1997/2/26
2	《关于执行 1982 年 12 月 10 日〈联合国海洋法公约〉第十一部分的协定》 Agreement relating to the Implementation of Part XI of the United Nations Convention on the Law of the Sea of 10 December1982	1994/8/10	1997/2/26
3	《执行 1982 年 12 月 10 日〈联合国海洋法公约〉有关养护和管理跨界鱼类种群和高度洄游鱼类种群的规定的协定》 Agreement for the Implementation of the Provisions of the United Nations Convention on the Law of the Sea of 10 December 1982 relating to the Conservation and Management of Straddling Fish Stocks and Highly Migratory Fish Stocks	1996/2/15	未批准
4	《国际海底管理局特权与豁免议定书》 Protocol on the Privileges and Immunities of the International Seabed Authority	1999/9/9	未批准

（二）缔结与加入的其他海洋海事条约

类别	条约名称	签署/批准/加入/ 接受日期 （年/月/日）	对巴基斯坦 生效日期 （年/月/日）
与海上安全相关的条约	《1974 年国际海上人命安全公约》 International Convention for the Safety of Life at Sea, 1974	1985/4/10	1985/7/10
	《1974 年国际海上人命安全公约 1978 年议定书》 Protocol of 1978 relating to the International Convention for the Safety of Life at Sea, 1974, as Amended	1985/4/10	1985/7/10
	《1974 年国际海上人命安全公约 1988 年议定书》 Proctocol of 1988 relating to the International Convention for the Safety of Life at Sea, 1974	2001/12/6	2002/3/6
	《国际移动卫星组织业务协定 1998 年修正案》 1998 Amendments of Operating Agreement on the International Mobile Satellite Organization	1976/9/3	2000/9/15

续表

类别	条约名称	签署/批准/加入/接受日期（年/月/日）	对巴基斯坦生效日期（年/月/日）
与海上安全相关的条约	《国际移动卫星组织公约》 Convention on the International Mobile Satellite Organization	1985/2/6	1985/2/6
	《国际移动卫星组织公约1998年修正案》 1998 Amendments of the Convention on the International Mobile Satellite Organization	2000/9/15	2001/7/31
与海洋环境保护相关的条约	《1973年国际防止船舶造成污染公约的1978年议定书》 Protocol of 1978 Relating to the International Convention for the Prevention of Pollution from Ships, 1973	1994/11/22	1995/2/22
	《1972年防止倾倒废物及其他物质污染海洋的公约》 Convention on the Prevention of Marine Pollution by Dumping of Wastes and other Matter, 1972, as Amended	1995/3/9	1995/4/8
与船舶及船员相关的条约	《1966年国际载重线公约》 International Convention on Load Lines, 1996	1968/12/5	1969/3/5
	《〈1966年国际载重线公约〉1988年议定书》 Protocol of 1988 Relating to the International Conventionon Load Lines, 1996	2002/4/25	2002/7/25
	《1969年国际船舶吨位丈量公约》 International Convention on Tonnage Measurement of Ships, 1969	1994/10/17	1995/1/17
	《联合国班轮公会行动守则公约》 Convention on A Code of Conduct for Liner Conference	1975/6/27	1983/10/6
	《1999年国际扣押船舶公约》 International Convention on Arrest of Ships, 1999	2000/7/11	未批准
	《1978年海员培训、发证和值班标准国际公约》 International Convention on Standards of Training, Certification and Watchkeeping for Seafarers, 1978	1985/4/10	1985/7/10
与渔业管理相关的条约	《1948年建立印度洋—太平洋渔业委员会协定》 Agreement for the Establishment of the Indo-Pacific Fisheries Council, 1948	1949/8/1	1949/8/1
	《1992年亚洲和太平洋水产养殖中心网络的协定》 Agreement on the Network of Aquaculture Centers in Asia and the Pacific, 1992	1990/1/28	1990/1/28
	《1993年建立印度洋金枪鱼委员会协定》 The Agreement for the Establishment of the Indian Ocean Tuna Commission, 1993	1995/4/27	1996/3/27